ANALYZING RHETORIC

A Handbook for the Informed Citizen in a New Millennium

ROBERT C. ROWLAND
THE UNIVERSITY OF KANSAS

FIFTH EDITION

Kendall Hunt
publishing company

*Thanks go to all of the many fine graduate students
who have worked with me teaching rhetorical criticism.*

For Donna

Cover images:
Ronald Reagan © AP/WIDE WORLD PHOTOS
Barack Obama © UniversalImagesGroup/Universal Images Group/Getty Images

Kendall Hunt
publishing company

www.kendallhunt.com
Send all inquiries to:
4050 Westmark Drive
Dubuque, IA 52004-1840

Copyright © 1999, 2002, 2008, 2012, and 2019 by Robert C. Rowland

ISBN 978-1-5249-9401-3

Published in the United States of America

CONTENTS

CHAPTER 3
Understanding Context and Judging Effectiveness . . . **43**

RHETORICAL STRATEGIES **73**

CHAPTER 4

Rational Argument **75**

CHAPTER 5

Narrative Forms of Rhetoric **111**

CHAPTER 6
Credibility Strategies **131**

CHAPTER 7
Aesthetic Strategies **159**

CHAPTER 8
Generating an Emotional Response:
Tapping Into Values, Needs and Symbols **191**

CHAPTER 9
Confrontative Rhetoric and Social Movements **227**

CHAPTER 10
Generic Analysis **253**

CHAPTER 11

The Informed Citizen

INTRODUCTION

INTRODUCTION

The most common use of the word *rhetoric* is negative. People often associate rhetoric with overblown language or with deception. For example, in a speech contained in this book Mario Cuomo distinguishes between "rhetoric" and "reality." Cuomo's usage reflects the common perception that rhetoric is both unimportant and generally used to deceive or manipulate. It is for this reason that political commentators often place the adjective *mere* in front of the word *rhetoric*. They do so to distinguish mere rhetoric from something truly important, like public policy. Perhaps unsurprisingly, in the decades after 9/11 as American politics became ever more strident, the perception that rhetoric is a negative force has grown stronger.

That perception, the view that rhetoric is either unimportant and therefore not worthy of serious consideration or is actually a dangerous force in society, is misguided. To make this point clear, it is first important to understand what the term rhetoric means. *Rhetoric involves the use of symbols (primarily language) to persuade or inform.* Any time one person uses speech (or writing or an object or a film and so forth) to influence another person, he/she is relying on the resources of rhetoric. As long as the person presenting the rhetoric (the rhetor or rhetorician) relies on "symbol use," rhetoric is being presented.

A symbol is an object that means something to both the rhetor and the audience. Our most common symbol system is language, but tangible objects (a cross for example), places (such as the FDR Memorial in Washington, D.C.), songs, pictures, and so forth also may function as symbols. People engage in rhetoric whenever they use symbols to communicate with others.

Perhaps the most common use of the term rhetoric is to refer to a political speech. But rhetoric is found in other kinds of speeches as well. When a manager tries to motivate or explain a principle to employees, he or she is using rhetoric. When a doctor explains to a patient the importance of taking all of a certain prescription, that doctor is using rhetoric. Rhetoric is also found in other forms. A book that informs or persuades us is rhetorical, as are many newspaper, magazine, and Internet articles. Many television programs and films use symbols to make an important point. Steven Spielberg's award-winning film *Saving Private Ryan* made a powerful point about the heroism and sacrifice of soldiers in World War II. The movie was so powerful that the media reported instances of veterans overcome with emotion at the conclusion of the film. Music, too, may be rhetorical. Beethoven's *Ninth Symphony* has been treated as a symbol for international peace and is played every year at the United Nations on United Nations Day.

And art may be rhetorical as well. A photograph or a drawing of a murdered child in Rwanda, Kosovo, or Darfur may bring home the horrors of genocide more powerfully than a thousand speeches. In a time when millions of Americans are constantly in touch with people around the world through email, twitter accounts, Facebook, and other new technologies, the importance for good or ill of rhetoric should be obvious.

The important point to remember is that any time we use symbols to persuade or inform, we are using rhetoric.

THE IMPORTANCE OF RHETORIC

The foregoing analysis should make clear the importance of rhetoric. Any time people use "talk" to make decisions, they are engaged in rhetoric. In this way, rhetoric is the primary vehicle through which all democratic decisions are made. In any democratic organization (from the church special events committee to the United States Congress), the business of the group gets done through the give and take of rhetoric.

In a fundamental sense, democracy might be understood as the "rhetorical form of government," for the most essential definition of democracy is that decisions are made via discussion and debate. In totalitarian organizations at all levels, by contrast, it is the "Big Boss" who decides; there is no place for rhetoric in such a society. This is true in organizations where one person makes all the decisions and it was true in Hitler's Germany and Stalin's Russia. In a sense, the hallmark of totalitarianism is that there is *no need for rhetoric* in making decisions. After the decision is made, rhetoric may be used to motivate the public, but rhetoric is not needed at the decision-making stage.

In a sense, rhetoric can be understood as both the blood and bone in any democratic society. It is the bone, because it is our words (like the Constitution, the Declaration of Independence, and the Gettysburg Address)[1] that hold us together. The power of rhetoric to create a sense of shared identity was evident in the reaction to then–state Senator Barack Obama's address to the 2004 Democratic National Convention, which is included in the *Workbook*. It is no exaggeration to say that before he spoke he was virtually unknown and after the speech millions of Americans hoped that one day he would be president. It surely is a testament to the power of rhetoric that only four years and a few months later that hope became a reality. But rhetoric is also the blood in any democratic society, because it is through rhetoric that the work of any democratic society gets done. When that blood circulates effectively, rhetorical give and take occurs and the society can solve its problems. In any democratic organization, prior rhetoric acts as the skeleton holding the organization together and current rhetoric functions as the lifeblood, leading to action.

Rhetoric is also important because rhetorical failure means institutional failure, inaction, and gridlock. Over the winter of 1995–1996, the U.S. government was shut down because President Clinton and the Republican-led Congress could not agree on a budget to fund government programs. Many attacked Clinton and the Republicans for various mistakes in this dispute, but what was not recognized was that the government shutdowns were failures of rhetoric.

Our system of rhetoric had broken down to the point that Clinton and the Republicans could not talk through the budget issues sensibly. Something similar has happened several times in Washington since the election of Barack Obama to the presidency. When rhetoric fails, government or any other organization is unable to address the problems confronting it and ordinary people suffer. Rhetorical failure is devastating. And this is just as true at the local level or in a business or other organization as it is for a nation. Many organizations have failed because the boss couldn't effectively use rhetoric to motivate his/her employees to achieve a given aim. Where the individuals in any group fail to use rhetoric effectively in making decisions, the result is likely to be a crisis for that group, whether it is a small business, a Fortune 500 corporation, a local government, a state, or a nation.

Thus, rhetoric is anything but trivial. It is the means through which decisions are hammered out at all levels in our society. When rhetoric fails, so does the organization or society.

And yet, the critics of rhetoric are not completely off base in associating rhetoric with deception and manipulation. Many leaders use rhetoric not to facilitate rational decision-making, but simply to get their way. The practice of using rhetoric to deceive an audience is so common that we have invented a special word to describe it—*spin*. It is common to hear political commentators discuss how one politician or another used "spin" to persuade an audience, often while the commentator is trying desperately to spin the audience him- or herself.

Even worse, sometimes rhetoric is used to create hatred or otherwise harm society. Hitler used rhetoric to take over Germany. He did not have vast wealth or power, but he used the resources of rhetoric to build a movement that eventually killed millions of innocent people and nearly captured all Europe. For every Winston Churchill who used rhetoric to warn of the Nazi threat, there is a Hitler using rhetoric to mislead, deceive, and manipulate. And this is true at every level of society. The leaders of cults are skilled rhetoricians who use their words to gather a group of followers. Rhetoric can be powerful (and dangerous) stuff.

The aim of this book is to provide students with a means of critically analyzing and evaluating rhetoric. The ability to break down a work of rhetoric—whether an essay, a speech, Spike Lee's latest film, or Sarah Palin's most recent tweet or Facebook posting—into its constituent rhetorical parts is essential for any informed and involved citizen. Therefore, this book provides the tools for the student to accomplish this aim—in other words to act as a rhetorical critic.

What is the role of the critic? To many a critic is someone who criticizes other people's creations, often unfairly. Criticism is therefore often thought of as inherently negative. In this view, artists create while critics criticize. To others, criticism is a simple yes/no judgment about quality. Does the film get a "thumbs up" or a "thumbs down"? Each of these meanings of "criticism" is partially correct, but inadequate.

Criticism (at least in the area of rhetoric) is best understood as a type of careful analysis. The goals of rhetorical criticism are to understand what is being said, how it is presented, whether and why it is persuasive for an audience, whether it can be considered good or just or moral rhetoric, and what that rhetoric tells us about related issues, including historical, political, and sociological questions.

In the sense developed throughout this book, a rhetorical critic is an informed analyst, someone who breaks a work of rhetoric into stylistic and substantive categories and fairly judges that rhetoric. To be a critic does not mean simply to criticize (in the negative sense), although there is much rhetoric that calls for negative criticism, but to understand the way that rhetoric functions in any community.

Why is rhetorical criticism an important subject? Some might react to the description of criticism in the previous paragraph and label it a purely academic endeavor. They would doubt that real people need to analyze or evaluate rhetoric. In fact, they are wrong. Skill at rhetorical analysis is one of the essential elements in becoming an informed and engaged citizen.

FUNCTIONS OF RHETORICAL CRITICISM

Training in rhetorical analysis serves three important goals. First, skill at rhetorical analysis helps the individual understand how people use symbols to persuade. Rhetoric, like all arts, involves a number of forms and strategies. The third section of this book focuses on six main strategies for using rhetoric to persuade. However, the strategies in a given work of rhetoric may not be immediately obvious to someone hearing, reading, or observing the rhetoric. Training in rhetorical analysis helps the individual identify the strategic pattern present in any given work of rhetoric.

An example clarifies this point. In their analysis of a 1980 debate between President Jimmy Carter and Republican nominee Ronald Reagan, the press almost universally concluded that Carter had better substance and Reagan better style. A *New York Times* reporter said simply, "It was a contest of content against style."[2] Many others in the media came to a similar conclusion.[3] The problem is that a close analysis of the debate shows that it was not a contrast between Reagan's style and Carter's substance. Analyzed as an academic debate, Reagan clearly was more substantive. He did a better job of answering questions, presenting evidence, and countering the claims of the other side than did Carter.[4] Why did many in the press miss Reagan's substantive success? The answer seems to be that they saw what they expected to see. They knew that Carter was extremely bright and had been a hands-on manager of every detail of U.S. policy during his term as president. And they knew that Reagan was a former actor. So they expected Reagan to be stylish and Carter substantive. But that wasn't what happened in the debate. The press needed training in rhetorical analysis to understand what really happened in the debate.

How does this purpose apply to average people who are not evaluating presidential debates? The ability to analyze rhetoric helps the individual in dealing with the school board, the city council, his or her boss, in fact, anyone who uses rhetoric. You cannot appropriately and effectively respond to rhetoric if you do not understand both what is said and how it is said. On the other hand, once you understand not only what is being said, but the strategy behind it, you are in a better position both to respond to and protect yourself from unethical rhetoric.

Second, skill at rhetorical analysis is essential to protect the individual from manipulative and deceptive rhetoric. There are many in politics, business, and elsewhere in society who skillfully use rhetoric to get their way. Some lie or deceive to accomplish their aims. Others use rhetoric to create hatred or attack some group in society. One of the essential skills needed to be an informed and empowered citizen is the ability to identify deceptive or manipulative rhetoric. Thus, rhetorical criticism serves as a self-protective function for the ordinary person. Later in this book, I develop what I call the "Informed Citizen" system for identifying deceptive and manipulative rhetoric. Through the application of that system, people can protect themselves from those who would manipulate or deceive them.

Third, skill at rhetorical analysis helps individuals become more effective persuaders. I said earlier that democracy can be understood as a form of government in which people use rhetoric to make their decisions. There is a corollary to this definition. To be an effective citizen, one must be a skilled rhetorician. For it is through rhetoric, whether talking to the city council or testifying before a congressional committee, that people protect their rights and interests. Training in rhetorical analysis helps one become a more effective persuader. If you understand how other people use language to persuade, that understanding helps you develop effective (and ethical) strategies for building a persuasive case, whether you are asking your boss for a raise or giving an inaugural address.

Rhetorical criticism is, therefore, not merely an academic undertaking. It is a crucial skill that ordinary people use every day in conducting their business. A skillful critic understands what others are saying to him or her, is able to distinguish between strong arguments and deceptive claims, and is capable of developing effective rhetorical strategies for use in any occasion.

It is instructive that when the Greeks invented the liberal arts, they treated rhetoric as the first of those arts. They knew that the most fundamental skill needed by any person living in a democracy was the ability to use rhetoric to state a case. With the rise of the Internet, rhetoric is, if anything, even more important today.

1   Gary Wills makes a similar argument in his book about the Gettysburg address. Gary Wills, *Lincoln at Gettysburg: The Words That Remade America.* New York: Simon & Schuster, 1992.

2   Hedrick Smith, "No Clear Winner Apparent," *The New York Times,* October 19, 1980, A1.

3   This literature is summarized in Robert C. Rowland. The Substance of the 1980 Carter–Reagan Debate. *Southern Speech Communication Journal, 51*(Winter 1986), 142–165.

4   See my analysis cited above.

CHAPTER ONE
A System For Rhetorical Criticism

In order to understand the way a given work of rhetoric functions, one needs a system for breaking down that rhetoric into its constituent parts and for placing the rhetoric in a context. Fulfilling the self-protection function of rhetorical analysis further requires a means of testing rhetoric to see if it is deceptive or manipulative. In order to accomplish these aims, I have developed the "I CARE" system.

The remainder of this book will develop the "I CARE" system and apply it to sample works of rhetoric. In this chapter, I provide an overview of the system. Chapters two and three focus on the "analysis" and "research" stages in more detail. Chapters four through nine then examine the six main strategies for persuading an audience. In chapter ten, I discuss how some groups of rhetorical acts are best understood as aspects of a broader category of rhetoric called a "genre." Finally, in chapter eleven, I discuss how an "Informed Citizen" can use standards for identifying deceptive or manipulative rhetoric.

THE "I CARE" SYSTEM

The "I CARE" system of rhetorical analysis is made up of a series of stages through which the critic (remember, we are all critics any time we hear or read or see a work of rhetoric) proceeds in carrying out rhetorical criticism. By following these stages, the critic can analyze a speech by former President Barack Obama, a comedy routine on *Saturday Night Live*, an editorial in The *New York Times*, or a speech delivered in 16th-century London. The point is that the stages provide the steps for analyzing any work of rhetoric.

The "I" in the "I CARE" system refers to each individual. "I" (and you) should care about rhetorical analysis because of the central role played by all forms of persuasion in our society. We are all rhetorical critics (or at least we should be) because we are constantly exposed to rhetoric aimed at influencing or manipulating us. Every time we listen to a politician, a manager, or a salesperson, or read a posting on the Internet, or receive rhetoric from anyone else who wants us to act in a certain way, we should be, but often are not, acting as informed rhetorical critics. An informed rhetorical critic is aware of how another person is attempting to persuade him or her and skillfully tests that persuasion to make sure that it is ethical and sensible. One goal of rhetorical criticism as a discipline is to make individuals more informed critics in order that they can understand, appreciate, and protect themselves from other people's use of rhetoric. Therefore, rhetorical criticism is our foremost tool for understanding and evaluating why and how people persuade each other.

CARE

In order to analyze any work of rhetoric, whether a speech by Lincoln, a music video by a contemporary artist, or a tweet by a reality TV star, the critic must move through four research stages prior to the final analysis. These four stages are represented in the acronym "CARE." CARE stands for:

- Choice
- Analysis
- Research
- Explanation and Evaluation

CHOICE

The first stage in any rhetorical analysis is *choice*, which relates to the selection of an appropriate work of rhetoric for analysis. There are four possible principles that can be used for choosing a work to analyze. The first and most important principle is *immediacy*. The critic analyzes the work because it has been presented (or assigned) to him or her. It is immediately in front of you. You are at the city council meeting and a developer argues for changing zoning to put in a bowling alley near your home. The rhetoric of the developer is immediately in front of you and you must respond. The same is true when you hear a politician give a speech or listen as a doctor advises a friend concerning therapy. In most cases in the classroom and real life, immediacy guides our choice of works for analysis.

It is crucially important that citizens not reject the "choice" to act as a critic. In late 2002 and the first three months of 2003, President Bush and others in his administration made a number of speeches and other presentations justifying a preemptive war in Iraq. In retrospect, (and admittedly hindsight is 20/20), poll data now makes it clear that many Americans wish that they had tested the rationale for war more carefully. The broader point is that the nation and all of us as individuals will be more likely to make informed choices if we make the *choice* to carefully examine rhetoric based on the principle of immediacy.

In some instances, however, the critic is not faced with a work of rhetoric immediately in front of him or her. For example, a person might want to analyze the rhetoric of a politician (whether a national figure like Ronald Reagan or a local leader) in order to understand or evaluate that person's effectiveness. In that situation, you cannot analyze all of the politician's rhetoric, so you must consider a selection of that material. How should the critic choose works to analyze? The second, third, and fourth principles of choice provide the tools to make that selection.

The second principle of choice is *representativeness*. If you want to understand someone's rhetoric, the most obvious method is to choose representative works that reflect the entire volume of the person's rhetorical output. Using this principle, the critic should attempt to choose works that are in some sense normal or average and avoid those that clearly are atypical. If you were looking at the rhetoric of former President George H.W. Bush, for example, you would want to choose works that broadly represented everything that he said during his presidency. This might mean choosing a representative sample of rhetoric concerning domestic and foreign policy, as well as some ceremonial works, such as his inaugural address. Representativeness is not the same as average or random. It would not be wise to choose rhetoric of the former president to analyze by randomly opening pages in volumes of his presidential papers and speeches.

The third principle of choice is *distinctiveness*. Here, the critic chooses a work of rhetoric because it is distinctive in its composition or effect. The distinctiveness principle is in a way the opposite of the representativeness principle. Sometimes the critic should choose to analyze a work of rhetoric precisely because it is quite different from the norm. This explains why rhetorical critics focus on major speeches by Lincoln, Reagan, or Franklin Roosevelt. Most speeches, even by presidents, have little effect. For major speeches by the presidents mentioned, however, there is little doubt about their impact both with an immediate audience and over time. These major speeches may not in every case have been representative of all of the rhetoric of the person, but they are distinctive in what they contain and the effects they produced. Therefore, they merit analysis. For example, later in this book, I analyze President Reagan's famed address honoring the Challenger astronauts on the night of the terrible accident that took their lives. This address occurred at a moment of extraordinary tragedy and President Reagan handled the situation with more than even his normal grace and eloquence. The Challenger address was hardly typical of Reagan's work, but a full understanding of his rhetoric would require a consideration of it and other *distinctive* speeches.

How should the critic balance the principles of representativeness and distinctiveness? There is no simple answer to this question. All the critic can do is recognize that both principles are important, but also recognize that either can be misapplied. For example, it probably would not make sense to choose works to analyze for a book on Ronald Reagan by simply choosing three or four works from each year of his two terms. That approach would be representative, but it hardly seems likely to produce much insight, because it might skip over the most important speeches. But then again it also wouldn't make sense to focus only on those important speeches. As someone who has written about Reagan for more than twenty-five years, one of the characteristics that is most evident in his speeches is that all of his rhetoric speaks with a similar voice. A focus on just the major speeches might lead one to conclude that Reagan had great speech writers. The discovery that he sounds so similar in speeches of many different types and over many different years (and thus with many different writers) suggests that Reagan himself was heavily involved in writing and editing his speeches, something that I have verified in my own research.[1] Thus, by applying both the principles of *representativeness* and *distinctiveness*, we as rhetorical critics can gain a greater understanding of what made Reagan such an effective public persuader.

The final principle of choice is *relevance*. In some cases, the critic chooses to analyze a given work, not because of that work's intrinsic importance, but because it helps him or her get at another question. The rhetorical historian Barnet Baskerville makes the point that rhetoric is not only an instrument that humans use for persuasion, but also a "window" on the society in which the rhetoric was presented.[2] One way to understand the United States in the 1950s, for example, would be to focus on rhetoric of the time. Looking at speeches from that era undoubtedly would reveal a much more conservative moral climate than in the United States today. It also would reveal a public sphere in which almost all of the leaders were white males. In other words, by looking at the rhetoric of the 1950s, we might be able to learn a lot about the entire society. A look at the rhetoric of the United States in the first and second decades of the new millennium would reveal very different rhetorical practices and a very different society. It is a long way from the rhetoric of Dwight Eisenhower to the rhetoric of Donald Trump. But just as an historian might learn a lot about the 1950s by studying Eisenhower's speeches, a contemporary cultural critic might learn a lot about cultural practices in the late two thousand teens by studying rhetoric at Trump rallies.

A study of rhetoric might be used to get at other questions as well. For example, some theorists argue that all rhetoric in one way or another tells a story.[3] If a critic were interested in testing this claim, he or she would pick rhetoric that is "relevant" to the theoretical issue under debate. The critic probably would analyze several works on the same topic (in order to hold that issue constant), only one of which explicitly told a story. The critic then would consider whether all of the works on the topic really could be considered stories.[4]

In sum, the principle of *relevance* is most important when the critic uses rhetorical analysis to answer questions relating to a purpose other than explaining or evaluating the particular piece of rhetoric, for example, using rhetorical analysis to illuminate history or culture.

The four principles of choice have been listed in descending level of importance. For most citizens, the principle of immediacy is far and away the most important. You need to understand what your boss is saying so that you can write a persuasive letter asking for a raise. In many cases, we need to analyze a work of rhetoric because if we do not do so, we may not be able to understand what is being said, or, worse, we may be manipulated by that rhetoric. In some circumstances, however, the principles of representativeness, distinctiveness, and relevance also are important because we are interested in identifying larger rhetorical patterns or interested in what the rhetoric tells us about history or other aspects of society.

ANALYSIS

The second stage in rhetorical criticism is *analysis*. Here, the goal is to see clearly what is being said and how the rhetor is saying it. The analyst identifies the explicit and implicit message, the supporting reasoning and evidence, the role played by the speaker or writer (the rhetor), the implied relationship between the rhetor and the audience, and all of the various strategies present in the rhetoric.

Why is such a system needed? The short answer is that humans tend to see what they expect to see. Take the 1996 presidential election as an example. Republicans tended to think that Senator Dole did a better job than President Clinton in various debates while partisans of President Clinton drew the opposite conclusion. The same point could be made about any political campaign. In 2004, Democrats thought that John Kerry won the debates, while Republicans tended to believe that they had been won by President Bush. In 2016, Democrats praised Hillary Clinton for her performance, while many Republicans thought that Donald Trump was the superior debater. This point is generalizable. We all have predispositions that shape what we see. A system of rhetorical analysis is needed to help us break through the "rhetorical blinders" that we all wear in order to see clearly what is being said and how it is supported.

The three most important principles operating in the analytical stage are *critical distance*, *completeness*, and an *audience-centered* approach. Critical distance means that the critic should try to be as objective as possible in putting aside his/her feelings and prior experience relating to the rhetoric. The goal is to see as clearly as possible what was in the words and other symbols used by the rhetor. Loss of critical distance often leads to misunderstanding the rhetoric. At the analytical stage, a critic takes off his/her hat as a Republican or Democrat, liberal or conservative, and so forth and becomes as much as is possible a pure analyst. This is a hard principle to meet, but especially important. Even the briefest look at the partisans on TV commentary shows makes it clear that they rarely have anything of interest to say because they always take the party line. The principle of critical distance should help a liberal Democrat see that Ronald Reagan was quite effective and help a conservative Republican make the same judgment about the rhetoric of Barack Obama.

Some people argue that objectivity is impossible or even unimportant.[5] They note that everyone has biases and assert that achieving perfect objectivity is a pipe dream. Some even argue that attempting to be objective is a bad thing because it privileges "reason" over feelings. On that last point, the critics of objectivity are clearly right. The idea of "critical distance" does assume that human reason is the best available tool for discovering the strategies in any work of rhetoric. It is in their judgment that reliance on "reason" is a bad thing that the critics of objectivity get wrong. Of course, the ideals of objectivity and critical distance are impossible to achieve in a perfect sense. Everyone has their biases. But we should strive to put aside those biases as much as possible. Would you want your worst enemy evaluating your job performance? Would it be fair for the prosecution in a criminal trial to pick all the jurors? These simple questions

© RON FOSTER SHARIF/SHUTTERSTOCK.COM

make clear the danger posed by bias. It is because that same danger exists in rhetorical analysis that critics should strive for critical distance. Critical distance helps the rhetorical critic put aside wishful thinking, first impression, prior opinions, and so forth to take a hard look at the rhetoric. Critical distance, therefore, helps us test the rhetoric for what it really is, not what we want it to be. It is hard to achieve, but an important goal at which the critic should aim.

Completeness is also a crucial goal of the critic at the analytical stage. Oftentimes people see part of the message or part of the strategy, but miss other parts. For example, in the 1992 presidential election, many in the media noted that independent candidate Ross Perot relied on charts and "plain Texas talk." And Perot did use charts and he did talk like a Texan. But Perot did other things as well. He drew on enormous public displeasure with government. He also appealed to the populist sentiment that ordinary people could fix things if they only could get into office. And Perot also built strong arguments that the budget deficit threatened the economic well-being of this nation.[6] An analysis that focused on Perot's charts and his "Texas talk," but ignored the anti-government, anti-deficit, and pro-populist appeals, would have been an incomplete analysis. In order to see clearly what is present in rhetoric, the rhetorical critic needs to see "completely." That requires the critic to identify all of the important components in a given work of rhetoric.

How can the critic achieve both critical distance and completeness in carrying out the analytical stage? The answer is to systematically apply a set of overlapping and in some cases inconsistent descriptive categories. The use of these categories can "force" the critic to put aside his/her blinders and conduct a complete analysis of all facets of the rhetoric. I will present a detailed system of analysis categories in the next chapter. In many contexts, appropriate categorization means defining categories so that they are discrete from each other. Such an approach is not practical in rhetorical analysis because words and other symbols can influence audiences in multiple ways. For example, in many works of rhetoric a story works as a powerful narrative making a point, but also as an argument and an appeal to core societal values. The same words function in three different strategy categories. Application of the analysis system developed in the next chapter would reveal each of these strategies and also how they work together.

The final principle that should guide critical analysis is to take an audience-centered approach. The goal of the rhetorical critic is not to discover a hidden pattern in the rhetoric, as in the plot of a Dan Brown novel. Rather, the goal is to explain the way that rhetoric resonated (or failed to resonate) for the real people who experienced it. For example, a critic not guided by an audience-centered approach might use a complex literary or psychological theory to look at the rhetoric of a recent president. But such theories are focused on literary principles or perhaps Freudian psychology, theories that do not necessarily apply to how people experience presidential rhetoric. As a starting point, it makes sense to begin with a focus on the kinds of rhetorical patterns that influence (or sometimes fail to influence) real people at the time the rhetoric is presented.

RESEARCH

The third stage in preparing a rhetorical critique is research. Here, the critic is concerned with learning as much as possible about the situation in which and the audience to whom the rhetoric was presented. It might seem that the research stage should come before the analytical one. Other than spoiling the acronym, however, there is a good reason that analysis should come before research. The problem is that research may act as a set of blinders limiting what the critic sees. If research reveals that several experts have written about the emotional appeals in a given speech, this information could cause the critic to miss other aspects of the speech. He or she would see the emotional rhetoric, because he/she expected to see it. Recall the example cited in the introduction of the 1980 Carter-Reagan debate. In their analysis of the debate, the media saw what they expected to see: Carter was better on the facts and Reagan better in his delivery. Of course, that was not what actually happened in the presidential debate. However, if I had researched press coverage of the debate prior to conducting my own analysis of it, I might have been influenced to conclude that Carter made stronger arguments than did Reagan. By doing the analysis prior to the research stage, however, my judgment was not influenced by the newspaper coverage and I saw (much to my surprise at the time) that Reagan had been a much better arguer than had Carter.

Research should be conducted after analysis in order to avoid the risk that previous research will bias your consideration of the message, as it biased the media analysts of the Carter-Reagan debate. Put more simply, you should look for yourself before reading what others have written about the rhetoric.

There is one exception to the rule that analysis should come before research. There are rare cases in which it is impossible to understand the rhetoric without some knowledge of the context in which it was presented. This situation occurs most frequently when the rhetoric was presented in a culture or at a time radically different than present-day America. In that case, the critic has to do enough research to understand the rhetoric prior to carrying out the analysis.

Goals of the Research Stage

In the research stage the critic has four main goals. First, research often is necessary to understand the time/place/culture in which the rhetoric was presented. The greater the difference in time/place/culture from our own, the more research the critic needs to do in order to place the rhetoric into perspective. So, for example, more research would be needed to understand a speech presented in medieval France than a speech given in the 2016 presidential campaign.

Second, the research stage is important for discovering as much as possible about the mindset of the audience to whom the rhetoric was presented. In order to explain and evaluate why a given work of rhetoric was or was not effective, the critic has to be able to see through the eyes of the audience. One of the most fundamental principles in rhetoric is that the successful rhetor must begin with where the audience already is. You persuade them to change their views by starting with where they are. In order to apply this principle, the critic must understand the mindset of the audience at the time the rhetoric was presented.

In accomplishing the first two goals the most important theoretical concepts are rhetorical barriers and rhetorical advantages. A "rhetorical barrier" *is an attitude, belief or other problem that a rhetor must overcome in order to persuade an audience to accept a given position.* For example, in the 1996 presidential campaign, Republican nominee Robert Dole had to overcome the perception of some that he was too old to run for president. In 2004, John Kerry had to persuade the American people that he was not a flip-flopper on the issues. In 2008, then Senator Obama had to persuade the American people that he had enough experience to be president. In 2016, Donald Trump had to persuade people that a businessman and reality TV star had the qualifications to be president. Neither Dole, nor Kerry overcame these barriers, which partially explains their failure to win the election. Obama and Trump obviously overcame the barriers they faced, leading to their elections as president.

A "rhetorical advantage" is precisely the opposite of a rhetorical barrier. A "rhetorical advantage" *is an attitude, belief, or other position that gives the rhetor assistance in persuading an audience.* For example, immediately after the Gulf War, General Colin Powell was immensely popular. That popularity functioned as a "rhetorical advantage" that helped him every time he spoke to an audience. After his resignation as Secretary of State in the first term of the second Bush administration, this rhetorical advantage had dissipated to some extent, especially among people who questioned the need to go to war with Iraq. The larger point is that one could not understand how Powell's rhetoric functioned between 1991 and 2006 without understanding the rhetorical advantage he possessed in the 1990s and how that advantage partially had disappeared by 2005.

In the research stage, the critic should be concerned with gathering adequate information to explain the barriers and advantages that the rhetor faced in attempting to persuade a particular audience. By focusing on rhetorical barriers and advantages, the critic will be able to get a good idea of both the context in which the rhetoric was presented and the mindset of the audience. In chapter three, I develop a category system for describing the various types of rhetorical barriers and advantages.

Third, the critic needs to be able to place him/herself in the position of the rhetor. For example, research might reveal that a given political candidate did not seriously expect to win a particular election, but instead wanted to use his or her rhetoric to rouse public interest in an issue. Some argue that this is often the case when a protest candidate campaigns for president. This discovery might cause a critic to judge the candidate's rhetoric as successful, where otherwise it would have been labeled a failure. Even if the candidate only received ten or fifteen percentage points of the vote, he/she may have accomplished his/her aim, which was to bring an issue to the attention of the public. Precisely that judgment could be made about the influence of Ross Perot in the 1992 election.

Finally, the critic needs to gather all data relevant to the evaluation of any work of rhetoric. As I explain in chapter three, in nearly all cases the rhetorical critic should base evaluation of the effectiveness of the rhetoric upon the rhetoric itself. That is, the critic asks whether the rhetor did as good a job as possible of responding to the audience in a given situation. In some cases, however, external data on audience reaction or some other aspect of the issue can be very useful in supporting an evaluation of a given work. For example, there was vast public reaction to the testimony of Oliver North before Congress during the Iran-Contra affair at the end of the Reagan presidency. North was called a national hero. There were Ollie North for President bumper stickers, Ollie North drinks, Ollie North sandwiches (a hero of course), and many other events illustrating strong support for North. This material is strong evidence that the main question in relation to North's rhetoric was not "whether" it was effective, but "why" it was so effective.[7] A similar point could be made about the influence of Donald Trump's speeches to core supporters at rallies. It is clear that his rally speeches work effectively for his supporters. The key issue is to explain why they work for that audience.

As the North and Trump examples illustrate, it is important to gather any available external data on the impact of a given work of rhetoric. Oftentimes, there will be no such data. But in some cases there may be opinion polls, press reports on audience reaction to a speech, newspaper editorial responses to a statement, letters to the editor, or other information that gives a strong hint about public reaction. If that data exists, it is important to find it. It also is important to gather data to test the quality and ethicality of the argument in any work of rhetoric. I will explain how to conduct that research when I discuss the "Informed Citizen" in chapter eleven.

FOUR FUNCTIONS OF THE RESEARCH STAGE

1 Clarify the context in which the rhetoric was presented.
2 Gather information on the mindset of the audience.
3 Discover the motives of the rhetor.
4 Gather information on public response to the rhetoric and the quality of the argument made in the rhetoric.

In order to fulfill the four functions of the research stage, the critic needs to gather as much research material relating to the rhetoric as is relevant. If the rhetoric comes from the present day, the research required may not be very much, only enough to support claims about audience attitudes, beliefs, values, interest, and knowledge. If, however, the rhetoric comes from another time/place/culture, then large amounts of research may be required. For example, the rhetorical practices in the United States in the 19th century were different in important ways from today. Significant research would be needed in order to understand the cultural norms of the time, audience attitudes, and so forth. There is a general rule in regard to research. The farther away in time, place, culture, or issue from the present day, the greater the research burden.

The key to the research stage is to recognize that the goal is not to research the person's biography per se or all aspects of the issues involved in the rhetoric. Rather, the critic should look for material in that biography, in information about the issue, and elsewhere that helps him or her understand, explain, and evaluate how the rhetoric worked for the particular audience. The research process is discussed in more depth in chapter three.

EXPLANATION AND EVALUATION

The final stage in rhetorical analysis is explanation and evaluation. Here, the critic takes the materials gathered in the previous three stages and uses them to explain why the rhetoric resonated or failed to resonate, and evaluates the ethicality and truthfulness of the rhetoric.

The goals of the evaluative stage are to judge the effectiveness, truth, and/or ethical quality of the rhetoric. It is important to note that the focus is on the rhetoric, not on evaluating the policy or ideology in the rhetoric. One can praise the rhetoric of President Reagan or President Obama without endorsing their political views. In many cases, the focus is less on evaluating effectiveness than it is on explaining why a given work of rhetoric resonated or failed to resonate. For example, there is no question that the address that then state Senator Barack Obama presented at the 2004 Democratic National Convention had enormous influence. Before the address, Obama was virtually unknown. By the time he left the podium commentators were talking about him as a potential president.[8] The interesting question about Obama's speech is not whether it was effective; that it was effective is obvious. The interesting question is why it had such enormous influence.

In relation to effectiveness, the critic asks whether the rhetor did as good a job as possible in developing strategies to persuade an audience in a particular situation. In relation to truth and the ethical quality of the discourse, the critic asks whether the rhetor built a strong case for his/her position and whether he/she used ethical means of persuasion. Principles for evaluating effectiveness are developed in chapter 3. Standards for evaluating truth and ethics are found in chapter 11.

Why is it important to evaluate or explain effectiveness and evaluate truth and ethicality? The short answer is that rhetoric matters. As I explained in the introduction, rhetorical failure often means that a group of some kind failed to address a major problem confronting them. On the other hand, unethical or untruthful rhetoric can create enormous problems, sometimes for an entire nation. Consequently, it is important for the rhetorical critic to evaluate (or explain) both the effectiveness of a given work of rhetoric and to judge whether that work made a strong and ethical case for a position.

It is vital to note that in these three types of evaluation, the critic is concerned with the rhetoric and not primarily the position being advocated in the rhetoric. In considering a speech about gun control, for example, the issue would not be whether gun control is a good idea, but whether the rhetor did as good a job as possible of supporting the position and did so in an ethical manner.

CONCLUSION

The "I CARE" system of analysis provides a systematic approach for rhetorical criticism. It can be used to critique a speech by President Trump, a music video advocating aid to the poor, an editorial in *The New York Times*, a feminist science fiction novel, or any other work of rhetoric. The next chapter lays out in more depth the analysis stage in the system.

1   This research is summarized in Robert C. Rowland and John M Jones, *Reagan at Westminster: Foreshadowing the End of the Cold War* (College Station: Texas A & M University Press, 2010). I had an opportunity to present the research in the primary paper on Reagan's rhetoric at a conference celebrating the centennial of his birth. See Robert C. Rowland, "Principle, Pragmatism, and Authenticity in Reagan's Rhetoric," The Ronald Reagan Centennial: An Academic Symposium 'Leadership and Legacy,'" University of Southern California School of Policy Planning and Development, February 2, 2011, http://www.youtube.com/watch?v=Ec485RYa3D4.

2   See Barnet Baskerville, "Must We All Be 'Rhetorical Critics'?" *Quarterly Journal of Speech* 63 (1977): 107–116.

3   Walter Fisher makes this argument. See "Narration as a Human Communication Paradigm: The Case of Public Moral Argument," *Communication Monographs* 51 (1984); 1–22.

4   I carried out this project in "On Limiting the Narrative Paradigm: Three Case Studies," *Communication Monographs* 56 (1989): 39–54.

5   The view that objectivity is unimportant and impossible to achieve is quite common in the philosophical movement called postmodernism. I explain and refute that position in "In Defense of Rational Argument: A Pragmatic Justification of Argumentation Theory and Response to the Postmodern Critique," *Philosophy and Rhetoric* 28 (1995): 350–364.

6   See Ross Perot, *United We Stand: How We Can Take Back Our Country* (New York: Hyperion, 1992).

7   See Robert C. Rowland, "The Strange Case of Ollie North: Rhetoric, Politics, and Criticism," paper presented at the Iowa Scholars Workshop on the Rhetoric of Political Argumentation, Spring 1991.

8   See Robert C. Rowland and John M. Jones, "Recasting the American Dream and American Politics: Barack Obama's Keynote Address to the 2004 Democratic National Convention," *Quarterly Journal of Speech* 93 (2007): 425–448.

CHAPTER 2
Tools for Analyzing Rhetoric

In order to understand the way that any work of rhetoric functions to persuade (or fails to persuade) a given audience, the analyst needs two sets of tools. The first set of tools is used to break the rhetoric down into constituent parts. A system of analysis is needed that can be applied systematically to any work of rhetoric. That system needs to be applicable to a speech, an essay, a film, a comedy show, and so forth. Such a system is developed in this chapter.

The second set of tools is a system for placing a given work of rhetoric in its context. Any work of persuasion exists in a particular context and cannot be understood apart from that context. For example, Franklin Roosevelt's advocacy of the "New Deal" must be understood in the context of the Great Depression. And Ronald Reagan's conservative rhetoric opposing large government is only understandable as a response to the expansion of Federal Government social programs, beginning with Roosevelt and continuing for almost five decades. The "tea party" movement at the end of the first decade of the 21st century can only be understood as a response to both the election of President Barack Obama and the bailout of the financial industry that occurred at the end of the second term of President George W. Bush. Even the very meaning of words may change over time. The word "gay" had a very different meaning in the 1930s, when it primarily was used as an adjective to describe someone who was full of fun, than it does today.

However, before placing rhetoric in its context, it is first necessary to identify the constituent parts of that rhetoric. Consequently, the focus of this chapter is on a descriptive system that can be applied to any work of rhetoric; a system for describing the context in which rhetoric is presented is developed in the following chapter.

ANALYSIS

The second stage in the "I CARE" system of rhetorical criticism is "analysis." The purpose of this stage is to see clearly all of the main elements present in the rhetoric, while putting aside any predispositions. Again, the focus is on characteristics as they relate to audience. While a literary critic might identify a complex stylistic pattern in a work, the focus of the rhetorical critic is on patterns as they relate to real audiences. In order to fulfill these purposes, it is important systematically to apply a broad set of categories designed to reveal the significant features in the rhetoric.

To carry out the analytical stage, the critic initially should familiarize him/herself with the "I CARE" categories. Then, he or she should carefully go over the rhetoric making appropriate notes. These notes then should be integrated into the system, usually in the form of an outline of the key characteristics in the rhetoric. Such an outline of the analysis categories is included at the end of the chapter. This outline can be used to analyze any work of rhetoric, from a YouTube video, to a speech by Al Gore, to a political cartoon, or a rhetorical work of art.

The following section defines each category and cites an example of how to apply it, drawing from the speech that President Donald Trump presented from the White House on January 8, 2019. At the time of the speech, the nation was dealing with a shutdown of the federal government that had been brought on by the failure of Congress to fund a border wall that President Trump insisted was needed to protect the nation from a crisis brought on by high levels of undocumented immigration. He delivered the speech in an effort to create public pressure on Congress to provide funds to build the wall. Peter Baker noted that Trump's aim was "to reframe the debate" in order "to pressure Congress into paying for his long-promised border wall, even at the cost of leaving the government partly closed."[1] It was "one of the biggest gambles of his presidency" that "changed no minds in Washington."[2] The failure of the speech ultimately led Trump to capitulate to Democrats in Congress and reopen the government without funding for the border wall. He followed by declaring a national emergency and taking funds for a wall from other priorities.

Despite its failure to pressure Congress to fund a border wall or to create a groundswell of public support for that wall, the speech is important. It meets the standards of both representativeness and distinctiveness that were discussed in chapter one. The speech is representative of the anti-immigration rhetoric that energized Trump's victory in first the Republican primaries in 2016 and then the general election campaign. More than any other issue, Trump used his anti-immigration rhetoric to win the presidency. Works of rhetoric rarely meet both the standards of representativeness and distinctiveness. In this case, however, the speech was not only representative of his rhetoric as a candidate and as president, but also distinctive because he most often presented his anti-immigration message in a campaign rally. The Oval Office speech, in contrast, was a formal presidential policy speech. For these reasons, it is an appropriate work for identifying the message that candidate and then President Trump used to energize his supporters and a starting point for explaining why that message not only failed to persuade, but often outraged Democrats and many independents as well.

President Donald J. Trump, "Address to the Nation on the Crisis at the Border," January 8, 2019[3]

1 My fellow Americans: Tonight, I am speaking to you because there is a growing humanitarian and security crisis at our southern border.

2 Every day, Customs and Border Patrol agents encounter thousands of illegal immigrants trying to enter our country. We are out of space to hold them, and we have no way to promptly return them back home to their country.

---

3   America proudly welcomes millions of lawful immigrants who enrich our society and contribute to our nation. But all Americans are hurt by uncontrolled, illegal migration. It strains public resources and drives down jobs and wages. Among those hardest hit are African Americans and Hispanic Americans.

4   Our southern border is a pipeline for vast quantities of illegal drugs, including meth, heroin, cocaine, and fentanyl. Every week, 300 of our citizens are killed by heroin alone, 90 percent of which floods across from our southern border. More Americans will die from drugs this year than were killed in the entire Vietnam War.

5   In the last two years, ICE officers made 266,000 arrests of aliens with criminal records, including those charged or convicted of 100,000 assaults, 30,000 sex crimes, and 4,000 violent killings. Over the years, thousands of Americans have been brutally killed by those who illegally entered our country, and thousands more lives will be lost if we don't act right now.

6   This is a humanitarian crisis—a crisis of the heart and a crisis of the soul.

7   Last month, 20,000 migrant children were illegally brought into the United States—a dramatic increase. These children are used as human pawns by vicious coyotes and ruthless gangs. One in three women are sexually assaulted on the dangerous trek up through Mexico. Women and children are the biggest victims, by far, of our broken system.

8   This is the tragic reality of illegal immigration on our southern border. This is the cycle of human suffering that I am determined to end.

9   My administration has presented Congress with a detailed proposal to secure the border and stop the criminal gangs, drug smugglers, and human traffickers. It's a tremendous problem. Our proposal was developed by law enforcement professionals and border agents at the Department of Homeland Security. These are the resources they have requested to properly perform their mission and keep America safe. In fact, safer than ever before.

10 The proposal from Homeland Security includes cutting-edge technology for detecting drugs, weapons, illegal contraband, and many other things. We have requested more agents, immigration judges, and bed space to process the sharp rise in unlawful migration fueled by our very strong economy. Our plan also contains an urgent request for humanitarian assistance and medical support.

11 Furthermore, we have asked Congress to close border security loopholes so that illegal immigrant children can be safely and humanely returned back home.

12 Finally, as part of an overall approach to border security, law enforcement professionals have requested $5.7 billion for a physical barrier. At the request of Democrats, it will be a steel barrier rather than a concrete wall. This barrier

is absolutely critical to border security. It's also what our professionals at the border want and need. This is just common sense.

13   The border wall would very quickly pay for itself. The cost of illegal drugs exceeds $500 billion a year—vastly more than the $5.7 billion we have requested from Congress. The wall will also be paid for, indirectly, by the great new trade deal we have made with Mexico.

14   Senator Chuck Schumer—who you will be hearing from later tonight—has repeatedly supported a physical barrier in the past, along with many other Democrats. They changed their mind only after I was elected president.

15   Democrats in Congress have refused to acknowledge the crisis. And they have refused to provide our brave border agents with the tools they desperately need to protect our families and our nation.

16   The federal government remains shut down for one reason and one reason only: because Democrats will not fund border security. My administration is doing everything in our power to help those impacted by the situation. But the only solution is for Democrats to pass a spending bill that defends our borders and re-opens the government.

17   This situation could be solved in a 45-minute meeting. I have invited Congressional leadership to the White House tomorrow to get this done. Hopefully, we can rise above partisan politics in order to support national security.

18   Some have suggested a barrier is immoral. Then why do wealthy politicians build walls, fences, and gates around their homes? They don't build walls because they hate the people on the outside, but because they love the people on the inside. The only thing that is immoral is the politicians to do nothing and continue to allow more innocent people to be so horribly victimized.

19   America's heart broke the day after Christmas when a young police officer in California was savagely murdered in cold blood by an illegal alien, who just came across the border. The life of an American hero was stolen by someone who had no right to be in our country.

20   Day after day, precious lives are cut short by those who have violated our borders. In California, an Air Force veteran was raped, murdered, and beaten to death with a hammer by an illegal alien with a long criminal history. In Georgia, an illegal alien was recently charged with murder for killing, beheading, and dismembering his neighbor. In Maryland, MS-13 gang members who arrived in the United States as unaccompanied minors were arrested and charged last year after viciously stabbing and beating a 16-year-old girl.

21   Over the last several years, I've met with dozens of families whose loved ones were stolen by illegal immigration. I've held the hands of the weeping mothers and embraced the grief-stricken fathers. So sad. So terrible. I will never forget

the pain in their eyes, the tremble in their voices, and the sadness gripping their souls.

22 How much more American blood must we shed before Congress does its job?

23 To those who refuse to compromise in the name of border security, I would ask: Imagine if it was your child, your husband, or your wife whose life was so cruelly shattered and totally broken?
To every member of Congress: Pass a bill that ends this crisis.
To every citizen: Call Congress and tell them to finally, after all of these decades, secure our border.

24 This is a choice between right and wrong, justice and injustice. This is about whether we fulfill our sacred duty to the American citizens we serve.

25 When I took the Oath of Office, I swore to protect our country. And that is what I will always do, so help me God. Thank you and goodnight.

Application of Analysis Categories

I. Goal—The goal refers to the aim either stated or implied in the rhetoric. The critic infers the goal from the rhetoric itself and not from any knowledge of the subject or the rhetor. Within the goal it is important to consider the themes that are presented and the action that the rhetor requests from the audience.

A. Themes

Themes are the main points made in the work. There may be multiple themes presented in a work of rhetoric or there may be a single main point (the thesis of the work) that is backed up by supporting themes. In this case, the overarching theme was that a massive shift in support of his administration's immigration policy was needed to deal with a crisis at the border. Trump supported this message with four primary themes, two related to immigration and two related to politics.

The first theme was that the nation faced an immigration crisis. He identified several dimensions of that crisis. In the first paragraph, he pointed to "a growing humanitarian and security crisis at our southern border." The humanitarian crisis involved "20,000 migrant children" who in the previous month "were illegally brought into the United States" by human traffickers, who he labeled "vicious coyotes and ruthless gangs" (7). He also noted that "One in three women are sexually assaulted on the dangerous trek up through Mexico. Women and children are the biggest victims, by far, of our broken system" (7). At the same time, his focus was not on the addressing the needs of the undocumented immigrants, many of whom were fleeing violence in Central America. If that had been his focus, he would have proposed expanding shelters for these people in the United States, expediting asylum hearings for them, or providing additional aid to nations in Central America to address the problems leading them to attempt the arduous journey to the U.S.

Rather, his focus was on the threat that these undocumented immigrants posed to the American people. In paragraph 3, he claimed that "all Americans are hurt by uncontrolled, illegal migration. It strains public resources and drives down jobs and wages." He added that "Among those hardest hit are African-Americans and Hispanic Americans" (3). Trump claimed that one major problem was that the border acts as "a pipeline for vast quantities of illegal drugs, including meth, heroin, cocaine, and fentanyl" (4). He also stated that "Every week, 300 of our citizens are killed by heroin alone, 90 percent of which floods across from our southern border" (4). Another problem was crime. President Trump claimed that in the previous two years, the government made "266,000 arrests of aliens with criminal records, including those charged or convicted of 100,000 assaults, 30,000 sex crimes, and 4,000 violent killings" (5). He added that "thousands of Americans have been brutally killed by those who illegally entered our country, and thousands more lives will be lost if we don't act right now" (5).

Trump labeled the problem as "a humanitarian crisis" (6) that was "the tragic reality of illegal immigration" (8). While Trump mentioned the suffering experienced by many of the undocumented immigrants, his real focus was on the claim that these immigrants posed a serious danger to the American people. He claimed that the result was a "cycle of human suffering" (8).

The second theme in the speech was that his immigration proposals, especially a wall, would address the problem. He did not describe his proposal in detail or explain how it would address all of the problems that he ascribed to immigration. He simply said that his plan included "cutting-edge technology for detecting drugs, weapons, illegal contraband, and many other things" (10) and also included funding for "more agents, immigration judges, and bed space" as well as "an urgent request for humanitarian assistance and medical support" (10). In addition he called for closing "border security loopholes so that illegal immigrant children can be safely and humanely returned back home" (11). In supporting this theme, Trump simply described his proposal in general terms and did not cite evidence that it would succeed. Moreover, several of the proposals that he mentioned had received bipartisan support and were not the proximate cause of the government shutdown.[4]

Trump's major focus in developing the second theme was on the need for spending "$5.7 billion" on a "steel barrier" that would be the "border wall" (11, 12) that he had promised throughout his campaign and the first two years of his presidency. Trump did not describe the wall in any detail, identify the sections of the border where it would be built, or cite evidence proving that the wall would effectively address any of the problems that he had described. Rather, he claimed that it was "what our professionals at the border want and need" and called it "just common sense" (12). He also claimed that the wall "would very quickly pay for itself" since "The cost of illegal drugs exceeds $500 billion a year—vastly more than the $5.7 billion" (13) cost of the wall. He added that "The wall will also be paid for, indirectly, by the great new trade deal we have made with Mexico" (13). He did not explain how the wall would stop drug traffickers who mostly get their product into the country through legal ports of entry or indicate how the trade deal would save money for the federal government.[5] The rationale for this theme can be boiled down to his phrase, "just common sense" (12).

The third theme in the speech was that Democrats in Congress were responsible for the government shutdown and were hypocrites since they previously had supported funding for a wall. In paragraph 14, he attacked the leader of the Democrats in the Senate, Senator Chuck Schumer of New York, claiming that Schumer "has repeatedly supported a physical barrier in the past, along with many other Democrats." Trump made it clear that he believed that Democratic opposition to a wall was based in politics, observing "They changed their mind only after I was elected president." In the following paragraph, he attacked Democrats because "they have refused to provide our brave border agents with the tools they desperately need to protect our families and our nation." He then placed blame for the continued shutdown of the government on Democrats in Congress. He said, "The federal government remains shut down for one reason and one reason only: because Democrats will not fund border security" (16). Trump amplified this point by noting that he had invited the leaders of both parties in Congress to meet at the White House and added, "Hopefully, we can rise above partisan politics in order to support national security" (17). While this statement called for "rising above" partisanship, it in fact was highly partisan since he was not offering to compromise, but calling on Democrats to simply give in to his demands for wall funding.

The final theme was that he cared about protecting the American people, while those opposed to wall funding did not. He began to develop this theme by drawing an analogy between a border wall and the "walls, fences, and gates" around the homes of politicians (18). He claimed that those barriers were built by people not "because they hate the people on the outside, but because they love the people on the inside" (18). The implication was that unlike Democrats, Trump loved the American people. He said it was "immoral. . . [for] politicians to do nothing and continue to allow more innocent people to be so horribly victimized" (18) and then went on to describe "a young police officer," "an Air Force Veteran," and others who were murdered by "an illegal alien" (20). He added that he had "held the hands of the weeping mothers and embraced the grief-stricken fathers" of those who lost family members murdered by an undocumented immigrant. The implication was that he cared deeply about the people of the nation, while the heartless Democrats did not.

B. Requested Action

The requested action concerns what the rhetor wants to be done and what he/she wants the audience to do in order to achieve that aim. In many cases, the rhetoric explicitly will call on the audience to take some action. A fund-raising letter will conclude by asking for money. In other cases, the action that should be taken by the audience is implied, but not explicitly stated. An editorial attacking gun violence might imply that strengthened gun control laws are needed, without ever stating that point explicitly.

In rare cases, the requested action may be the opposite of what is actually stated in the rhetoric. Imagine a situation in which a politician has been accused of misconduct. A speaker might lay out all of the reasons why the politician had every right to fight the charges, despite the harm to his/her career. In so doing, the speaker explicitly would be saying that the politician had the right to fight to the end, but implicitly would be saying that the sensible thing to do would be to resign. Such rhetoric, where the implied conclusion is the opposite of what is stated, is uncommon.

In this case, the requested action was quite obvious and precisely the same as the thesis to the speech. At the end of the speech, Trump made it very clear that achieving border security justified a temporary government shutdown. He asked, "How much more American blood must we shed before Congress does its job?" (22). He then instructed members of Congress, "Pass a bill that ends this crisis" and spoke "To every citizen: Call Congress and tell them to finally, after all of these decades, secure our border" (23). He said the "choice" was "between right and wrong" (24). Thus, the requested action was for the American people to pressure Congress into fully funding Trump's border wall.

I have developed the primary themes and supporting sub-themes in the speech in some detail because they inform other aspects of the analysis that I will discuss in a moment. In outline form, these themes and sub-themes could be summarized with a few key phrases and references to particular paragraphs in the speech.

II. Organization—It is very important to lay out the organizational pattern found in any work of rhetoric. In some cases, the organization itself may be one of the characteristics defining the rhetoric. For example, a critic of the economic policies of President Obama might first remind the audience of the strong growth that occurred in the last five years

of the Reagan administration and then juxtapose that record with slow growth following the stimulus package that passed Congress in 2009. In this case, the organization would be crucial to the themes and strategies present in the speech. In essence, that would be true because the speech or essay would be organized around two stories, one involving fast growth in the Reagan Administration and one involving much slower growth during Obama's presidency. As this example indicates, organization is likely to be most important in works that tell a story. For example, the organization of the speech by John Anjain, which is considered in chapter five, is the core of his rhetoric. It only makes sense that the organization (plot) of a story is more important than in cases where the organization is based in a topical or problem-solution pattern.

Even when the organizational pattern does not fully dominate the work, it is important to lay out the organization in order to reveal the emphasis that the rhetor places on different points. By carefully outlining the development of the rhetoric, the critic can discover the main points in the rhetoric and determine what receives the most emphasis. Put simply, the points that get the most emphasis are likely to be the most important. In Trump's immigration speech, for instance, he spent more time accusing Democrats of hypocrisy and not caring about protecting the American people than he did explaining how a wall would solve the various problems he discussed. Trump's emphasis on the political, as opposed to detailed explanation of how the policy would work, indicates that one of his primary goals was to score political points against Democrats in Congress and also that strongly defending his proposal as sensible was a less important message.

The key to identifying the organization of any work is to go through it paragraph by paragraph, listing the main points in each section. If the rhetoric is a film, then the critic would go through it scene by scene. A song could be broken down verse by verse. And a picture could be described from top to bottom or side to side, depending on what was most convenient.

After the critic has identified the points in each unit of the rhetoric, he/she should then place those points in the following subcategories.

A. **Introduction**—Introductions are important for leading into the main body, establishing the credibility of the rhetor, and gaining the attention of the audience. As a general rule, the introduction (along with the conclusion) is proportionally more important than the main body of the rhetoric. It is, therefore, important for the rhetorical critic to identify the illustrative devices in the introduction and also where the rhetor moves into the main body of his/her rhetoric.

In this case, the introduction is quite brief, comprising only the first sentence of the speech where the president points to the existence of "a growing humanitarian and security crisis at our southern border" (1). As I've noted, Trump's primary focus was not on the humanitarian crisis experienced by those fleeing to the United States, but on how those people threatened American citizens. He used the brief introduction and then the discussion of "migrant children" and migrant women who "are sexually assaulted" (7) in order to claim that he was concerned about the safety of the immigrants in order not to appear to be totally heartless. One reason that the introduction was so short may have been that his real focus was not on expressing concern for the immigrants, a group that he had demonized at many rallies and that he would attack as including many vicious criminals later in the speech, but on masking his lack of concern for this group.

B. **Conclusion**—In general, the function of a conclusion is to summarize the main points that have been made, call upon the audience to act, and use some form of illustrative material to keep the attention of the audience. Conclusions are often very important for building a strong emotional response that will cause the audience to act in some way.

In this case, the conclusion begins in paragraph 22 when he used a rhetorical question to demand that Congress act. He asked "How much more American blood must we shed before Congress does its job?" He followed that question by explicitly calling on Congress to act and urging ordinary people to pressure Congress. He concluded by claiming that his action in causing a government shutdown was required by "the Oath of Office, I swore to protect our country" (25). In this passage, Trump not only called for action, but also placed blame for the shutdown on Democrats in Congress and attempted to label his own actions as based in a patriotic commitment to fulfilling his responsibilities as president.

C. **Main Body**—While the introduction and the conclusion are often proportionally more important than the main body, the main body can be considered the core of the rhetoric. It is in the main body that the dominant themes and strategies of the rhetoric are developed. People remember speeches and other rhetoric with memorable introductions and conclusions, but without an effective main section, they do not act on them.

In relation to the main body, it is important to identify the overarching organizational pattern that dominates the work in order to discover the evolution of the claims made in the rhetoric. This also will help reveal the strategies that dominate the work. In some cases there may not be a clear organizational pattern. That is also a revealing discovery. If the organizational pattern is not clear, that implies strongly that the rhetoric either is argumentatively flawed *or* that it works through non-argumentative strategies.

There are many possible organizational forms: topical, problem-solution, problem-cause-solution, chronological, geographical, and so forth. In this case, the organization is largely topical, built around the four main themes I described. After the introduction, in paragraphs 1 through 8, Trump focused on the theme that the immigration situation was a crisis. He discussed the second theme that his policies would solve the problem in paragraphs 9–13. It is notable that his discussion of the solution was so brief and as I noted almost without explanation or evidence, but instead based largely in the claim that it was "just common sense" (12). Trump's focus was not to build a strong argument that his plan would work, but to create fear and then label his approach as obviously sensible. The third theme that Democrats were acting hypocritically and did not care about their fellow citizens was developed in paragraphs 14 through 17 and also to some degree in the final section where he developed the fourth theme by juxtaposing his concern for the American people with the implicit claim that since Democrats did not favor a wall that they must not care about ordinary people (18–21).

The description of the organization of the speech, along with my earlier description of themes, is important. The focus of the speech was clearly not on building a strong case for his administration's immigration policy. In fact, he discussed policy quite briefly in only a few paragraphs and the discussion was quite general. Clearly, the absence of detailed policy discussion is suggestive of the strategies found in the speech, which I will discuss in a moment.

III. Role of the Rhetor—Humans play many roles. For example, a president of the United States may speak to the nation as a grandfather figure (Uncle Sam), as a partisan politician, as leader of all the people, as a cheerleader, as Commander in Chief, and so forth. Ordinary people also assume roles in their rhetoric. For example, there is a major difference between the roles of teacher and priest.

Role identification is important for two reasons. First, the role that one assumes strongly limits what you can say. A person playing the role of minister or priest will be expected to act and speak accordingly. If he/she violates those role assumptions, his/her rhetoric is likely to fail. Second, the choice of a role is important, because it may influence the audience's evaluation of the rhetor's credibility. We would not necessarily find it credible if a politician who had been convicted of some ethical wrongdoing attempted to play a role of "political priest" and judged others in the political system. In that case, the role of the rhetor would not be consistent with our knowledge of the person and we would doubt his/her honesty. In general, skillful rhetors assume only those roles that they credibly can play.

Roles can matter a great deal. Bill Clinton had a gift for feeling the pain of his fellow citizens, of coming across as an ordinary guy who understood their concerns. Both Ronald Reagan and Barack Obama were particularly skillful at assuming a patriotic role, a kind of modern version of the role played by the Founders of the nation, and providing a unifying vision of the nation that transcended issues of race, gender, and identity. Clinton, Reagan, and Obama were most effective when they played a role that particularly fit their rhetorical approaches.

There are two subparts of the role of the rhetor. As a first step in discovering this role, it is important to consider the *implied relationship* between the rhetor and the audience. There are three possible general relationships: peer to peer, superior to inferior, and inferior to superior. First, a rhetor may speak to an audience as a peer. President Clinton often assumed this relationship when he attended town hall meetings and talked to ordinary people, citizen to citizen. As a peer, he was able to "feel their pain" and "hear where they were coming from." Second, in the relationship of superior to inferior, the rhetor tells an audience what to think or what to do. When a general issues orders, he/she assumes a superior to inferior relationship with his/her troops. The general is not seeking input; he/she is simply telling the troops what to do. The third possible relationship is inferior to superior. Sometimes rhetors speak to an audience more powerful than they are. When the convicted criminal speaks to the jury, he/she is an inferior (a convicted felon) speaking to superiors (citizens on the jury). Political figures often assume this role when they have committed some moral transgression and must seek forgiveness from the public.

There are two key signs in rhetoric that help the critic identify the *implied relationship* in the rhetoric. The first relates to the evidence cited. If the rhetor seems to assume that his/her audience is well-informed on a subject, that indicates that he/she is not acting as a superior. In contrast, if the rhetor seems to be teaching the audience about the subject, that is a strong indication of a superior to inferior relationship. Second, a similar point can be made about the moral tone of the rhetoric. If the rhetor tells his/her audience how to think, that indicates a superior to inferior relationship. On the other hand, if the rhetor either assumes that the audience agrees with a point or actually asks for their assistance, that indicates either a relationship as a peer or even an inferior speaking to a superior.

It is important to identify the general relationship between the rhetor and the audience because that relationship places limits on other aspects of the rhetoric. For example, it may be difficult for a leader to move from the role of peer to a more commanding role. Some have argued, for instance, that this problem made it difficult for President Clinton to mobilize support for programs, such as his health care initiative. Precisely the opposite criticism was leveled against President Obama. He was seen as much more skillful in a superior to inferior role and was criticized for an inability to speak with ordinary people as a peer. That view is behind the common criticism of Obama as too "professorial."

The second subpart of the role of the rhetor is the *specific role* played in the rhetoric (if any). After the general relationship is identified, it should be possible to nail down more specifically the role or roles being played by the rhetor. As I noted, the president of the United States often plays roles such as Commander in Chief, Moral Leader, First Mourner, or Uncle Sam. Again, identification of the specific role is important because that role limits other rhetorical choices. And choice of an inappropriate role may doom a work of rhetoric to failure.

In this case, the Trump speech can be broken down in relation to both the *implied relationship* and *specific role* played by the rhetor. In relation to the *implied relationship*, for the bulk of the speech Trump assumes the role of superior to inferior. He does this by citing a great many statistics that would not be known to ordinary people. Fact checkers noted that in reality undocumented immigrants commit fewer crimes than American citizens, but the actual facts are not at issue in determining the role played by the rhetor.[6] Trump assumed the role of someone who was much more knowledgeable than ordinary citizens. The same is true in relation to his expression of moral outrage. Although he mentioned meeting with "dozens of families whose loved ones were stolen by illegal immigration" and holding "the hands of weeping mothers" (21), he did so not do so to come across as an ordinary man, but to express outrage at those who opposed his policies. He judged those who blocked the wall as failing to serve the American people.

In terms of the particular role, Trump assumed the role of defender of ordinary people. He defined the problem in black and white terms, labeled those who opposed his policy as uncaring and essentially un-American, and described himself as making decisions based in "common sense" with the aim of protecting those who could not protect themselves. If others would not do their duty, he would fulfill his oath and protect the people. The difficulty with the role that Trump assumed was that for it to ring true, the nation needed to be experiencing the kind of crisis that he described. While I will discuss the steps in evaluating rhetoric in the next chapter, at this point it is important to recognize that most Americans did not see their nation as facing a crisis brought on by undocumented immigration. Undocumented immigrants did commit crimes, but as I've noted, at a lower rate than American citizens. Opioids were a real problem, but many of the deaths were associated with legal drugs, and as I noted, the vast majority of illegal drugs came across the border at border crossings where there was already considerable security. The facts I've mentioned undoubtedly played a role in the failure of the speech to build public support for his program and his ultimate decision to end the government shutdown without gaining congressional funding for a wall. The role he assumed would only ring true for the minority of the country who saw undocumented immigration as a real crisis.

IV. Linguistic or Aesthetic Tone—Linguistic tone refers to the "feel" of the language (or the other symbols) in a given work of rhetoric. In a speech on gun control, a rhetor could be sarcastic, professorial, angry, or even satirical. Normally, the appropriate tone that should be used will be shaped by the combination of the topic, the purpose of the rhetor, and the particulars of the audience and situation. The choice of tone is important since it limits the other options available to the rhetor. An inappropriate tone may prevent a work from being effective. For example, many people are offended by a sarcastic or satirical tone on issues of grave public concern.

Non-linguistic works of rhetoric also have a tone, which I label aesthetic tone. A song may sound romantic, militaristic, or even sarcastic. Similarly, a film, a TV show, or a painting also may possess a specific aesthetic tone. For example, romantic comedies often have a gauzy feel to the way that scenes are shot, while documentaries often have a stark tone. The stark aesthetic of the documentary would not work in a romantic comedy and in fact might tip off the audience that the comedy was really about to become a tragedy.

In this case, the tone is passionate throughout. Trump claimed that the immigration crisis he describes was serious enough that he was willing to close the government in order to get funding for the wall. Trump also attempted to use language to portray himself as informed, caring, and reasonable. In the opening paragraphs he cited a number of statistics in order to depict himself as well-informed about the issue. He also described meetings he had with families who had a loved one killed by an undocumented immigrant. In claiming to have "held the hands of the weeping mothers" and "having embraced the grief-stricken fathers," Trump presented himself as both knowledgeable and compassionate (23). He also tried to use language to show that he was reasonable. He spoke of inviting "Congressional leadership to the White House" and claimed that "The situation could be solved in a 45-minute meeting" (17). With this language, Trump presented himself as the caring and reasonable adult in the room.

The difficulty with this use of tone to portray himself as knowledgeable, compassionate, and patriotic is that it may not have rung true for people who remembered instances when as a candidate or president he presented wild allegations, called an opponent a name, or made claims that were widely debunked by the media and fact-checking sites. In the process of doing the descriptive analysis, it is important to as much as possible put aside personal preconceptions. Thus, the critic would note Trump's tone as manifesting the four characteristics I've mentioned. At the same time, the knowledgeable critic would file away the sense that the tone didn't ring true and test that judgment in the research and evaluation stages of the complete analysis.

V. Implied Audience—The idea of an "implied audience" at first may seem silly. After all, there is a real audience for any rhetoric, in this case the millions of people who watched, heard, or read Trump's speech, as well as those who read about it in the media or online, or heard or saw clips in other media. The research steps needed to identify the rhetorical barriers and advantages present in the real audience will be considered in the next chapter.

In contrast to the real audience, the implied audience consists of those people for whom the rhetoric is best adapted as a work of persuasion. In order to identify the implied audience, the critic can think of the rhetoric as an arrow and ask, "Who would be the perfect target group for this arrow?" For example, if a scientist spoke about complex mathematical formulas and referred to material known only to those who read obscure scientific journals, then the implied audience for that speech would be other experts in the field. If that same scientist relied on comparisons and homey examples to make his/her point, then the implied audience would be the general public. The implied audience is a useful concept for identifying the target group at which the rhetor was aiming.

In discovering the implied audience, the critic should consider the complexity of the message, the knowledge that the rhetor assumes the audience to possess, any values or principles that the rhetor takes for granted that the audience accepts, and the language (or aesthetic) patterns in the rhetoric. The way that the rhetor presents his/her message in regard to those points tells us a great deal about the implied audience of the rhetoric. For example, if the rhetor cites complicated information without explaining it, this indicates that he/she assumes that the audience already understands the material. He/she may not be correct in that assumption or may not have made it consciously, but that is what is indicated by the way the material is presented.

After the implied audience has been discovered, it can be compared to the actual or empirical audience. Major inconsistency between the implied and the actual audience in almost every case will doom the rhetoric to failure. One common problem in many speeches, editorials, and other works of rhetoric is that the rhetor assumes the audience has knowledge about (or even interest in) a subject, when in fact the audience lacks that knowledge or interest. In that situation, the rhetoric is unlikely to be successful.

In this case, the implied audience consists of people who are core supporters of President Trump and thus likely to oppose immigration, as well as those who fear demographic change and/or are uninformed about undocumented immigrants. One sign that the speech is aimed at those who already oppose immigration and are likely to be supporters of Trump is that he made almost no effort to explain how building a wall would solve the various immigration problems that he discussed. In particular, it is difficult to see how a wall would prevent drug cartels from trying to find a way to get their product into the country. Nor would a wall be a solution to the increase in those seeking asylum, since they simply surrender to authorities at the border. Moreover, the research cited earlier indicating that undocumented immigrants actually commit fewer crimes on average than American citizens also provides a clue about the implied audience. Trump cites quite scary statistics that are likely to resonate most strongly with people who are either not aware of the actual crime rate among undocumented immigrants and/or have had very little contact with that group. It is for that reason that opposition to immigration is strongest in areas with few immigrants.[7] An audience that is either informed about the issue or that has had substantial experience with undocumented immigrants is far less likely to be scared by Trump's depiction of alien criminals than is an uninformed audience.

A final group in the implied audience is those who are uncomfortable with demographic change. Trump's description of undocumented immigrants as gang members and brutal killers could be particularly powerful for older white voters who associate high crime with African Americans and Hispanics. Such stereotypical views are inaccurate and arguably based in racist stereotypes, but they are widely held by many in this group. An analysis of Trump's actual audience in the next stage of rhetorical analysis, the research stage, would verify that many Trump supporters in fact are older white male voters.

VI. **Strategy Categories**—The most important category in the analysis system is "strategy." A strategy is a major plan of attack, one of the key ways that the rhetor appeals to the audience. Strategies are the way that the rhetor attempts to overcome rhetorical barriers and maximize rhetorical advantages to persuade the audience.

How can a critic identify strategies? In sports, the coach often will reveal what his/ her strategy was. In rhetoric, however, we do not have access to the mind of the speaker/ writer/creator and, even if we did, there is no guarantee that he or she consciously could identify the main strategies in the work. This means that the critic must identify the strategy from the work itself.

Two clues for identifying main strategies are emphasis and distinctiveness. If a given appeal is really important, then the speaker/writer/creator is likely to spend a substantial amount of time or space on it. For example, if a speaker refers once to a given metaphor, then that comparison may not be very important. But if, as in the case of Martin Luther King's "I Have a Dream Speech," a metaphor recurs throughout the rhetoric, than it is likely to be quite important. In addition, the more distinctive that a given component of rhetoric is, the more likely it is that the component reflects an important strategy in the work.

Rhetorical strategies can be placed in one or more of the following strategy categories: rational argument, narrative, aesthetic strategies, appeals to values, needs, or symbols, credibility, and confrontation. These strategies are briefly defined below and will be considered in much more detail in chapters four through nine. In carrying out the sixth sub-stage in the analysis system, the critic carefully should consider which of the sub-strategy types are present. Here, the critic should remember the general rules that rhetoric rarely contains more than three or four main strategies and that the same words may serve more than one strategic function. In the next section, I apply the six strategy categories to the speech.

A. **Rational Argument**—If the rhetor relies heavily on stated or implied evidence and reasoning, then he/she is utilizing a rational argumentative strategy for persuading the audience. There are three sub-types of rational argument. Evidence-oriented argument relies on the citation of evidence (some form of data) to persuade the audience. The main types of support are authoritative evidence, statistics, examples, and comparisons. The second sub-type is enthymematic argument. An enthymeme is a kind of argument in which the audience fills in some part of the evidence or reasoning or the claim itself is implied by the evidence and reasoning. The third sub-type is refutative argument. Refutative argument occurs when the rhetor explains why his/her position is superior to that of the other side. He/she "refutes" the views of the opposition with argument.

Where a rational argumentative strategy is present, the critic should identify the main arguments present in a piece of rhetoric, note the different types of reasoning used, and identify the kinds of support materials used to back up the arguments.

B. Narrative—If the rhetoric either directly tells a story or draws upon commonly known stories of one type or another, then it is built around a narrative strategy. Narratives work rhetorically because of the normal human pleasure in a good story and also because narrative form can create a strong sense of identification between the characters in the story and the audience, thus bringing home the message. One sign of the power of narrative is its presence throughout all aspects of contemporary society and in the historical and anthropological records throughout history and pre-history.

C. Aesthetic—Aesthetics is the theory of beauty. In rhetoric, an aesthetic strategy relies upon the power of language or other aesthetic forms to persuade the audience. In his Inaugural Address, President John F. Kennedy used an aesthetic strategy to emphasize the importance of citizens aiding their government. Kennedy said, "ask not what your country can do for you—ask what you can do for your country." Here, Kennedy appealed to his audience with a strategy called antithesis in which two opposed ideas are juxtaposed against each other. It was not the power of Kennedy's idea which made this passage so important. After all, that idea was merely a conventional call to serve the community. It was the way he said it.

There are many sub-categories of language and other aesthetic strategies that will be considered later. In general, language-based strategies rely on the appeal of a well-turned phrase or the capacity for rhetorical figures (metaphors, antithesis, and so forth), to both create interest and let us see the world in a different way. Other aesthetic strategies include physical objects, photographs, paintings, film, graphic formatting (such as bullet points), and so forth.

D. Values, Needs, and Symbols—The press often writes about politicians who appeal to our emotions. This is not as simple as it sounds. The emotions are not a spot in the brain at which a rhetor can aim. Rather, speakers and writers often create strong emotional reactions by appealing to basic societal values and attitudes or to essential human needs. Thus, a speaker might draw on patriotism as a value or the need for security in order to energize the audience. Or a writer might draw on human needs through a fear appeal focused on the danger posed by a given pollutant. Alternatively, the rhetor could use symbols that indirectly energize the values or needs. Thus, in the United States, the flag is a powerful symbol that taps into patriotism as a value.

E. Credibility—In some cases, the strategy and the speaker are one. In other words, the rhetor relies upon his or her authority in order to persuade the audience to act. Credibility plays a crucial role in persuasion in two different ways. It is a necessary condition for persuasion and occasionally developing a strong sense of credibility can persuade an audience by itself.

In rare cases, we may be willing to act simply because someone tells us to. If Michael Jordan suggests a technique for shooting a jump shot or Warren Buffett provides investment advice, most of us will go along. In many other cases, credibility is a necessary precondition for persuasion. After his resignation, few would have listened to a speech by Richard Nixon on honesty in politics because he had lost all credibility on the subject. The more recent case of Tiger Woods, who quickly fell from national icon to late-night punch line after it became clear that he had been unfaithful to his wife with multiple women is a good indication of what happens when a person loses credibility. In the analysis stage, the critic looks for evidence in the text that the rhetor is either attempting to build credibility or draw upon pre-existing credibility.

F. Confrontation—More than two thousand years ago Aristotle noted that in order to persuade an audience, the speaker must start with where the audience already is.[7] He meant that in successful rhetoric, the rhetor must begin with points of agreement in order to lead the audience to a new conclusion. In most cases, Aristotle's insight about audience adaptation is clearly correct, but in some instances, the rhetor relies on disagreement in order to persuade the audience.

In confrontative rhetoric, the rhetor "confronts" the audience by intentionally offending them or even attacking them directly, in order to get their attention and ultimately change their views. Confrontation is a dangerous rhetorical strategy that is (and should be) rarely used. It is much less common than the other five strategies, precisely because it often produces backlash in the audience. Few people like to be attacked. But there are cases where confrontation is a necessary strategy because one must get the attention of the audience prior to changing their views. Almost all movements that call for and ultimately produce major social change are forced to rely on confrontative strategies at some point in their effort to reform society. One obvious example illustrating this point is that the civil rights movement relied heavily on civil disobedience to get the attention of and create guilt within the white audience. The use of civil disobedience shocked many Americans at the time of its first use, but it also focused attention on the evils of racism and discrimination and ultimately played a crucial role in reforming laws governing civil rights.

Strategies in Trump's Speech

In the speech by President Trump, the most important strategies were evidence-oriented and refutative argument, narrative, and appeals to the need for safety and the value of family. In the opening section of the speech, Trump used an evidence-oriented argument to make a case that a failure to control immigration leads to drug overdoses, crimes, and other problems. In paragraphs four and five, he cited six different statistics. As I've noted, these statistics are quite misleading and some are simply inaccurate, but judgments about accuracy and persuasiveness come in the last stage of rhetorical analysis, the explanation and evaluation stage. At the end of the speech, he cited the examples of three people who were murdered by undocumented immigrants. He also briefly referenced authoritative evidence when he claimed that his immigration proposal "was developed by law enforcement professionals and border agents at the Department of Homeland Security" (9). Thus, Trump relied on three of the four forms of evidence to support his proposal.

Trump also relied on refutative argument when he claimed that the opposition of Democrats to his proposal to build a wall was based in politics, not principle. He noted that Senator Schumer, "along with many other Democrats" "supported a physical barrier in the past" (14). Notably, he used refutation not to defend his policy proposal, but to score a political point.

At the same time, Trump also depended on narrative to make his case. This was most evident at the end of the speech when in paragraphs 19 and 20, he told the stories of three people who were murdered by undocumented immigrants. Note, these stories functioned both as examples within Trump's argument and as part of an underlying story that immigrants are foreign and dangerous. Trump used the three cases to draw on a broader story that criminals are people who don't look like us (regardless of who the us is). As I've noted, the story (or argument) that immigrants are more likely to be criminals than are American citizens is untrue, but it clearly resonated for many Americans, especially those who rarely interact with immigrants.

Trump's argument and his use of narrative were designed to anger the public and cause them to pressure Congress to act by drawing upon the values and needs of the audience. With his claims about opioid deaths and crimes committed by immigrants, Trump tapped into the most basic need of all, the need for life. He also drew upon one of the most strongly felt societal values, love of family.

At this point, someone might object that I've cited the same statements in my discussion of Trump's use of rational argument, narrative, and appeals to values, needs, and symbols. In a way, that criticism is entirely accurate, but it isn't a fault in the analysis. Trump's speech was designed to come across as based in strong evidence. He also depicted Democrats as hopelessly inconsistent for previously supporting proposals to build barriers at the border, but now opposing funding for a wall. In addition, he used narrative to connect with his audience and to scare them about the danger posed by dangerous immigrants, a danger tied to their status as Other than his core supporters among white voters. In the speech, he used each of these three strategy categories, but the categories also overlapped. Something similar often happens in rhetoric. In this case, the overlap among these three categories is a sign that the speech was well adapted to appealing to those who already strongly supported Trump's agenda. In the evaluation stage, the critic also might argue that the speech was not well adapted to changing the minds of those who either opposed that agenda or were uncertain about it. It is because he only spoke effectively to core supporters that the speech did not move public opinion and he ultimately was forced to acquiesce to the demands of Democrats (and some Republicans) and reopen the government without gaining any funding for his wall.

The other three strategy categories were much less evident in the speech. One might think that there was a great deal of confrontation in the speech because of the attacks on Senator Schumer and other Democrats. However, it is important to recognize that confrontation is a strategy in which the rhetor intentionally attacks or offends the audience to get their attention in order to persuade them to change their mind. In this case, Trump attacked Democrats not to get their attention (he had been attacking them constantly as president), but rather to build support in his base. Senator Schumer and other Democrats were not a key audience for his rhetoric; they were a foil that he used to maximize support among his own followers.

Trump also did not rely to any significant degree on either aesthetic or credibility strategies. There are aesthetic strategies in the speech. I noted earlier that in paragraph 22, he used a rhetorical question to call for Congress to provide funding for his border wall. He also used metaphor when he spoke of the system as broken. A complex system such as immigration cannot be broken in the same sense that a chair or a watch is broken. But it should be obvious that these strategies were much less important than the argument, narrative, and value appeals in the speech. In fact, it makes more sense to attribute Trump's use of metaphor to the fact that a great deal of language is based in metaphor, rather than see it as an important strategy.

There also was no significant attempt to develop credibility as a strategy. One could say that he built credibility by showing his knowledge of the immigration system and also demonstrating with the examples he cited and his story of holding the hands of those who had lost a loved one that he genuinely cared about the people. However, these comments functioned much more directly as arguments, stories, and value appeals than they did as devices designed to raise his credibility. His decision to rely on argument, narrative, and value appeals was probably wise given the highly polarized nature of public attitudes about his presidency.

The analysis of the Trump speech illustrates the general principles that should be applied in the analysis stage for any work of rhetoric. I systematically analyzed all aspects of the speech, using the six categories within the system. In each case, I described all of the components that were present in the speech that were relevant to the sub-category. I did this as objectively as possible with the goal of identifying the characteristics that ultimately meant that the speech did little to move public opinion. Finally, the analysis was focused on aspects of the speech that could resonate with an audience, although they did not move public opinion in this case, rather than applying literary or other theory to his remarks.

One final point is important. The same analysis could have been condensed into a two page outline, such as the sample outlines included later. In that case, the analyst would, in application to each sub-category, briefly note the characteristic and add references (paragraph or page) along with very brief quotations from the rhetoric. Those notations would be made onto an outline such as the following example.

OUTLINE OF RHETORICAL ANALYSIS CATEGORIES

I. Goals

    A. Themes

    B. Requested Actions

II. Organization

    A. Introduction

    B. Conclusion

    C. Main Body—identify the organizational pattern

III. Role of the Rhetor

    A. Implied Relationship

    B. Specific Role

IV. Linguistic Tone

V. Implied Audience

VI. Strategy Categories—use all that are relevant and identify sub-strategies as specifically as possible.

    A. Rational Argument

    B. Narrative

    C. Aesthetic

    D. Values, Needs, and Symbols

    E. Credibility

    F. Confrontation

CONCLUSION

The analysis system developed in this chapter can be applied to any work of rhetoric. It can be used to discover the defining rhetorical elements of a speech, an editorial, a film, a television show, and so on. By applying the six categories, the critic (and that means all of us) can break the rhetoric down into its parts in order to better understand how it functions. In chapters four through nine, I focus in detail on the six strategy categories to illuminate their functioning.

It is important to remember, however, that analysis is only the second step toward fully understanding any work of rhetoric. In the next chapter, I explain how rhetoric must be understood in the context of the time in which it was presented. For example, in his Farewell Address that is included in the Workbook, President Ronald Reagan spoke memorably about his vision of the United States as a "shining city upon a hill," a phrase that he borrowed from Pilgrim leader John Winthrop. Reagan added that "in the mind it was a tall proud city built on rocks stronger than oceans, wind-swept, God-blessed, and teeming with people of all kinds living in harmony and peace, a city with free ports that hummed with commerce and creativity, and if there had to be city walls, the walls had doors and the doors were open to anyone with the will and the heart to get here."[9] Reagan, who was the greatest hero for Republicans and other conservatives for a generation, described a nation that wasn't afraid of immigrants, but that welcomed them. It should be obvious that Trump's rhetoric would not have resonated in the same way when Reagan was president and also that Reagan's description of a welcoming "shining city upon a hill," had lost resonance by the 2016 campaign. The ultimate conclusion is that analysis is only one stage in the full explanation of a work of rhetoric and must be followed by the research and evaluation stages.

To illustrate the application of the system, I have included below a weekly address from then-President Obama, and a sample outline showing how the address would be described with the analysis system.

Remarks of President Barack Obama

Weekly Address, December 17, 2016

Hi, everybody. If you've ever played a game of basketball in a gym, or entered a contest in school, or started a small business in your hometown, you know that competition is a good thing. It pushes us to do our best. And you know that a fight is fair only when everybody has a chance to win, when the playing field is level for everybody, and the rules are clear and consistent.

1

President Barack Obama, Weekly Address on Ensuring a Fair and Competitive Marketplace, December 16, 2016

That's important to our consumers, our workers, our employers, and our farmers. 2
You deserve a fair shake, even though there might be much bigger players in the market. Without a truly competitive marketplace, those big companies can raise costs, or slack off on offering good service, or keep their workers' wages too low. And in an era when large corporations often merge to form even larger ones, our leaders have an even greater responsibility to look out for us as consumers.

To keep America's economy growing and America's businesses thriving, we need 3
to protect the principle of fair competition. That's not, by the way, a Democratic idea or a Republican idea—it's an American idea, because it's the best way to make sure the best ideas rise to the top.

My administration has done a lot to keep the marketplace fair. We defended a free, 4
open, and accessible Internet that doesn't let service providers pick winners and losers. We cracked down on conflicts of interest by making sure professionals who give you retirement advice do so in your best interest, not in theirs. And in the last few months, we've made even more progress.

This week, my Department of Agriculture took major steps to protect farmers from 5
unfair treatment by bigger processors. These rules will help swine, beef cattle, and especially poultry growers who have fewer choices in where they sell their products.

This month, the FDA started taking steps to make hearing aids more affordable 6
for more than the nearly 30 million Americans suffering from the frustration of hearing loss. We think people with moderate hearing loss should be able to buy a hearing aid over the counter as easily as you can buy reading glasses at your local pharmacy.

This year we also addressed two other problems that keep workers and wages 7
down: the overuse of non-compete agreements that hurt workers in the job market, and the unfair practices of companies that collude to set wages below the market rate. And we backed new steps, including a law I just signed to fight robot scalpers that artificially drive up ticket prices, and a rule that requires airlines to reimburse your baggage fees if your bags don't make it to your destination when you do.

Finally, it's this principle of competition that's at the very heart of our health reform. 8
In fact, it's the reason we call it the Affordable Care Act; it makes insurance companies compete for your business, which is helping millions afford the care that helps them get and stay healthy. By the way, it's open enrollment season right now. You can still sign up on HealthCare.gov until January 31st and get covered for 2017.

Our free-market economy only works when there's competition. And competition 9
only works when rules are in place to keep it fair and open and honest. Whether you're building the next big thing or just want to be treated right as a customer, that's good for you and good for the country.

Thanks everybody, and have a great weekend. 10

ANALYSIS OF OBAMA WEEKLY ADDRESS

I. Goals

    A. Themes

    Competition is valuable across society and especially in the marketplace.

    Appropriate regulation is needed to make competition fair.

    The Obama administration has promoted fair competition and helped many people.

    B. Requested Actions

    Support regulation to make the free market function.

II. Organization

    A. Introduction

    The opening paragraph introduces the argument with examples from sports and business that emphasize both the value of competition and the importance of making sure that "the playing field is level for everybody, and the rules are clear and consistent."

    B. Conclusion

    The conclusion is the last two paragraphs that emphasize the theme that "competition only works when rules are in place to keep it fair and open and honest."

    C. Main Body—identify the organizational pattern

    The organization is topical. Paragraphs 2 and 3 defend the main point of the speech that it is important "to protect the principle of fair competition," a conclusion that Obama claims is not "a Democratic idea or a Republican idea—it's an American idea."

    The remainder of the main body is organized around a series of Obama administration policies that are claimed to have protected or improved competition related to the Internet, farmers selling animal to processors, regulation of hearing aids, non-compete labor agreements, scalping of event tickets, and health insurance under the Affordable Care Act.

III. Role of the Rhetor

    Implied Relationship

    Obama provides information that the audience is unlikely to have and therefore plays the role of a superior to inferior.

Specific Role

Obama tries to come across as essentially an informed and reasonable referee. This role is implied in both paragraph 1 where he references sports and in his discussion of the specific policies of his administration.

IV. Linguistic Tone

The tone is positive and reasonable. He defends his administration's policy as based in common sense and fairness.

V. Implied Audience

The implied audience is broad. He makes this clear when he claims that the values he supports are not Republican or Democratic, but American. The policies that he discusses aid both small business and ordinary people. The only people who would be excluded from the implied audience are fervent Republicans who oppose essentially all Obama policies and those who reject all government regulation.

VI. Strategy Categories—use all that are relevant and identify sub-strategies as specifically as possible

A. Rational Argument

He cites multiple examples of his administration's policies to support the idea that regulation is needed to promote a strong and fair society. He also uses an evidence-oriented argument when he draws an analogy between government regulation and the need for referees to guarantee a level playing field in sports.

B. Narrative

There is no developed narrative in the speech. He discusses how the policies he describes help people but does not flesh that out into stories.

C. Aesthetic

He relies on the metaphor of a level playing field in order to emphasize the importance of reasonable regulation.

D. Values, Needs, and Symbols

He appeals to the value of fairness and also to the self-interest of all those members of the audience who might be helped by the policies he describes.

E. Credibility

He uses the various policies to demonstrate that he is knowledgeable and also that he supports reasonable positions. Credibility is not a particularly important strategy in the speech.

F. Confrontation

Confrontation is not used in the speech.

FOR FURTHER DISCUSSION

Given the events of September 11, 2001, it is difficult to recall that issues other than terrorism and national security were dominant in the summer of 2001. One of the key issues that President George W. Bush faced that summer concerned whether the federal government should allow government funds to be spent on stem cell research. In a brief speech made in early August, President Bush tried to please both conservatives who opposed the research and others who believed that the research could produce important benefits. Carefully read and do an analysis outline of Bush's speech.

Excerpts From Bush Address on U.S. Financing of Embryonic Stem Cell Research

The issue of research involving stem cells derived from human embryos is increasingly the subject of a national debate and dinner-table discussions. The issue is confronted every day in laboratories as scientists ponder the ethical ramifications of their work. It is agonized over by parents and many couples as they try to have children or to save children already born. The issue is debated within the church, with people of different faiths, even many of the same faith, coming to different conclusions. 1

Many people are finding that the more they know about stem cell research, the less certain they are about the right ethical and moral conclusions. My administration must decide whether to allow federal funds, your tax dollars, to be used for scientific research on stem cells derived from human embryos. 2

A large number of these embryos already exist. They are the product of a process called in vitro fertilization, which helps so many couples conceive children. When doctors match sperm and egg to create life outside the womb, they usually produce more embryos than are implanted in the mother. Once a couple successfully has children, or if they are unsuccessful, the additional embryos remain frozen in laboratories. Some will not survive during long storage, others are destroyed. A number have been donated to science and used to create privately funded stem cell lines, and a few have been implanted in an adoptive mother and born and are today healthy children. 3

Based on preliminary work that has been privately funded, scientists believe further research using stem cells offers great promise that could help improve the lives of those who suffer from many terrible diseases, from juvenile diabetes to Alzheimer's, from Parkinson's to spinal cord injuries. And while scientists admit they are not yet certain, they believe stem cells derived from embryos have unique potential. . . . 4

Scientists further believe that rapid progress in this research will come only with federal funds. Federal dollars help attract the best and brightest scientists. They insure new discoveries are widely shared at the largest number of research facilities and that the research is directed toward the greatest public good. 5

President George W. Bush, Excerpts from Address on U.S. Financing of Embryonic Stem Cell Research

The United States has a long and proud record of leading the world toward advances in science and medicine that improve human life. And the United States has a long proud record of upholding the highest standards of ethics as we expand the limits of science and knowledge.

6

Research on embryonic stem cells raises profound ethical questions because extracting the stem cell destroys the embryo and thus destroys its potential for life. Like a snowflake, each of these embryos is unique with the unique genetic potential of an individual human being.

7

As I thought through this issue, I kept returning to two fundamental questions. First, are these frozen embryos human life and therefore something precious to be protected? And second, if they're going to be destroyed anyway, shouldn't they be used for a greater good, for research that has the potential to save and improve other lives?

8

I've asked those questions and others of scientists, scholars, bioethicists, religious leaders, doctors, researchers, members of Congress, my cabinet and my friends. I have read heartfelt letters from many Americans. I have given this issue a great deal of thought, prayer and considerable reflection, and I have found widespread disagreement.

9

On the first issue, are these embryos human life? Well, one researcher told me he believes this five-day-old cluster of cells is not an embryo, not yet an individual, but a pre-embryo. He argued that it has the potential for life, but it is not a life because it cannot develop in its own.

10

An ethicist dismissed that as a callous attempt at rationalization. Make no mistake, he told me, that cluster of cells is that same way you and I and all the rest of us started our lives. One goes with a heavy heart if we use these, he said, because we are dealing with the seeds of the next generation.

11

And to the other crucial question, if these are going to be destroyed anyway, why not use them for good purpose? Many argue these embryos are byproducts of a process that helps create life and we should allow couples to donate them to science so they can be used for good purpose instead of wasting their potential. Others will argue there's no such thing as excess life. And the fact that a living being is going to die does not justify experimenting on it or exploiting it as a natural resource.

12

At its core, this issue forces us to confront fundamental questions about the beginnings of life and the ends of science. It lies at a difficult moral intersection juxtaposing the need to protect life in all its phases with the prospect of saving and improving life in all its stages.

13

As the discoveries of modern science create tremendous hope, they also lay vast ethical minefields. As the genius of science extends the horizons of what we can do, we increasingly confront complex questions about what we should do. We have arrived at that brave new world that seemed so distant in 1932 when Aldous Huxley wrote about human beings created in test tubes in what he called a hatchery.

14

In recent weeks, we learned that scientists have created human embryos in test   15
tubes solely to experiment on them. This is deeply troubling and a warning sign that
should prompt all of us to think through these issues very carefully. Embryonic stem
cell research is at the leading edge of a series of moral hazards. The initial stem
cell researcher was at first reluctant to begin his research, fearing it might be used
for human cloning. Scientists have already cloned a sheep. Researchers are telling
us the next step could be to clone human beings to create individual designer stem
cells, essentially to grow another you to be available in case you need another heart
or lung or liver.

I strongly oppose human cloning, as do most Americans. We recoil at the idea of   16
growing human beings for spare body parts or creating life for our convenience. And
while we must devote enormous energy to conquering disease, it is equally important
that we pay attention to the moral concerns raised by the new frontier of human
embryo stem cell research. Even the most noble ends do not justify any means.

My position on these issues is shaped by deeply held beliefs. I'm a strong supporter   17
of science and technology and believe they have the potential for incredible good,
to improve lives, to save life, to conquer disease. Research offers hope that millions
of our loved ones may be cured of a disease and rid of their suffering. I have friends
whose children suffer from juvenile diabetes. Nancy Reagan has written me about
President Reagan's struggle with Alzheimer's. My own family has confronted the
tragedy of childhood leukemia. And like all Americans, I have great hope for cures.

I also believe human life is a sacred gift from our creator. I worry about a culture   18
that devalues life and believe, as your president, I have an important obligation to
foster and encourage respect for life in America and throughout the world ...

As a result of private research, more than 60 genetically diverse stem cell lines   19
already exist. They were created from embryos that have already been destroyed
and they have the ability to regenerate themselves indefinitely, creating ongoing
opportunities for research.

I have concluded that we should allow federal funds to be used for research on   20
these existing stem cell lines, where the life-and-death decision has already been
made. Leading scientists tell me research on these 60 lines has great promise that
could lead to breakthrough therapies and cures. This allows us to explore the promise
and potential of stem cell research without crossing a fundamental moral line by
providing tax-payer funding that would sanction or encourage further destruction of
human embryos that have at least the potential for life.

I also believe that great scientific progress can be made through aggressive   21
federal funding of research on umbilical cord, placenta, adult and animal stem cells
which do not involve the same moral dilemma. This year, your government will spend
$250 million on this important research.

I will also name a president's council to monitor stem cell research, to recommend   22
appropriate guidelines and regulations and to consider all of the medical and ethical

ramifications of biomedical innovation. This council will consist of leading scientists, doctors, ethicists, lawyers, theologians and others and will be chaired by Dr. Leon Kass, a leading biomedical ethicist from the University of Chicago. This council will keep us apprised of new developments and give our nation a forum to continue to discuss and evaluate these important issues.

As we go forward, I hope we will always be guided by both intellect and heart, by both our capabilities and our conscience. I have made this decision with great care and I pray it is the right one.   23

1   Peter Baker, "Trump's National Address Escalates Border Wall Fight," *New York Times*, January 8, 2019, https://www.nytimes.com/2019/01/08/us/politics/donald-trump-speech.html.

2   Baker, "Trump's National Address Escalates Wall Fight."

3   Donald J. Trump, "Address to the Nation on the Crisis at the Border," January 8, 2019, https://www.whitehouse.gov/briefings-statements/president-donald-j-trumps-address-nation-crisis-border. Future references to the speech will be made by parenthetical reference by paragraph number.

4   "Trump's Speech to the Nation: Fact Checks and Background," *New York Times*, January 8, 2019, *https://www.nytimes.com/2019/01/08/us/politics/trump-speech.html*.

5   "Trump's Speech to the Nation: Fact Checks and Background," *New York Times*.

6   See Christopher Ingraham, "Two charts demolish the notion that immigrants here illegally commit more crime," *Washington Post*, June 19, 2018, https://www.washingtonpost.com/news/wonk/wp/2018/06/19/two-charts-demolish-the-notion-that-immigrants-here-illegally-commit-more-crime/?utm_term=.876c9f940947.

7   Ronald Brownstein, "Places with the fewest immigrants push back hardest against immigration," CNN, August 22, 2017, https://www.cnn.com/2017/08/22/politics/immigration-trump-arizona/index.html.

8   See Aristotle, *The Rhetoric* in *The Basic Works of Aristotle*, ed. Richard McKeon (New York: Random House, 1941), pp. 1325–1451.

9   Ronald Reagan, "Farewell Address to the Nation," January 11, 1989, https://www.reaganlibrary.gov/011189i.

CHAPTER 3
Understanding Context and Judging Effectiveness

The third stage in the consideration of any work of rhetoric is research concerning the context in which the rhetoric was presented. No work of rhetoric can be understood or judged apart from its context. For example, prior to 9/11, a politician who said that terrorism was the greatest threat to the United States might have been perceived as somewhat kooky. After 9/11, the same idea became the conventional wisdom. At one point, the war in Iraq was quite popular and seen as a sign of the nation's power to change the world. Over time, the situation reversed and the war became quite unpopular and was seen as an example not of American power, but of arrogance and overreach.

The key point is that all rhetoric is presented at a specific time and place and cannot be understood apart from that time and place. Even our understanding of the meaning of words and phrases is shaped by the context in which they were presented. For example, a comment about Mr. Potato Head in a speech in the 1970s would simply have been a reference to the children's toy, probably used to label someone as childish or stupid. But a reference to the same toy in the early 1990s would have a totally different meaning, especially if the word potato were misspelled with an e on the end. In that case, the comment would be a reference to an instance in the first Bush administration when Vice President Dan Quayle famously misspelled potato by adding an e to the end. When then Senator Obama talked about hope and change in the 2008 election, the words became powerful symbols of a new political order that his election could bring. When the same words were used by Republicans in the 2010 midterm campaign, they often conveyed a sarcastic message indicting President Obama.

The focus of this chapter is on developing tools that the critic can use to illuminate the context in which a given work of rhetoric was presented. In the first section, I discuss the goals of contextual analysis. I then lay out the stages in the research process, develop a system for identifying rhetorical barriers and rhetorical advantages, and explain the proper method for evaluating the effectiveness of any work of rhetoric. I conclude the chapter with an analysis of one of the most famous speeches of the 19th century, Booker T. Washington's "Atlanta Exposition Address," to illustrate the principles discussed throughout the chapter.

GOALS OF CONTEXTUAL RESEARCH

The contextual research stage has four goals. The first goal is to understand the cultural context in which the rhetorical interchange occurred. In order to fairly judge any speech, essay, or other rhetorical artifact, one must understand the culture in which it was presented. Contemporary American culture is, for example, quite different from contemporary Japanese culture. It also is quite different from the culture found in this country in an earlier period. To understand any rhetorical artifact, the critic must have some understanding of the society in which it was presented. Obviously, this goal increases in importance in relation to works of rhetoric that come from cultural situations quite different from the United States today. One of the reasons that I have included an analysis of the Washington speech in this chapter is that the cultural conditions he faced were quite different from contemporary America.

The second goal is to understand the mindset of the actual audience that heard/read/saw the rhetoric. In the analysis stage, the critic focused on the "implied audience" for a given piece of rhetoric. In the research stage, the focus shifts to the actual audience of people who heard a speech, read a magazine article, saw a film, and so forth. It is important to understand the mindset of the audience because of the general principle that effective rhetoric must be adapted to the views of the audience.

An illustration may make this point clear. Imagine that during his presidency President Bill Clinton made a major speech calling for equal rights for all soldiers, regardless of their sexual preference. If that speech had been presented at a meeting of the American Civil Liberties Union (ACLU), it is easy to predict that President Clinton would have received a standing ovation. The ACLU strongly supports equal rights for all Americans in general and gay rights in particular. On the other hand, if the speech had been presented at one of the service academies, President Clinton probably would have received a very cold response, due to negative attitudes among many in the military about both homosexuality and President Clinton himself. The key point is that it is not possible to evaluate the hypothetical Clinton speech, without knowing the audience to which it was presented. The same speech would be effective in one case and ineffective in the other. Now, think about the evolution of attitudes about gay rights over the period after Clinton left office. Even in the military, there clearly has been an evolution with many senior officers, including the Joint Chiefs, now saying that they see no problem with gay soldiers serving their nation. Rhetoric must always be understood in relation to the attitudes, beliefs, knowledge, and interest of the audience who heard, saw, or read it.

The third goal of the contextual stage is to gain an understanding of the goals of the rhetor. It is difficult to judge the effectiveness or ethics of a work of rhetoric without knowing what the person who created that work wanted to accomplish. For example, there is an important difference between protest rhetoric that is designed to rouse public attention and political campaign rhetoric that is designed to win an election. The former may be considered successful even if it does not persuade the people to support a given cause. But campaign rhetoric is successful only if the candidate wins the election. However, some candidates may be running for the purpose of "protest," rather than because they really expect to win the election. In that case, it is possible that their rhetoric might be considered successful, even if they only received a small percentage of the vote.

As I noted earlier, Ross Perot's 1992 presidential campaign illustrates this point. Was Perot's rhetoric successful? If his goal was to be elected president, clearly it failed. But if his goal was to focus attention on the budget deficit and other issues, then his campaign must be labeled a great success. Precisely the same point can be applied to recent campaigns by Representative Ron Paul for the Republican nomination. The key point is that it is important to discover the goals of the rhetor in order to adequately and fairly evaluate his/her rhetoric.

The final goal in the contextual research stage is to gather any relevant data concerning the actual influence that the work of rhetoric had on the audience. In some instances, there may be public opinion polls or other audience surveys indicating a strong reaction to a given speech, essay, or film. Alternatively, media reports may indicate how the actual audience responded to the rhetoric. In other cases, editorial reaction and letters to the editor may provide data indicating that a given work influenced (or failed to influence) a given audience. Film or book reviews may provide information about the impact of a movie or a novel. In the present day, one may be able to gauge reaction based on social media response.

In some cases there may be a wealth of information indicating that the audience was moved by a given work. For example, there is a great deal of data indicating that Ronald Reagan's "Star Wars" address, which advocated building a missile defense system to protect the nation, had vast influence both on the public and also on debate in Congress.[1] In the first chapter, I made a similar point about the speech that then state Senator Obama gave at the Democratic National Convention. There is no question that the speech instantly made him into a national figure. This data would be important in evaluating the rhetoric. On occasion, external data tells us a great deal about the effect of a speech or other work, as well as how and why the rhetoric functioned. It is important for the critic to search for that data.

In most instances, however, there probably won't be much, if any, external data indicating the impact of the rhetoric. Even when important figures present speeches, there is rarely significant media coverage. Consequently, there probably won't be any opinion polls, newspaper editorials, news stories, or other information indicating the effectiveness of the rhetoric. To make matters worse, even if there is such information, it may be difficult to tell what it means. For example, a newspaper might report that the audience responded to a speech by President George W. Bush by applauding twelve times. While this data is useful, it may not be at all clear whether twelve rounds of applause means that Bush was especially effective or that the audience was polite to the ex-president. The key point is that it is important to consider all of the available data about a given work of rhetoric and that means looking to see if there is any useful information bearing on the actual impact of that rhetoric.

1. Gain an understanding of the cultural context.
2. Discover the mindset of the actual audience.
3. Isolate the goals of the rhetor.
4. Gather external data on the impact of the rhetoric.

RESEARCH STAGES

In order to fulfill the four goals of contextual research, the analysis should progress through four research stages. The first stage is to identify the necessary level of research on the subject. There is a simple rule in relation to this stage: the farther away that one is in time, place, culture, and so forth from the rhetoric, the more research that is needed. For example, someone who is active in local politics probably would not need to do any research in order to analyze and evaluate a speech by a city councilperson. At the opposite extreme, an enormous amount of research would be needed to analyze a work presented hundreds of years ago in a foreign culture.

The second research stage is immersion in the context concerning the rhetoric. This requires research on a number of subjects. First, all relevant material on the rhetoric itself should be reviewed. This means checking for articles or editorials about the work. There also may be useful information in online comments about an article or editorial or in looking at Twitter data or some other aspect of social media commentary. If one were looking at a film, it would mean looking at all the reviews of the film, as well as press reports about ticket sales. If you were looking at a television series, you would look at both reviews of the series and information concerning ratings. Similar research should be done in source materials relevant to the particular type of rhetoric.

Second, the analyst should research the life of the person creating the rhetoric, if that is relevant. To understand Rudy Giuliani's rhetoric in the 2008 presidential campaign, it would be important to research Giuliani's life, especially his time as Mayor of New York. On the other hand, if the subject of the analysis were an unsigned newspaper editorial, then research on the author probably would not be necessary. It also might be impossible.

Third, the critic should look for relevant historical and cultural material to explain how the rhetoric worked for the actual audience that heard/read/watched the rhetoric. In particular, the critic should research the cultural situation in which the rhetoric was presented, the particular issue or issues that the rhetoric dealt with, and audience attitudes concerning those issues. The success or failure of a given work of rhetoric can be judged only in relation to a particular audience. This means that it is important to discover as much as possible about the audience that witnessed the rhetoric. In particular, it is important to discover information about the demographic characteristics of the audience and group membership. Demographic characteristics include age, sex, region of the country, educational and income status, and so forth, and they tell us a great deal about likely attitudes and beliefs of not individual audience members, but the audience as a whole.

Information about group membership is even more important. An example clarifies this point. If a critic knew that the audience for a given speech was composed primarily of highly educated white men over sixty with high incomes, he or she might leap to the conclusion that the audience was quite conservative and Republican. Each of the demographic characteristics I mentioned is an indicator that the audience member is more likely to be conservative than liberal and more likely to be Republican than Democratic. On the other hand, now imagine that one more piece of information is added to the mix: the audience members are all American Civil Liberty Union (ACLU) local chapter leaders. With this information, the critic would reason that most ACLU members are liberal Democrats and discount the importance of the demographic data.

The crucial point is that it is important to gather as much information as possible about the actual audience for the rhetoric, including demographic and group membership data, because that data allows the critic to draw inferences about the attitudes, beliefs, and values of the audience.

Information about the audience can be discovered by considering where the rhetoric was presented and then reasoning to the nature of the audience that was present. If the rhetoric under consideration were an essay published in *Time*, then the critic would research the characteristics of readers of that magazine. This same process can be used to gain information about the audience for any work of rhetoric.

An example may make the three steps clearer. In order to evaluate a speech advocating a strong global warming policy by someone like Al Gore, the critic would need to take the following steps. First, the critic would look for any articles or editorials on the speech. After winning an Oscar, former Vice President Gore received a great deal of press attention, so there might be press commentary. On the other hand, Gore has been talking about global warming for many years. It is not very likely that a speech given while he was a senator would have received the same coverage as a speech in the period after the Oscar. In the second step, the critic would research the life of the speaker. This research might turn up additional material on the speech. It also might tell the critic about the general ideas of the speaker and how people often respond to them. In this case, research about Gore undoubtedly would reveal strongly positive and negative attitudes about him from different segments of the audience. He is widely admired by many environmentalists, but many conservatives view him as an alarmist. Then, the critic would look at all available information on the particular audience to whom Gore spoke and draw inferences about their attitudes, beliefs, values, and interests. I will describe how to draw those inferences in a moment in the discussion of rhetorical barriers and advantages.

The fourth step is to research the cultural context and the particular issue. For a speech presented in the United States in the present day, research about culture probably wouldn't be very important. We all swim in the sea of our culture. While in the case of a speech about global warming, cultural research might not matter much, but research on the issue could be very important. Global warming is a very complicated subject and research might be needed to clarify the message in the speech. Research on the issue also could reveal audience attitudes and values concerning the subject. In some cases, articles might summarize poll data on what Americans think about the environment in general and global warming in particular. In others, the article might indirectly tell the critic about the audience. So, for example, an article might report on the complexities associated with the debate over global warming. That article tells the critic that "complexity" is likely to be an important rhetorical barrier that a pro-environment speaker on global warming must overcome. A wealth of poll data about American attitudes and to a lesser degree attitudes of citizens of other nations is now available on a number of websites that focus on opinion polling.

Gun control is a topic that illustrates the importance of issue research for identifying rhetorical barriers. For example, many Europeans find American public policy on gun control to be incomprehensible. Most European countries tightly regulate gun ownership and, consequently, given the epidemic of gun violence in this country, they do not understand the failure of the United States to implement similar laws. To understand why the NRA has been so successful in blocking gun regulation in this country, it would be necessary to research gun control as an issue. The goal of that research would be to discover audience beliefs, attitudes, and values that relate to gun ownership. This would require looking at research material that explains what people think about gun control as an issue. After looking at that material, it should be possible to explain why pro gun control rhetoric only has been successful on a few issues.

SUMMARY OF THE RESEARCH STAGE

1   Gather information relating to the particular rhetoric that was presented.
2   Gather information concerning the rhetor.
3   Gather information relating to the specific audience that was exposed to
    the rhetoric.
4   Gather information concerning the cultural context and the particular issue
    under consideration.

RHETORICAL BARRIERS AND ADVANTAGES

In conducting the research stage, the rhetorical analyst should be particularly aware of material relating to *rhetorical barriers* and *rhetorical advantages* facing the rhetor. In chapter one, I defined a rhetorical barrier as *an attitude, belief, or other problem that a rhetor must overcome in order to persuade an audience to accept a given position.* In contrast, a rhetorical advantage is *an attitude, belief, or other position that gives the rhetor assistance in persuading an audience.*

An illustration may make these terms clearer. On an emotional issue like gun control, advocates of both sides face difficult rhetorical barriers, but also possess significant rhetorical advantages. For example, a pro gun control speaker must overcome barriers relating to public fear of crime and attitudes against government regulation of guns in order to persuade an audience to support strengthened gun control laws. On the other hand, an advocate of gun control also has certain rhetorical advantages, particularly on issues like assault rifles and concealed weapons. In relation to these policies, many in the public doubt that ordinary people need to carry either a concealed weapon or an assault rifle. Consequently, the pro gun control speaker starts out with a considerable rhetorical advantage. Particular events also may create barriers or advantages. After the shootings at Virginia Tech, Tucson, Charleston, and unfortunately many other instances, proponents of gun control had rhetorical advantages in advocating tighter controls on allowing gun sales to the mentally ill. After the Gulf Oil disaster, advocates of more drilling faced an enormous rhetorical barrier that had not existed prior to the blowout.

How does the critic discover rhetorical barriers and advantages? The critic uses the material gained through the four research steps and the category system developed in the following section to draw conclusions about the barriers/advantages that faced a rhetor in a particular situation. For example, in relation to gun control, knowledge that a particular audience was composed primarily of women and that women tend to support gun control more strongly than men, would suggest the presence of rhetorical advantages relating to the attitudes that guns are very dangerous and that gun regulations are sensible. It is through the combination of the four research steps and the category system for rhetorical barriers/advantages that the critic can isolate particular barriers/advantages for a given work of rhetoric.

Types of Barriers/Advantages

There are four main types of rhetorical barriers/advantages: audience-related, situational, occasion-related, and those that are tied to the rhetor's reputation.

Audience-Related Barriers/Advantages

The most important barriers and advantages relate to the mindset and interests of the audience. The mindset of the audience can be divided into three related categories: beliefs, attitudes, and values. A belief is a statement of fact that is in principle testable. A person might believe, for example, that many homeowners use guns to protect their property. This belief could be tested against statistics. While it could be tested in that manner, beliefs are difficult to change, even when they are not supported by the best data.

An attitude is an evaluation of a belief. In this case, the attitude would be a statement such as, "I have a right to own a gun to defend myself" or "only criminals need assault rifles." The first attitude is based on the belief that guns are an effective means of home defense, but it also includes an evaluative component, in this case support for the right to gun ownership. The second attitude is tied to a belief that ordinary people have no use for assault rifles and the evaluation that we should not help criminals arm themselves with dangerous weapons. Attitudes are harder to change than beliefs because they relate not only to factual material, but also to personal evaluation of those facts. In common language, attitudes contain a strong emotional component and strongly held emotional attitudes are very difficult to change.

Values are basic principles of right and wrong, good and bad. In a sense, a value is a more basic version of an attitude. Basic values in the United States include support for freedom, peace, prosperity, progress, and so forth. In relation to gun control, the pro gun control speaker or writer faces barriers relating to public values concerning limits on government regulation of the individual. Opponents of gun control tend to value personal independence and devalue government control. However, the pro gun control speaker has the advantage of being able to appeal to the value of life.

© NATE A./SHUTTERSTOCK.COM

In relation to any work of rhetoric, the analyst should identify barriers/advantages related to the beliefs, attitudes, and values of the audience. These barriers and advantages are generally the most important ones facing any rhetor. Public opinion data (polls and other surveys) are especially important in discovering barriers/advantages related to beliefs, attitudes, and/or values. It is helpful to keep in mind that of the three types of barriers/advantages that reflect the audience mindset, those related to values are the most powerful and those tied to beliefs the least powerful. Basic values are so ingrained in the individual that it is extremely difficult to change them. The rhetor either must adapt to the values or recognize that he/she is unlikely to fully persuade the audience.

Beliefs are more easily changed because they are based on a factual understanding of the world. With enough information (and time), one often can convince someone to change their beliefs, although this is by no means an easy process. Belief change comes most easily where a dramatic event (such as the Gulf oil spill) undercuts the previously held belief. Even in a case such as the oil spill, however, beliefs are not easily changed, as the continuing debate in Congress about loosening regulation of offshore oil development illustrates.

The final barrier falling in the audience category is attention. On some issues it will be difficult to gain or keep the attention of the audience because they do not care about the subject or find it uninteresting. On the other hand, there are issues where it is easy to get the attention of the audience. Far more press attention was focused on the deaths of Caylee Anthony and Anna Nicole Smith than on the dangers posed by antibiotic resistance. Most people find a discussion of causes of and risks posed by antibiotic resistance to be difficult to understand and quite dull. By contrast, tens of millions of Americans were fascinated by the Smith and Anthony cases. There is a similar fascination with the lives of many celebrities. Of course, there is no question that the threat of antibiotic resistance is vastly more important to the world than the tragic death of any individual person, but a rhetor discussing this issue faces serious problems relating to attention. On the other hand, when a rhetor can link his/her position to a subject about which there is intense public interest, that gives him/her a rhetorical advantage.

Situational

The second type of rhetorical barrier/advantage is tied to the situation in which the rhetoric is presented. There are three main types of situational barriers/advantages. The first relates to culture. Different cultures have varying expectations concerning rhetorical practice. This is most obvious in relation to foreign cultures, but is also true in this country. For example, greater formality is still the norm in the East and the South, as opposed to the Midwest or West. Culture also influences attitudes. There have been major controversies in recent years in several Southern states concerning displays of the Confederate flag and statutes honoring Confederate Civil War heroes. Obviously, there have been no such controversies in Minnesota. Therefore, the critic should consider whether the culture either creates a barrier or provides an advantage for the rhetor.

The second situational barrier/advantage relates to complexity. If the topic of the rhetoric is complicated, then the rhetor often faces a major barrier in persuading the audience. Nuclear power is a good example. Many experts believe that nuclear power is actually much safer than producing electricity in coal-fired plants, although the safety advantages may not apply in areas such as Japan, which are subject to major earthquakes and tsunamis.[2] In this view, the number of deaths from mining and transporting coal, when added to the deaths caused by air pollution coming from the coal plant and the impacts of global warming, is much larger than a similar figure for nuclear power. But this argument is complex and runs up against fear of a nuclear accident. Many people somehow equate nuclear power and nuclear weapons as similar. The nuclear catastrophe in Japan in 2011 certainly added to those fears, although relatively few American power plants are subject to the tsunami risk that led to the crisis in Japan. In this case, the argument of many scientists that the most modern nuclear plants are extremely safe has not been enough to change public attitudes concerning the energy source. The result of this rhetorical situation has been to make it impossible for most utilities to order new nuclear power plants.

On the other hand, if the issue is a very simple one, that gives the rhetor a significant advantage. In relation to gun control, for example, both sides of the debate try to simplify the issue. The pro gun control advocates may reduce the issue to a picture of a dead loved one killed in a gun accident. The pro NRA side, in contrast, will simplify the issue by focusing on horrible crimes that might have been prevented if the homeowner had owned a gun.

On rare occasions, complexity also may be an advantage. Sometimes political leaders support complicated positions in order to avoid taking actual action to solve a major problem. Thus, a conservative might propose a market-based health insurance reform proposal not with the goal of actually passing it, but with the goal of blocking a more liberal plan. In this case, complexity might be an advantage for the advocate of the market-based plan. The public might have difficulty understanding the complexities of the two plans, leaving them with the impression that both parties were equally concerned with taking action to provide health insurance reform. In such an instance, which only occurs rarely, complexity would be an advantage for the advocate of the market-based program, because it would make it easier for that person to obscure the fact that the market by itself provides no incentive to provide health insurance for Americans who have a pre-existing health condition. Covering people with significant health risks is expensive and insurance companies only will do it when either regulation requires it or there are adequate subsidies to offset the costs.

The third type of situational barrier/advantage relates to specific events that sometimes occur immediately prior to or during a rhetorical interchange. In the spring of 1996, Republicans in Congress were attacking President Clinton for accepting illegal campaign contributions from foreign sources. It then was discovered that the Republicans had accepted similar illegal donations. That discovery made it much more difficult for Republican leaders to maintain their attacks on the Democrats. Perhaps the most dramatic recent example of how a specific event can change the rhetorical situation would be the 9/11 attacks. Prior to 9/11, many Americans saw terrorism as a mere inconvenience, something that was unlikely to impact them or their family. After 9/11, that attitude changed dramatically.

Occasion

The third main type of barrier/advantage relates to the general occasion in which the rhetoric is presented. Barriers/advantages related to occasion are especially important for speeches. One subtype relates to standards for appropriateness. For example, the standards of appropriateness in a church service and a political pep rally are somewhat different. A speaker would have many more options when speaking at the pep rally as opposed to the church service. Sometimes the rhetor is also limited by the expectations of the audience related to the category of the rhetoric. For example, the expectations of an audience for the category "after dinner speech" are different than for the category "academic lecture." If a speaker presents an academic lecture in the after dinner situation, he or she is likely to bore the audience to tears. On the other hand, an after dinner speech might be perceived as mere fluff if the audience expected an academic lecture.

It is important to recognize, however, that standards for what is appropriate in a given occasion can change. Standards for how to dress and act while attending a religious service are much less formal than they were a half century ago. Moreover, President Trump has demonstrated that the standards for how a political figure should talk in formal and less formal settings also can change.

Reputation of the Rhetor

The final category of rhetorical barriers/advantages relates to the audience's perception of the rhetor. In some cases, a main barrier may be that the audience does not trust the person creating the rhetoric. After his resignation from the presidency, Richard Nixon always faced barriers related to the audience perception that he had lied to the American people and broken the law. Nixon had to overcome that perception before anyone would listen to him. Once a reputation is harmed, it may be extremely difficult to persuade an audience that the person has changed and should be forgiven. It is doubtful, for example, that Tiger Woods will ever be able to rebuild his reputation to what it was before the scandal that ended his marriage. He remains a highly respected and in some cases beloved golfer, but is not seen as a perfect role model as he was in the past. In other cases, the rhetor may face an audience perception that he/she is not qualified to speak about the subject. It would be difficult for President Trump to present a major speech on "Growing Up in Poverty," because he did not do so. On the other hand, former President Reagan would have had no trouble on that subject because of his life experiences.

Just as there are barriers relating to the reputation of the rhetor, in some cases there are rhetorical advantages. After the Gulf War, Colin Powell was admired by nearly all Americans. He possessed a particular rhetorical advantage when he spoke in that period. After the Iraq war initiated in the second Bush administration turned into a debacle, Powell's reputation changed dramatically, mainly because of the perception that he did not do enough to make sure that there was a strong case for going to war with Iraq in 2003. The key point is that it is quite hard to build up such a strong reputation that it serves as a rhetorical advantage and quite possible to lose that reputational advantage with a single misstep or scandal.

A TYPOLOGY OF RHETORICAL BARRIERS AND ADVANTAGES

A Audience
  1 Beliefs
  2 Attitudes
  3 Values
  4 Attention
B Situational barriers
  1 Cultural factors
  2 Complexity of the issue
  3 Specific events occurring immediately before or during the presentation
     of the rhetoric
C The occasion
  1 Standards of appropriateness
  2 Categorical expectations
D The reputation of the rhetor

Summary of the Research Stage

At the end of the research stage, the critic should have a good understanding of the context in which the work of rhetoric was presented, the goals of the rhetor in presenting the work, and the barriers/advantages that he/she faced. The critic also should be aware of any data concerning the effect that the work had on the actual audience to which it was presented. With both the analysis and research steps complete, the critic now can evaluate the effectiveness of the rhetoric as a work of persuasion.

EVALUATING EFFECTIVENESS

One of the most important issues in rhetorical analysis concerns the effectiveness of a work of rhetoric. Rhetoric, unlike literature, is always concerned with persuasion. The whole point of rhetoric is to persuade an audience to change their views or reinforce views that they already hold. Politicians and others producing rhetoric do not speak just to hear their own voices, although in a few cases one wonders. They speak (or write or produce films or art) because it is through rhetoric that the business of the nation and every democratic organization small or large gets done. Democracy is a system where we talk, that is produce rhetoric, first and then decide. That makes it important to discover if a given piece of rhetoric was effective and why or why not. It might seem that evaluating effectiveness should be a very straightforward process. The analyst simply would check to see if the rhetoric persuaded the audience. Unfortunately, it isn't that simple.

Here, the main problems relate to obtaining and interpreting "external" data on the effectiveness of a work of rhetoric. As noted earlier, in most cases, there will be no data relating to the impact of a particular work of rhetoric on an audience. Even in the case of a speech by an important political figure, rarely will there be opinion polls directly bearing on the address. Nor are there likely to be newspaper articles or editorials on the speech or useful data drawn from social media. With the exception of the State of the Union Address and a few other speeches, even addresses by the president of the United States are largely ignored by the press.

Second, it is important to remember that even if there is data, it may be very difficult to tell what it means. Does the fact that three people wrote favorable letters to the editor about a given editorial mean that the editorial was effective? There is no clear answer to that question. The same point applies to all of the other types of external data. Of course, there are exceptions to this rule. In the last major section of this chapter, I evaluate Booker T. Washington's "Atlanta Exposition Address." There is an enormous amount of information proving that the speech was effective, but that case is the exception that proves the general rule that evaluation based on external data is rarely possible.

Therefore, since in most instances the critic will not be able to rely on external data concerning the effectiveness of a speech, essay, film, and so forth, another approach to evaluation must be taken. If evaluation based on "external" data is not feasible, then the alternative is an "internal" form of evaluation. In this view, the critic should ask a simple question:

> *Does the rhetor present strategies that are well-designed to overcome the rhetorical barriers (and maximize the rhetorical advantages) in order to achieve his/her purpose?*

This question pulls together material gathered in the analysis and research stages in order to make an evaluation of the effectiveness of the rhetoric. In essence, the critic is considering whether the rhetoric was well-designed to persuade the audience, given the rhetorical barriers and advantages that the rhetor faced.

In answering this question, the critic first would outline the purpose of the rhetoric. This purpose would be identified in the goal section of the analysis stage (the themes and requested actions) and backed up with material gathered in the research stage. In most instances, the purpose of the rhetoric simply can be summarized as the actions that the rhetor hoped the audience would take in relation to the themes. The analyst then would lay out the barriers/advantages that the rhetor faced. Of course, these barriers/advantages would have been discovered in the research stage. At that point, he/she would identify the main strategies present in the rhetoric, based on the outline created in the analysis stage. Finally, the strategies would be compared to the barriers/advantages in order to judge whether the rhetor did as good a job as possible in overcoming the barriers and using the advantages.

In the substage where the strategies are compared to barriers and advantages, the key is for the analyst carefully to consider whether the strategies responded to each important barrier and maximized each advantage. If the rhetor accomplished these aims, that suggests the rhetoric was well-designed and should be judged as quite effective. The acronym PBS is helpful in summarizing the evaluation stage. First, think about Purpose, then identify Barriers (and advantages), then identify Strategies, and finally compare the strategies to the barriers and advantages. Serious evaluation of public policy is often founded on the PBS network and serious evaluation of rhetoric can be done through the PBS system.

Two final points are important here. A judgment of effectiveness (or failure) based on the internal evaluating system I have outlined is not a scientific one. Rather, that judgment must be based on strong arguments for whatever conclusion is drawn. Second, in addition to applying the PBS system of internal evaluation, the analyst should consider whether the internal evaluation of effectiveness is consistent with any data about the impact of the work that was discovered in the research stage. In most cases, there will be no such data, but in a few instances, such as the "Atlanta Exposition Address," which I will discuss in the next section, there will be obvious external data. Clearly, the internal and external data should support the same conclusion. If they don't, something is seriously wrong.

WASHINGTON'S ATLANTA EXPOSITION ADDRESS

On September 18, 1895, Booker T. Washington spoke at the Cotton States and International Exposition in Atlanta. Washington, an African American, was the head of the Tuskegee Institute in Alabama and one of the leading black educators of his era. At the Exposition, Washington spoke to an all-white audience at a time when not only segregation, but outright racism, often involving violence against people of color, was the norm in the South and to a large part in the rest of the nation as well.

Washington's Atlanta Exposition Address has been praised as one of the greatest speeches ever presented by an American. An early biographer reports that "Journals of the North and South vied with each other in giving it [the address] praise" and concludes that "as a classic it passed into the realm of the world's famous orations."[3] Public reaction at the time was overwhelming. Washington himself reported that "I received so many and such hearty congratulations that I found it difficult to get out of the building."[4] The speech caused such a stir that Washington was offered $50,000 to go on a speaking tour.[5] Of course, in 1895, $50,000 was an enormous amount of money. Another sign of the influence of the speech is that President Grover Cleveland wrote a personal note to Washington in which he explained, "I think the exposition would be fully justified if it did not do more than furnish the opportunity for its [the speech's] delivery."[6]

More recently, the speech has been widely criticized as a sellout to the white establishment. Thomas Harris and Patrick Kennicott claim that Washington "told the majority what they wanted to hear" and consequently his rhetoric "disregarded many of the immediate social and political needs of the people for whom Washington spoke."[7] If their judgment is correct, then Washington's address merits criticism, not praise. Robert L. Heath makes a similar judgment. He argues that "The hostile and bleak rhetorical atmosphere surrounding the race question in 1895 was not a time for Washington's Exposition address; it was a time for silence."[8] Harris, Kennicott, and Heath base their criticism of the address on passages in the speech in which Washington seemed to accept unequal treatment for black Americans. In famous passages, Washington emphasized the need for economic opportunity as more important than political and social rights.

Given the contrasting viewpoints, it is important to ask: Who is right about the Washington speech? This question cannot be

© BETTMAN/CORBIS

answered without a careful analysis of the historical context in which the speech was presented. Clearly, if Washington's speech were presented in contemporary America, we would label him an "Uncle Tom" who had sold out to the white establishment. But Washington did not present his speech in today's America. He presented it in the deep South in 1895. In that time and place, Washington sensibly adapted to an impossible rhetorical situation.

The following analysis will show that Washington did not sell out to Southern racists. I also will demonstrate the importance of judging any rhetoric in the context of the time in which it was presented. In accomplishing these aims, I also illustrate the stages in the internal evaluation scheme described in the previous section. The Washington address is a good one to illustrate internal evaluation of effectiveness both because the context of the time played such a major role in the reaction to the speech and because the address is one of the very small group of rhetorical acts about which we have enough data to judge effectiveness externally.[9] There is no question that the address was successful for the immediate audience and the larger national audience. Internal evaluation should come to a similar judgment.

"Progress of the American Negro" Atlanta Exposition Address

Booker T. Washington

Mr. President and gentlemen of the board of directors and citizens: One-third of the population of the South is of the Negro race. No enterprise seeking the material, civil, or moral welfare of this section can disregard this element of our population and reach the highest success. I but convey to you, Mr. President and Directors, the sentiment of the masses of my race when I say that in no way have the value and manhood of the American Negro been more fittingly and generously recognized than by the managers of this magnificent Exposition at every stage of it's progress. It is a recognition that will do more to cement the friendship of the two races than any occurrence since the dawn of our freedom.

Not only this, but the opportunity here afforded will awaken among us a new era of industrial progress. Ignorant and inexperienced, it is not strange that in the first years of our new life we began at the top instead of at the bottom; that a seat in Congress or the state legislature was more sought than real estate or industrial skill; that the political convention or stump speaking had more attractions than starting a dairy farm or truck garden.

A ship lost at sea for many days suddenly sighted a friendly vessel. From the mast of the unfortunate vessel was seen a signal, "Water, water; we die of thirst!" The answer from the friendly vessel at once came back, "Cast down your bucket where you are." A second time the signal, "Water, water; send us water!" ran up from the distressed vessel, and was answered, "Cast down your bucket where you are." And a third and fourth signal for water was answered, "Cast down your bucket where you are." The captain of the distressed vessel, at last heeding the injunction, cast down his bucket, and it came up full of fresh, sparkling water from the mouth of the Amazon river. To those of my race who depend on bettering their condition in a foreign land or who underestimate the importance of cultivating friendly relations with the Southern white man, who is their next-door neighbor, I would say: "Cast down your bucket where you are"—cast it down in making friends in every manly way of the people of all races by whom we are surrounded.

Cast it down in agriculture, mechanics, in commerce, in domestic service, and in the professions. And in this connection it is well to bear in mind that whatever other sins the South may be called to bear, when it comes to business, pure and simple, it is in the South that the Negro is given a man's chance in the commercial world, and in nothing is this Exposition more eloquent than in emphasizing this chance. Our greatest danger is that in the great leap from slavery to freedom we may overlook the fact that the masses of us are to live by the productions of our hands, and fail to keep in mind that we shall prosper in proportion as we learn to dignify and glorify common labor and put brains and skill into the common occupations of life; shall prosper in proportions as we learn to draw the line between the superficial and the substantial, the ornamental gewgaws of life and the useful. No race can prosper till it learns that there is as much dignity in tilling a field as in writing a poem. It is at the bottom of life we must begin, and not at the top. Nor should we permit our grievances to overshadow our opportunities.

To those of the white race who look to the incoming of those of foreign birth and strange tongue and habits for the prosperity of the South, were I permitted I would repeat what I say to my own race, "Cast down your bucket where you are." Cast it down among the eight millions of Negroes whose habits you know, whose fidelity and love you have tested in days when to have proved treacherous meant the ruin of your firesides. Cast down your bucket among these people who have, without strikes and labor wars, tilled your fields, cleared your forests, builded your railroads and cities, and brought forth treasures from the bowels of the earth, and helped make possible this magnificent representation of the progress of the South. Casting down your bucket among my people, helping and encouraging them as you are doing on these grounds, and, with education of head, hand, and heart, you will find that they will buy your surplus land, make blossom the waste places in your fields, and run your factories. While doing this, you can be sure in the future, as in the past, that you and your families will be surrounded by the most patient, faithful, law-abiding, and unresentful people that the world has seen. As we have proved our loyalty to you in the past, in nursing your children, watching by the sick-bed of your mothers and fathers, and often following them with tear-dimmed eyes to their graves, so in the future, in our humble way, we shall stand by you with a devotion that no foreigner can approach, ready to lay down our lives, if need be, in defense of yours, interlacing our industrial, commercial, civil, and religious life with yours in a way that shall make the interests of both races one. In all things that are purely social we can be as separate as the fingers, yet one as the hand in all things essential to mutual progress.

There is no defense or security for any of us except in the highest intelligence and development of all. If anywhere there are efforts tending to curtail the fullest growth of the Negro, let these efforts be turned into stimulating, encouraging, and making him the most useful and intelligent citizen. Effort or means so invested will pay a thousand percent interest. These efforts will be twice blessed—"blessing him that gives and him that takes."

There is no escape through law of man or God from the inevitable:

The law of changeless justice bind
Oppressor with oppressed;
and close as sin and suffering joined
We march to fate abreast.

Nearly sixteen millions of hands will aid you in pulling the load upward, or they will pull, against you, the load downward. We shall constitute one-third and more of the ignorance and crime of the South, or one-third its intelligence and progress; we shall contribute one-third to the business and industrial prosperity of the South, or we shall prove a veritable body of death, stagnating, depressing, retarding every effort to advance the body politic.

Gentlemen of the Exposition, as we present to you our humble effort at an exhibition of our progress, you must not expect overmuch. Starting thirty years ago with ownership here and there in a few quilts and pumpkins and chickens (gathered from miscellaneous sources), remember the path that has led from these to the inventions and production of agricultural implements, buggies, steam-engines, newspapers, books, statuary, carving, paintings, the management of drug-stores and banks, has not been trodden without contact with thorns and thistles. While we take pride in what we exhibit as a result of our independent efforts, we do not for a moment forget that our part in this exhibition would fall far short of your expectations but for the constant help that has come to our educational life, not only from the Southern states, but especially from Northern philanthropists, who have made their gifts a constant stream of blessing and encouragement.

8

The wisest among my race understand that the agitation of questions of social equality is the extremist folly, and that progress in the enjoyment of all the privileges that will come to us must be the result of severe and constant struggle rather than of artificial forcing. No race that has anything to contribute to the markets of the world is long, in any degree, ostracized. It is important and right that all privileges of the law be ours, but it is vastly more important that we be prepared for the exercise of those privileges. The opportunity to earn a dollar in a factory just now is worth infinitely more than the opportunity to spend a dollar in an opera-house.

9

In conclusion, may I repeat that nothing in thirty years has given us more hope and encouragement, and drawn us so near to you of the white race, as this opportunity offered by the Exposition; and here bending, as it were, over the altar that represents the results of the struggles of your race and mine, both starting practically empty-handed three decades ago, I pledge that, in your effort to work out the great and intricate problem which God has laid at the doors of the South, you shall have at all times the patient, sympathetic help of my race; only let this be constantly in mind, that, while from representations in these buildings of the product of field, of forest, of mine, of factory, letters, and art, much good will come, yet far above and beyond material benefits will be that higher good, that, let us pray God, will come, in a blotting out of sectional differences and racial animosities and suspicions, in a determination to administer absolute justice, in a willing obedience among all classes to the mandates of law. Thus, this, coupled with our material prosperity, will bring into our beloved South a new heaven and a new earth.

10

INTERNAL EVALUATION OF THE ATLANTA EXPOSITION ADDRESS

Internal evaluation of any work of rhetoric proceeds through four steps: purpose identification, outlining rhetorical barriers and advantages, strategy analysis, and comparison of strategies to the rhetorical barriers/advantages. In the PBS acronym, the S does double duty reminding the critic to first identify the Strategies and then compare those Strategies to the rhetorical barriers and advantages. In the following analysis, I illustrate the application of each stage via an analysis of Washington's address.

Washington's Purpose

The primary goals of Washington's address are quite clear. He wants to protect black jobs in the South, obtain the good will of the white southern audience, and seek assistance from northern philanthropists. The most important of these goals relates to jobs. In the third paragraph, Washington uses a long figurative analogy based on the example of the crew of a ship lost at sea and running out of water being told to "cast down your bucket where you are." The ship was in the mouth of the Amazon and when the crew "cast" down their bucket, they came up with pure, clean water. Similarly, Washington argues that black Southerners should "cast it [their metaphorical bucket] down in agriculture, mechanics, in commerce, in domestic service, and in the professions" (paragraph 4). In the next paragraph, he juxtaposes the "loyal" black population with new foreign immigrants or labor. Clearly, Washington hopes that the white population will provide jobs to African Americans in the South.

The interpretation that Washington's primary concern was jobs is supported by Washington's emphasis upon "work" as the most important means of helping black Americans. In paragraph 9, he both emphasizes the crucial value of work and suggests that having a productive job is more important than having complete equality with the white population. Washington says, "The opportunity to earn a dollar in a factory just now is worth infinitely more than the opportunity to spend a dollar in an opera house." With this statement, Washington indicates that he believes work opportunity is far more important than social equality with white Americans.

The second goal in the speech is clearly to create good will with the white audience. Throughout the address, Washington relies on a strategy of ingratiation. He praises the accomplishments of the white audience and sometimes puts down those of his own people. In the first paragraph, he refers to "this magnificent Exposition." A little later, he returns to a discussion of the Exposition itself stating, "Gentlemen of the Exposition, as we present to your our humble effort at an exhibition of our progress, you must not expect overmuch" (paragraph 8). Two paragraphs later, he concludes that "nothing in thirty years has given us more hope and encouragement and drawn us so near to you of the white race, as this opportunity offered by the Exposition." Clearly, Washington hopes that his rhetorical adaptation will produce a positive reaction among white Southerners.

Finally, Washington appeals to a very specific sub-audience—rich potential grant givers. In paragraph 8, he comments about the "constant help that has come to our educational life, not only from Southern states, but especially from Northern philanthropists." Here, his aim seems to be to generate additional revenues.

It is easy to see why some academics and others object to the tone and content of Washington's address. He praises the South and the Exposition shamelessly and demeans black Americans. As I will note in the analysis of strategies, he also praises Southern history and rejects attempts to change the Southern system. From our vantage point today, his rhetoric is disgusting. But Washington did not have the luxury of living in a nation in which the African American population has both significant political influence and legal restrictions that protect their rights.

The Situation Facing Washington in 1895

In 1895, Washington faced immense rhetorical barriers and possessed essentially no rhetorical advantages. In relation to barriers, the most important was extreme racism throughout society. In his book, *Anti Negro Thought in America*, I. A. Newley explained that "Southerners and other Americans too were especially receptive to racist doctrine and accepted without question the whole complex of anti-Negro ideas."[10] Even the title of Newley's book is an indication of the extent of racism in society of the time. It was a time in which terrible racism was the norm. Robert Brisbane puts it this way: "White people were united as never before in their determination to compel the Negro to begin from the bottom."[11] Brisbane also notes that even many Northern liberals supported strongly racist views.[12]

The second barrier Washington faced was the threat of white violence. In this period, black Americans, especially in the South, often were beaten and sometimes lynched. According to Thomas Dye, "A virtual reign of terror began in the 1890s and extended to the beginning of World War I."[13] A study done for the NAACP found that in this "reign of terror," more than 3,000 black Americans were lynched.[14] Black men and women who seemed the least bit threatening to the white establishment often were simply murdered. In truth, at this time an African American could be killed because a white person found offensive anything that he/she did. It was a very hard time to be a black American.

The third primary rhetorical barrier was that black Americans had essentially no political power. The Civil War had been over for thirty years and, as I noted earlier, many Northern liberals were racists. To make matters worse, black Americans were not allowed to vote. The distinguished historian August Meier writes that "By 1895 disenfranchisement had been pretty well accomplished by various devices ... in most of the South."[15] It is difficult to appeal to people who strongly believe that you are inferior, when you lack the protections of law and have essentially no political power. It is also important to note that black Americans could not effectively use violence to defend themselves against racism. Not only were black Americans on average quite poor (and thus less likely to be armed than their white counterparts), but fighting back could provoke still worse racist violence.

As should be clear, Washington possessed no rhetorical advantages. He was coming "hat in hand" to ask for jobs and money to an audience that thought him and other black Americans to be inferior. He had no power over his audience. It was in this context that Washington presented the Atlanta Exposition Address.

Strategies in the Address

Washington's overall strategy was to adapt to the attitudes and values of the audience, but underneath the surface state a case for fair treatment for black Americans. This last aspect of the address largely has been ignored by those who attack Washington.

Washington adapts to the Southern audience in several ways. First, as I noted earlier, he praises the Exposition in the strongest terms. Of course, everyone loves to be praised. Washington pushes this about as far as he can, without making the strategy painfully obvious. Second, and more fundamentally, Washington appeals to dominant attitudes of the age concerning the importance of business and hard work. The long "cast down your bucket" section of the introduction is both a wonderful use of metaphor, parallel structure, and repetition, and also an appeal to the ideal of "work." This same strategic adaptation is also evident in Washington's negative comments about labor unions and foreign immigrants. With these statements, Washington appeals to business attitudes about labor and immigrants. He also is subtly suggesting to the audience that they would be better off with black workers than other alternatives.

Third, Washington adapts to Southern attitudes about race. Perhaps the most famous statement of the address occurs at almost exactly the midpoint. He uses the metaphor of the fingers and the hand to suggest that blacks and whites can work together but still be separate. He says "In all things that are purely social we can be as separate as the fingers, yet one as the hand in all things essential to mutual progress" (paragraph 5). With this statement, Washington clearly adapts to Southern racism. He returns to this theme in the conclusion, where he says that "The wisest among my race understand that the agitation of questions of social equality is the extremist folly, and that progress in the enjoyment of all the privileges that will come to us must be the result of severe and constant struggle rather than of artificial forcing" (paragraph 9). In these statements, Washington seems to accept segregation.

Washington also adapts to Southern attitudes about history. In a long passage in paragraph 5, he depicts the past as a time in which the black population of the South was extremely loyal to the white population:

> As we have proved our loyalty to you in the past, in nursing your children, watching by the sick-bed of your mothers and fathers, and often following them with tear-dimmed eyes to their graves, so in the future, in our humble way, we shall stand by you with a devotion that no foreigner can approach, ready to lay down our lives, if need be, in defense of yours, interlacing our industrial, commercial, civil, and religious life with yours in a way that shall make the interests of both races one.

In this statement, Washington almost seems nostalgic about the pre-Civil War period. Of course, in that time Washington and other African Americans were slaves in the South. One can imagine the satisfaction that the Southern audience would have with Washington's description. Even here, however, the strategic character of Washington's adaptation is obvious. He not only appeals to Southern history, but sneaks in a negative comment about foreign workers. Washington clearly was doing everything possible to generate jobs for black Americans.

In addition to adaptation to Southern attitudes, Washington relies on a number of aesthetic strategies. I already have mentioned the two dominant metaphors of the fingers on a hand and the sailor casting down his bucket for water. Washington also relies on depiction in the passage concerning Southern history, as well as repetition, parallel structure, and rhythm. In this speech, Washington uses language strategies to make his message more appealing and memorable. The language strategies are not, however, the core of the speech.

Finally, Washington includes with the adaptive strategy an implicit call for justice and equality for all Americans. Recognizing the rhetorical situation, Washington does not make this conclusion explicit. Rather, he makes his argument for justice by implication. The implicit argument for justice for African Americans takes two forms. The first is an implied threat that the South must help black Southerners or face severe problems. After completing the introduction, Washington comments:

> Nearly sixteen millions of hands will aid you in pulling the load upward, or they will pull, against you, the load downward. We shall constitute one third and more of the ignorance and crime of the South, or one third its intelligence and progress; we shall contribute one third to the business and industrial prosperity of the South, or we shall prove a veritable body of death, stagnating, depressing, retarding every effort to advance the body politic. (paragraph 7)

With this statement, Washington appeals to the self-interest of the audience. He warns them that they could be much worse off if they do not assist the black population.

In the conclusion, he uses a somewhat different strategy. While rejecting demands for immediate social equality, Washington also emphasizes that eventually all rights must be guaranteed. For example, after downplaying the importance of social equality, Washington states "No race that has anything to contribute to the markets of the world is long, in any degree, ostracized" (paragraph 9). He then adds that "It is important and right that all privileges of the law be ours, but it is vastly more important that we be prepared for the exercise of those privileges" (paragraph 9). While he emphasizes the importance of responsibility in this statement, he also clearly says that black Americans should have the same rights as others. Washington does not call for immediate action on civil rights, but he makes it clear that eventually change must come.

Washington's rhetoric has been labeled a rhetoric of compromise or even appeasement. While there is no doubt that his focus was on adapting to his audience, he also clearly warned them that ultimately society must change. There is a strong argument that under the circumstances this was the only strategy open to him. A more forceful address or outright confrontation certainly would not have worked with the Southern audience. And there was no caring national audience to whom Washington could appeal. Moreover, a more forceful strategy very possibly could have caused white backlash, perhaps violence against the black population. Given the situation, there is a strong argument that Washington went about as far as he could go in pushing his agenda.

INTERNAL EVALUATION

There is no question that Washington's address was a success with both the immediate audience and the larger audience. The secondary data on this is quite clear. The question then becomes: Does an internal evaluation of effectiveness yield the same judgment concerning the speech as an external evaluation? The answer is clearly yes. It is important to remember that the primary rhetorical barriers faced by Washington were intense racism, the complete absence of political allies, and lack of power in any form to influence his audience. He also lived in an extremely violent Southern culture in which lynchings were quite common. In that circumstance, adaptation was his only choice.

Washington brilliantly adapted to Southern history, the dominant attitudes of the age concerning work, and especially to Southern attitudes about race. He used metaphor, depiction and other aesthetic strategies to get and keep the attention of the audience. But he also included an implicit threat and stated that the day must come when equal rights are provided to black Americans. In essence, he was willing to make a tactical retreat in order to protect black Americans from violence and obtain jobs for them. It must have sickened him to say some of the things he said, but he had no alternative.

WASHINGTON'S ADDRESS AND UNDERSTANDING CONTEXT

Booker T. Washington's Atlanta Exposition Address illustrates the importance of conducting adequate contextual research prior to judging any work of rhetoric. Today, a speech like Washington's rightly would be labeled a sellout or worse, but in 1895 it was an act of courage. The analysis of the address also illustrates the steps in the process of internal evaluation. By first identifying the goals of a work of rhetoric, then considering barriers (and advantages) to achieving those goals, next laying out the strategies in the work, and finally comparing the strategies to the barriers/advantages and making an on-balance judgment, the critic can evaluate the effectiveness of any work of rhetoric. Precisely the same steps could be taken to evaluate a speech by President Trump or a contemporary blog or Twitter message.

One final point is illustrated by the analysis of the Washington address and its later impact. Ethical evaluation also is dependent on the context. After presenting the speech, Washington became the most powerful black American, until his death in 1915. For decades after his death, the conventional wisdom was that Washington had followed a policy of accommodating white America. Reasonable people differed on whether that policy was required by the times or was a sellout. However, after Washington's private papers became available, a different picture emerged. It was discovered that while publicly seeming to accept segregation, Washington secretly attacked it. Louis Harlan writes:

> Washington in these circumstances decided to launch a secret but direct attack on racially restrictive laws. He secretly paid for and directed a succession of court suits against discrimination in voting, exclusion of Negroes from jury panels, Jim Crow railroad facilities, and various kinds of exploitation of the black poor. In all of this secret activity it is clear that Washington was not merely trying to make a favorable impression on his militant critics or to spike their guns, for he took every precaution to keep information of his secret actions from leaking out.[16]

It would seem that Washington, who had been attacked for being too passive, a sort of rhetorical chicken, was in fact a rhetorical fox. He did what he could under very difficult circumstances. When he saw the chance to launch a legal attack on racism and racist laws, he did so, but secretly, so that he could maintain his other strategy of adaptation. In contemporary America, we would label what Washington did as deceptive, manipulative, and very possibly money laundering. But in the context of his time, his actions should be labeled as a wonderful example of rhetorical skill and moral courage.

CONCLUSION

In this chapter, I explained the process of contextual research, the goals which this research serves, and the main and subcategories of barriers (and advantages) facing rhetors. I also developed the PBS system for evaluating the effectiveness of any work of rhetoric and applied that system to Booker T. Washington's "Atlanta Exposition Address." The most important conclusion developed in this chapter is that a fair understanding of how any rhetoric works or a fair evaluation of that rhetoric requires an understanding of the context in which the rhetoric was presented.

FOR FURTHER DISCUSSION

One of the most important foreign policy initiatives of the Obama administration was an agreement negotiated with the government of Iran in which Iran agreed to cease efforts to produce nuclear materials that could be used to construct nuclear weapons in exchange for relief from sanctions that the United States and other Western nations had applied to the Iranian economy. The Iran agreement was immensely controversial with some arguing that it lessened the chance that Iran would get nuclear weapons and also the risk of war and others arguing that it was a terrible deal that created major security risks. On July 14, 2015, President Obama made a statement defending the agreement. Carefully read and do an analysis outline of Obama's statement. Then consider the following questions:

1   What are the explicit and implicit themes and requested actions of Obama's statement?
2   What strategies does Obama present to support these positions?
3   What barriers would Obama have faced at the time in presenting this message?
4   How should Obama's statement be judged in terms of persuading this audience? Why or why not?

Statement by the President on Iran
President Barack Obama

Today, after two years of negotiations, the United States, together with our inter-   1
national partners, has achieved something that decades of animosity has not—a comprehensive, long-term deal with Iran that will prevent it from obtaining a nuclear weapon.

This deal demonstrates that American diplomacy can bring about real and   2
meaningful change—change that makes our country, and the world, safer and more secure. This deal is also in line with a tradition of American leadership. It's now more than 50 years since President Kennedy stood before the American people and said, "Let us never negotiate out of fear, but let us never fear to negotiate." He was speaking then about the need for discussions between the United States and the Soviet Union, which led to efforts to restrict the spread of nuclear weapons.

In those days, the risk was a catastrophic nuclear war between two super powers.   3
In our time, the risk is that nuclear weapons will spread to more and more countries, particularly in the Middle East, the most volatile region in our world.

Today, because America negotiated from a position of strength and principle, we   4
have stopped the spread of nuclear weapons in this region. Because of this deal, the international community will be able to verify that the Islamic Republic of Iran will not develop a nuclear weapon.

This deal meets every single one of the bottom lines that we established when we   5
achieved a framework earlier this spring. Every pathway to a nuclear weapon is cut off. And the inspection and transparency regime necessary to verify that objective will be put in place. Because of this deal, Iran will not produce the highly enriched uranium and weapons-grade plutonium that form the raw materials necessary for a nuclear bomb.

Because of this deal, Iran will remove two thirds of its installed centrifuges—the   6
machines necessary to produce highly enriched uranium for a bomb—and store them

President Barack Obama, Statement by the President on Iran, July 15, 2015

under constant international supervision. Iran will not use its advanced centrifuges to produce enriched uranium for the next decade. Iran will also get rid of 98 percent of its stockpile of enriched uranium.

To put that in perspective, Iran currently has a stockpile that could produce up to 10 nuclear weapons. Because of this deal, that stockpile will be reduced to a fraction of what would be required for a single weapon. This stockpile limitation will last for 15 years.   7

Because of this deal, Iran will modify the core of its reactor in Arak so that it will not produce weapons-grade plutonium. And it has agreed to ship the spent fuel from the reactor out of the country for the lifetime of the reactor. For at least the next 15 years, Iran will not build any new heavy-water reactors.   8

Because of this deal, we will, for the first time, be in a position to verify all of these commitments. That means this deal is not built on trust; it is built on verification. Inspectors will have 24/7 access to Iran's key nuclear facilities.   9

Inspectors will have access to Iran's entire nuclear supply chain—its uranium mines and mills, its conversion facility, and its centrifuge manufacturing and storage facilities. This ensures that Iran will not be able to divert materials from known facilities to covert ones. Some of these transparency measures will be in place for 25 years.   10

Because of this deal, inspectors will also be able to access any suspicious location. Put simply, the organization responsible for the inspections, the IAEA, will have access where necessary, when necessary. That arrangement is permanent. And the IAEA has also reached an agreement with Iran to get access that it needs to complete its investigation into the possible military dimensions of Iran's past nuclear research.   11

Finally, Iran is permanently prohibited from pursuing a nuclear weapon under the Nuclear Non-Proliferation Treaty, which provided the basis for the international community's efforts to apply pressure on Iran.   12

As Iran takes steps to implement this deal, it will receive relief from the sanctions that we put in place because of Iran's nuclear program—both America's own sanctions and sanctions imposed by the United Nations Security Council. This relief will be phased in. Iran must complete key nuclear steps before it begins to receive new sanctions relief. And over the course of the next decade, Iran must abide by the deal before additional sanctions are lifted, including five years for restrictions related to arms, and eight years for restrictions related to ballistic missiles.   13

All of this will be memorialized and endorsed in a new United Nations Security Council resolution. And if Iran violates the deal, all of these sanctions will snap back into place. So there's a very clear incentive for Iran to follow through, and there are very real consequences for a violation.   14

That's the deal. It has the full backing of the international community. Congress will now have an opportunity to review the details, and my administration stands ready to provide extensive briefings on how this will move forward.   15

As the American people and Congress review the deal, it will be important to consider the alternative. Consider what happens in a world without this deal. Without this deal, there is no scenario where the world joins us in sanctioning Iran until it completely dismantles its nuclear program. Nothing we know about the Iranian government suggests that it would simply capitulate under that kind of pressure. And the world would not support an effort to permanently sanction Iran into submission. We put sanctions in place to get a diplomatic resolution, and that is what we have done.

16

Without this deal, there would be no agreed-upon limitations for the Iranian nuclear program. Iran could produce, operate, and test more and more centrifuges. Iran could fuel a reactor capable of producing plutonium for a bomb. And we would not have any of the inspections that allow us to detect a covert nuclear weapons program. In other words, no deal means no lasting constraints on Iran's nuclear program.

17

Such a scenario would make it more likely that other countries in the region would feel compelled to pursue their own nuclear programs, threatening a nuclear arms race in the most volatile region of the world. It would also present the United States with fewer and less effective options to prevent Iran from obtaining a nuclear weapon.

18

I've been president and commander in chief for over six years now. Time and again, I have faced decisions about whether or not to use military force. It's the gravest decision that any president has to make. Many times, in multiple countries, I have decided to use force. And I will never hesitate to do so when it is in our national security interest. I strongly believe that our national security interest now depends upon preventing Iran from obtaining a nuclear weapon—which means that without a diplomatic resolution, either I or a future U.S. president would face a decision about whether or not to allow Iran to obtain a nuclear weapon or whether to use our military to stop it.

19

Put simply, no deal means a greater chance of more war in the Middle East. Moreover, we give nothing up by testing whether or not this problem can be solved peacefully. If, in a worst-case scenario, Iran violates the deal, the same options that are available to me today will be available to any U.S. president in the future. And I have no doubt that 10 or 15 years from now, the person who holds this office will be in a far stronger position with Iran further away from a weapon and with the inspections and transparency that allow us to monitor the Iranian program.

20

For this reason, I believe it would be irresponsible to walk away from this deal. But on such a tough issue, it is important that the American people and their representatives in Congress get a full opportunity to review the deal. After all, the details matter. And we've had some of the finest nuclear scientists in the world working through those details. And we're dealing with a country—Iran—that has been a sworn adversary of the United States for over 35 years. So I welcome a robust debate in Congress on this issue, and I welcome scrutiny of the details of this agreement.

21

But I will remind Congress that you don't make deals like this with your friends. We negotiated arms control agreements with the Soviet Union when that nation was committed to our destruction. And those agreements ultimately made us safer.

22

I am confident that this deal will meet the national security interest of the United States and our allies. So I will veto any legislation that prevents the successful implementation of this deal. 23

We do not have to accept an inevitable spiral into conflict. And we certainly shouldn't seek it. And precisely because the stakes are so high, this is not the time for politics or posturing. Tough talk from Washington does not solve problems. Hard-nosed diplomacy, leadership that has united the world's major powers offers a more effective way to verify that Iran is not pursuing a nuclear weapon. 24

Now, that doesn't mean that this deal will resolve all of our differences with Iran. We share the concerns expressed by many of our friends in the Middle East, including Israel and the Gulf States, about Iran's support for terrorism and its use of proxies to destabilize the region. But that is precisely why we are taking this step—because an Iran armed with a nuclear weapon would be far more destabilizing and far more dangerous to our friends and to the world. 25

Meanwhile, we will maintain our own sanctions related to Iran's support for terrorism, its ballistic missile program, and its human rights violations. We will continue our unprecedented efforts to strengthen Israel's security—efforts that go beyond what any American administration has done before. And we will continue the work we began at Camp David to elevate our partnership with the Gulf States to strengthen their capabilities to counter threats from Iran or terrorist groups like ISIL. 26

However, I believe that we must continue to test whether or not this region, which has known so much suffering, so much bloodshed, can move in a different direction. 27

Time and again, I have made clear to the Iranian people that we will always be open to engagement on the basis of mutual interests and mutual respect. Our differences are real and the difficult history between our nations cannot be ignored. But it is possible to change. The path of violence and rigid ideology, a foreign policy based on threats to attack your neighbors or eradicate Israel—that's a dead end. A different path, one of tolerance and peaceful resolution of conflict, leads to more integration into the global economy, more engagement with the international community, and the ability of the Iranian people to prosper and thrive. 28

This deal offers an opportunity to move in a new direction. We should seize it. 29

We have come a long way to reach this point—decades of an Iranian nuclear program, many years of sanctions, and many months of intense negotiation. Today, I want to thank the members of Congress from both parties who helped us put in place the sanctions that have proven so effective, as well as the other countries who joined us in that effort. 30

I want to thank our negotiating partners—the United Kingdom, France, Germany, Russia, China, as well as the European Union—for our unity in this effort, which showed that the world can do remarkable things when we share a vision of peacefully addressing conflicts. We showed what we can do when we do not split apart. 31

And finally, I want to thank the American negotiating team. We had a team of   32
experts working for several weeks straight on this, including our Secretary of Energy,
Ernie Moniz. And I want to particularly thank John Kerry, our Secretary of State,
who began his service to this country more than four decades ago when he put
on our uniform and went off to war. He's now making this country safer through his
commitment to strong, principled American diplomacy.

History shows that America must lead not just with our might, but with our   33
principles. It shows we are stronger not when we are alone, but when we bring the
world together. Today's announcement marks one more chapter in this pursuit of a
safer and more helpful and more hopeful world.

Thank you. God bless you. And God bless the United States of America.   34

1   See Robert C. Rowland and Rodger A. Payne, "The Effectiveness of Reagan's 'Star Wars' Address,"
    Political Communication and Persuasion 4 (1987): 161–178.

2   See Bertram Wolfe, "Why Environmentalists Should Promote Nuclear Energy," *Vital Speeches of the Day*
    1 November 1996: 52–56.

3   B. F. Riley, *The Life and Times of Booker T. Washington* (New York: Fleming H. Revell, 1916), pp.
    206–207.

4   Booker T. Washington, *Up From Slavery* (New York: Doubleday, 1901).

5   Riley, p. 207.

6   President Cleveland is cited in Samuel R. Spencer, Jr., *Booker T. Washington and the Negro's Place in
    American Life* (Boston: Little, Brown, 1955), p. 103.

7   Thomas E. Harris and Patrick C. Kennicott, "Booker T. Washington: A Study of Conciliatory Rhetoric,"
    Southern Speech Journal 37 (1971), pp. 58, 59.

8   Robert L. Health, "A Time For Silence: Booker T. Washington in Atlanta," *Quarterly Journal of Speech*
    64 (1978), p. 399.

9   A good description of the enormous impact of the speech is found in Riley, *The Life and Times of Booker
    T. Washington.*

10 I. A. Newley, *Anti Negro Thought in America 1900–1930* (Baton Rouge: LSU Press, 1965), p. 126.

11 Robert H. Brisbane, *The Black Vanguard* (Valley Forge: Johnson Press, 1970), p. 29.

12 Brisbane, p. 29.

13 Thomas R. Dye, *The Politics of Equality* (Indianapolis, The Bobbs-Merrill Company, 1971), p. 18.

14 Cited in Dye, pp. 18–19.

15 August Meier, *Negro Thought in America. 1880–1915: Racial Ideologies in the Age of Booker T. Washington*
    (Ann Arbor: University of Michigan Press, 1964), p. 162.

16 Louis R. Harlan, "The Secret Life of Booker T. Washington," *Booker T. Washington and His Critics*, Ed.
    Hugh Hawkins (Lexington: D.C. Heath, 1974), p. 187.

RHETORICAL STRATEGIES

INTRODUCTION

In the next six chapters, I discuss the six main strategy categories that were identified earlier. In each case, I define the characteristics of the strategy category, identify subtypes of the strategy (if relevant), and lay out the strengths and weaknesses of the strategy type as a means of persuasion.

CHAPTER 4
Rational Argument

The most common meaning of "argument" is a verbal fight or disagreement. In this view, argument is a bad thing, something to be avoided as mere bickering. While that meaning is the most common, it is not the correct interpretation of the term when it is considered a type of rhetorical strategy. As a strategy category, rational argument consists of the use of evidence and reasoning to persuade an audience with the logical power of the data and reasoning presented.

Why is rational argument important enough that I treat it as the first strategy category? The short answer is that while rational argument is not always the most effective strategy, it must be present if people are to use rhetoric to make effective decisions in a democratic society. Rational argument is based on the power of human reason. Through the give and take of argumentative discussion, people can come to a reasoned democratic decision on any issue from questions of war and peace to zoning. The alternative—an unreasoned decision—is certainly not very appealing.

In this chapter, I first lay out the functions of argument in any democratic society. I then discuss the formal components of argument and the three ways that argument can be used as a persuasive device. This section is followed by a consideration of the strengths and weaknesses of the four main types of supporting evidence. I then illustrate the way that argument functions as a strategy via analysis of a speech by President Barack Obama advocating for the health care reform that eventually passed Congress in 2010. In the final section of the chapter, I consider the conflicting data on whether argument is a generally effective persuasive strategy.

THE FUNCTIONS OF RATIONAL ARGUMENT

Rational argument serves two primary functions. First, it is a method of persuasion. People often use argument to try and persuade each other to act in some way or believe in something. In the last section of the chapter, I describe the somewhat conflicting research tradition on whether argument is an effective means of persuasion. Second, argument is the preferred method of resolving disagreements and making decisions in a democratic organization of any type, whether a large nation such as the United States, a lower level of government, or an organization of any size. Initially, it may seem odd to label argument as a key component of democracy. After all, most people hate having arguments. It is important, however, to remember that by argument I do not mean the common definition of the term—*a verbal fight*. Rather, I mean the use of data and reasoning to support a claim. Viewed in this manner, argument is not remotely similar to bickering.

Argument is essential in a democracy for two related reasons. First, argument is the primary method that humans have developed for solving problems of any kind. Through the give and take of argument, through testing evidence and reasoning, people can come to the best judgment possible about a given issue. Viewed in this manner, science, the law, and so on are merely places where specific types of rational argument are used to make decisions. In argument of all kinds, we test each other's evidence and reasoning. This method is quite flawed, but a lot better than **not** testing evidence and reasoning. Two rhetorical questions may make this point clear. What is the alternative to rational argument? Would it be better to rely on "irrational" means of persuasion? For all the flaws associated with argument as a method of decision-making, it clearly is better than any of the alternatives.

Second, argument is at the core of democratic decision-making at all levels because in argument all that matters is what you have to say. In rational argument, every individual is the same, regardless of status. It doesn't matter if you are president of the United States, the Queen of England, or a janitor from Manhattan, Kansas. All that matters in argument is what you have to say. Argument is also an empowering form because all judgments are based on the power of the argument, a principle that outlaws discrimination based on race, gender, ethnicity, religion, class, or any other characteristic. When judged based on the standards of argument alone, all people are equal. In addition, name-calling and other divisive and unpleasant forms of rhetoric are not legitimate forms of argument. Despite the common definition of argument as bickering, once someone stops relying on evidence and reasoning, one stops using rational argument. Thus, rational argument is valued not only because it is the basic human method for making reasonable decisions, but also because it is consistent with democratic theory that values people for what they do and say and not their class, wealth, race, gender, religion, or any other characteristic. Even the most skillful arguers often do not live up to this standard, but it is important that everyone strives to create a democratic society in which all are treated fairly and with respect. A reliance on rational argument moves us closer to that goal.

Faith in reason as an instrument of democratic decision-making has been ingrained in the American system since the very beginning. In the debate about the Constitution, the primary author of both the Constitution and the Bill of Rights and later president of the United States, James Madison, recognized the dangers posed by special interest domination and also by simple irrationality, but also saw that these dangers

© ONUR ERSIN/SHUTTERSTOCK.COM

could be turned against themselves in order to produce "a republican remedy for the diseases most incident to republican government."[1] Sheehan notes that Madison's faith in representative democracy was based in his faith in "the reason of the public."[2] Madison wrote in Federalist Number 49, that "it is the reason of the public alone that ought to controul [sic] and regulate the government."[3] Why did he have such faith, given the dangers posed by faction, human irrationality, and the dearth of enlightened leaders? Madison's faith was based in his view expressed in Federalist 51 that free and open debate among competing advocates would produce a political system in which "Ambition ... [would] counteract ambition."[4] The forces of ambition, Madison's "republican remedy," in turn would force faction leaders on all sides to support their views in open debate. It was that process of open debate that would protect the system because as he observed in Federalist Number 41, "A bad cause seldom fails to betray itself."[5] As Mathews has noted, Madison believed that "over the long run ... cool and calculated rational argument would win out over passion and hyperbole," ultimately producing what Madison labeled in commentary in the *National Gazette* on December 5, 1791 an "Empire of Reason."[6] We are far from that Empire of Reason and the dangers posed by special interest domination, racism, and other forms of prejudice, and simple irrationality are obvious across American society and yet the power of rational argument to win out in the end remains a key guarantor of American democracy.

THE DEFINING CHARACTERISTICS OF ARGUMENT FORM

A rhetor uses rational argument any time he or she backs up a claim with evidence and reasoning. Thus, the three defining characteristics of argumentative form are *a claim supported by evidence and reasoning*. It is important to understand how these three terms fit together. A claim is the conclusion that is drawn. The evidence is the supporting data the backs up the claim. And the reasoning is the premise that links the evidence to the claim.

Consider the following hypothetical argument:

> After Newt Gingrich was elected Speaker of the House, Republicans succeeded in passing welfare reform and achieved an historic budget deal that was praised by several Nobel Prize winning economists. He forced Congress to consider 100 percent of the items in the Contract with America and, in terms of his conservative legacy, can only be compared to Ronald Reagan. The party should not forget this record in 2012.

On the surface, the claim in this argument is that Republicans should remember Gingrich in the year 2012. But because a presidential election will occur that year, the obvious implication is that Gingrich deserves support for the Republican nomination for president. Four types of evidence are cited to back up this claim: the expert opinion of Nobel Prize winning economists, examples of legislation passed under his leadership, a statistic about the legislation from the Contract with America that was passed, and a comparison to Ronald Reagan, who is, of course, a much admired figure for conservatives. In this case, the reasoning linking the evidence to the conclusion is implied but not stated. The reasoning includes the value judgment that passing the listed legislation was a good idea, as well as the assumption that the Speaker of the House deserves credit for legislation passed during the time of his/her service, and general rules for when statistics, examples, and other evidence types are acceptable forms of proof.

The Gingrich example illustrates both the simplicity and complexity of argument. Argument is simple in that it is built on three building blocks: evidence, reasoning, and claims. It is complex in that the relationship among those three elements can occur in many ways. Before considering the ways that argument can be used as a persuasive device, it is important to understand each component part of argumentative form.

Claims

A claim is the conclusion drawn from the evidence and reasoning. Newt Gingrich should be elected president is a claim, as is a statement such as "Meryl Streep is the greatest actress in the history of film." It is important to recognize that not all claims are explicitly stated. In some instances the conclusion may be *implied*, but not stated. When Republicans attacked President Clinton with statements such as "I'm not saying that he should be impeached, but we do have to weigh whether we want a perjurer in the White House," they really meant "Of course, he should be impeached." In rare cases, the real claim may be the opposite of what is explicitly stated.

Evidence

Evidence is the data that supports an argument, which explains why it is sometimes labeled as "support material." The architectural analogy in the words "support material" is on point. It is the evidence that supports any argumentative claim. Evidence can be either explicitly presented or implicitly referenced.

There are four types of evidence: examples, statistics, comparisons, and statements of authority. An example is a specific instance that is used to prove a broader conclusion. A statement—"I had wonderful risotto at Lidias. What a great restaurant"—is an argumentative claim supported by an example. A statistic is a compilation of examples into a category. When someone cites Derek Jeter's lifetime batting average or the more than 3,000 hits he amassed in his career to support the claim that he was a great ballplayer, that person is using statistics to back up an obviously true conclusion. The third type of evidence—all forms of comparison, including metaphors, similes, analogies, and so forth—backs up a conclusion by noting the points of similarity between two objects, books, ideas, or whatever. Thus, when someone said in 2011 that "We shouldn't send troops to Libya because it could be the new Vietnam," that person was supporting the conclusion that the United States should not send ground troops into Libya based on a claim that a war with Libya in 2011 and the Vietnam War of the 1960s and 1970s were similar. The final evidence type is a statement of authority. In argument from authority, the rhetor cites the expertise or experience of someone to support a claim. Authoritative evidence can be used as a way to simplify a complex argument and to draw on positive audience attitudes about someone's credentials on a given topic. People listen to what Bill Gates and Warren Buffett say because their success in business is seen as a sign of their underlying knowledge about business.

Reasoning

Reasons serve a linking function between evidence and claims. There are three types of reasons. The first type is a simple rule for interpreting what evidence means. Consider the following statement: "Joe Jones, of the National Weather Service concludes that thunderstorms are likely." The claim and authoritative evidence in this statement are readily apparent. What is the reasoning? The reasoning is so obvious that it is hard to see: "The opinions of experts in a given field function as strong evidence for claims within the field." In many similar cases, reasoning either stated directly or implied provides the justification to trust a given type of evidence. Thus, more examples are better than fewer examples and comparisons in which there are many points of similarity are stronger than comparisons with few points of similarity.

The second form of reasoning is as a rule for interpreting what evidence means in a context. Imagine the statement, "Sam Kelly is a great basketball player. He is hitting 37 percent of his three point shots." Clearly, the argument about Sam is based on the general principle that statistics are a valid form of evidence *and* the rule of thumb known by basketball fans that a 37 percent shooting percentage for three point shots is a very good one. That figure—37 percent—would not constitute a good completion rate for a football passer or a good conviction rate for a prosecutor or a good score on a college exam. And a hockey player who scored on 37 percent of the shots he took would be better than even Wayne Gretsky. Thus, the second type of reasoning is a shared rule for what evidence means in a specific context.

The third form of reasoning is a value principle labeling something, someone, or some idea as good or bad. The statement—"Thousands are dying in Syria. We must act"—illustrates this point. In this case, the conclusion that the United States should act is supported by evidence of thousands of people dying and implied reasoning that it would be immoral for this nation to allow mass murder if we can prevent it. Put simply, this argument depends upon the shared value assumption that mass killings are not acceptable.

THREE WAYS THAT ARGUMENT WORKS AS A PERSUASIVE STRATEGY

There are three primary ways that rational argument works as a persuasive strategy. The first way is evidence-oriented argument, in which the primary strategy is to provide information to persuade the audience to support a position. The second way is enthymematic argument. As noted earlier, an enthymeme is a kind of argument in which the audience fills in some portion of the evidence or reasoning, or even the claim. In an enthymeme, the audience participates in creating the argument. The final way argument works to persuade is refutation, which occurs when the rhetor identifies a claim made by someone with whom he/she disagrees and then systematically refutes that claim.

The three forms of argument have somewhat different persuasive purposes. Evidence-oriented argument is used primarily when the issue is factual and the presentation of new information can persuade the audience to take a particular stand. Enthymematic argument draws upon pre-existing audience knowledge. It works best when reinforcing a view already shared to some extent by the audience. Refutation is used to deny the position of the other side. Refutation is most likely to be effective when appealing to an undecided audience that is considering two different perspectives or when reinforcing the views of an audience that already supports a claim. One is unlikely to be able to use refutation to change the mind of someone on the other side of an issue. For example, it is extremely unlikely that a strong supporter of President Trump could use refutation to persuade a Hillary Clinton supporter that Secretary Clinton should have been indicted for her email practices as Secretary of State. The Clinton supporter's likely view that Secretary Clinton had sloppy email practices, but committed no crimes is too firmly established for it to be changed easily. On the other hand, refutation may be quite effective when it is used with an undecided audience and when the arguer is refuting someone on the other side and not refuting the views of the audience. Alternatively, it can be used to shore up support among people who already endorse a position, but who may not be well-informed about details of the issue.

THE THREE PERSUASIVE FUNCTIONS OF ARGUMENT

1 Evidence-oriented argument persuades people by giving them new evidence about an issue.

2 Enthymematic argument reinforces positions that an audience already accepts.

3 Refutative argument exposes the weakness in the views of the other side in order to support a particular position.

Evidence Types

Earlier, I cited an example to illustrate each of the four main types of evidence. It is now important to consider in more depth the strengths and weaknesses of these evidence types as persuasive devices. It is important to note that in this section I am *not* discussing strengths and weaknesses of the four evidence types as forms of proof. Here, my focus is on the persuasive value of the four types of evidence. In the final chapter, as part of the Informed Citizen system, I will lay out tests for the rational quality of each evidence type.

Examples

Examples are individual instances of some larger category. Thus, I might cite examples of how homeowners had used guns to protect their homes to defend current gun laws and oppose stricter regulation. Examples have several strengths. In many cases, the example includes an interesting tidbit that helps keep the attention of the audience. In addition, examples can be used to personalize an issue. Citing an example of an AIDS victim might humanize the issue for people who knew intellectually about the horror of AIDS, but had not internalized that horror. Even a hypothetical example can accomplish that end. Tom Hanks' film *Philadelphia* is a powerful illustration of the impact that hypothetical examples can have, even in a work of fiction. Finally, examples may be cited to "bring home" an issue to someone, to make it real for them. A detailed description of a particular homeless person might do more to bring home the fate of the homeless than a hundred statistics.

At the same time, examples also have weaknesses. For instance, a specific example may be perceived as atypical and thus not taken seriously. And since examples are specific instances, they easily may be refuted with counterexamples. There is also some risk that a given example might be too interesting, causing the audience to miss the ultimate point. Oftentimes the media personalize the harm caused by a given disease by focusing on a celebrity who suffers from the disease. The problem from a persuasive perspective may be that the example of the celebrity is so interesting for the audience that the larger argumentative point gets lost.

Statistics

Statistics are "bunches" of examples combined in a category. A batting average, for instance, is calculated based on the batter's total number of hits in relation to the total number of at bats. All statistics are simply compilations of examples. Scientific and social scientific research studies are simply complex combinations of bunches of examples compiled into categories.

© WRANGLER/SHUTTERSTOCK.COM

One persuasive strength of statistics is that they show the size of a problem. It is one thing to cite an example of child abuse and quite another to show that there are many thousands of abused children. Another strength is the perception that statistics are both scientific and objective. Some people think that statistics are "hard facts" based on the best scientific research. Finally, by citing a number of statistics, the rhetor can add to his/her own credibility, since we tend to believe that someone who is aware of statistical data must be well-informed on the subject.

Statistics also have weaknesses as a category of evidence. First, statistics are impersonal and dull. No one reads statistical analyses for entertainment. And because statistics reduce individual cases to a numerical representation, they remove any personal dimension from the rhetoric. It often is easier to ignore a statistic showing many people hurt by some problem than a compelling example of a single victim. Third, statistics may be complicated and difficult to understand. Very few people understand the ins and outs of statistical analysis. Consequently, there may be problems getting an audience to understand exactly what a statistic means. Finally, while some people perceive statistics as objective, some have nearly the opposite perception, that statistics can be cited to prove anything. The saying that there are "lies," and still worse, "damn lies," and worst of all, "statistics," is illustrative of that attitude.

Authoritative Evidence

Authoritative evidence involves a citation of someone with either expertise or experience to support a point. An expert is someone who has extensive training in an area and thus can be quoted based on their knowledge. The other form of authoritative evidence is to cite someone with direct personal experience. In the area of prison reform, the expert might have an advanced degree in criminology or have worked in a prison for a decade. On the other hand, a former prisoner, while not an expert, could talk about prisons based upon his/her experience.

In general, experience is a more powerful form of authoritative evidence than expertise if the issue involves a specific event. The person with experience says "I saw it happen." It is difficult to deny such a statement. Expertise is the more powerful form if any kind of generalization is involved. In relation to a generalization, the expert is in a position to speak to the characteristics of the category. He/she has knowledge (expertise) on more than specific instances.

In terms of strengths as a general category of support, authoritative evidence may be used to simplify an issue. If a given position is difficult to explain because of complexity, one way to deal with the problem is to simply quote an expert. A second strength is that citation of authoritative testimony again adds to the rhetor's credibility. The audience is likely to conclude that someone who can quote many experts must him/herself be knowledgeable on the subject.

On the other hand, authoritative evidence can be dull. That is why so many more people watch tabloid news shows, rather than *The News Hour* on PBS or any other news program that often brings in experts to discuss issues. Authoritative evidence also depends upon the knowledge base of the audience. If the audience doesn't have a minimum understanding of the issue, the expert evidence will be meaningless. And finally, authoritative evidence does not work very well if the audience is not aware of the identity of the expert. Citing the greatest expert in the world on a given subject will not persuade an audience if they do not both know who the expert is and are impressed by his/her qualifications. In addition, some people react negatively against the very idea of expertise. That kind of backlash against experts has been quite evident in the debate about global warming, where nearly all climatologists support the theory and many ordinary people reject the views of the experts. Donald Trump successfully drew on populist backlash against experts and other elites in the 2016 presidential campaign.

Comparisons

Comparisons occur in many forms. Analogies, metaphors, similes, and simple comparisons all fall into this category. There are two main dimensions for understanding all of these different types of comparisons: literal versus figurative and developed versus undeveloped. A literal comparison is used when two ideas, objects, people, and so forth from the same category are compared. In a figurative comparison, in contrast, the two objects, ideas, or people being compared are from different categories. It would be a literal comparison to contrast President Reagan with President Obama. It would be a figurative comparison to say that "Bill Clinton was the Michael Jordan of politics."

Comparisons also differ in terms of degree of development. Sometimes, all of the points of similarity are laid out in great detail. In such a developed comparison, the rhetor makes crystal clear the relationship between the objects being compared. In an undeveloped comparison, in contrast, the comparison is not developed in detail. The comparison of President Clinton to Michael Jordan would be an undeveloped comparison if an arguer simply stated it. On the other hand, if the arguer developed the comparison point by point, then it would be a developed comparison. Obviously, undeveloped comparisons often are used in enthymematic argument. It should be noted that undeveloped comparisons cannot be used effectively unless the audience already has a great deal of knowledge on the subject. For this reason, a comparison of Kansas City Chiefs quarterback Patrick Mahomes to all-time great Johnny Unitas would likely not be effective for fans under the age of 70 because they would have no memory of watching Unitas play.

In terms of strengths, comparisons may be used to add interest to otherwise boring material. The comparison of Clinton to Jordan, for instance, draws on public knowledge of the two men and casts the former president in a very different light from normal political analysis. Comparisons also are valuable as a way of taking an unfamiliar concept and making it clear. When people first started seeing UFOs, they called them "flying saucers" because everyone could imagine what a flying saucer would look like.

On the other hand, comparisons also have weaknesses. Comparisons are generally perceived as the weakest form of evidence, because they only "compare" two different objects. A second weakness is that a comparison may become trite. For example, the figurative comparison of "life is a journey" has been used so much that it no longer has any power. The first time that comparison was used (probably thousands of years ago) it must have seemed striking and insightful. But it has been used so many times since that original use that it now is trite and boring. There is also a danger that a comparison will not "connect" with the audience. If a rhetor compares a contemporary scientist to J. Robert Oppenheimer, that comparison will be effective only if the audience knows that Oppenheimer was the head of the Manhattan Project, which developed the atomic bomb. Otherwise, they will say simply, "J. Robert-who?" Finally, as in the case of examples, there is some danger that a comparison can be too interesting. If the members of the audience become caught up in the comparison, they may miss the point that is being made.

Strengths and Weaknesses of the Four Types of Evidence

Examples

Strengths
- Add interest
- Personalize an issue
- Make the issue hit home

Weaknesses
- May be perceived as atypical
- Easily refuted
- May be "too" interesting and distract from the main message

Statistics

Strengths
- Show the magnitude of the problem
- Add to the credibility of the rhetor
- Perceived as hard data

Weaknesses
- Often are boring
- Impersonal
- Complicated and difficult to understand
- Perceived as a deceptive form of proof

Authoritative Evidence

Strengths
- Can be used to simplify complicated material
- Adds to the credibility of the rhetor

Weaknesses
- Often can be dull
- Depends upon the knowledge base of the audience
- Audience may be unaware of the identity of the expert

Comparisons

Strengths
- Add interest
- Explain complex material in terms that are familiar to the audience

Weaknesses
- Perceived as the weakest form of proof
- May become trite over time
- May not connect with the audience

Summary of Evidence Types

Which of the evidence types that I have discussed is the strongest? The answer is that none of them is inherently stronger than the other. Rather, the skilled rhetor should use a variety of types of support material in order to keep the attention of his/her audience and should tie that evidence usage to the particular strengths of each of the four types of support. For example, it almost always is smart to combine examples and statistics in support of a claim. The statistics demonstrate the breadth of the problem being discussed, while the examples personalize the issue and add interest. A similar point can be made about authoritative evidence and comparisons. Authoritative evidence can be used to simplify complex material, while comparisons make that complex material both more interesting and more understandable.

A good illustration of the strengths and weaknesses of the four types of evidence can be found in President Obama's opening statement at a health care town hall held at Northern Virginia Community College in Annandale, Virginia on July 1, 2009. The speech and the town hall discussion that followed it were part of the advocacy campaign that President Obama led in support of the health care reform law that eventually passed Congress and was signed into law in spring 2010. A number of presidents, both Democrats and Republicans, had tried since the time of President Theodore Roosevelt to get health care reform passed by Congress. Until Obama succeeded in the spring of 2010, each of the major reform efforts had failed in large part because of entrenched interest groups that opposed any reform that threatened them and strong opposition from conservatives who felt that any government effort would be a terrible failure. Like the other presidents who had supported reform, Obama faced strong opposition. In his advocacy for reform, Obama decided to use the resources of rational argument to respond to objections to his proposal in order to reassure the American people that the proposed legislation would not harm the citizen and would not be enormously expensive. More broadly, Obama was trying to win the case for health care reform on the merits and in a sense revitalize the very idea of public reason.[7] His remarks at the health care town hall meeting provide an excellent illustration of how rational argument functions as a persuasive strategy.

Excerpts from the Remarks of President Barack Obama in a Health Care Town Hall

Northern Virginia Community College Annandale, Virginia[8]

1   It's also not too soon to reform our health care system, which we've been talking about since Teddy Roosevelt was president.

President Barack Obama, Remarks at Health Care Town Hall in Annandale, VA, 2009

2 We are at a defining moment for this nation. If we act now, then we can rebuild our economy in a way that makes it strong, competitive, sustainable, and prosperous once more. We can lead this century the same way that we led the last century. But if we don't act, if we let this moment pass, we could see this economy just sputter along for decades—a slow, steady decline in which the chances for our children and our grandchildren are fewer than the opportunities that were given to us. And that's contrary to the history of America. One of our core ideas has always been that we leave the next generation better off than us. And that's why we have to act right now.

3 I know that people say the costs of fixing our problems are great—and in some cases, they are. The costs of inaction, of not doing anything, are even greater. They're unacceptable. And that's why this town hall and this debate that we're having around health care is so important.

4 Let me just give a few statistics. Many of you already know these. In the last nine years, premiums have risen three times faster than wages for the average family. I don't need to tell you this because you've seen it in your own lives. Even if you've got health insurance—and 46 million people don't—if you've got health insurance, you have seen your costs double. They've gone up three times faster than wages. If we do nothing, then those costs are just going to keep on going higher and higher.

5 In recent years, over one third of small businesses have reduced benefits and many have dropped coverage altogether since the early 90s—not because small business owners don't want to provide benefits to their workers, but they just simply can't afford it; they don't have the money. If we don't act, that means that more people are going to lose coverage and more people are going to lose their jobs because those businesses are not going to be competitive.

6 Unless we act, within a decade, one out of every $5 we earn will be spent on health care. And for those who rightly worry about deficits, the amount our government spends on Medicare and Medicaid will eventually grow larger than what our government spends today on everything else combined— everything else combined.

7 The Congressional Budget Office just did a study that showed that when you look at the rising costs of entitlement, 90 percent of it is Medicare and Medicaid—it's not Social Security—90 percent of it comes from the federal share of health care costs. So if we want to control our deficits, the only way for us to do it is to control health care costs.

8 Now, those are all abstractions, those are numbers. But many of you know that this translates into pain and heartache in a very personal way for families all across America. I know because during the two years that I campaigned for President every town hall meeting I had, people would raise horrible stories about their experiences in the medical system. And now that I'm president, I'm hearing those same stories. I get 10 letters a day—out of the 40,000 or so that the White House receives, my staff selects 10 for me to read every single day. And at least half of them relate to a story about somebody who has been denied coverage because of a pre-existing condition, or somebody who finds out that what they thought was going to be a $500 bill ends up being a $25,000 bill.

9   I was at a town hall meeting in Green Bay, Wisconsin, met a young woman, 36 years old, has breast cancer that's metastasized. She's got two small children. Her and her husband are both employed, both have health insurance, and yet she still has $50,000 worth of debt. And all she's thinking about right now is, instead of thinking about how to get well, she's thinking, if I don't survive this, my main legacy to my children may be another $50,000 worth of debt.

10   Everybody here knows stories like that. Some of you have experienced them personally. So this is a problem that we can't wait to fix. It's not something that we're going to keep on putting off indefinitely. This is about who we are as a country. And that's why we are going to pass health care reform—not 10 years from now, not five years from now; we are going to pass it this year. (Applause.) That is my commitment. We're going to get it done. (Applause.)

11   Now, we've already started to see some progress in Washington. Those who said we couldn't do it, they're already being surprised, because as a consequence of us pushing, suddenly the drug companies and the insurance companies and the hospitals, all of them are starting to realize this train is leaving the station, we better get on board.

12   So just a few weeks ago, the pharmaceutical industry agreed to $80 billion in spending reductions that we can use to close the so-called "doughnut hole." Some of you know what the "doughnut hole" is, right, where senior citizens who are on the prescription drug plan under Medicaid, they get their drugs reimbursed up to a certain point, and then suddenly there's a gap until it reaches thousands of dollars in out-of-pocket costs.

13   And so we've struck a deal with the drug companies; they're willing to cut those costs for seniors in half. Already we're seeing that when we put pressure to reform the system, then these industries are going to have to respond. Last month, doctors and hospitals, labor and business, insurers and drug companies all came together and agreed to decrease the annual rate of health care growth by 1.5 percent—that would translate into $2 trillion or more of savings over the next decade. And that would mean lower costs for everybody, for ordinary families.

14   In the past two weeks, the committee in the Senate, led by Senator Kennedy and Senator Dodd, have made tremendous progress on a plan to hold down costs, improve patient care, and ensure that you won't lose your coverage even if you lose your job, or if you change your job, or you've got a preexisting medical condition.

15   But now we need to finish the job. There's no doubt that we have to preserve what's best in the health care system, and that means allowing Americans who like their doctor and their health care plan to keep their plan. And that's going to be a priority for us. (Applause.) But we also have to fix what's broken about the system, and that means permanently bringing down costs and giving more choice for everyone.

16   And to do this, we've got to do a couple of things. We have to build on the investments that we've made in electronic medical records. We already made those investments in the Recovery Act—because when everything is digitalized, all your records—your privacy is protected, but all your records on a digital form —that reduces medical errors. It means that nurses don't have to read the scrawl of doctors when they are trying to figure out what treatments to apply. That saves lives; that saves money; and it will still ensure privacy.

17   We need to invest in prevention and wellness that help Americans live longer, healthier lives. We know this saves money. If we can help somebody control obesity, they are less likely to get diabetes. And if they are less likely to get diabetes that means that we are going to be saving a whole lot of money in hospital costs.

18   The biggest thing we can do to hold down costs is to change the incentives of the health care system that automatically equates expensive care with good care. Now, this is an important concept, so I want everybody to really focus on this. We are—we've been under the illusion that the more health care we get, the healthier we become. And it turns out that every study shows that the question is, are you getting the right care, are you getting the best care, the high-quality care, rather than are you having a whole bunch of tests ordered that are unnecessary, getting a bunch of treatments that are unnecessary, staying in hospitals longer than may be necessary—all of which drives up your costs, but doesn't make you better.

19   We have to ask ourselves why there are places like Geisinger Health Care Systems in rural Pennsylvania, or Intermountain Health in Salt Lake City, that offer high-quality health care at costs that are well below average, in some cases 30 percent lower than in other communities. If they can do it, there's no reason why all of America shouldn't do that. We've got to identify the best practices across the country; we've got to learn from those successes, and then we've got to replicate those successes elsewhere.

20   And we should change the warped incentives that reward doctors and hospitals based on how many tests or procedures they prescribe, even if those tests and procedures aren't shown to actually make people better, or if they result in medical mistakes. Doctors across this country did not get into the profession just to be bean-counters or paper-pushers, but more and more time that doctors should be spending with patients are spent on administration and worrying how do they deal with how they're reimbursed. We've got to create a simplified, more effective system where they are reimbursed for quality care, as opposed to having to distort their practices in ways that don't actually make their patients better.

21 It's also time to provide Americans who can't afford health insurance with more affordable options. I believe this is a moral imperative and it is an economic imperative. (Applause.) It's a moral imperative because in a country as wealthy as ours, if people are working and holding up their responsibilities, they shouldn't be bankrupted just because they get sick. On the other hand, it's an economic imperative because every single one of us who do have health insurance, our families, on average, are paying an extra $1,000 in premiums for uncompensated care.

22 Hospitals and doctors are adding those costs to your premiums—insurance companies are adding those costs to your premiums, even if you don't know it. And if we can get a system in which people are getting regular checkups, mammograms, all the things that we know prevent disease from occurring over the long term, or at least allow us to catch those diseases early, that's going to allow us to drive down costs for everybody.

23 So what we have been working on is the creation of something called the Health Insurance Exchange. And this is going to be a marketplace which would allow you to one-stop-shop for health care plans and compare benefits and prices in simple, easy-to-understand language, and then choose the best plan for you. None of these plans would be able to deny coverage on the basis of a pre-existing condition. All of them would include an affordable, basic benefit package. If you couldn't afford these plans, then we could provide you a little bit of help so that you can afford these plans.

24 I also strongly believe that one of the options in the exchange should be a public option, in order for us to create some competition for the private insurers to keep them honest. If they are in fact giving good service and providing high-quality coverage, then that's where people will want to go. But there should be a benchmark there of a public plan, non-for-profit plan, that keeps administrative costs low and is focused on providing good service. And that way you can make the decision which deal is going to be better for you and your family.

25 Now, I know one of the biggest questions on everybody's mind is how do we pay for all this, how do we finance reform? And I have made a commitment, because our deficit is a genuine problem, that whatever we do we have to pay for it. This can't add to our deficits. It's got to be deficit-neutral over the next 10 years.

26 Here's the good news: About two thirds of the costs of the reforms that we are proposing will come from reallocating money that is already being spent in the health care system but isn't being spent wisely. So it doesn't involve more spending; it just involves smarter spending. A lot of the money that's being spent in the health care system right now adds nothing to the quality of patient care.

27 And I'll just give you one example. We spend right now about—over the next 10 years, we will spend $177 billion—$177 billion over the next decade—in unwarranted subsidies to insurance companies under something called Medicaid Advantage—Medicare Advantage. Now, this does not make seniors healthier. People who are signed up for this private insurance subsidized program don't get any better care than those who aren't. The subsidies don't go to the patients; they go to the insurance companies. Now, think if we took that $177 billion and helped families so that they could have insurance, and that we could have preventive care.

28 So about two thirds of the cost of the reform we're proposing is just reallocating money that's already in the system you, the taxpayers, are already paying for.

29 Now, one third of it we're going to have to pay for by increased revenues. And what I've proposed is, is that if we capped the itemized deductions that very wealthy people do—the top 2 percent use on their income tax—so that they're getting the same tax breaks as everybody else, as opposed to getting higher tax breaks because they've got a bigger house, then we can pay for the rest of reform.

30 We've already identified $950 billion over 10 years—a little less than $100 billion a year—in order to pay for reform; two thirds of it reallocating money, one third of it with increased revenues. That's a sensible investment for us to make in solving an intractable problem that has been dragging down family finances, businesses, and the federal government for far too long.

31 Now, keep in mind, by the way, what we've identified as paying for the system, that doesn't even include the savings that we're going to get from prevention, or the savings that we're going to get from health IT—because in using congressional jargon, which I'm never supposed to do because nobody understands it—it's not scorable. And what that means is, is that the Congressional Budget Office can't identify exactly how much you would save— even though everybody believes that it will end up saving a lot of money, we can't put a hard number on it.

32 So we will get additional savings that will drive down costs. In the meantime, the costs of reform will be paid for with hard dollars that we've identified.

33 So here's the bottom line. Now we're going to—I'm almost done here, but this is a big, complicated topic, so I hope you forgive me. We're starting to make

progress on Capitol Hill. We're identifying ways not only to reform the system, to make it smarter and more efficient, more user-friendly, better for American families, but also ways to pay for it in a way that doesn't bloat our deficit.

34 But the hardest part is yet to come—because everybody here knows that the easiest thing to do when you're looking at big policy questions like health care is just to be saying it can't be done. And the naysayers are already starting to line up and finding every excuse and scare tactic in the book for why reform is not going to happen. This is going on as we speak. And what I say to these critics is, well, what's your alternative? Is your alternative just to stand pat and keep on watching more and more families lose their health care, more and more families with higher out-of-pocket costs for less insurance; businesses who are not able to compete internationally; a Medicare and a Medicaid system that is run amok? Is that your alternative?

35 What do you say to all those families who can't pay their medical bills? What do we tell those businesses that are having to choose between closing their doors or eliminating benefits for their workers? What do you say to every taxpayer whose dollars are propping up a system that doesn't work and that's driving us into debt?

36 This isn't just about those Americans without health care. It's about every American—because if we do not act to bring down costs, everybody's health care will be in jeopardy. If you lose your job, or if you've got a pre-existing condition, you don't know that your family is going to be secure. All of us are in this together.

37 So when it comes to energy, when it comes to improving our schools, and when it comes to health care, I don't accept the status quo. And you shouldn't either. And I don't think that the American people want to just stand pat. They know that change isn't easy. They know there are going to be setbacks and false starts. But they also know this—that we're in one of those rare moments where everybody is ready to move into the future. We just can't be scared. We've got to stop clinging to a broken system that doesn't work, and we've got to have the courage to reach out for a future that's going to be better for our children and our grandchildren.

38 I believe we can accomplish it this year. But in order to make it happen, I'm going to need ordinary Americans to stand up and say, "Now is the time." You are what are going to drive this process forward—because if Congress thinks that the American people don't want to see change, frankly, the lobbyists and the special interests will end up winning the day. But when the American people decide that something needs to happen, nothing can stop us.

39 So I hope you'll join me. Thank you very much, everybody.

ANALYSIS OF RATIONAL ARGUMENT IN PRESIDENT OBAMA'S HEALTH CARE TOWN HALL

President Obama expresses the thesis of his speech in the first paragraph of the section on health care reform, where he references the Republican charge that his administration was trying to act "too quickly" on health care and responds, "It's also not too soon to reform our health care system, which we've been talking about since Teddy Roosevelt was President." In the second paragraph, he explains the underlying rationale for health care reform, arguing that ultimately reform is about preventing "a slow, steady decline in which the chances for our children and our grandchildren are fewer than the opportunities that were given to us." Here, he makes the point that health care reform can have major economic impacts that go far beyond simply providing health coverage to the uninsured. The remainder of the speech makes a positive argument for health care reform and a refutative argument responding to both arguments that had been made against health care reform and doubts about reform that were in the minds of many Americans. He concludes the speech, which was followed by a town hall discussion, with a series of enthymematic arguments in which he reminds the audience of the excitement of his campaign for the presidency and asks "ordinary Americans to stand up and say, 'Now is the time'" (38). Given Obama's use of all three forms of rational argument and all four forms of evidence, his remarks provide a very clear illustration of the power (and weaknesses) of rational argument.

Before considering the various forms of argument in Obama's address, it is important to consider the three primary barriers that Obama faced. It is crucial to understand that the health care town hall occurred prior to the period when a series of what can only be called wild charges were made against his proposal, including most notably the charge that the plan might deny care to some seniors, resulting in their deaths, and the claim that the plan would essentially take over the health care industry. These charges were specious, but they dominated later debate.[9]

At the time when Obama spoke, he faced three main barriers. The first was worry about cost, worry that the plan would produce massive deficits. There was a sense among many in the public that the United States simply couldn't afford health care reform during a terrible recession. One of the most important liberal magazines in the nation, *The New Republic*, noted in March 2009 that "As far back as the fall, skeptics were warning that Barack Obama would have to abandon his hope of overhauling American health care. There was no money to fund such a transformation, they said."[10] The second barrier was closely related to the first, the sense that government programs don't work very well. For example, David Leonhardt noted in an analytical article in *The New York Times*, despite the fact that "a solid majority of Americans support the stated goals of health reform," those same "polls also show that people are worried about the package emerging from Congress."[11] Many of the outlandish charges that would come later resonated with the public, despite being refuted again and again, because of the strength of the attitude shared by many Americans that government simply isn't very competent and often makes problems worse. This problem may have been greater simply because Obama was a

Democrat. Citing polls, Charles M. Blow noted that "Americans seem to trust the government substantially more after a Republican president is elected than they do after a Democratic one is elected."[12]

The third barrier came out of the fact that something over 75 percent of Americans had health insurance in one form or another. For this group, the fear was that reform efforts to provide coverage to others might somehow threaten their coverage. Leonhardt noted "on the subject of health care reform, most Americans probably don't have a good answer to the question 'What's in it for me?'" He added that "obviously, is a problem for" Obama in selling health reform and then concluded that because of this situation, "Our health care system is engineered, deliberately or not, to resist change."[13] Here, seniors were a particularly potent political group. They possessed universal coverage through Medicare and if they could be convinced that their coverage might be threatened by the new plan, they might turn strongly against it.

One might think that Obama would have had significant rhetorical advantages, including relatively strong polling numbers, remaining excitement from the 2008 presidential campaign, and the simple fact that the American health care system faced severe problems. Labeling the problems in health care as severe actually understates the situation. More than 45 million Americans were uninsured and perhaps 25 million had what the Commonwealth Fund labeled "woe-fully inadequate policies." The lack of adequate insurance produced according to the Institute of Medicine 18,000 unnecessary deaths a year.[14] These problems were predicted to worsen dramatically with the number of uninsured and under-insured rising to as many as 92 million by 2019,[15] leading to 275,000 unnecessary deaths over the next decade.[16] These terrible results occurred despite the fact that the United States spent approximately half again as much as any other nation in the developed world.[17] Yet, this vast spending produced poor health outcomes with the United States ranking 39th in infant mortality, and 42nd and 43rd in adult male and adult female mortality and 31st in life expectancy.[18]

Why given Obama's popularity and the terrible status of the American health care system did this not produce significant rhetorical advantages for Obama? The answer relates to the seriousness of the barriers that I described. Liberals and experts on health care had supported reform for literally generations. At one point, that support also included many thoughtful conservatives and major health care initiatives in the late 1980s and early 1990s were supported even by organizations as conservative as the Heritage Foundation.[19] However, by 2009, there was unified conservative opposition to Obama's reform effort. This meant that his proposal would take constant criticism for many months as it was debated in Congress. In that context, what otherwise would have been Obama's rhetorical advantages did not count for much.

Obama does not rely exclusively on rational argument in the health care town hall. He also ties his arguments to basic values including health, life, fairness, and the chance to build a better life and a better country. He also links to one of the most important American narratives, the American Dream, when in paragraph 2, after noting the danger that the nation might face decline, he adds "And that's contrary to the history of America. One of our core ideas has always been that we leave the next generation better off than us." Arguably, he also relies on narrative in paragraph 9 when he describes a woman in Wisconsin whose insurance company denied her care, producing horrible results. At the same time, Obama's overall focus is heavily on argument. It is through argument that he links to the values I mentioned. In relation to narrative, the case of the woman in Wisconsin is better understood as a form of evidence-oriented argument (an example) than as a narrative.

As I noted, Obama relies on all three forms of rational argument. In the first half of the speech, he builds a positive argument for health reform that is based almost exclusively in evidence-oriented argument. In the next roughly 40 percent of the speech, he uses a combination of evidence-oriented and refutative argument to respond to objections to his proposal and reassure his audience. In the conclusion, he uses mainly enthymematic argument as he shifts from making a case for health reform to trying to energize his audience.

In making the positive case for health reform, Obama makes a variety of claims about problems in the present system and how his proposal could address those problems. He notes that 46 million Americans lack health insurance and adds that "if you've got health insurance, you have seen your costs double. They've gone up three times faster than wages" (4). He points to the fact that "one third of small businesses have reduced benefits and many have dropped coverage" (5) and then goes on to note how health care costs are bankrupting the government with "90 percent" of the "rising costs of entitlement" coming from Medicare and Medicaid (7). He also notes that insurance companies often deny coverage because of a "pre-existing condition" (8), often resulting in terrible medical debt, which in the case of the woman with cancer in Wisconsin amounted to $50,000.

Immediately following his description of the problems in the present system, he began his defense of his program, first arguing that the drug industry had "agreed to $80 billion in spending reductions" (12) and then adding that doctors, hospitals, insurance companies, and others had agreed to "decrease the annual rate of health care growth by 1.5 percent," a savings that could "translate into $2 trillion or more of savings over the next decade" (13). He then argues that the proposed legislation would improve the health care system by investing in "electronic medical records" and "prevention and wellness" programs (16, 17), as well as by changing "the incentives of the health care system" (18). He backs up the last claim by citing two particular hospital systems, one in Pennsylvania and one in Salt Lake City, that "offer high-quality health care at costs that are well below average, in some cases 30 percent lower than in other communities" (19). At that point, he claims that his plan would provide people "with more affordable options" through the creation of a Health Insurance Exchange on which they could choose among a number of high quality programs, including "a public option" (24).

In the first half of the speech, Obama lays out a strong positive case for health care reform in which he relies on all four forms of evidence to support his position. Most obviously, he relies on statistics. I've only cited a few of the many statistics that Obama cites. Here, Obama hopes to convince his audience that the magnitude of the various health care problems facing the nation means that we have to pass real reform. He also builds his own credibility as someone who is obviously well-informed on the issue and tries to demonstrate that the health care crisis faces all Americans, not just the uninsured. One potential problem with the use of statistics is that they can be difficult to understand, but in this case Obama does a good job of clearly explaining how the statistics relate to ordinary people.

Another main weakness of statistics is that they are impersonal. Obama attempts to respond to this problem with use of examples. I've already mentioned his description of the terrible case of the woman in Wisconsin who had breast cancer and more than $50,000 in medical debt, despite having health insurance. This is a powerful example, although it would be stronger if Obama more clearly explained how the spread of the cancer and the debt were related to bad acts by insurance companies. In the previous paragraph, (8), he mentioned receiving many letters from people who had "been denied coverage because of a pre-existing condition, or somebody who finds out that what they thought was going to be a $500 bill ends up being a $25,000 bill." While these letters function as hypothetical examples, it is obvious that real examples would do a much better job of personalizing the issue. Obama's use of examples of ordinary people harmed by the current health care system is not nearly as strong as his use of statistics.

Obama combines examples and comparisons with his citation of the "Geisinger Health Care Systems in rural Pennsylvania" and "Intermountain Health in Salt Lake City" (19). The two hospital systems are examples proving his point that there is a great deal of waste in the system that could be eliminated, thus reducing costs. But they are also comparisons, since Obama is juxtaposing these hospital systems against others throughout the nation that do not do a good job of cost control. His point is that if a rural health system in Pennsylvania and a system in a major city can cut costs by 30 percent without harming care, then other hospital systems should be able to do it too. Obviously, examples of hospital systems don't work to personalize his argument in the same way that examples of real people do. And the fact that two hospital systems have cut costs might not persuade many people that such cost cutting can be done everywhere without harming care.

In addition to the two hospital systems, Obama also uses a number of figurative comparisons to support his positive argument. He refers to the health care system as "broken" (15) and later says that many of the problems in the present system come from "the warped incentives that reward doctors and hospitals based on how many tests or procedures they prescribe" (20). Clearly, the "broken" and "warped" comparisons function more as a minor aesthetic strategy than they do as strong evidence supporting a claim.

It might seem that Obama cites no authoritative evidence in developing the positive argument, but that is not true. When the president references the agreement of the pharmaceutical industry to cut drug costs by $80 billion and then cites the fact that doctors, hospitals, insurance companies, and others have agreed to reduce the "annual rate of health care growth by 1.5 percent" (13), he is implicitly noting that people in various health care industries who obviously know a great deal about the system agree that health care reform can reduce costs. He is also using a form of authoritative evidence called reluctant testimony. Reluctant testimony occurs when someone says something that appears to go against their self-interest. One would not expect health care companies to cut costs since that might cut their profits. Thus, the fact that they support the claim that his plan could reduce costs can be viewed as a powerful form of reluctant testimony.

While the president clearly builds a powerful indictment of the health care system and a case for reform, it is also clear that his use of the resources of evidence-oriented argument could have been stronger. He relied predominantly on statistics to make his case, a reliance that can confuse an audience and depersonalize the issue. His persuasive case would have been stronger if he had used more personal examples to bring home the statistics. He also could have relied more on comparisons, especially of U.S. spending versus the rest of the developed world, to make the point that there is enormous waste in the American system. And he could have relied more heavily on authoritative evidence to explain complex issues such as how an insurance exchange would work. In an argumentative sense, the case he built was a strong one, but in a persuasive sense it could have been stronger with a better balance of evidence types.

On the other hand, evidence-oriented argument depends on more than the evidence presented, but also on the quality of the reasoning—the explanation of how the evidence is linked to the conclusion—in this case that health care reform was needed and could work. In terms of explanatory reasoning, Obama was quite skillful. For example, he built a strong case for the cost-effectiveness of his proposal in explaining how electronic medical records and more investment in "prevention and wellness" (17) could save substantial amounts of money. He also did a good job explaining how the insurance exchange would work.

In addition to evidence-oriented argument, Obama relied heavily on refutation to answer potential objections to his proposal and reassure the audience that health care reform would not harm them. This section of the speech extends from paragraph 25 to 34. Early in this section, he refutes the idea that the cost of reform would be excessive, first arguing that "two thirds of the costs of the reforms that we are proposing will come from reallocating money that is already being spent" (26), including "$177 billion over the next decade—in unwarranted subsides" (27) to Medicare Advantage (private insurance versions of Medicare). He then refutes the claim that the remaining one third of the cost will come from ordinary Americans by saying that it will come from capping "the itemized deductions that very wealth people do—the top 2 percent" (29). Thus, the bottom 98 percent would not have to pay higher taxes. He then adds that these cost figures do not even take into account "the savings that we're going to get from prevention, or the savings that we're going to get" (30) from health care information technology. He adds the somewhat confusing comment that he isn't counting these savings because according to the Congressional Budget Office they aren't "scorable" (31).

Obama also attempted to refute "scare tactics," by asking the opponents of reform "what's your alternative?" (34). His point was that the present system was not sustainable and could not be worse than a reformed system. In addition, his discussion of the health care exchange in the first half of the speech also functioned indirectly as refutation of the charge that the new government program would harm people. He said, "None of these plans [in the system] would be able to deny coverage on the basis of a pre-existing condition. All of them would include an affordable, basic benefit package" (23).

One primary problem with refutation is that it is very difficult to persuade people who have negative attitudes about something to change their mind. It seems obvious that for people with fears that the plan would cost too much, provide bad care, or harm their coverage that Obama's refutative arguments were inadequate. It is not that what he said was inaccurate. As I've noted, experts who reviewed the controversy concluded that many of the charges against what became known as "Obamacare" were simply false. And in fact, the intellectual roots of Obama's plan came from conservative sources, not liberal ones.[20] Obama's refutation did little to change the minds of people with doubts about costs or how a government program would work for two reasons. First, when one confronts entrenched attitudes, the only way to overcome them is by citing evidence so new and striking that the audience cannot deny it. Obama clearly did not do that. Second, Obama's refutation was much less skillful than his development of a positive argument for health reform. Consider his reference to the fact that his plan could produce additional savings, but he wasn't counting them because the Congressional Budget Office did not consider them to be "scorable." Obama was quite right argumentatively, but his explanation was so complex and depended upon such a high level of knowledge about how the Washington bureaucracy worked that it is difficult to see how it could have been persuasive to anyone. He meant that the Congressional Budget Office will not count savings that come from improved practice, if there is not direct evidence for those savings. That meant that the likely savings were even greater than the estimates, but this conclusion depended upon a quite complex and esoteric explanation. His claim that two thirds of the cost could come from reallocation of funds also illustrates this point. Again, Obama was right intellectually to focus on waste in the system, but anyone who was the least bit skeptical about health care reform would be likely to doubt that reallocation of waste would be as easy as the president indicated. One also suspects that the millions of seniors in the heavily subsidized Medicare Advantage programs would not see that subsidy as wasteful.

While Obama's refutation was unlikely to change the minds of those who had substantial doubts about his plan, it may have served a different persuasive function. Refutation can be important for providing supporters of a proposal with the argumentative ammunition that they need when they later confront criticism of the proposal. In that way, refutation sometimes functions in a way similar to how a vaccine inoculates someone against later exposure to a disease. The refutation protects the person against the danger of exposure to a counterargument. I think this was Obama's primary focus. He knew that convincing strong opponents of health care reform to change their minds would be extremely difficult. Obama was much more successful with his use of refutation in producing that inoculation effect than he was in providing enough data to change the mind of someone who opposed or had major doubts about reform.

In the last few paragraphs of his address, Obama also relies on enthymematic argument. Here, Obama reminds his audience of the promise he made during the campaign to bring real change and a sense of hope to the presidency. In paragraph 37 he says:

> So when it comes to energy, when it comes to improving our schools, and when it comes to health care, I don't accept the status quo. And you shouldn't either. And I don't think that the American people want to just stand pat. They know that change isn't easy. They know there are going to be setbacks and false starts. But they also know this—that we're on one of those rare moments when everybody is ready to move into the future. We just can't be scared. We've got to stop clinging to a broken system that doesn't work, and we've got to have the courage to reach out for a future that's going to be better for our children and our grandchildren.

Here, Obama attempts not to change the mind of those who have doubts about health care reform, but to reinforce those who already support his administration. He references the myriad of problems facing the nation and implicitly calls for them to continue the fight, just as they fought during the 2008 campaign for hope and change. He also enthymematically draws on memories of the presidential campaign when he says, "But in order to make it happen, I'm going to need ordinary Americans to stand up and say, 'Now is the time'" (38).

Enthymematic argument serves two primary persuasive functions. In some cases, the rhetoric allows the audience to fill in data known to them so that they will draw the conclusion without the rhetor explicitly making that conclusion. This strategy is useful when the conclusion is an unpleasant diagnosis, whether medical or on some other topic. Obama does not rely on this substrategy. Rather, he uses enthymematic references to reinforce views already held by a portion of his audience. At a time when it was particularly important to be able to mobilize supporters on an issue, Obama's use of enthymematic argument was obviously skillful, even though it was unlikely to change a single person's mind.

In most ways, Obama's use of rational argument was quite skillful. It is true that he could have done a better job of including examples and authoritative evidence both to provide a better mix of support materials and also to humanize and simplify his claims. Overall, he clearly did a good job in wielding rational argument as a strategy. The question then becomes to consider how effective he was.

The answer here is quite mixed. Obama's rhetorical campaign for health care reform ultimately resulted in the passage of the most sweeping reform legislation since Medicare. On the other hand, polling data indicates that by late summer 2009, a plurality (and at some points an outright majority) of the American people opposed health care reform.[21] And yet, while polling found a plurality opposed to the reform plan, the public continued to support most of the key parts of the reform.[22] Consequently, *The New Republic* editorialized, "People may not like the Affordable Care Act, per se, … they like nearly all of its component parts, in some cases by huge margins."[23] At that point, it would seem that the public favored what the law did, but not the law itself. In that situation, it is understandable that over time support might increase. By July 2010, 48 percent favored the law with unfavorable at 41 percent.[24] Polling also revealed that "a large portion of the respondents who disapprove of health care reform are upset that reform didn't go far enough."[25]

This conflicting data indicates that Obama's rhetorical campaign for health care reform initially succeeded most strongly with people who were already supporters. For this group, it was his enthymematic cheerleading and the way that he used refutation to inoculate against counterarguments that was most important. But, over time, the power of Obama's evidence-oriented argument gradually increased support for the law, although much opposition still remained.

These findings make perfect sense when Obama's rational-argument strategy is compared against the barriers of perceived high cost, opposition to government, and fear of losing coverage for those with good insurance. In the short term, rational argument could not overcome strongly held beliefs or even doubts of those who were fearful they could lose their Medicare. But over time, rational argument could gradually change minds, because being right is a very powerful thing indeed. It should be remembered that when Medicare was passed, it too was immensely controversial. That controversy largely disappeared when ordinary people experienced the benefits provided by the program. Something similar began to happen once the Affordable Care Act actually went into effect and the predictions of denied care, high cost, and government incompetence largely did not occur.

The legislation became still more popular after the election of Donald Trump, when Republicans in Congress attempted to repeal it without having a clear alternative. At that point, 53% of Americans had a favorable view of the law, against 40% unfavorability. Opposition to the law was concentrated among Republicans and the primary components of the law were much more popular than the law itself, ranging from 65% to 82% support.[26] The lesson is that evidence-oriented rational argument works most effectively when the importance of the argument is made tangible for the audience because they are either personally experiencing it or know of others who are experiencing that impact. When Republicans threatened to repeal Obamacare and therefore take coverage away from more than twenty million Americans and eliminate the rule that prevented insurance companies from denying coverage based on a pre-existing condition, the potential loss of those benefits was found threatening by tens of millions of Americans. Evidence-oriented argument cannot work effectively without new data. By the summer of 2017, the new data that many millions were about to lose basic coverage began to hit home, resulting in increased support for the law. Why did 76% of Republicans continue to view the law unfavorably, while supporting many of the major provisions of the law?[27] The most likely answer is that partisan identification led this group to oppose the law because the leaders of their party did so, but at the same time they did not want to lose the benefits the law provided. Of course, Democrats are subject to a similar partisan reaction. Given these attitudes, it seems quite plausible that if Congress had simply renamed the law as "Trumpcare," public support would have shot up among Republicans and declined among Democrats.

Strengths and Weaknesses of Rational Argument as a Rhetorical Strategy

The foregoing discussion raises a fundamental question: How powerful is rational argument as a strategy for producing persuasion? There is inconsistent evidence on this point. On the one hand, there is a large amount of research indicating that rational argument is rarely an effective strategy for producing persuasion. A great deal of research in political science indicates that the public in general is not very well-informed and rarely makes decisions based on the issues.[28] Certainly, advertisers (in politics and elsewhere) apparently do not believe that most people are heavily influenced by rational argument. If they believed that people made choices based on rational argument, they would orient their advertising towards argumentative strategies and take a kind of *Consumer Reports* approach to selling candidates, products, and services. Clearly, few commercials use this kind of argumentative approach. Instead, they tend to rely on humor, sexuality, and mini-narratives that tie to basic needs and values of the audience.

There is also social scientific research indicating that rational argument has relatively little impact on the perceived persuasiveness of a given work of rhetoric.[29] Research in this tradition has focused on whether citing evidence adds to the persuasiveness of the message. Several researchers have found no significant effect, a conclusion that would seem to deny that rational argument is a powerful persuasive strategy. It is certainly disquieting that a speech without adequate rational support is often perceived as just as persuasive as a speech containing that support.

On the other hand, there is a great deal of evidence indicating that people are heavily influenced by rational means of persuasion. A research tradition has developed in political science that indicates that rational argument often makes a great deal of difference in politics.[30] Supporting this view is a considerable amount of research on public opinion and political knowledge that found beginning in the 1960s a large percentage of the public began to pay attention to the issues and make decisions based on them, rather than on long-time party association. Proponents of the issue-oriented perspective argue that while the public may not know the details about specific issues, they are informed about the big picture. Research in this tradition suggests that rational argument is often extremely important, even decisive, in political campaigns.

There is also research about what is known as "persuasive argument theory," which indicates that people are moved by the weight of available evidence when attempting to solve a particular problem. This research, which has been conducted on "problem-solving" groups, suggests that people in the group are likely to choose the particular alternative that is supported by the largest number of valued arguments and that new information is particularly important in this process.[31] Persuasive argument theory seems to suggest that people are highly rational and that, therefore, rational argument is a very powerful strategy.

How can the two research traditions concerning the power of rational argument be reconciled? One possibility is that both sides are partially right. Rational argument is an extremely powerful means of persuasion, but only in limited circumstances.

What are those limitations? First, rational argument does not work very well on issues that are tied to basic values. The reason is that rational argument applies to the world of facts. Value claims, by contrast, are not fundamentally about facts. In the debate about abortion, for example, the fundamental conflict is between the values of freedom and life. Pro-choice advocates say that the woman's right to choose is the preeminent value. Anti-abortion advocates say that life is the preeminent value. There is no argumentative means of resolving this conflict.

Second, rational argument also fails, especially in the short term, if the audience already possesses a strongly-held position on the subject. This is why rational argument works better in the problem-solving group context than in politics. Regardless of the quality of the argument, no Democrat is going to persuade Newt Gingrich to change his mind on a major point. Nor is Gingrich going to persuade Barack Obama to change his views and become a Reagan Republican. The same point could be said of any issue on which people already have a fixed point of view. However, when people either have not decided what they think or are not fixed in their viewpoint, rational argument can be very persuasive. In the problem-solving group context the aim is to solve some problem (finding the cheapest pizza for a large party, for instance). In such a situation, rational argument can be quite persuasive, because everyone wants the same goal, good pizza at a cheap price.

Third, rational argument does not work very well if the issue is highly complicated. On highly complex issues, the audience may not be able to understand the details of the argument being presented. This is one reason that advocates have had such difficulty justifying nuclear power with argument. The complexity of the issue makes it almost impossible to effectively use rational argument as a primary strategy.[32] Global warming is another example of an issue on which rational argument has been relatively ineffective, despite the consensus of climate scientists that the theory is true. This result, which seems inexplicable, becomes understandable when the role of complexity as a mediating factor influencing the power of rational argument is considered. Moreover, public support for action on global warming began to rise when people experienced the impact of the problem in extremely hot summers and an increase in major storms, including hurricanes. Their experience of these effects in essence simplified the issue and made it more persuasive.

Fourth, rational argument is unlikely to be effective if the audience is not at least somewhat concerned with the issue. If the audience lacks interest, they are likely to tune out the argumentative discussion. This point is illustrated in relation to issues such as the ozone layer. Few people find a discussion of the ozone layer to be extremely exciting. This means that it is difficult to get the attention of the public in relation to that issue. If there were some dramatic incident involving ozone depletion, however, then it might be possible to influence public attitudes via rational argument. That is precisely what happened after 9/11 with the issue of terrorism. It was not as if the risks of terrorism were unknown before the attacks. Experts and a few leading politicians, notably Senator Richard Lugar of Indiana and former Senator Sam Nunn of Georgia, had been pointing to the threat for many years. But, it was extremely hard to get people's attention on an issue which seemed to be more a movie plot than a serious threat. After 9/11 that situation changed.

Finally, rational argument is unlikely to be effective if the issue is a familiar one and there is no new data to be presented. On an issue like capital punishment, for example, the basic positions of the two sides are quite familiar. The pro side says that capital punishment is justified by horrible crimes and deters criminal behavior. The anti side denies that capital punishment is effective, labels it as barbarous, and says that innocent people sometimes are executed. We all have heard these arguments many times. Therefore, rhetoric presenting one of these positions is unlikely to change anyone's minds, unless some new material is added. This principle is directly supported by persuasive argument theory, which finds that new information is especially important in influencing group attitudes. If there were new information, even on a tired issue like capital punishment, it might be possible to alter public opinion. And that is precisely what has happened over the last two decades as DNA evidence has been discovered proving that a number of the inmates on death row were innocent of the crimes for which they were convicted. This dramatic new data influenced a number of states to declare a moratorium on capital punishment or even eliminate the death penalty.

Of course, the above principles can be turned around to define when rational argument is likely to be effective. It will work best on factual (non-value) issues which are not too complicated, on which the audience has some interest, but does not yet have a firm position, and where there is new material to be considered.

One other point is relevant. Rational argument is especially powerful over time. When Tiger Woods turned pro, some doubted that he would be one of the dominant golfers on the PGA tour. Others said he would be good, but it would take time. After he won the Masters in his first try, these critics of Woods said, "Never mind!" Tragically for Woods, something similar happened with the revelations about his personal life. Prior to that time, Woods was viewed as a role model. The new information led many people to a radically different conclusion. In the long term being right is a powerful thing indeed.

CONCLUSION

In this chapter, I defined the characteristics of argumentative form, identified the three primary ways that argument can function as a persuasive device, discussed the strengths and weaknesses of the four types of evidence as persuasive devices, and outlined the situations in which rational argument is likely to be persuasive. Ultimately, rational argument is the most powerful persuasive strategy because positions supported by strong argument are more likely to work in solving problems than are positions not supported by strong arguments. This means that in the long run, strong arguments generally win out over weaker arguments. Of course, this result only occurs in the long run (sometimes the very long run) and only occurs if there is free and full debate on the issue. Rational argument works much better in the United States, despite all the flaws in our political system, than it does in China or North Korea, because all sides can debate a given issue. In that context, what John Stuart Mill called the "free marketplace of ideas," rational argument is ultimately an extremely powerful force. I began this chapter by noting that argument is essential for democracy to function. The opposite of that point is also true. For argument to work properly there must be some sort of democratic process in which all sides of a dispute are presented. Thus, effective argument and democratic decision-making are inherently intertwined.

FOR FURTHER DISCUSSION

On September 20, 2011, J.D. Foster testified before the Committee on the Budget of the United States Senate. Mr. Foster is an economist who works for the conservative think tank, The Heritage Foundation. In his testimony, Mr. Foster argued for a conservative approach to fostering growth in the economy and attacked the economic policies of the Obama administration. Carefully read and do an analysis outline on Foster's testimony. Then consider the following discussion questions:

1   What argumentative strategies does Foster rely on in his testimony?
2   Does Foster effectively present new data to the Congressional committee?
3   What barriers will Foster face in attempting to persuade the committee?
4   On balance, does Foster do a good job of presenting arguments in order to persuade the committee? Would other strategies have been more appropriate?

Promoting Job Creation and Reducing Unemployment in the U.S.
By J.D. Foster, Ph.D.
September 21, 2011

Chairman Conrad, Ranking Member Sessions, Members of the Senate Budget   1 Committee, thank you for the opportunity to testify today. My name is J.D. Foster. I am the Norman B. Ture Senior Fellow in the Economics of Fiscal Policy at The Heritage

J.D. Foster, Testimony before the Budget Committee of the Senate, September 21, 2011

Foundation. The views I express in this testimony are my own, and should not be construed as representing any official position of The Heritage Foundation.

The risks to the economy are great, and so the focus today on jobs and economic growth is critical. Two years after the end of the Great Recession, as the economy should be accelerating smartly, economic growth and job growth have ground to a halt. Speculation, argumentation, theorizing, and models are now irrelevant on this point—the data before us agree with the underlying message from the President's recent jobs speech. They all attest to the simple, incontrovertible fact that the President's stimulus policies have failed utterly and completely. I take no pleasure in pointing out this inescapable reality, nor in the fact that we predicted this policy failure two years ago. I would much rather have been wrong, and for millions of my fellow citizens to be gainfully employed in all those jobs the President promised to create.

Nor is the worst necessarily behind us. Left to our own, I believe the economy would pick up soon despite, not because of, the President's policies. But we will not be left to our own. Europe is about to go through a cataclysmic paroxysm as it suffers the inevitable penalty of a failed monetary system. We are about to learn, once again, how important Europe is to the United States as Europe's troubles present us with the stark reality of a certain, large, near-term and a still larger medium-term economic shock only the exact proportions of which remain uncertain.

To understand what policies might be helpful today and which harmful, it's important to assess why the economy is not yet recovering. The fundamentals of our economy remain sound. The natural productive tendencies of America's workers, investors, and entrepreneurs remain undiminished. The economy is poised to grow. Why, then, does it hold back?

There are, of course, the unusual headwinds, such as the follow-on effects of Japan's devastating earthquake and tsunami. But the economy faces and overcomes such headwinds even in the best of times. Headwinds there are, to be sure, but they do not explain the economy's lethargy.

The economy suffers from two categories of troubles. The first are structural troubles, which today primarily reflect a housing sector still in deep disequilibrium in many areas of the country. There is very little substantively that government can do to return housing markets to normal, and heaven knows Congress and the President have tried just about everything. And that is part of the problem. Government's well-intentioned meddling has delayed and distorted the essential requirement for normalization—price discovery. On balance, these policies have set back the housing recovery by months, perhaps a year or more. There is an important lesson here.

The second category of trouble is what might be termed environmental—not the natural environment, but the economic environment. Missing from most economics textbooks are the true animating forces of prosperity. Most relevant for our discussion is alternatively a shortage of confidence or an excess of bad uncertainty.

Those who could make the decisions and take the actions that would grow the economy lack the confidence to do so. Even today, the economy abounds in opportunities for growth. But turning potential into reality requires action, and action requires confidence—confidence in the future, confidence in the specific effects in government policy, and confidence that government can properly carry out its basic functions, like agreeing to a budget. America suffers a confidence shortage, and Washington is overwhelmingly the cause.

Confidence, in turn, is lacking because of an excess of uncertainty: Uncertainty about the future, but also uncertainty about the effects of government policies—tax policies, regulatory policies, monetary policies, trade policies.

9

Uncertainty is natural, of course. The future is always uncertain. But there is good uncertainty and bad uncertainty, much as there is good cholesterol and bad cholesterol. Good uncertainty, for example, presents opportunities for profit. Bad uncertainty arises largely when investors and entrepreneurs have very real questions about the consequences of government policy.

10

Tax policy provides a good example of bad uncertainty. The President's repeated insistence on raising taxes on high-income workers and investors slows the economy even without the policy being enacted. It does so by raising the uncertainty about the tax consequences of various actions. It does not stop all such actions, but it stops some, and therein lies the difference between growth and stagnation.

11

Moreover, the President's insistence is a twofer in terms of bad uncertainty. The specific is that taxpayers don't know what their tax liability will be. The general is that suggesting raising taxes on anyone in the face of high and possibly rising unemployment suggests a gross lack of understanding about how an economy works. That's a source of bad uncertainty that afflicts the entire economy, not just those threatened with higher taxes. In this environment, Congress need not enact bad policy to weaken the economy. Threats suffice to do real damage.

12

Guiding Principle: Do Less Harm

The federal government should adopt a very simple guiding principle for deciding what to do next. That principle is to do less harm. There is very little in terms of concrete actions government can do at this stage that would help, and a great deal of intended help that would harm, either by raising the deficit to no good effect or by creating more uncertainty and slowing the economy's natural healing process.

13

Do less harm means getting spending under control and thereby cutting the budget deficit. Americans are worried about spending and the deficit. That worry by itself is holding us back.

14

Do less harm means policymakers should stop threatening higher taxes. We can have debates about who should pay what when we're at full employment. In the meantime, this threat is debilitating.

15

Do less harm means stop the onslaught of new regulations. The recent pullback of the EPA's ozone regulation was a good example. Even the threat of new regulations creates bad uncertainty for those affected, freezing them in place. Again, we can work through these regulations when Americans are back to work.

16

Do less harm means policymakers should stop meddling with the economy. There is almost no limit to the harm Washington can do *to* the economy in its efforts to do something *for* the economy. The patient is in recovery, slowed by the incessant proddings and procedures of Washington's policy doctors. The patient doesn't need another procedure or a new nostrum. Let it heal. Do less harm. 17

Keynesian Alchemy

What policies meet this criterion? Under the circumstances, very few. Consider, for example, the policy of increasing the budget deficit to spur the economy. The argument is fairly simple: the economy is underperforming; demand is too low; the government deficit is part of aggregate demand, so just increase the deficit. It's an equation. How can it be wrong? 18

The answer, of course, is that the economy is more complicated than this simple equation. Government borrows the money, so every deficit dollar spent by the government is a dollar less available to the private sector. The answer, in other words, is that the macroeconomic model ignores financial intermediation which is the bread and butter of financial markets. 19

Proponents will counter by saying that people are saving more, and corporations are sitting on mounds of cash. True, but it changes nothing. All this saving is not lying dormant in some vault or stuffed in some mattress. Ironically, even if it were, irresponsible deficit spending would surely not draw it out. On the contrary, this saving is deposited with the financial system, which then takes the resources from those who do not currently need them and makes them available to those who do need them. In terms of aggregate flows, this process works just as well today in recession as it does at full employment. 20

Thus, Keynesian demand-side stimulus does not help. It is fiscal alchemy. And by adding to the deficit and thus fears about the future, it surely adds to the economy's headwinds. 21

Infrastructure

Increased infrastructure spending, as the President and others have advocated, is an example of a double folly. To be clear, the issue here is not whether the nation needs more or less infrastructure spending. I am not expressing an opinion on that one way or another. 22

The issue is whether it acts as a short-term stimulus. It does not. First, assuming the additional spending was financed by additional borrowing, the policy runs afoul of the Keynesian fallacy. To be sure, once a project is underway one can point to the people working, but just as surely the borrowing that made that project possible reduced employment elsewhere. 23

The second folly is just as plain. Infrastructure spending on projects is capital 24
intensive and stretches over years. It cannot, even if enacted, swiftly affect employment
in the next year plus.

Payroll Tax Holiday

The irony of another payroll tax holiday to create jobs is that reducing payroll taxes 25
would increase employment when the economy is at full employment yet cannot accelerate hiring in periods of high unemployment. The key to this irony is incidence—
who bears the tax.

The payroll tax is borne by workers. It subtracts from their total compensation, 26
leaving them less after-tax wage income. This is equally true of the "employer's
share," because, of course, the employer has no share. The tax is all paid by the
worker, but the worker unfortunately is aware of only half the tax, so extending the tax
relief to the invisible part of the tax does not improve the outcome. Nor are weak labor
markets the environment in which workers would gain a new ability to force employers
to bear part of the tax.

Thus, a reduction in the payroll tax rate does not reduce the employer's costs, 27
but rather raises the worker's after-tax wage. During periods of full employment, this
means an additional supply of workers to be absorbed into the economy, thereby
raising output. During periods of high unemployment, the increase in labor supply
resulting from a payroll tax cut, temporary or otherwise, results in an increase in the
number of unemployed workers. Thus, a policy intended to reduce the ranks of the
unemployed is likely to produce an increase in the unemployment rate.

Repatriation Tax Holiday

Another policy under consideration that does not create jobs is a repatriation tax 28
holiday. The issue here is not whether tax cuts are good or bad per se, but whether this particular tax cut would increase domestic employment and domestic jobs.
Again, the answer is that it would not.

A repatriation tax holiday would result in a sizable influx of corporate profits from 29
abroad. Tax policy does matter. Companies do respond to this extent. But no new
jobs would result. The key to understanding why this policy and its undoubted influx of
capital would not increase investment and jobs at home lies in the following question:
Are these repatriating companies capital-constrained today?

No, they are not. These large multinational companies have enormous sums of 30
accumulated earnings parked in the financial markets already. And those few if any
that might need additional financing have ready access to the capital markets at
remarkably low prices. Thus, they can meet all their financing needs out of available
domestic resources. Adding to those resources will not increase the extent of their
investment opportunities. Parallel to the payroll tax holiday that would increase the

supply of workers without increasing the number of jobs available, the repatriation tax holiday would increase the supply of saving without increasing the range or amount of investments to which the saving could be applied.

Unemployment Benefits

Yet another ineffective or even counterproductive policy for increasing employment   31
is extension of unemployment benefits. This policy may be defended on humanitarian grounds, but not as economic stimulus because it, too, runs afoul of the Keynesian fallacy. The extension of benefits will certainly increase the purchasing power and purchases of the recipients, but the borrowing needed to fund these benefits will with equal certainty reduce other areas of private spending.

Further, to the extent the resulting increased budget deficit adds to the depth of the   32
bad uncertainty, it adds to this important economic headwind. And the research on the issue strongly suggests, as recent papers by both the Heritage Foundation and the Brookings Institution made clear, that extending unemployment benefits actually raises the unemployment rate.

Conclusion

In light of the ongoing high unemployment, policymakers should be keenly fo-   33
cused on what they can do for the economy. But they must also recognize the limita-tions of policy initiatives. As difficult as this may be to implement, the guiding principle should be: Do less harm.

1   James Madison, *Writings* (New York: Library of America, 1999), 167.

2   Colleen A. Sheehan, *James Madison and the Spirit of Republican Self-Government* (Cambridge: Cambridge University Press, 2009), 10.

3   Madison, *Writings*, 290.

4   Madison, *Writings*, 295.

5   Madison, *Writings*, 230.

6   Richard K. Matthews, *If Men Were Angels: James Madison and the Heartless Empire of Reason* (Lawrence: University of Kansas Press, 1995), 144, Madison, *Writings*, 500.

7   I develop these ideas in some depth in Robert C. Rowland, "Barack Obama and the Revitalization of Public Reason," *Rhetoric and Public Affairs*, 14(2011): 693–726.

8   "Remarks by the President in an Online Town Hall on Health Care," Northern Virginia Community College, Annandale, Virginia, July 1, 2009, http://www.whitehouse.gov/the-press-office/remarks-president-online-town-hall-health-care-reform. The excerpt includes all of the president's opening statement that discussed health care and only excludes a few introductory comments that are not relevant to a discussion of how rational argument works as a rhetorical strategy.

9   See Jim Rutenberg and Gardiner Harris, "Conservatives See Need for Serious Health Debate," *The New York Times*, September 3, 2009, A19.

10   "Dr. Obama's Waiting Room, *The New Republic*, March 18, 2009, 1.

11   David Leonhardt, 'Real Challenge to Health Bill: Selling Reform," *The New York Times*, July 22, 2009.

12   Charles M. Blow, "Imbalance of Trust," *The New York Times*, August 29, 2009, A17.

13   Leonhardt, A1.

14   "The Uninsured," *The New York Times*, August 23, 2009, WK7.

15   "If Reform Fails," *The New York Times*, March 7, 2010, WK9.

16   Reed Abelson, "The Cost of Doing Nothing," *The New York Times*, February 28, 2010, WK8.

17   Trudy Rubin, "Other nations make universal care work," *Lawrence Journal World*, March 2, 2010, 7A.

18   Nicholas D. Kristof, "Do We Really Want the Status Quo on Health Care?" *The New York Times*, February 18, 2010, A21; Nicholas D. Kristof, "Unhealthy America," *The New York Times*, November 5, 2009, A31.

19   See Stuart M. Butler, *Assuring Affordable Health Care for All Americans*, Heritage Foundation, October 2, 1989. AP writer Ricardo Alonso-Zaldivar noted that the individual mandate "is a Republican idea that has been around at least two decades." See "Health Insurance Requirement a Republican Idea," *Lawrence Journal World*, March 28, 2010, 5A.

20   Paul Krugman, "Missing Richard Nixon," *The New York Times*, August 31, 2009, A17.

21   Henry J. Kaiser Family Foundation, "Kaiser Health Tracking Poll," May 2010, 1.

22   Henry J. Kaiser Family Foundation, "Kaiser Health Tracking Poll," January 2010, 5. And public support also remained strong for a public option. Even at the nadir of support for reform in the late fall of 2009, a CBS/*New York Times* poll found that support for a "public option." PollingReport.Com, *http://pollingreport.com/health.htm*, downloaded January 25, 2010.

23   "Healthy Respect," *The New Republic*, October 28, 2010, 1.

24   The results of the Kaiser Health Tracking Poll were cited by Ruy Teixeira, "Public Opinion Snapshot: Public Warms to Health Care Reform Law," *Center for American Progress*, July 6, 2010, *http://www.americanprogress.org/issues/2010/07/snapshot070610.htm*.

25   "Healthy Respect," *The New Republic*, October 28, 2010, 1.

26   See Ashley Kirzinger, Cailey Muñana, and Mollyann Brodie, "6 Charts About Public Opinion On The Affordable Care Act," *Kaiser Family Foundation*, December 19, 2018, https://www.kff.org/health-reform/poll-finding/6-charts-about-public-opinion-on-the-affordable-care-act.

27   Kirzinger, Muñana, and Brodie, "6 Charts About Public Opinion On The Affordable Care Act."

28   A classic work in this area is Angus Campbell, Philip E. Converse, Warren E. Miller and Donald E. Stokes, *The American Voter* (New York: Wiley, 1960). Also see Gerald Pomper, *Voter's Choice* (New York: Harper & Row, 1975).

29   Most of this research was conducted in the 1950s and 1960s. For a review see James C. McCroskey, "A Summary of Experimental Research on the Effects of Evidence in Persuasive Communication," *Quarterly Journal of Speech* 55 (1969): 169–176.

30   The classic work on this theme is Norman H. Nie, Sidney Verba, and John R. Petrocik, *The Changing American Voter* (Cambridge: Harvard University Press, 1976).

31   See, for instance, Eugene Burnstein and Amiram Vinokur, "What a Person Thinks Upon Learning He Has Chosen Differently From Others: Nice Evidence for the Persuasive-Arguments Explanation of Choice Shifts," *Journal of Experimental Social Psychology* 11 (1975): 412–426.

32   In "A Reanalysis of the Argumentation at Three Mile Island," I considered public debate and discussion about the Three Mile Island nuclear disaster. I discovered that the accident had been misunderstood by the public through no fault of their own. In fact, rather than a catastrophe, the accident at Three Mile Island indicated that the nuclear safety systems at the reactor site worked well. The essay can be found in *Argument in Controversy: Proceedings of the 7th SCA-AFA Conference on Argumentation*, Donn Parson ed., (Annandale, Virginia: SCA, 1991): 277–283.

CHAPTER 5
Narrative Forms of Rhetoric

Throughout human history, and the evidence of cave paintings suggests that this may be true of pre-history as well, human beings have told stories for amusement, as a way of making sense of the world, and to persuade. There is no question that narrative is one of the most effective forms of persuasion.[1] One piece of evidence for this claim is the fact that some of the most powerful rhetoricians in human history have been storytellers. For example, Jesus told stories in the form of parables to his disciples. The result of these stories was the creation of one of the world's great religions. This example is not unique. In fact, much of our most powerful religious rhetoric in Christianity and other religions has been narrative. Earlier, I cited Jesus, but I just as well might have cited Moses, Mohammad, Buddha, or some other religious leader. The same is true all across human society. Narrative has been and is a powerful rhetorical form in politics, business, mass movements, and elsewhere.

The power of narrative rhetoric to bring a point home to an audience is illustrated by the success of one of the most powerful contemporary rhetoricians, Steven Spielberg. Thousands of books have been written about the Holocaust and World War II, some of them by distinguished scholars and academics. Yet, it is two movies that have made these subjects come alive for most Americans: *Schindler's List* and *Saving Private Ryan*. Spielberg is not our greatest historian or expert on the Holocaust or D-Day. But he is unquestionably our greatest contemporary rhetorician on those topics. What Spielberg understands is the power of a well-told narrative to bring a subject alive for an audience. While Spielberg is an accomplished storyteller and a powerful rhetorician, he is not unique. Throughout human history, there have been many storytellers who used the power of narration to influence a group, a tribe, a city, or a nation.

Another contemporary example illustrating the power of narrative can be found in the rise of then-state Senator Barack Obama from the Illinois legislature to president of the United States in only 53 months. One major factor in what is one of the most amazing stories in American history is Obama's skill as a storyteller. Obama demonstrated this power (along with his gift for clear argument) in his memoir *Dreams from My Father* and in a different way in a book he wrote as a United States senator, *The Audacity of Hope*.[2] The book tour for this work played a part in creating the mass movement that later played a pivotal role in his election as president in 2008. This same gift for the creation of an empowering story was also evident in Senator Obama's presidential campaign. At the core of this campaign was a narrative of how the American Dream could be reinvigorated in order to provide ordinary Americans with a better life.[3] While the power of this narrative has been evident throughout American history, Obama's ascendance from Illinois state senator to president of the United States in a little over five years is strong evidence of its continuing influence and more generally the power of a well-told story.

The power of narrative rhetoric makes it important to understand the components of narrative and the way that narrative functions. It is also important to recognize that narrative is not always a force for good, as it was in Spielberg's wonderful films about the Holocaust and World War II. Sometimes, narrative can be used for evil ends. It must be remembered that Hitler was an accomplished storyteller. He created a story in which Germany was a victim of terrible mistreatment from the Allies at the end of the First World War and from one group of her own citizens, the Jews. In this story, a revitalized Aryan people would cleanse Germany of those who had weakened her and bring the nation to dominance in the world. Hitler's story was not remotely accurate, but it certainly was effective in creating a mass movement that ultimately took control of Germany and caused World War II and the Holocaust. Stories can be powerful forces for good *and* evil. Given this power, it is very important to understand the components that make up a narrative as well as the functions that narrative often fulfills.

In this chapter, I sketch the characteristics of narrative rhetoric, beginning with a discussion of narrative form. I then identify the functions fulfilled by narrative and apply the formal/functional components of narrative to the testimony of John Anjain, a native of a small island in the Pacific near where the United States conducted atomic bomb tests, before a United States Senate Committee.

FORMAL COMPONENTS OF NARRATIVE RHETORIC

In narrative rhetoric a story is told in order to make some point. In some cases, the entire work of rhetoric is a story and the main point is implied. For example, Harriet Beecher Stowe's novel, *Uncle Tom's Cabin* was a biting attack on slavery. In other instances, the rhetor may use a number of small stories to make a point. Ronald Reagan often used these micro-narratives[4] to back up his conservative perspective. In still other instances, the rhetor may refer to a widely known story, but not retell it in any detail. This type of narrative is somewhat similar to enthymematic argument and is used most often in reference to the dominant stories in an organization or society. For the United States as a whole, for instance, this approach might be used with stories of the pioneers, the founding of the nation, or the American Dream, because these narratives are familiar to everyone.

What makes up a narrative? Narrative rhetoric is defined by four components: plot, setting, characters, and theme. These components are found in all stories, whether the story is in a speech, an editorial, a film, or a picture on the wall of an art gallery, although these various narratives differ in the degree to which the components are explicit or are in some way implied by the work.

Plot

The plot is the story line. It is what happens in the tale. While there are many possible types of plots, it is important to recognize that principles of plot development demand that a story be introduced in some sort of scene that sets the stage for the plot that follows. The plot then builds gradually to greater and greater conflict. Ultimately, a point of greatest conflict or tension is reached (the climax), and the conflict or tension is then resolved. This is followed by a return to normalcy. Often, in this final period, the narrative will draw implicit or explicit conclusions. In a fairy tale, for example, this is the "moral of the story."

The basic plot pattern I have described can take many specific forms, but the overall design is found in most narrative rhetoric. The pattern typifies adventure stories (the *Star Wars* films for instance), serious drama, and even comedy (from Shakespeare to *Friends*, *The Big Bang Theory*, or *Modern Family*). This general plot pattern is tied to the logic of storytelling. Clearly, the story would not be very exciting if the biggest point of conflict occurred in the first scene. In that case, there would be no conflict to resolve, no interesting character development, and so on. At the same time, the logic of telling a good story requires that the point of greatest conflict must come near the end. Crucially, the pattern of rising action, which I have described, is generally present, not because life always works that way, but because that pattern works best to gradually increase tension and excitement in the audience over time.

It is important to note at this point that what makes a good plot is not necessarily what makes a true story. Real life rarely develops in the set pattern of plot development I have described. For example, in real life, the point of greatest conflict may be in the beginning, the end, or any-where in between. In addition, while minor incidents are often crucial clues in a good story, in real life the minor incident may be simply one more random thing that happens. The point is that causality works differently in the real world than it does in narrative. A trash truck coming unexpectedly through a neighborhood may in a given story be a sign of some great conspiracy. In real life, the trash truck may be in the neighborhood early simply because the route changed or the crew got lost.

Scene

The second component of narrative rhetoric is a scene. This is the place/time where the story occurs. The scene can be literally anywhere. For example, at the beginning of the story, Robert A. Heinlein's acclaimed science fiction novel, *Job: A Comedy of Justice* appears to be set in the United States in the near future. In fact, as becomes clear in the middle of the book, the story is set in an alternative universe. As this example makes clear, a story can be set in any place that can be imagined by the human mind. Many stories have been set, for example, in heaven or hell. The key to understanding a scene from the perspective of rhetoric is to consider the "work" that the scene does in carrying forward the message of the story. Often the scene carries an im-portant message. For example, many American novels are set in a generic suburb or small town because the message in the story is about life in Everytown, U.S.A.

At the same time, one of the reasons that narrative rhetoric is so important is that it can transport the reader/viewer/listener to a very different place and time. It can take us out of the contemporary United States and transport us mentally to witness ethnic cleansing in Kosovo, Rwanda, or Darfur or to see what life was like in the death camps or in Elizabethan England.

The scene is also important because some places carry more cultural resonance than other places. A narrative set at the site where formerly the World Trade Center stood would have special power because of the terrible acts that occurred at the site on September 11, 2001.

Characters

The third component of any narrative consists of the characters. Narratives generally revolve around the conflict between the protagonist (also known as the hero) and the antagonist or villain. Other characters may serve a variety of functions including as helpers of the hero/villain, innocent victims of some act of the villain, people to represent a given viewpoint, and so forth. While literary critics focus on characterization for a variety of reasons, rhetorical critics are most concerned about how characters enact the message (the theme) of the narrative or add interest/emphasis to that theme.

One point concerning characterization is particularly important from a persuasive point of view. As a rule, the protagonist will be either a hero who is greater than average people or he/she will be a representative of the people. The first type of protagonist serves as a model to be followed or emulated. In the language of a popular television commercial at the height of his career as an NBA star, we all want to "be like Mike." Mike (Michael Jordan) is a hero to be imitated. The second type of protagonist is used in a rhetoric of identification. In that case, the protagonist is not greater than all of us, but he/she is one of us and serves as an example of what an average person can accomplish. We don't so much admire this second type of protagonist as identify with them. We see the similarity between their life and our own. The first type of protagonist (the hero) often serves as a model to be followed. The second type, because he/she is one of us, can be used to create a sense of shared identity between the character and the audience. Thus, characters both act in and are acted upon in the plot and serve as models to be imitated or as average folk with whom to identify.

Theme

The final component of narrative rhetoric is the theme. The theme is the message; it is the point of the story. The theme is built by the combination of the actions of the characters in a given setting. Put another way, it is constructed out of the previous three elements. Some stories have powerful and quite explicit persuasive messages. For example, the theme of the 1980s TV movie, *The Day After*, was that nuclear war would be a very bad thing and the United States should work harder to avoid any risk of it. While in some works of rhetoric the theme may be immediately obvious, in others, the theme may be less obvious, but still present. Tim Allen's television show, *Home Improvement*, got laughs by telling stories about how Allen's character was always getting into trouble by trying to be macho. On the surface, the show gloried in everything that is male. Below the surface, it had almost a feminist message in the way it made fun of male stereotypes. Another example of an implicit theme can be found in the classic television show *Star Trek*. While the series did not explicitly present a theme that commented on

American society of the time, by implication it supported ideals of racial tolerance and integration, investment in science and technology, and support for international organizations.

It is in relation to theme that narrative rhetoric and narrative literature differ most notably. Narrative rhetoric of necessity has a persuasive theme. That is in fact what makes it rhetoric. In contrast, while some narrative literature has such a persuasive theme, that it is not required. At some level, narrative rhetoric is always about persuasion and audience; this is not true of all literature. This means that a work of narrative may fall into the classification of both literature and rhetoric. For example, Mark Twain's novel *Huckleberry Finn*, which has been called the greatest American novel, is both a work of fiction and a work of rhetoric. As rhetoric, Twain among other things, attacked racism.

It might seem odd that a work of fiction can serve a persuasive function, but that can occur because while the work is fictional, in another sense it provides commentary on the real world. In fact, a fictional story may contain a strong element of implied truth. The details of the plot may not have occurred, but the themes reflected in the story may present a larger truth about society. This sort of narrative functions as an implied enthymeme in which the "fictional" actions of characters in the plot imply a "factual" message. In the case of *Huckleberry Finn*, the obvious humanity of the character Jim sent a powerful message about the need for racial justice, a message that still resonates in the United States today. *To Kill a Mockingbird* sent a similar message making Scout and Atticus heroes for millions.

One more point about theme is important. In literature, there is often great virtue in complexity and nuance. A great novelist may show us the contradictions present in a character, a society, an organization, and so forth. Such complexity generally works less effectively in rhetoric, where a complex message may be misunderstood or simply missed by an audience. In order to get a point across to an audience, narrative rhetoric often reinforces a quite simple message. This simplicity may not make great literature, but it is necessary to get a message across to an audience. One of the great virtues of Upton Sinclair's novel, *The Jungle*, from a rhetorical perspective is its clarity in displaying dreadful conditions in meat packing plants in Chicago.

Functions of Narrative Rhetoric

Narrative rhetoric can function in six different ways to produce persuasion. First, narratives add interest to material that otherwise might bore an audience. Rhetorical theorist and critic Walter Fisher argues that humans are inherently story-telling animals.[5] He means that one of the defining characteristics of being human is telling stories. Fisher is clearly onto something. In all cultures and throughout history, human beings have told stories to amuse, inform, and persuade.

One sign of the human affection for stories is the dominance of the form in the media. When was the last time that a hit TV show or a big summer movie concerned a topic like "Statistics on a Major Issue," or "Harvard Experts Talk for Three Hours?" This point could have been made at any point in human history. One hundred years ago, there was no television or radio, but other forms of stories played a crucial role in U.S. culture. People like stories because they add

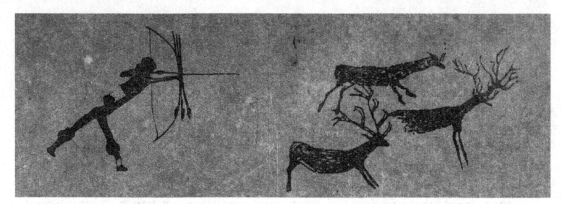

interest to our lives. Research on early humans seems to indicate that this always has been true. Cave paintings, for example, appear to be stories about events that were crucial in the lives of the people who painted them.

Second, narrative rhetoric can create identification between the characters and the members of the audience. In so doing, it can break down barriers to understanding. By identification I do not mean the ability to identify different objects. Identification in a rhetorical sense is an understanding of shared commonality among people. The rhetorical theorist Kenneth Burke argues that creating a sense of shared identity, which he sometimes calls consubstantiality, is essential to persuasion.[6] Stories can make us understand that people growing up in Africa or Asia or in America 200 years ago are or were people just like us.

Identification is important in two ways. First, identification is essential to breaking down barriers between people who come from different backgrounds. Two people may be very different in terms of birthplace, race, gender, age, and so forth, but a rhetoric of identification may make it quite clear that in other more fundamental ways they are quite similar. These two people may discover that they have had similar life experiences, love the same books, have the same values, or support the same causes and so forth. In so doing, the barriers between them may be eliminated. At that point, these two very different people may become friends or work together for some cause.

Second, identification is linked to identity. We all need an identity, a sense of who we are. People define themselves as Republicans, or feminists, or Cowboys fans, or labor union members, or of Italian ancestry, and so forth. These definitions of the self often have both a literal and a symbolic dimension. A person may literally be the son or daughter of an Italian immigrant. But that person also may symbolically define him/herself as an Italian-American, even though his/her actual parents were from somewhere else. It should be obvious that the symbolic sense of identity is more important than the literal one. I may not have been closer to Italy than a dinner at the local pizza joint, but still define myself as an Italian-American.

A symbolic definition of self provides the person with an identity. Ronald Reagan often spoke of the importance of being an American, sometimes with a reference to early Pilgrim John

Winthrop's label of the new society as a "shining city on a hill." Clearly, Reagan understood the power of identification. He believed that by revitalizing a sense of shared national identity as Americans that he also could revitalize the nation. His many political successes over his two terms demonstrate that he was right.

Narrative rhetoric is one of the most powerful means of creating a sense of shared identity. A good story can show people of different races or cultures that they really are in some ways the same. The award-wining movie *Philadelphia* illustrates this point. The film told the story of a young lawyer with AIDS who was fired by his law firm when they found out that he was gay and had the terrible disease. The lawyer, played by Tom Hanks, sues and eventually wins a judgment, but the tragedy remains, for he is dying. One primary message of the film is that anti-gay discrimination is wrong. In order to get that point across, the film narrative creates a sense of identification between Hanks' character and other characters in the film and those of us in the audience. The film shows us that the young lawyer has a loving family and partner. It shows us that he is a hard-working lawyer and a good person. It shows us that he had the same kinds of hopes and dreams that all of us have. The attorney for Hanks' character, played by Denzel Washington, starts out as homophobic. Over the course of the film, however, he gradually identifies with his client, leading to a change in his ideas about gay people. The film was designed to produce the same impact on theatergoers. As the *Philadelphia* example indicates, narratives are a powerful way of creating identification. Stories that created a sense of identification between gay Americans and their neighbors have played a major role in this nation's move toward becoming a more enlightened, caring, and egalitarian society over the last thirty years.

Third, stories are important forms of persuasion in part because they sometimes possess aesthetic qualities that make a message far more appealing than it otherwise would be. The message in a story may be powerful, not only because of what it is, but also because of how it is told. The movie *The China Syndrome* illustrates this point. The film drew a chilling picture of the danger of a nuclear meltdown. In the film, the fine acting of Jane Fonda and Jack Lemmon made the threat of a nuclear accident come alive. For many people, the film, which opened at roughly the same time as the accident at Three Mile Island, came to symbolize what a nuclear accident would be like. The aesthetic quality of the film, including the acting, camera angles, the way the plot developed, and so forth, made the threat of a nuclear power accident seem very real to many Americans. Many narratives used the events of 9/11 to similarly enliven their storyline.

In actuality, the accident at Three Mile Island produced very little radioactivity and almost no harm.[7] There is even an argument that the greatest negative effect of the accident was unnecessary stress among the residents around the plant. Despite the reality that no significant harm was produced, most Americans saw the accident as a major disaster. This message was reinforced by the film's treatment of a nuclear accident. In that way, the aesthetic qualities of *The China Syndrome* played a role in influencing public opinion in a direction not supported by the actual experience with a real nuclear power accident. On the other hand, the terrible (and true) events of 9/11 have been used to give power to factual arguments about the terrorist threat to the United States.

Fourth, narratives persuade not with proof in the sense of formal logic, but by encapsulating a point. The story functions as a rhetorical whole, rather than as a supporting example. For many years, Ronald Reagan and other conservative politicians told stories about welfare cheaters as part of an attack on "big government." Their stories of people using welfare or food stamps to buy liquor or otherwise waste the government money struck a nerve with the American people. No one wants his/her hard-earned money to go to a welfare cheat, who is about to go off on a drunken spree. In this case, the stories encapsulated the point and made it very difficult to answer. The fact that statistical evidence suggested that there were relatively few welfare cheaters did not make much difference. Many people had seen an example similar to one told by Reagan or others, and so that example encapsulated the point for them. The capacity of narrative to encapsulate a point makes it very difficult to refute the claims in a narrative.

Fifth, narrative rhetoric provides a powerful vehicle for creating an emotional response, especially through the creation of pity and guilt. For example, a narrative can show us a wholly innocent victim being hurt by monstrous evil. Or it can create guilt by showing us the terrible effects on innocent people of some action by the government. Think for a moment about the works in contemporary popular culture that produce the strongest emotional response. For kids, the all-time greatest may be the Disney film, *Bambi*. More recently, movies like *Titanic, Brokeback Mountain,* and *Schindler's List* have created very powerful emotional reactions. The key point is that every one of the artifacts I have cited is a story. If you want to move people emotionally, one powerful means of doing so is to tell a story.

Finally, narrative has the power to break down barriers to understanding. It does this by taking us out of our here and now and placing us in someone else's life in a different place/time. One of the wonders of modern science is technology that allows a people to put on advanced goggles and suddenly find themselves seeing a different reality. This modern miracle isn't really that modern. Stories have always had the capacity to take us out of our mundane lives and transport us to another world. The worldwide sensation of J.K. Rowling's *Harry Potter* stories is good evidence that even in a culture besotted with the powers of technology, there is almost nothing as powerful as a well-told tale. Narrative can lift us out of our lives and place us in the midst of the Holocaust or in the Depression or even on a different world. In so doing, narrative can make real the evils of slavery, the Nazi system, or Stalin's Soviet Union in a way that argumentative rhetoric cannot.

One sign of the power of narrative to transport us to a different place or time is the way that people respond to characters in fictional narratives. Rowling's novels are not unique in producing this reaction. For millions of people, Captain James T. Kirk of the Starship Enterprise is a real person that they care about. So is Han Solo or Yoda. Everyone knows that Kirk, Solo, and Yoda are just characters, but over time they have become trusted friends and even role models. The narratives have made these people quite real to us. If narrative can make us feel close to invented characters who "live" in a time that is still hundreds of years away or in "a galaxy far far away," then think about how narrative can bring home to us actual events and/or people in the real world.

1 Narratives add interest.
2 Narratives create identification.
3 Narratives function aesthetically to persuade.
4 Narratives encapsulate claims.
5 Narratives can be used to create an emotional response.
6 Narratives transport us to another place/time.

JOHN ANJAIN AND NARRATIVE FORM

The four components of narrative form and the six functions served by narrative are readily apparent in John Anjain's testimony to Congress. Anjain and his family were victims of fallout from a 1954 hydrogen bomb blast in the South Pacific. He appeared before the Senate Committee on Energy and Natural Research on June 15, 1977 to ask for compensation.

Statement by John Anjain before the Senate Committee on Energy and Natural Resources

Mr. Chairman and members of this committee: 1

My name is John Anjain. I am a citizen of the Marshall Islands District of the   2 Trust Territory. I am here today to speak to you in support of a bill which will provide compensation for the people of Rongelap and Utirik Atolls in my district. I welcome this opportunity to appear before you. I ask for your support of this bill. My only regret is that English is a second language for me, I cannot speak directly to you in your own language.

I am here today to tell you of my experiences as one of the Marshallese who was   3 exposed to radiation because of the bomb in 1954.

In 1954, I was the Chief Magistrate of Rongelap Island, in Rongelap Atoll. At that   4 time your country was making tests of atomic bombs at Bikini and Enewetak. Our people did not fully understand about these tests, or about the bombs. But we had learned to trust the Americans after the Japanese had gone. We believed they would do nothing to harm us. We believed that they were on our islands to help us.

In March of 1954, I was on Rongelap with my wife and family, including one year   5 old son, Lekoj. Lekoj was just learning to walk.

John Anjain, Statement before Senate Committee on Energy and Natural Resources, 1977

We were very happy with Lekoj. He was a happy child. But as a father, a husband and provider, and as a magistrate I was worried. I was worried because of what one Hawaiian had said to me when the field trip ship came to our island. He said that "Your life is about that long." He said this and placed his thumb half way down his first finger. I asked him why. He said because of the tests. He did not explain. He just made a statement. 6

On March 1, 1954, there were 64 people on Rongelap. There were another 18 of our people on nearby Ailihghae. They were cutting copra, and catching fish. 7

In the morning, the sun rose in the east. And then something very strange happened. It looked like a second sun was rising in the west. We heard noise like thunder. We saw some strange clouds over the horizon. But the sun in the west, which we know now was the bomb, faded away. We heard no more noise. But we did see the cloud. 8

In the afternoon, something began falling from the sky upon our island. It looked like ash from a fire. It fell on me, it fell on my wife, it fell on our infant son. It fell on the trees, and the roofs of our houses. It fell on the reefs, and into the lagoon. 9

We were very curious about this ash falling from the sky. Some people put it in their mouths and tasted it. One man rubbed it into his eye to see if it would cure an old ailment. People walked in it, and children played with it. 10

An airplane passed by our island. Some people thought that the plane was spraying for mosquitoes. The Americans had done that after the war. We thought maybe the ash came from the plane. But we did not really know. We did not understand. No one told us what to expect. We were not prepared. 11

Later on, in the early evening it rained. The rain fell on the roofs of our houses. It washed away the ash. The water mixed with the ash which fell into our water catchments. Men, women, and children drank that water. It did not taste like rainwater, but some people drank it anyway. 12

Then the next day, I think it was the next day, some Americans came to our island in a boat. They had a machine with them. They went around the island. They looked very worried, and talked rapidly to each other. They told us we must not drink the water in our catchment tanks. They left. They did not explain anything. 13

On the second day, some ships came. Americans again came on our island. They explained that we were in great danger because of the ash. They said if we did not leave, we would die. They told us to leave everything and to only take our clothes. Some people were very afraid and fell into the water trying to get into the landing boat. Some people were taken away to Kawjaleih by airplane. The rest of us went by boat. 14

We looked at our island as we left. We did not know that we would never see our island again for three years. We did not know that the people of Utirik 100 miles to the east, had the same experience. 15

We still did not understand what had happened, but now we were afraid. 16

Some people were feeling sick. Some people had an itching on their skin where 17
the ash was. Later, some people got very sick. They threw up. They felt weak. Later,
the hair of men, women and children began to fall out. A lot of people had burns on
their skin. There were doctors at Kwajaleih and they examined us. Now we were very
afraid.

We thought we were going to die. But we did not die. We got better and we were 18
sent to an island in the Hajuro Atoll. We were told that we could not go back for a long
time. The people of Utirik also could not go back soon.

We waited. We were given some new clothing. Houses were built. We were also 19
given some money every month. This money was to take the place of the copra we
could not make. It was not much money and the people were unhappy. We were
given some food, but we were still not happy. We were not living on our island. We
had left our ancestral lands. We left behind our houses, and possessions. We left our
pigs and chickens. We did not know when we would return.

Three years passed very slowly. The American doctors came to examine us from 20
time to time. Many people complained that they did not feel well. Many women said
that they had miscarriages, and that the babies did not look like human babies. Some
babies were born dead. The doctors said that they did not know why. They did not
see the dead babies, so they said they could not tell why.

In 1957, we returned to Rongelap. The Utirikese were returned after only three 21
months. We were happy to return. The Americans were very kind. They built us new
homes, a school, a dispensary. They built new water catchments. But they told us not
to eat certain foods, especially coconut crabs. Coconut crabs are one of our favorite
foods. But we could not eat any, until a couple of years ago. We still cannot eat
coconut crabs from the north part of our lagoon. We can eat other coconut crabs, but
only one crab for one person, in one day. They say that they still have some poison in
them from the bomb. We were home and we were still afraid.

But even though the Americans were kind, we were still not happy. Some people 22
still did not feel good. We could not eat the food we wanted to eat. The American
doctors came every year to examine us. Every year they came, and they told us
that we were not sick, and then they would return the next year. But they did find
something wrong. They found one boy did not grow as fast as boys his age. They
gave him medicine. Then they began finding the thyroid sickness.

My son, Lekoj was 13 when they found his thyroid was sick. They took him away 23
to a hospital in America. They cut out his thyroid. They gave him some medicine and
told him to take it every day for the rest of his life. The same thing happened to other
people. The doctors kept returning and examining us. Several years ago, they took
me to a hospital in America and they cut out my thyroid. They gave me medicine, and
told me to take it every day for the rest of my life.

A few years after the bomb, Senator Ahata Kabua tried to get some compensation 24
for the people of Rongelap. He got a lawyer and the lawyer made a case in court. The
court turned our case down. The court said it could not consider our case because

we were not part of the United States. Dwight Heine went to the United Nations to tell them about us. People from the United Nations came to see us and we told them how we felt. Finally, in 1964, the U.S. Congress passed a bill. The bill gave us money as a payment for our experience. Some of the people spent all their money, some of them still have money in the bank. After we got the money, they began finding the thyroid sickness.

In 1972, they took Lekoj away again. They said they wanted to examine him. They took him to America, to a big hospital near Washington. Later, they took me to this hospital near Washington because they said he was very sick. My son Lekoj died after I arrived. He never saw his island again. He returned to our home in a box. He is buried on our island. The doctors say he had a sickness called Leukemia. They are quite sure it was from the bomb. 25

And I am positive. 26

I saw the ash fall on him. I know it was the bomb. I saw him die. 27

Now, it is 22 years after the bomb, and I am here to ask for your help. I know that money cannot bring back my thyroid. It cannot bring back my son. It cannot give me back three years of my life. It cannot take the poison from the coconut crabs. It cannot make us stop being afraid. 28

But it can help us. It will tell us that the Americans are sorry, and that they want to help. It can help our islands, our people, and our children. We can build things. We can send our children to school. We can do many things. We ask for your help. 29

The doctors still come every year, sometimes two times a year. But the people are not happy. They are still afraid. The doctors tell us that we are not sick. Then they take someone away and cut out a thyroid. Then they return. The people ask, if we are not sick, why do you come? If we are sick, why don't you tell us? The doctors say they just want to check on us. 30

It is 22 years after the bomb. They are still finding thyroid sickness. Now they are finding it on Utirik, too. We are still afraid. They said it was an accident that the ash fell on us. They say that we are not being used for an experiment. 31

We like the Americans. They have been kind to us. We are not angry, only afraid. When we get sick, we think of the bomb. When people die, we think of the bomb. May God forgive America for what it has done to our people. 32

I have lost my health, I have lost three years of my life, and I have lost my son. 33

Please help us. 34

Thank you. 35

NARRATIVE FORM IN ANJAIN'S TESTIMONY

A close reading of his testimony reveals the plot pattern of rising action I described, along with how Anjain depicts the scene in his story, and his use of characterization. These components are combined to produce Anjain's themes, which are to place the blame for sickness among his people on the United States, emphasize the innocence of the islanders, and ask for compensation.

Plot

The first three paragraphs of Anjain's testimony introduce the story. He tells the committee who he is and why he is testifying before the committee. In paragraph 4, he begins the story itself, by setting the scene for the action to follow. He describes his family and their almost idyllic life on the island of Rongelap. In paragraph 6, he forecasts the crisis to come by telling of how a man from Hawaii warned him that his life was threatened.

In paragraph 8, the first crisis of the story—the bomb being exploded—begins. He tells of how the islanders saw "a second sun" in the west and then of how they were so innocent about the bomb that they played in the atomic ash that fell on their island (paragraph 10). They drank water that had been contaminated with the ash because no one had told them "what to expect" (paragraph 11). It is at this point that the Americans come to the island. "They went around the island. They looked very worried, and talked rapidly to each other." Following that visit, Anjain and the other islanders were taken away from their beloved island. The first crisis ends in paragraph 18 after the islanders begin to get sick. "We thought we were going to die. But we did not die."

The second main aspect of the plot, which might be labeled "Exile," is discussed in paragraphs 19–21. Here the plot plateaus. The islanders did not die because of the bomb, but they did face continuing illness, miscarriages, and unhappiness at being away from their home. In paragraph 21, Anjain describes the return of the islanders to Rongelap. This paragraph stands as a point of transition to the last great crisis in the story—the thyroid sickness. In paragraphs 22–27, Anjain tells us about how his child Lekoj got sick with the "thyroid sickness." Later, Anjain himself had to have his thyroid removed. In paragraph 24, Anjain tells of how the islanders received compensation from the government, before people started getting the thyroid sickness. His obvious point is that past compensation was not adequate because it did not take into account the thyroid problem.

The final portion of the main body is found in paragraphs 25–27, which tell the story of how Lekoj became ill again, was taken to the United States, and eventually died. In paragraphs 26 and 27, Anjain states his certainty that it was the bomb that made Lekoj sick. "And I am positive. I saw the ash fall on him. I know it was the bomb. I saw him die." Paragraphs 28 through 35 constitute the conclusion, the epilogue to the story. In them, Anjain pulls together the themes from the story and asks for compensation.

Anjain's narrative develops in precisely the pattern noted earlier. Initially, he sets the stage for the story. He then begins with the second greatest crisis in the narrative, the explosion of the bomb and the aftermath of the explosion. The plot then plateaus with the exile stage, before it moves to a climax with the death of Lekoj. The conclusion pulls together the themes that drive the narrative.

Scene

The primary scene for the story is obviously the island of Rongelap. In relation to scene, Anjain's most important goal is to make the place seem real. In the first few paragraphs of the story itself, he gives us a picture of an Edenic place where people are one with nature. They live and work in this beautiful island environment. With this description, Anjain breaks down barriers to understanding the terrible thing that the United States did to the people of Rongelap. He also is setting up the appeal to guilt that I will discuss in relation to the functions of narrative, by describing the islanders as innocent and trusting.

Characters

The protagonist of Anjain's narrative is obviously Anjain himself. He is an ordinary person caught in an impossible situation. Anjain describes himself as a family man, who loved his wife and child, and as village magistrate trying to take care of his people. Clearly, Anjain is not heroic. Rather, he is an ordinary person trying to do his best; he is someone with whom the audience can identify.

The antagonist is not a person, but the bomb and the American government. The radiation from the bomb threatens to destroy not only their island, but their life. But in Anjain's narrative, the greater threat is really American indifference. Anjain describes the government of the United States as largely unconcerned about the welfare of the island people. After the fact, the government tries to take care of them, but beforehand the government did not consider the danger that the ash might float over the island. Clearly, that failure was unconscionable.

The other main character is Anjain's son Lekoj, whose function in the story is to create sympathy for Anjain and all of the islanders and guilt about the failure of the United States to protect these innocent people. Other characters in the story primarily serve plot functions. For example, Anjain tells us about a man who "rubbed it [the atomic ash] into his eye to see if it would cure an old ailment." In narrative terms, this man demonstrates the innocence of the island people. They knew so little about the bomb that they played in nuclear ash.

Theme

The dominant theme of the story is that the United States harmed the people of Rongelap and should compensate them for that harm. Obviously, this theme is divided into two sub-themes: the people of Rongelap were harmed and the United States was responsible for harming them. Along with these themes and sub-themes, Anjain aims at creating guilt in the audience. Very early in the story, Anjain says, "But we had learned to trust the Americans after the Japanese had gone. We believed they would do nothing to harm us. We believed that they were on our islands to help us." With this statement, Anjain distinguishes Americans from Japanese in order to create guilt about how badly the islanders were treated by the United States. He is saying: we trusted you, but you let us down.

THE FUNCTIONS OF NARRATIVE IN ANJAIN'S TESTIMONY

Anjain's testimony to the Senate committee fulfills all six of the functions of narrative rhetoric. First, the story is much more interesting than a similar argument would have been. Building an interesting argument about the failures of U.S. policy at Rongelap, some twenty-five years after the bomb blast, would have been nearly impossible. When he testified, Anjain faced the danger that the events would be viewed as ancient history. To counter that risk, Anjain's narrative adds interest to keep the attention of the audience.

Second, Anjain breaks down barriers to understanding and creates identification with his narrative. One problem that Anjain faces in his testimony is stereotyping about "primitive" people on a South Pacific island. By describing himself as a family man who loved his son and worked to protect his people, Anjain demonstrates to the senators that he is a person just like them. He uses the story of his son's death to force senators to think about how they would have felt if it had been their child. In one way, senators have little in common with the inhabitants of a small Pacific island. But in another way, as Anjain demonstrates in his story, senators and the people on the island are exactly the same.

Third, the aesthetic character of Anjain's testimony gives him great credibility. In the first third of his testimony in particular, Anjain's presentation is quite choppy. He uses a number of very short sentences and a simple vocabulary that fits his role as village magistrate. This style fits who Anjain is. It adds to his credibility. For someone else, this style might have undercut his message, but for Anjain it was the perfect way to demonstrate his authenticity to the audience.

Fourth, Anjain uses the story to encapsulate his point. In the story, he can state with great certainty that "I saw the ash fall on him. I know it was the bomb." In medical terms this makes no sense. Seeing the ash fall on his son does not prove that the bomb caused him to get cancer. Do some kids get cancer without being exposed to the bomb? Of course they do. In a purely logical way, there is no certainty that the bomb caused Lekoj's death, although it does seem highly likely that the bomb was the cause. The key point is that in a narrative, Anjain can encapsulate the point and make it impossible to refute. In the story, Anjain saw the ash fall and he knows with absolute certainty in his heart that it killed Lekoj. That kind of certainty is rarely if ever possible in the world of science or argument, but can be attained in narrative.

Fifth, Anjain skillfully creates both pity and guilt. Both emotions are produced when Anjain describes the simple innocence of the people on the island and contrasts them with the United States government, which did not even warn the islanders of the risk they faced. A simple warning would have told the islanders to avoid contact with ash from the bomb. The failure of the government to do so is shameful, something that clearly comes through in Anjain's testimony. He also creates guilt by comparing the actions of the United States to those of Japan. On a couple occasions, he tells the senators that the people on the island had come to trust the United States forces, because they weren't like the Japanese, who apparently had mistreated the islanders during the Second World War. Of course, his real point was that the United States should have done a much better job of protecting the islanders from the bomb.

Finally, Anjain uses the power of setting to take us out of the contemporary United States to his island home on that fateful day when the hydrogen bomb test took place. He uses close description to break down barriers to acceptance of his views. He also humanizes the people of the island with this description. After Anjain describes them and their life, they are no longer part of an event that happened twenty-five years ago and many thousand miles away; they are instead real people whose lives were destroyed by our thoughtlessness.

SUMMARY OF ANJAIN'S USE OF NARRATIVE DRAMATIC FORM

Anjain faced a difficult situation in his testimony before the Senate committee. He was asking for compensation for an event that had happened roughly twenty-five years before. It is hard to get people to care about something that happened so long ago. To make matters worse, the people harmed were not American citizens (as Anjain himself notes), although they were under the protection of the United States. And there weren't very many who were harmed. Anjain told the committee that there were 82 total people on the two islands and not all of these people were harmed. Thus, Anjain faced a major barrier in relation to getting the attention of the committee and also an attitudinal barrier in that the committee members could have concluded that the issue was no longer very important, if it ever was. He may also have faced an attitudinal barrier relating to American stereotypes of island people. And since the islanders were not Americans, there was no electoral interest in helping them.

Anjain also faced the problem that the United States already had compensated the islanders previously. Thus, it would be quite easy for a senator to respond to his plea by shrugging and saying, "We already paid you." Finally, Anjain had to deal with a problem of proof. It isn't possible to identify the specific cause of a given cancer in the same way that you can prove that bad potato salad caused food poisoning. Some people just get cancer for no apparent reason. Thus, Anjain could not prove in a scientific sense that Lekoj or anyone else got cancer from the bomb.

While Anjain faced significant barriers, he had no rhetorical advantages. He had no political power base with which to influence the senators. And he had no way to threaten them with bad publicity. It is important to recognize that before the Internet, someone like Anjain had very few means to spread his message. Clearly, he had to deal with a very difficult rhetorical situation.

Anjain could have confronted these barriers by building a strong rational argument. He could have laid out the statistical data on the cancer rates among islanders, cited experts on the effects of the ash, and so forth. But if he had taken this tack, he would have magnified the attention problem. Rational argument is not a good way to get the attention of a group that believes your problem to be insignificant. And rational argument provides no way around the problem of proof.

With narrative, in contrast, Anjain had a good strategy for persuading the committee. Anjain responded to the problem of attention by telling the story of real people who were harmed by the United States. He showed the audience that those on the island were people just like them. In so doing, he made the numbers issue less important. Yes, there were fewer than 100 of the islanders, but they still were real people. He also created both pity for the islanders and guilt about our inaction.

In relation to the barrier that the islanders already had been compensated, Anjain carefully noted that they began finding the thyroid disease after the compensation had been received. This meant that the compensation couldn't have been adequate.

Finally, Anjain used the story to prove in an absolute sense that Lekoj was killed by the bomb. While nothing can be demonstrated absolutely in science, in the context of the story, he clearly proved that the bomb caused the terrible disease. Who could respond to his statement— "I saw the ash fall on him. I know it was the bomb. I saw him die."—by challenging causation?

In summary, Anjain did a masterful job of using narrative to respond to the rhetorical barriers that he faced. In so doing, he also successfully fulfilled all six of the functions of narrative rhetoric. His testimony before the Senate Committee remains a strong illustration of the enormous power of narrative rhetoric.

CONCLUSION

Narrative is a very powerful form of rhetoric. A person who controls the stories told in any culture would have a great deal of influence over the culture. At the same time, the influence of narrative should not be overstated. Walter Fisher, who was cited earlier, goes so far as to argue that all forms of rhetoric are really types of narrative, a conclusion that obviously goes against the way that stories are used in the real world.[8] The *News Hour* is obviously not a narrative in the same sense as *Mad Men* or *Battlestar Galactica*.

The major weakness of narrative rhetoric is that it may be perceived as just a story, not something that typically happens in the real world. This means that narrative will be most powerful when it is understood as either a "true" story or as telling a fictional story about a real situation. As a consequence, in most situations, to be effective narrative will need to be combined with rational argument in order to achieve all of the six functions that I have described.

FOR FURTHER DISCUSSION

Former Miss America, Marilyn Van Derbur, testified before Congress on October 26, 1995 about sexual abuse of children. In her testimony, Van Derbur used a personal narrative in order to oppose legislation before Congress that had been labeled as a "shield" for parental rights and privacy. She feared that such legislation could be used to block action to prevent sexual abuse of children. Carefully read and do an analysis outline on Van Derbur's narrative. Then consider the following questions:

1 What narrative strategies does Van Derbur rely on in her testimony?
2 Does Van Derbur effectively use the resources of narrative to present her case? If so, how?
3 What barriers will Van Derbur face in attempting to persuade the committee?

4   On balance, does Van Derbur do a good job of presenting a narrative in order to persuade the committee? Would other strategies have been more appropriate?

Testimony of Marilyn Van Derbur

My name is Marilyn Van Derbur Atler. I grew up in a wealthy, socially prominent family. I graduated from the University of Colorado with Phi Beta Kappa honors. I skied on the University of Colorado's ski team down hill. I broke and trained my own horses. I was tough and smart and fearless. I was also an incest victim from age 5 to age 18. I was terrified and helpless and powerless. My father owned me and my three older sisters. He could do anything he wanted with us, and he did, and there was no one to hear us or help us and there was no hope of it ending, ever. I was pried open, violated, traumatized for 13 years.

In order to stop the physical and sexual violations of children, we need to know it's happening. Children have to tell an adult they trust, someone who will believe them, protect them, fight for their rights. To not support those who try to protect a child is to doom that child.

When I was about 4, my father was beating my eldest sister Gwen and my mother cried out, "Van, you're going to kill her." I'm sure I believed my mother that he was going to kill her. When I was 7, Gwen was 13 and ready to start ninth grade as an honor student. Because she was defiant to my mother, my father sent her to a boarding school in Kansas City. I learned only recently that he would then fly to Kansas City and take her to the Muelbach Hotel, the most luxurious hotel in Kansas City, for weekends.

I learned as a very small child, if you defy, you get beaten and sent away. I am pleading with you to never send a message to parents that it is acceptable to hit or spank a child. It was the physical violence that my father would have called reasonable, corporal punishment that terrorized us into submission for the sexual violations. I am speaking for millions of today's children, pleading with you to never allow my past to be any child's future. We were his property. He could hit us at will and no one, no one ever told him this was wrong.

In the airport recently, I saw a woman hit her child, yelling, "I have told you to never hit your sister." Do we allow a man to hit his wife or is that domestic violence? Then how could we allow an adult to hit a child? Where is the sense of it?

The first time a reporter asked me, "Why didn't you tell as a child," I just stared at him. I couldn't believe anyone would ask such an uneducated question. Who in the world would I have told? My father and I had never spoken of it. I had always pretended to be asleep.

Marilyn Van Derbur, Testimony in Hearing before the Subcommittee on the Constitution of the House of Representatives Judiciary Committee, 1995

When I was 40, after being released from the hospital, I called my father and asked to speak with him at the home in which I had grown up. When he realized why I was there, he said, "I'll be back in a minute." He came back immediately and I knew he had a gun in his pocket. After our conversation, as I rose to leave, he said, "If you had come in any other way, I would have killed myself." The message was very clear: if you are even thinking about exposing me, take a good look at the consequences. If he said this to me when I was 40, what do you think he would have done to me as a child?

I was 48 years old when I told my mother, a year after my father had died. With gut-retching sobs, I brought up the words. My mother said, "I don't believe you. It's in your fantasy." If my mother would not believe me, a successful adult, with my father dead, do you think she would have believed me as a child with my father alive, powerful, intimidating and in charge? There was no one in my family to protect me. Please do not make it more difficult than it already is for child protection services to intercede in a family where children are being raped and beaten.

My mother called it spanking. What reasonable corporal punishment might mean to you, I can promise you it had a different meaning for my mother and father.

During the past 4 years, I've been in personal contact with more adults physically and sexually violated as children than anyone else in America. I've spoken in 163 cities and personally answered over more than 7,000 letters, over 95 percent never reported.

Representative Parker said this is a shield for parents. Where is the shield for children? Please do not pass this bill.

1   On the importance of narrative see Alisdair MacIntyre, *After Virtue: A Study in Moral Theory* (Notre Dame: University of Notre Dame Press, 1981); Wallace Martin, *Recent Theories of Narrative* (Ithaca, New York: Cornell University Press, 1986).

2   Barack Obama, *Dreams from My Father*, (New York: Three Rivers, 2004, originally published 1995); Barack Obama, *The Audacity of Hope: Thoughts on Reclaiming the American Dream* (New York: Crown, 2006).

3   See Robert C. Rowland and John M. Jones, "Recasting the American Dream and American Politics: Barack Obama's Keynote Address to the 2004 Democratic National Convention," *Quarterly Journal of Speech* 93 (2007): 425–448

4   See William F. Lewis, "Telling America's Story: Narrative Form and the Reagan Presidency," *Quarterly Journal of Speech* 73 (1987): 280–302.

5   Walter R. Fisher, "Narration as a Human Communication Paradigm: The Case of Public Moral Argument," *Communication Monographs* 51 (1984): 1–22.

6   For a discussion of identification and consubstantiality see Kenneth Burke, *A Rhetoric of Motives* (Berkeley: University of California Press, 1969, pp. 20–29, 45–46, 55–59. For an analysis of Burke's views on identification see Sonja K. Foss, Karen A. Foss, and Robert Trapp, *Contemporary Perspectives on Rhetoric*, 2nd ed. (Prospect Heights, Illinois: Waveland, 1991), pp.174–178.

7   See *Report of the President's Commission on the Accident at Three Mile Island: The Need For Change: The Legacy of TMI* (Washington: Government Printing Office, 1979).

8   For an analysis of Fisher's views see Robert C. Rowland, "Narrative: Mode of Discourse or Paradigm," *Communication Monographs* 54 (1987): 264–275.

CHAPTER 6
Credibility Strategies

The third main rhetorical strategy is credibility. Since the Greeks invented the study of rhetoric more than two thousand years ago, we have known that the credibility of the rhetor plays a crucial role in the effectiveness of any work of rhetoric. In fact, Aristotle labeled ethos, which today we would define as credibility, as one of the three modes of persuasion.[1]

An example makes the importance of credibility clear. Colin Powell was a national hero in the aftermath of the first Gulf War. People clamored to hear him speak or read things he wrote. He was mentioned as a possible Republican candidate for president or vice president. And in that period the Democrats would have loved for him to switch parties. Where did this popularity come from? The obvious answer is that he had enormous credibility with the American people because of his leadership role during the Gulf War and at other times in his military career. Powell had so much credibility, especially on military issues, that many people believed him simply because of who he was. They didn't demand strong arguments or powerful narratives from him.

The power of credibility was evident when prior to the invasion of Iraq, during the second Bush administration, he went to the United Nations to present evidence that Iraq had an active program to create weapons of mass destruction (WMD). Many people found the testimony to be especially compelling because it came from Colin Powell. On the other hand, after no WMD were found and the invasion of Iraq gradually turned into a quagmire, Powell's credibility suffered. No longer was he the media star that he had been before. The key point is that credibility can be a very powerful persuasive tool, but once lost, the absence of credibility can pose a major barrier for persuading an audience. Senator Al Franken was a hero to many liberals until allegations that he had touched women inappropriately led to his resignation. Franken, like Tiger Woods and many others, demonstrates that it is quite possible to move from idolized icon to punch line quite quickly.

As these examples indicate, in some cases rhetoric persuades not because of the power of the argument or a compelling narrative, but via the credibility of the rhetor. That is, people are persuaded by the expertise or good character which is presented in the rhetoric. The remainder of this chapter explores the way that credibility functions in persuasion. In the first section, I explore the influence of credibility, draw a distinction between internal and external credibility, and identify the dimensions that make up credibility. I then analyze two speeches to illustrate how credibility functions as a persuasive strategy: anti-Vietnam War testimony to Congress by John Kerry, then a leader of the Vietnam Veterans Against the War and later a United States

Senator from Massachusetts, 2004 Democratic nominee for president, and Secretary of State in Obama's second term, and Representative Barbara Jordan's acclaimed keynote address at the 1976 Democratic National Convention.

THE INFLUENCE OF CREDIBILITY ON PERSUASION

Credibility is rarely the dominant strategy found in a work of rhetoric. It is only in exceptional cases (such as Colin Powell after the Gulf War during the administration of George H.W. Bush) that a person has so much credibility that we accept their comments immediately. If it is Michael Jordan talking about basketball or Peyton Manning on football, we might accept their words without comment. In the public square, however, there are almost no cases in which we accept someone's views simply because of their credibility. In the immediate aftermath of the 2008 presidential election, President Obama's popularity with liberals was quite high, but this did not stop them from disagreeing with him on a host of policies. And Republicans opposed virtually every policy he proposed. Thus, it is only in rare and usually specialized instances in which the speaker/writer will have so much credibility that the audience simply accepts their views. With those rare exceptions in mind, credibility is best understood as both a supporting strategy and, at some minimum level, a necessary requirement for persuasion to occur.

While credibility is rarely a sufficient strategy for persuasion, it is always a necessary one. If a rhetor lacks a minimum level of credibility, the audience simply will ignore him or her. Occasionally, someone will lose their credibility in some sort of scandal. When that happens, the person also loses their audience. When the Watergate tapes finally were released, many people who previously had supported Richard Nixon were confronted with clear evidence of a cover-up. The result was that Nixon lost all credibility and was forced to resign. A similar result has occurred in U.S. politics, on many occasions. Thus, credibility can be understood as always necessary for persuasion and only in very rare cases sufficient to produce that persuasive effect.

Credibility is also a supporting strategy. Thus, a rhetor may back up a claim with language strategies, strong arguments, and so forth, and also by demonstrating that he/she has high credibility on a given subject. A great deal of research has been conducted to back up this claim. This research has measured the importance of credibility by keeping constant the content of a speech or essay, but varying the characteristics of the rhetor. While there are many complexities to this research, the general conclusion is that credibility makes a difference. One survey of this literature concluded:

> For most persuasive communication situations, however, sources who are perceived as having either high-positive or high-negative source credibility *can* make a difference in the attitude change of a receiver or group of receivers.[2]

Many researchers have drawn similar conclusions. One summary of experimental findings concluded some years ago that "The finding is almost universal that the ethos of the source is related in some way to the impact of the message."[3]

At this point, it is important not to overstate the importance of credibility. Only in rare cases is credibility the decisive factor, either in a positive or negative sense. In most instances, credibility is one among several important persuasive strategies. It rarely is as important as the primary triad of persuasive strategies: argument, narrative, and value-laden appeals.

Finally, one additional limitation on credibility as a strategy should be recognized. Credibility is in a sense derivative of rational argument. We tend to trust someone if we perceive that person as both honest and expert on a subject. Similarly, we value a friend because our experience with them leads us to trust their judgment or expect them to be fun. In this way credibility is at the core of authoritative proof and is also based in our experience with or knowledge of someone. But it is important to recognize that credibility is, therefore, built on the storehouse of examples, statistics, and metaphors at the disposal of the authority, as well as our experience with that person. And that storehouse of previous experience/knowledge can be overwhelmed by stronger data. An example may make this point clear. Imagine that the world's greatest expert on UFOs is arguing that there are in fact no aliens visiting the earth. This person might have enormous credibility based upon their experience and training. But all that credibility could be overwhelmed immediately if another researcher said, "Yes that nice, but here is my friend ET the Alien." Credibility is a crucial strategy, but it is not as basic or powerful a strategy as rational argument, narrative, or appeals to values or needs.

INTERNAL AND EXTERNAL CREDIBILITY

Credibility may be brought to a work of rhetoric or created in it. Extrinsic (external) credibility exists when the rhetor has credentials that are well-known to the audience. Michael Jordan was for many years the world's most famous athlete; he continues to bring that credibility with him whenever he speaks. His credibility has sold a great quantity of athletic wear. While many similar examples could be cited from the world of sports and entertainment, it is much harder to think of someone who has that level of credibility relative to public policy. Is there anyone who has so much credibility that we simply trust their judgment on foreign policy? There was a time when respected news anchors, especially Walter Cronkite, had that level of credibility. After Cronkite broadcast about failures of U.S. policy in Vietnam, President Lyndon Johnson was quoted as saying, "If I've lost Cronkite, I've lost Middle America."[4] Cronkite's last broadcast was decades ago and there has been no one with his level of credibility since at least the Clinton administration. Even highly respected figures such as the first President Bush or Senator Edward Kennedy were distrusted by a large percentage of the people.

In contrast, intrinsic or internal credibility is created in a work of rhetoric, when the rhetor demonstrates his/her competence, honesty, and so forth. Any time a rhetor mentions his or her credentials or relevant work on the topic, he or she is building intrinsic credibility. A rhetor also may build internal credibility by showing commonality with the audience or demonstrating likability or good character.

Of the two forms, extrinsic credibility is probably more powerful, but intrinsic credibility more important. It is when someone possesses enormous extrinsic credibility, as in the cases of

Michael Jordan or Warren Buffett, that credibility becomes sufficient for persuasion. Obviously, such occurrences are far more the exception than the rule. Thus, the primary focus of rhetorical analysis is on internal credibility and more specifically how the speaker/writer/director convinces the audience that he/she is a highly credible source.

TYPES OF CREDIBILITY

There are four subtypes of credibility, three of which have been recognized at least since Aristotle.[5] The four types of credibility are: expertise/experience, good character, good will, and charisma.

Expertise/Experience

The first subtype of credibility is expertise/experience. I discussed these concepts earlier in the consideration of the types of authoritative evidence. To recapitulate, an expert is someone with training in a content area. Thus, we give more credibility to a person who has studied an issue for decades than to someone who spent thirty minutes on the Internet looking up a subject. Experience relates to the life experience of the individual. An expert can study the Arctic, but a person who lived there has experience in the region. We treat a person who has had experience working in an area as more credible than someone who is new to the topic.

In relation to expertise and experience, it is important to remember that expertise is the more important subdimension when the issue under consideration is a generalization about a topic. Thus, we are more likely to believe a cardiologist about issues related to heart health than an ordinary person who has had heart problems. On the other hand, if the issue is a specific incident or fact, then experience is more important than expertise. This only makes sense. An expert on handguns can tell an audience in general about how guns are used. But only an eyewitness can tell the audience about how a particular gun was used in a particular incident.

It is important to recognize that a growing populist rejection of expertise and a broader anti-elitism in society may be undercutting the power of appeals to experience and expertise. Writing for *Scientific American*, Gleb Tsipursky cited polls indicating declining trust in higher education and science and observed that "Growing numbers of people claim their personal opinions hold equal weight to the opinions of experts." Tsipursky also noted that the recent rise in cases of measles can be attributed to an anti-scientific and anti-expertise attitude that led parents to not vaccinate their children.[6] The decline in trust in experts also has the effect of making personal experience a more powerful form of credibility even in cases where personal expertise provides little grounding for making broader judgments about some issue.

Good Character

The second subtype of credibility is good character. A person with good character is known for his/her trustworthiness, sincerity, integrity, honesty, and so forth. We all value people who we perceive to be trustworthy. This is true in relation to persuasive communication but also in our personal lives. There are some people who we perceive as honest and moral and, consequently, we tend to believe what they have to say. For example, despite his conservative views, many moderates and even liberals admired Arizona Republican Senator John McCain, at least prior to the 2008 presidential campaign.[7] They found him trustworthy because he seemed to speak his mind, regardless of the political implications. McCain was, for example, one of the two sponsors of a campaign finance bill (along with Wisconsin Democrat Russell Feingold) that was opposed by nearly every other Republican in the Senate. McCain's willingness to take a position, regardless of what others thought, was seen by many as a sign of his fundamental honesty. That is why many liberals and moderates admired McCain, even though they disagreed with him on most issues. The McCain example also illustrates the point that credibility is not eternal. After the 2008 campaign in which McCain and others working for him labeled then-Senator Obama a socialist and worse, many moderates and liberals lost their faith in him. But when McCain cast a crucial vote blocking repeal of the Affordable Care Act, many liberals and moderates again concluded that he was a fundamentally honest person.

Good Will

The third subtype of credibility is usually referred to as "good will." Good will includes attractiveness, similarity, and an ability to identify with the audience. Why do advertisers pick beautiful actresses or handsome actors for their commercials? The obvious answer is that humans like attractive people. It is not late breaking news to say that attractiveness counts for a lot in appealing to an audience. For example, any political candidate would love to have Leonardo DiCaprio, Scarlett Johansson, or Angelina Jolie accompany them on a speaking tour, even if DiCaprio Johansson, or Jolie knew nothing about the issues.

While attractiveness is an important subdimension of good will, it is less important than similarity and identification. We like people who are beautiful/handsome, but even more than that, we like people who are similar to us. In the last chapter, I cited the rhetorical theorist and critic Kenneth Burke, who argues that the ability to establish a connection with an audience is essential to persuasion. Burke understood that humans tend to be put off by people who seem to be different than they are. But if you can establish similarity between yourself and the audience, then that barrier evaporates. It is the need to establish similarity or identification with an audience that leads skilled speakers to talk about their background and experience. When a speaker says to a rural audience, "I was once a country boy/girl myself," he or she is trying to create identification with the audience.

The example of Ronald Reagan illustrates this point. In youth and for many years thereafter, Reagan was a handsome man, but his greatest success came in politics when he was well over sixty and had accumulated the inevitable signs of age. As President and then ex-President, Reagan was no longer the handsome young movie star, but he was beloved by millions in large part because of his ability to connect with them, to show that he understood how they lived and what they believed in. Attractiveness is important, but not nearly as important as the ability to create a sense of shared identity with the people in your audience.

Charisma

The fourth form of credibility is power or charisma. It is an ability to project an energetic and active image and, at the same time, adapt to the audience perspectives. Unlike the other three forms of credibility, charisma cannot be created, although it can be manifested in rhetoric. Some people have charisma, while most do not. There is little evidence that charisma can be manufactured or learned. The ability to produce a charismatic reaction seems to be closely tied to personality characteristics of the rhetor. Ronald Reagan had it; the first president Bush didn't. Bill Clinton has it; Al Gore doesn't. Barack Obama has vast charisma, as does Donald Trump.

What is charisma? The answer to that is somewhat uncertain. Charisma is not merely physical power or attractiveness. Nor is it verbal ability, although it may be related to all of these factors. More than anything else charisma seems to be tied to an empathic understanding of the audience. Some rhetors seem to have an ability to sense how an audience is reacting and adapt to those feelings. It is that ability, more than anything else that creates charisma.

Charisma is of course a powerful persuasive factor. Rhetors with charisma may be able to persuade an audience to support their views. But that also makes charisma dangerous. American presidents like Ronald Reagan and Franklin Roosevelt used their charisma to energize the country behind their agendas. Hitler did the same thing in Germany. Great religious leaders possess charisma, but so do the leaders of cults. Charisma is powerful, but dangerous. It is probably good for human society that so few leaders are strongly charismatic.

SUMMARY OF THE DIMENSIONS OF CREDIBILITY

Which of the dimensions of credibility is most important? The answer is that it depends upon the context. If a person is an eyewitness in a trial, then good character is the most important dimension of credibility. The key for the jury to believe him/her is their trust in his/her character. If the person is an expert witness in that trial, then both good character and expertise/experience will be critical. In these first two circumstances, goodwill and charisma are important, but not as crucial as the other dimensions of credibility. On the other hand, if the circumstance were a social event, then goodwill would be the most important dimension of credibility. And if the focus were on motivating a group, charisma might be the most important dimension. The key point is that the relative importance of the four dimensions of credibility will depend upon the context in which the rhetoric is presented and the purpose of the rhetor.

CREATING CREDIBILITY

Earlier in this chapter, I explained the difference between intrinsic and extrinsic credibility. From the perspective of rhetorical analysis, intrinsic (or internal) credibility is clearly the more important concept. Extrinsic credibility is an important persuasive factor only in rare cases. There are few people in society who bring massive amounts of credibility to a speech or essay presented to an average audience of Americans. It is revealing that several of my examples of people with external credibility came from the world of sports. All a sports star has to do to maintain credibility is succeed on the field and not be caught in scandal off it. Succeeding in the world of public policy is much more difficult than the world of sports. Plus, in the public world, ideology, values, religion, and a host of other factors influence our judgment. With the basketball or football star, our focus is narrower—their in-game performance and whether they come across as a nice person.

It is because intrinsic credibility is far more common than extrinsic credibility that it is important to focus on the ways that people increase credibility in a speech or other rhetoric. One clue that credibility is an important strategy in a work of rhetoric is if the rhetor focuses on his/ her personal characteristics or experiences, either as they relate to the subject or as they relate to the audience. If this happens, the rhetor probably is trying to show himself or herself as a bright/ capable/honest person whom the audience can trust.

In order to illustrate the ways that credibility may be created in a work of rhetoric, testimony before the Senate Foreign Relations Committee by John Kerry, then a leader of a veterans organizations against the war in Vietnam. The testimony was presented in April 1971 when the United States still was deeply involved in the Vietnam War. Kerry uses a number of strategies to develop his credibility, especially in relation to the common perception at the time that opponents of the war were in some way unpatriotic. The speech became a major issue in the 2004 presidential campaign when some veterans argued that Kerry had dishonored veterans in the speech. As you will see, that charge was entirely unfounded.

Vietnam Veterans against the War
Statement of John Kerry

Thank you very much. Senator Fulbright, Senator Javits, Senator Symington, Senator Pell. I would like to say for the record, and also for the men behind me who are also wearing the uniforms and their medals, that my sitting here is really symbolic. I am not here as John Kerry, I am here as one member of the group of 1,000, which is a small representation of a very much larger group of veterans in this country, and were it possible for all of them to sit at this table they would be here and have the same kind of testimony.   1

I would simply like to speak in very general terms. I apologize if my statement is general because I received notification yesterday you would hear me and I am afraid because of the injunction I was up most of the night and haven't had a great deal of chance to prepare.   2

I would like to talk, representing all those veterans, and say that several months ago in Detroit, we had an investigation at which over 150 honorably discharged and many very highly decorated veterans testified to war crimes committed in Southeast Asia, not isolated incidents but crimes committed on a day-to-day basis with the full awareness of officers at all levels of command.   3

It is impossible to describe to you exactly what did happen in Detroit, the emotions in the room, the feelings of the men who were reliving their experiences in Vietnam,   4 but they did. They relived the absolute horror of what this country, in a sense, made them do.

They told the stories at times they had personally raped, cut off ears, cut off heads, taped wires from portable telephones to human genitals and turned up the power, cut off limbs, blown up bodies, randomly shot at civilians, razed villages in fashion reminiscent of Genghis Kahn, shot cattle and dogs for fun, poisoned food stocks, and generally ravaged the countryside of South Vietnam in addition to the normal ravage of war, and the normal and very particular ravaging which is done by the applied bombing power of this country.   5

We call this investigation the "Winter Soldier Investigation." The term "Winter soldier" is a play on words of Thomas Paine in 1776 when he spoke of the Sunshine Patriot and summertime soldiers who deserted at Valley Forge because the going was rough.   6

We who have come here to Washington have come here because we feel we have to be winter soldiers now. We could come back to this country; we could be quiet; we could hold our silence; we could not tell what went on in Vietnam, but we feel because of what threatens this country, the fact that the crimes threaten it, not reds, and not redcoats but the crimes which we are committing that threaten it, that we have to speak out.   7

I would like to talk to you a little bit about what the result is of the feelings these men carry with them after coming back from Vietnam. The country doesn't know it yet, but it has created a monster, a monster in the form of millions of men who have been taught to deal and to trade in violence, and who are given the chance to die for the biggest nothing in history; men who have returned with a sense of anger and a sense of betrayal which no one has yet grasped.   8

As a veteran and one who feels this anger, I would like to talk about it. We are angry because we feel we have been used in the worst fashion by the administration of this country.   9

In 1970 at West Point, Vice President Agnew said "some glamorize the criminal misfits of society while our best men die in Asian rice paddies to preserve the freedom which most of those misfits abuse," and this was used as a rallying point for our effort in Vietnam.   10

But for us, as boys in Asia whom the country was supposed to support, his statement is a terrible distortion from which we can only draw a very deep sense of revulsion. Hence the anger of some of the men who are here in Washington today. It is a distortion because we in no way consider ourselves the best men of this country, because those he calls misfits were standing up for us in a way that nobody else in this country dared to, because so many who have died would have returned to this country to join the misfits in their efforts to ask for an immediate withdrawal from South Vietnam, because so many of those best men have returned as quadriplegics and amputees, and they lie forgotten in Veterans' Administration hospitals in this country which fly the flag which so many have chosen as their own personal symbol. And we   11 cannot consider ourselves America's best men when we are ashamed of and hated for what we were called on to do in Southeast Asia.

In our opinion, and from our experience, there is nothing in South Vietnam, nothing which could happen that realistically threatens the United States of America. And to attempt to justify the loss of one American life in Vietnam, Cambodia, or Laos by linking such loss to the preservation of freedom, which those misfits supposedly abuse, is to us the height of criminal hypocrisy, and it is that kind of hypocrisy which we feel has torn this country apart. 12

We are probably much more angry than that and I don't want to go into the foreign policy aspects because I am outclassed here. I know that all of you talk about every possible alternative of getting out of Vietnam. We understand that. We know you have considered the seriousness of the aspects to the utmost level and I am not going to try to dwell on that, but I want to relate to you the feeling that many of the men who have returned to this country express because we are probably angriest about all that we were told about Vietnam and about the mythical war against communism. 13

We found that not only was it a civil war, an effort by a people who had for years been seeking their liberation from any colonial influence whatsoever, but also we found that the Vietnamese whom we had enthusiastically molded after our own image were hard put to take up the fight against the threat we were supposedly saving them from. 14

We found most people didn't even know the difference between communism and democracy. They only wanted to work in rice paddies without helicopters strafing them and bombs with napalm burning their villages and tearing their country apart. They wanted everything to do with the war, particularly with this foreign presence of the United States of America, to leave them alone in peace, and they practiced the art of survival by siding with whichever military force was present at a particular time, be it Vietcong, North Vietnamese, or American. 15

We found also that all too often American men were dying in those rice paddies for want of support from their allies. We saw first hand how money from American taxes was used for a corrupt dictatorial regime. We saw that many people in this country had a one-sided idea of who was kept free by our flag, as blacks provided the highest percentage of casualties. We saw Vietnam ravaged equally by American bombs as well as by search and destroy missions, as well as by Vietcong terrorism, and yet we listened while this country tried to blame all of the havoc on the Vietcong. 16

We rationalized destroying villages in order to save them. We saw America lose her sense of morality as she accepted very coolly a My Lai and refused to give up the image of American soldiers who hand out chocolate bars and chewing gum. 17

We learned the meaning of free fire zones, shooting anything that moves, and we watched while America placed a cheapness on the lives of orientals. 18

We watched the U.S. falsification of body counts, in fact the glorification of body counts. We listened while month after month we were told the back of the enemy was about to break. We fought using weapons against "oriental human beings," with 19 quotation marks around that. We fought using weapons against those people which I do not believe this country would dream of using were we fighting in the European theater or let us say a non-third-world people theater, and so we watched while men charged up hills because a general said that hill has to be taken, and after losing one platoon or two platoons they marched away to leave the hill for the reoccupation by the North Vietnamese because we watched pride allow the most unimportant of battles to be blown into extravaganzas, because we couldn't lose, and we couldn't retreat, and because it didn't matter how many American bodies were lost to prove that point. And so there were Hamburger Hills and Khe Sanhs and Hill 881's and Fire Base 6's and so many others.

Now we are told that the men who fought there must watch quietly while American lives are lost so that we can exercise the incredible arrogance of Vietnamizing the Vietnamese.   20

Each day—

[Applause.]

The Chairman. I hope you won't interrupt. He is making a very significant statement. Let him proceed.

Mr. Kerry. Each day to facilitate the process by which the United States washes her hands of Vietnam someone has to give up his life so that the United States doesn't have to admit something that the entire world already knows, so that we can't say that we have made a mistake. Someone has to die so that President Nixon won't be, and these are his words, "the first President to lose a war."   21

We are asking Americans to think about that because how do you ask a man to be the last man to die in Vietnam? How do you ask a man to be the last man to die for a mistake? But we are trying to do that, and we are doing it with thousands of rationalizations, and if you read carefully the President's last speech to the people of this country, you can see that he says, and says clearly: 22

But the issue, gentlemen, the issue is communism, and the question is whether or not we will leave that country to the Communists or whether or not we will try to give it hope to be a free people.

But the point is they are not a free people now under us. They are not a free people, and we cannot fight communism all over the world, and I think we should have learned that lesson by now.   23

But the problem of veterans goes beyond this personal problem, because you think about a poster in this country with a picture of Uncle Sam and the picture says "I want you." And a young man comes out of high school and says, "That is fine. I am going to serve my country." And he goes to Vietnam and he shoots and he kills and he does his job or maybe he doesn't kill, maybe he just goes and he comes back, and when he gets back to this country he finds that he isn't really wanted, because the largest unemployment figure in the country—it varies depending on who you get   24 it from, the VA Administration 15 percent, various other sources 22 percent. But the largest corps of unemployed in this country are veterans of this war, and of those veterans 33 percent of the unemployed are black. That means 1 out of every 10 of the nation's unemployed is a veteran of Vietnam.

The hospitals across the country won't, or can't meet their demands. It is not a   25
question of not trying. They don't have the appropriations. A man recently died after he had a tracheotomy in California, not because of the operation but because there weren't enough personnel to clean the mucous out of his tube and he suffocated to death.

Another young man just died in a New York VA hospital the other day. A friend of   26
mine was lying in a bed two beds away and tried to help him, but he couldn't. He rang a bell and there was nobody there to service that man and so he died of convulsions.

I understand 57 percent of all those entering the VA hospitals talk about suicide.   27
Some 27 percent have tried, and they try because they come back to this country and they have to face what they did in Vietnam, and then they come back and find the indifference of a country that doesn't really care, that doesn't really care.

Suddenly we are faced with a very sickening situation in this country, because   28
there is no moral indignation and, if there is, it comes from people who are almost exhausted by their past indignations, and I know that many of them are sitting in front of me. The country seems to have lain down and shrugged off something as serious as Laos, just as we calmly shrugged off the loss of 700,000 lives in Pakistan, the so-called greatest disaster of all times.

But we are here as veterans to say we think we are in the midst of the greatest   29
disaster of all times now because they are still dying over there, and not just Americans, Vietnamese, and we are rationalizing leaving that country so that those people can go on killing each other for years to come.

Americans seem to have accepted the idea that the war is winding down, at least   30
for Americans, and they have also allowed the bodies which were once used by a President for statistics to prove that we were winning the war, to be used as evidence against a man who followed orders and who interpreted those orders no differently than hundreds of other men in Vietnam.

We veterans can only look with amazement on the fact that this country has   31
been unable to see there is absolutely no difference between ground troops and a helicopter crew, and yet people have accepted a differentiation fed them by the administration.

No ground troops are in Laos, so it is all right to kill Laotians by remote control. But   32
believe me the helicopter crews fill the same body bags and they wreak the same kind of damage on the Vietnamese and Laotian countryside as anybody else, and the President is talking about allowing that to go on for many years to come. One can only ask if we will really be satisfied when the troops march into Hanoi.

We are asking here in Washington for some action, action from the Congress of   33
the United States of America which has the power to raise and maintain armies, and which by the Constitution also has the power to declare war.

We have come here, not to the President, because we believe that this body can   34
be responsive to the will of the people, and we believe that the will of the people says
that we should be out of Vietnam now.

We are here in Washington also to say that the problem of this war is not just   35
a question of war and diplomacy. It is part and parcel of everything that we are
trying as human beings to communicate to people in this country, the question of
racism, which is rampant in the military, and so many other questions also, the use of
weapons, the hypocrisy in our taking umbrage in the Geneva Conventions and using
that as justification for a continuation of this war, when we are more guilty than any
other body of violations of those Geneva Conventions, in the use of free fire zones,
harassment interdiction fire, search and destroy missions, the bombings, the torture
of prisoners, the killing of prisoners, accepted policy by many units in South Vietnam.
That is what we are trying to say. It is part and parcel of everything.

An American Indian friend of mine who lives in the Indian Nation of Alcatraz put   36
it to me very succinctly. He told me how as a boy on an Indian reservation he had
watched television and he used to cheer the cowboys when they came in and shot
the Indians, and then suddenly one day he stopped in Vietnam and he said "My God,
I am doing to these people the very same thing that was done to my people." And
he stopped. And that is what we are trying to say, that we think this thing has to end.

We are also here to ask, and we are here to ask vehemently, where are the leaders   37
of our country? Where is the leadership? We are here to ask where are McNamara,
Rostow, Bundy, Gilpatric and so many others. Where are they now that we, the men
whom they sent off to war, have returned? These are commanders who have deserted
their troops, and there is no more serious crime in the law of war. The Army says they
never leave their wounded.

The Marines say they never leave even their dead. These men have left all the   38
casualties and retreated behind a pious shield of public rectitude. They have left the
real stuff of their reputations bleaching behind them in the sun in this country.

Finally, this administration has done us the ultimate dishonor. They have attempted   39
to disown us and the sacrifice we made for this country. In their blindness and fear
they have tried to deny that we are veterans or that we served in Nam. We do not
need their testimony. Our own scars and stumps of limbs are witnesses enough for
others and for ourselves.

We wish that a merciful God could wipe away our own memories of that service   40
as easily as this administration has wiped their memories of us. But all that they have
done and all that they can do by this denial is to make more clear than ever our
own determination to undertake one last mission, to search out and destroy the last
vestige of this barbaric war, to pacify our own hearts, to conquer the hate and the fear
that have driven this country these last 10 years and more, and so when, in 30 years
from now, our brothers go down the street without a leg, without an arm, or a face,
and small boys ask why, we will be able to say "Vietnam" and not mean a desert, not
a filthy obscene memory but mean instead the place where America finally turned
and where soldiers like us helped it in the turning.

Thank you. [Applause.]

ANALYSIS OF THE KERRY SPEECH

Kerry's goal in his statement to the Senate Foreign Relations Committee is to persuade the committee and, via press reporting to the country, to support a policy to end the war in Vietnam as quickly as possible. He makes this clear throughout the speech, but especially in the concluding paragraphs. In paragraph 40, he labels the mission of his anti-war veterans group as "to search out and destroy the last vestige of this barbaric war." Here, Kerry uses an allusion to the "search and destroy" tactic used by the military in Vietnam to argue for precisely the opposite policy, ending the war. Kerry also advocates increased support for Vietnam veterans

© SLAVKO SEREDA/SHUTTERSTOCK.COM

returning to the United States. In paragraphs 24 through 27 he describes problems facing returning veterans including unemployment, lack of medical care, suicide, and so forth. While he does not detail a solution, he clearly implies the need for increased governmental support.

In developing these positions, Kerry faced severe rhetorical barriers and lacked significant rhetorical advantages. One problem was that the Vietnam War had been the most important issue facing the nation since the middle 1960s. By 1971, people had heard every possible position on the war. Therefore, it would be difficult for Kerry to come up with new material to influence the audience. A second barrier was Kerry's lack of expertise. Kerry was not a foreign policy specialist. Nor was he a high officer in Vietnam. This left Kerry in the difficult position of speaking to a committee that over the years had heard testimony from the most qualified experts in the nation. Kerry seemed to recognize this problem when he noted in paragraph 13 that "I don't want to go into the foreign policy aspects because I am outclassed here."

Finally, Kerry faced the public perception that war protesters were unpatriotic, a problem that he faced again in the 2004 election. Throughout American history, those who opposed a given war have been labeled as unpatriotic. Kerry clearly was aware of this problem in regard to opposition to the war in Vietnam. In paragraph 10, he cited a statement attacking protesters by then Vice President Spiro Agnew.

It is important to recognize that pro-war attitudes were not a primary barrier facing Kerry because he was not aiming his rhetoric at those strongly on the other side of the Vietnam issue. Kerry would have had little chance of persuading a strong supporter of the war to change his/her mind. Thus, he focused on those whose views were not totally fixed, as well as on reinforcing the positions of those who already opposed the war. It is noteworthy that Kerry possessed no significant rhetorical advantages in presenting his testimony.

In confronting the barriers I have described, Kerry clearly relies on internal credibility as a primary strategy. He also utilizes a strategy closely related to credibility—rhetorical redefinition. Of course, Kerry relies on other strategies as well. He uses the language strategy of detailed depiction to make the conflict come alive for the audience. He also uses a powerful metaphor/allusion, which I will discuss in a moment, to support the redefinition strategy. And Kerry also appeals to the values of the audience. However, the dominant strategies are the attempt to increase credibility and the redefinition of the nature of the conflict.

Kerry's Use of Internal Credibility

Kerry builds internal credibility in several ways. First, he emphasizes that he is testifying as a member of a much larger group of veterans. In the first paragraph of his testimony, he states "I am here as one member of the group of 1,000, which is a small representation of a very much larger group of veterans in this country, and were it possible for all of them to sit at this table they would be here and have the same kind of testimony." With this statement, Kerry emphasizes that there are many more veterans who support the same position that he does on Vietnam.

Second, Kerry argues that the anti-war veterans did their duty and now have returned to this nation to do their duty again, by fighting to end the war. In the first paragraph, he refers to "the men behind me who are also wearing the uniforms and their medals." A picture of Kerry at the table in the Senate hearing room shows that he too was wearing a uniform with medals. Thus, Kerry is representing a group of veterans who were willing to sacrifice for the nation. In paragraph 7, he emphasizes that the sacrifice continues with his testimony. First, he notes that "we could be quiet; we could hold our silence." Later he adds that the veterans see the problem as so large that "we have to speak out."

Third, Kerry picks inclusive pronouns to consistently remind the committee that he is speaking for a host of other veterans. For example, in paragraph 7 alone, he uses "we" nine times to refer to the actions of his organization. In so doing, Kerry emphasizes that his testimony should be understood as reflecting the experiences of thousands of veterans.

Fourth, Kerry emphasizes the importance of experience over expertise in relation to understanding the Vietnam War. I already have noted that Kerry admitted to the committee that he was "outclassed" on foreign policy issues. But on the events in Vietnam, Kerry implicitly argues that those who have been there know more than those who haven't. He begins to emphasize this theme very early in the statement in the third paragraph, where he describes how his group "had an investigation at which over 150 honorably discharged and many very highly decorated veterans testified to war crimes committed in Southeast Asia." Then throughout the testimony, Kerry emphasizes that his experience and that of his fellow veterans does not match with what the "experts" or supporters of the Nixon administration were saying. For example, in paragraph 12, he explains, "In our opinion, and from our experience, there is nothing in South Vietnam, nothing which could happen that realistically threatens the United States of America." Later, in paragraphs 17 through 19, he describes the experience of veterans with destroying villages, free fire zones in which innocent people were killed, and falsified body counts. Implicitly, throughout the speech, Kerry emphasizes the fact that the veterans had been there and seen the war with their own eyes and that they were right, while the experts, who lacked personal experience, were wrong.

Fifth, Kerry uses reluctant testimony to add to the credibility of his group. Reluctant testimony is a special type of internal credibility strategy in which the rhetor states some sort of claim that goes against his/her interest to demonstrate the honesty of the position. It would be reluctant testimony if one of the members of the Coors family went to Congress to testify in favor of restrictions on beer sales. In this instance, Kerry uses reluctant testimony (as well as emphasizing the importance of experience over expertise), in paragraph 5, where he cites horrible actions committed by members of his group:

> They told the stories at times they had personally raped, cut off ears, cut off heads, taped wires from portable telephones to human genitals and turned up the power, cut off limbs, blown up bodies, randomly shot at civilians, razed villages in fashion reminiscent of Genghis Khan, shot cattle and dogs for fun, poisoned food stocks, and generally ravaged the countryside of South Vietnam.

It might at first seem that Kerry would damage his credibility by admitting that members of his group had committed these terrible acts. However, his very willingness to admit to the acts is a sign of his fundamental honesty. In addition, Kerry makes it very clear, as I will explain in a moment, that the primary cause of these actions was the war itself. In paragraph 4, immediately prior to the statement I just cited, Kerry refers to the "horror" experienced by the veterans, a "horror of what this country, in a sense, made them do."

In summary, Kerry utilizes internal credibility as a primary strategy in his testimony. He emphasizes that he is a representative of a large group of honorably discharged veterans who did their duty in Vietnam and who are doing it again. In so doing, he implicitly argues that priority should be given to experience over expertise. And he uses reluctant testimony to demonstrate that the veterans must be telling the truth.

Kerry's use of credibility strategies, especially his emphasis on the power of eyewitness testimony of people who were there, skillfully responded to the rhetorical barriers that he confronted. He used this strategy to provide new information to the senators and also to devalue any testimony that they might hear from "experts." The statement "we were there and the experts weren't" was then and remains a powerful strategy.

Kerry's Use of Redefinition

Redefinition occurs when a rhetor takes a commonly understood definition of a situation or concept and changes our understanding of it. He or she "re"defines what the situation means in order to give the audience a better way of understanding an issue. Redefinition is used to change the way the audience thinks about the claim. Kerry relies on three related instances of redefinition. He redefines what it means to be an American soldier. He redefines what it means to be a war protester. And he redefines what it means to be a military leader in the Vietnam War.

The first level of redefinition occurs in relation to American soldiers. For many, probably most Americans at the time, the dominant image of an American soldier had been established by World War II and the depictions of that war in the media. From that vantage point, an American soldier was brave, honorable, competent, and essentially moral. American soldiers did not commit atrocities; they helped kids. Many Hollywood movies reinforced this image. American soldiers were John Wayne or Jimmy Stewart, quintessentially American in terms of competence and morality. Kerry radically rejects the stereotype of who American soldiers are and what they do.

I already cited Kerry's discussion of the terrible atrocities committed in Vietnam. Crucially, Kerry does not argue that American soldiers are themselves evil. Rather, he argues that the war has "created a monster, a monster in the form of millions of men who have been taught to deal and to trade in violence, and who are given the chance to die for the biggest nothing in history" (paragraph 8). Kerry is arguing that the war is evil, not just because of what it is doing to the people of South Vietnam, but also because of what it is doing to our soldiers. In this way, he gives the senators a strong reason to oppose the war based on self-interest. Tragically, Kerry's view has been confirmed many times over the several decades since he testified, when veterans of the Vietnam War suffering from various mental illnesses have committed often terrible crimes. Kerry was right; it wasn't them, it was the war. The same thing happened during the wars in Iraq and Afghanistan and to veterans of those wars.

Kerry uses a similar strategy in relation to the image of war protesters. In my discussion of barriers, I noted the common perception that war protesters are unpatriotic. Kerry turns around this view and redefines protesters as the true patriots. He cites an attack on protesters by Vice President Agnew, who labeled protesters as "criminal misfits" (paragraph 10), and then states that "those he calls misfits were standing up for us [soldiers in Vietnam] in a way that nobody else in this country dared to, because so many who have died would have returned to this country to join the misfits in their efforts to ask for an immediate withdrawal from South Vietnam" (paragraph 11).

Kerry also uses the redefinition strategy in relation to his own group, Vietnam Veterans Against the War. In paragraph 6, he explains to the committee that:

> We call this investigation the "Winter Soldier Investigation." The term "Winter Soldier" is a play on words of Thomas Paine in 1776 when he spoke of the Sunshine Patriot and the summertime soldiers who deserted at Valley Forge because the going was rough.

In the next paragraph, he adds that "We who have come here to Washington have come here because we feel we have to be winter soldiers now." It is as "winter soldiers" that they oppose the war. They are doing their duty by telling the country about the hard truths of what really is going on in Vietnam.

The "winter soldier" section combines an allusion, a metaphor, and redefinition. The allusion is to the work of Thomas Paine, who was one of the most important writers during the American Revolution. Kerry draws on Paine to create the metaphor of the "winter soldier." A "winter soldier" was there at Valley Forge in the snow. The "sunshine patriot" marched in April and May, but was gone by December. But the "winter soldier" stayed and did his job. Kerry is arguing that like the soldiers at Valley Forge, his group of veterans is composed of "winter soldiers." They are not anti-American protesters, but the true patriots, who know the importance of telling the truth to the American people. It is ironic and tragic that in the 2004 election campaign, Kerry's words which expressed his patriotism in a profound way would be twisted to claim that he was anti-American. His point was that sometimes an American patriot opposes a war because it is a terrible idea.

The third level of redefinition relates to the country's military leaders in the war. Throughout our history, from Washington to Colin Powell to David Petraeus, Americans have tended to idolize our most successful military leaders. In contrast to the view of military leaders as heroes, Kerry redefines their role in Vietnam as decidedly unheroic. In fact, he says that the leaders in Vietnam are deserters. In paragraphs 37 and 38, he makes this redefinition quite clear:

> We are also here to ask, and we are here to ask vehemently, where are the leaders of our country? Where is the leadership? We are here to ask where are McNamara, Rostow, Bundy, Gilpatric and so many others? Where are they now that we, the men whom they sent off to war, have returned? These are commanders who have deserted their troops, and there is no more serious crime in the law of war. The army says they never leave their wounded.
>
> The Marines say they never leave even their dead. These men have left all the casualties and retreated behind a pious shield of public rectitude.

Here, Kerry attacks four of the main leaders who got the United States involved in the war. Robert McNamara was Secretary of Defense. Walt Rostow was Lyndon Johnson's chief of staff. McGeorge Bundy worked for the National Security Council and Roswell Gilpatric was Deputy Secretary of Defense.

At this point, the redefinition is complete. The leaders who sent the soldiers to Vietnam are not heroes, but deserters. The soldiers in Vietnam are not moral and heroic, but monsters in the making. And those who protest the war are not unpatriotic, but the true patriots. Kerry's redefinition was perfectly consonant with his credibility strategies and a powerful response to the rhetorical barriers he faced.

Evaluation of Kerry's Testimony

Kerry's use of redefinition, internal ethos, and other supporting strategies was well-designed to overcome the barriers that he faced in his testimony before the Senate committee. With the credibility and redefinition strategies, Kerry tried to give the committee a new way to think about the war. By privileging personal experience over other forms of evidence, he also gave the committee new information and undercut the view that experts knew best. In addition, Kerry's use of redefinition was well-designed to confront negative attitudes toward protesters. He showed the committee that members of his group and other protesters were anything but anti-American; they were true patriots.

Overall, Kerry's testimony was carefully crafted to overcome the barriers that he faced. This does not mean that Kerry actually changed a single mind, although he may well have done so. There is no external evidence that bears on this question. But it is fair to conclude that Kerry did a superior job of adapting to a difficult rhetorical situation.

Kerry's eloquence in his testimony in 1971 exists in contrast to what many viewed as a lackluster presidential campaign in 2004, in which Kerry's remarks generally sounded as if they had been carefully scripted by campaign consultants. Where was the eloquence that he demonstrated in 1971? The answer may relate to a lack of perceived authenticity. Agree with him or disagree with him, in 1971 Kerry came across as someone passionately committed to his cause. In 2004, in contrast, many found his rhetoric uninspiring. The difference between the two periods relates to authenticity. When we perceive someone as authentic, we tend to trust them, even if we also disagree with them on particular issues. On the other hand, if someone is perceived as telling us what we want to hear, this may harm their credibility by making them seem inauthentic. Kerry's inability to persuade the American people about his authenticity in 2004 clearly was a major factor in the election.

BARBARA JORDAN AND ENACTMENT

In 1976, Barbara Jordan, then a member of the House of Representatives from Texas, presented one of the most famous convention keynote addresses of the 20th century. According to Wayne Thompson, both press and public reaction were overwhelmingly positive. He cites a Harris poll that found 54 percent of those responding were positive about the speech against only 9 percent negative, along with strong praise from media commentators.[8] Thompson concludes that the address "held unusually high attention" and was a "most resoundingly heartfelt ovation."[9] The address is still remembered as one of the most important convention speeches of the second half of the 20th century. It made such an impact that Democrats invited her back at later conventions as one among several keynote speakers.

Barbara Jordan's Keynote Address to the Democratic National Convention

July 14, 1976

Thank you ladies and gentlemen for a very warm reception. 1

It was one hundred and forty-four years ago that members of the Democratic Party 2
first met in convention to select a presidential candidate. Since that time, Democrats
have continued to convene once every four years and draft a party platform and
nominate a presidential candidate. And our meeting this week is a continuation of
that tradition.

But there is something different about tonight. There is something special about 3
tonight. What is different? What is special? I, Barbara Jordan, am a keynote speaker.

A lot of years have passed since 1832, and during that time it would have been 4
most unusual for any national political party to ask a Barbara Jordan to deliver a
keynote address... but tonight here I am. And I feel that notwithstanding the past that
my presence here is one additional piece of evidence that the American dream need
not forever be deferred.

Now... now that I have this grand distinction, what in the world am I supposed to 5
say?

I could easily spend this time praising the accomplishments of this party and 6
attacking the Republicans but I don't choose to do that.

I could list the many problems which Americans have. I could list the problems 7
which cause people to feel cynical, angry, frustrated: problems which include lack
of integrity in government; the feeling that the individual no longer counts; the reality
of material and spiritual poverty; the feeling that the grand American experiment is
failing or has failed. I could recite these problems and then I could sit down and offer
no solutions. But I don't choose to do that either.

The citizens of America expect more. They deserve and they want more than a 8
recital of problems.

We are a people in a quandary about the present. We are a people in search of our 9
future. We are a people in search of a national community.

We are a people trying not only to solve the problems of the present: unemployment, 10
inflation... but we are attempting on a larger scale to fulfill the promise of America. We
are attempting to fulfill our national purpose; to create and sustain a society in which
all of us are equal.

Throughout... throughout our history, when people have looked for new ways to 11
solve their problems, and to uphold the principles of this nation, many times they have
turned to political parties. They have often turned to the Democratic Party.

What is it... what is it about the Democratic Party that makes it the instrument 12
the people use when they search for ways to shape their future? Well, I believe the

answer to that question lies in our concept of governing. Our concept of governing is derived from our view of people. It is a concept deeply rooted in a set of beliefs firmly etched in the national conscience of all of us.

Now what are these beliefs? 13

First, we believe in equality for all and privileges for none. This a belief, this is a belief that each American regardless of background has equal standing in the public forum, all of us. Because… because we believe this idea so firmly, we are an inclusive rather than an exclusive party. Let everybody come. 14

I think it no accident that most of those immigrating to America in the nineteenth century identified with the Democratic Party. We are a heterogenous party made up of Americans of diverse backgrounds. 15

We believe that the people are the source of governmental power; that the authority of the people is to be extended, not restricted. This, this can be accomplished only by providing each citizen with every opportunity to participate in the management of the government. They must have that, we believe. 16

We believe that the government which represents the authority of all the people, not just one interest group, but all the people, has an obligation to actively, underscore actively, seek to remove those obstacles which would block individual achievement… obstacles emanating from race, sex, economic condition. The government must remove them, seek to remove them. 17

We, we are a party of innovation. We do not reject our traditions, but we are willing to adapt to changing circumstances, when change we must. We are willing to suffer the discomfort of change in order to achieve a better future. 18

We have a positive vision of the future founded on the belief that the gap between the promise and reality of America can one day be finally closed. We believe that. 19

This, my friends, is the bedrock of our concept of governing. This is a part of the reason why Americans have turned to the Democratic Party. These are the foundations upon which a national community can be built. 20

Let all understand that these guiding principles cannot be discarded for short-term political gains. They represent what this country is all about. They are indigenous to the American idea. And these are principles which are not negotiable. 21

In other times, in other times, I could stand here and give this kind of exposition on the beliefs of the Democratic Party and that would be enough. But today this is not enough. People want more. That is not sufficient reason for the majority of the people of this country to decide to vote Democratic. We have made mistakes. We realize that. We admit our mistakes. In our haste to do all things for all people, we did not foresee the full consequences of our actions. And when the people raised their voices, we didn't hear. But our deafness was only a temporary condition, and not an irreversible condition. 22

Even as I stand here and admit that we have made mistakes, I still believe that as the people of America sit in judgment on each party, they will recognize that our mistakes were mistakes of the heart. They'll recognize that. 23

And now, now we must look to the future. Let us heed the voice of the people and   24
recognize their common sense. If we do not, we not only blaspheme our political
heritage, we ignore the common ties that bind all Americans.

Many fear the future. Many are distrustful of their leaders, and believe that their   25
voices aren't ever heard. Many seek only to satisfy their private work… wants, to
satisfy their private interests.

But this is the great danger America faces. That we will cease to be one nation and   26
become instead a collection of interest groups: city against suburb, region against
region, individual against individual. Each seeking to satisfy private wants.

If that happens, who then will speak for America?   27

Who then will speak for the common good?   28

This is the question which must be answered in 1976.   29

Are we to be one people bound together by common spirit sharing in a common   30
endeavor or will we become a divided nation?

For all of its uncertainty, we cannot flee the future. We must not become the new   31
puritans and reject our society. We must address and master the future together. It
can be done if we restore the belief that we share a sense of national endeavor. It
can be done.

There is no executive order; there is no law that can require the American people   32
to form a national community. This we must do as individuals, and if we do it as
individuals, there is no President of the United States who can veto that decision.

As a first step, as a first step, we must restore our belief in ourselves. We are a   33
generous people so why can't we be generous with each other? We need to take to
heart the words spoken by Thomas Jefferson:

"Let us restore the social intercourse, let us restore to social intercourse that
harmony and that affection without which liberty and even life are but dreary
things."

A nation is formed by the willingness of each of us to share in the responsibility for   34
upholding the common good.

A government is invigorated when each one of us is willing to participate in shaping   35
the future of this nation.

In this election year we must define the common good and begin again to shape   36
a common future. Let each person do his or her part. If one citizen is unwilling to
participate, all of us are going to suffer. For the American idea, though it is shared by
all of us, is realized in each one of us.

And now, what are those of us who are elected public officials supposed to do? We   37
call ourselves public servants, but I'll tell you this: we as public servants must set an
example for the rest of the nation. It is hypocritical for the public official to admonish
and exhort the people to uphold the common good if we are derelict in upholding the
common good. More is required, more is required of public officials than slogans and

handshakes and press releases. More is required. We must hold ourselves strictly accountable. We must provide the people with the vision of the future.

If we promise as public officials, we must deliver. If . . . if we as public officials propose, we must produce. If we say to the American people, it is time for you to be sacrificial, sacrifice, if the public official says that, we [public officials] must be the first to give. We must be. And again, if we make mistakes, we must be willing to admit them. We have to do that. What we have to do is strike a balance between the idea that government should do everything and the idea, the belief, that government ought to do nothing. Strike a balance. 38

Let there be no illusions about the difficulty of forming this type of national community. It's tough, difficult, not easy. But a spirit of harmony will survive in America only if each of us remembers that we share a common destiny. If each of us remembers, when self-interest and bitterness seem to prevail, that we share a common destiny. 39

I have confidence that we can form this kind of national community. 40

I have confidence that the Democratic Party can lead the way. I have that confidence. We cannot improve on the system of government handed down to us by the founders of the Republic, there is no way to improve upon that. But what we can do is to find new ways to implement that system and realize our destiny. 41

Now, I began this speech by commenting to you on the uniqueness of a Barbara Jordan making a keynote address. Well, I am going to close my speech by quoting a Republican president, and I ask that as you listen to these words of Abraham Lincoln, relate to them to the concept of a national community in which every last one of us participates: "As I would not be a slave, so I would not be a master. This . . . this, this expresses my idea of Democracy. Whatever differs from this, to the extent of the difference is no Democracy." Thank you. 42

Why did the speech produce such a strong reaction? One partial explanation undoubtedly relates to Jordan's powerful delivery. Jordan had such a rich, deep, resonant voice that in reporting on one of her speeches, the late Peter Jennings once compared her to "the voice of God." While delivery is rarely a major factor in the success of a speech, in this case it undoubtedly played a role.

Professor Thompson suggests that an additional reason for her success was a "skillful use of appeal to values."[10] There is no doubt that Jordan uses value appeals throughout her address. In paragraphs 7 and 8 she rejects a focus on problems alone and instead calls for a "search" for "a national community" (paragraph 9). Later, she endorses equality (paragraphs 10, 14), diversity (paragraphs 15–17), innovation (paragraph 18), a positive vision (paragraph 19), common sense (paragraph 24), unity and the common good (paragraphs 28–35), accountability for public officials (paragraphs 37–38), and confidence in the future (paragraphs 40–41).

Despite her reliance on value appeals, it seems unlikely that this strategy explains the success of her address. The problem is that everyone agrees with the values she endorses. A conservative Republican could have presented virtually the same speech, from the beginning of the focus on values to the conclusion. In fact, in the conclusion she memorably quotes a Republican, President Abraham Lincoln:

> As I would not be a slave, so I would not be a master. This. . . this, this expresses my idea of Democracy. Whatever differs from this, to the extent of the difference is no Democracy. (paragraph 42)

Lincoln's definition of democracy is eloquent, but hardly controversial. Given the standard character of Jordan's value appeals it is hard to see why they would energize her audience.

If the explanation of the success for Jordan's address cannot be found in the main body or conclusion, which both were dominated by the value appeals, it must lie in what she said in the introduction. In paragraphs 2, 3, and 4 of her address, Jordan uses the rhetorical strategy of enactment to create one of the most memorable moments in any American political speech of the last half century. Enactment is a strategy in which the speaker uses himself/herself as proof of the point he/she is making. In this case, Jordan's very presence on the podium as a keynoter is used to demonstrate the fact that the Democratic Party stands for equality, freedom, diversity, and the other values she identifies. Jordan uses the fact that she is a black woman from the South to prove her point.

> It was one hundred and forty-four years ago that members of the Democratic Party first met in convention to select a presidential candidate. Since that time, Democrats have continued once every four years and draft a party platform and nominate a presidential candidate. And our meeting this week is a continuation of that tradition.

> But there is something different about tonight. There is something special about tonight. What is different? What is special? I, Barbara Jordan, am a keynote speaker.

> A lot of years have passed since 1832, and during that time it would have been most unusual for any national political party to ask a Barbara Jordan to deliver a keynote address...but tonight here I am. And I feel that notwithstanding the past that my presence here is one additional piece of evidence that the American dream need not forever be deferred (paragraphs 2–4).

With these words, Jordan enacts her message in a way that establishes both her personal authenticity and that of her party. She is the proof that the Democratic Party has broken with a past in which minorities and women were not allowed representation. It was her presence and the wonderful introduction, especially her reference to the American Dream, that made the speech so memorable.

And Jordan herself seemed to recognize that it was her presence that was most important in sending a message about what it meant to be a Democrat. Immediately after the wonderful introduction, Jordan asks, "now that I have this grand distinction, what in the world am I supposed to say?" (paragraph 5). In actuality, it made little difference what she had to say from that point on in the speech. Her utterly conventional recital of basic values was perfectly appropriate, although hardly memorable. But the introduction where she enacted the basic message of the party was a very memorable use of enactment as a special type of credibility.

In the most eloquent line in the introduction, Jordan referred to her presence on the podium as "one additional piece of evidence that the American dream need not forever be deferred." On that point, she was surely right. Thirty-two years after her address, a very short period in the life of a great nation, Barack Obama would accept the Democratic nomination for president of the United States and later that fall be elected the first African American president of the United States.

CONCLUSION

One of the most important principles in understanding rhetoric is that it isn't just the words (and other symbols) that speak to an audience, but the person behind those words. In some cases, especially those in which a person possesses a great deal of external credibility, the mere fact that a given individual favors a position may be enough for an audience. The flip side of this principle is that once credibility has been lost, it matters very little what you have to say. The audience isn't going to listen to you. Thus, credibility is occasionally a decisive strategy, always necessary for persuasion, and in many cases an important strategy for producing persuasion.

FOR FURTHER DISCUSSION

The two samples of rhetoric from Senator John McCain and Secretary of Defense James Mattis that are included both testify to the power and importance of credibility in rhetoric. I noted earlier in this chapter that Senator John McCain was admired not just by Republicans but also by many Democrats and independents. Senator McCain fought for the United States in Vietnam and then served the nation for decades first in the House of Representatives and then the Senate. In a final statement just before he died from brain cancer, Senator McCain both drew upon and enacted credibility in speaking to the nation.

Secretary of Defense James Mattis was widely known for his honesty and commitment to serving the nation. In December of 2018, after President Trump ordered that American troops be pulled out of Syria where they were assisting in a battle against the terrorist group ISIS, Mattis resigned as principled protest against that policy decision and more generally because he believed that continued support for NATO and other American allies was essential and that President Trump was undercutting these alliances.[11] After carefully outlining the statements using the descriptive analysis form, answer the following questions:

1   What credibility strategies do Mattis and McCain use in their messages?
2   What non-credibility strategies do Mattis and McCain use? Are they consistent with their use of credibility?

3 What barriers will Mattis and McCain face in presenting their messages to the American people?

4 On balance, do Mattis and McCain successfully overcome the barriers to achieve their purposes?

Farewell Statement from Senator John McCain

My fellow Americans, whom I have gratefully served for sixty years, and especially my fellow Arizonans, 1

Thank you for the privilege of serving you and for the rewarding life that service in uniform and in public office has allowed me to lead. I have tried to serve our country honorably. I have made mistakes, but I hope my love for America will be weighed favorably against them. 2

I have often observed that I am the luckiest person on earth. I feel that way even now as I prepare for the end of my life. I have loved my life, all of it. I have had experiences, adventures, and friendships enough for ten satisfying lives, and I am so thankful. Like most people, I have regrets. But I would not trade a day of my life, in good or bad times, for the best day of anyone else's. 3

I owe that satisfaction to the love of my family. And I owe it to America. To be connected to America's causes—liberty, equal justice, respect for the dignity of all people—brings happiness more sublime than life's more fleeting pleasures. Our identities and sense of worth are not circumscribed but enlarged by serving good causes bigger than ourselves. 4

"Fellow Americans"—that association has meant more to me than any other. I lived and died a proud American. We are citizens of the world's greatest republic, a nation of ideals, not blood and soil. We are blessed and are a blessing to humanity when we uphold and advance those ideals at home and in the world. We have helped liberate more people from tyranny and poverty than ever before in history. We have acquired great wealth and power in the process. 5

We weaken our greatness when we confuse our nationalism with tribal rivalries that have sown resentment and hatred and violence in all the corners of the globe. We weaken it when we hide behind walls, rather than tear them down, when we doubt the power of our ideals, rather than trust them to be the great force for change they have always been. 6

We are three hundred and twenty-five million opinionated, vociferous individuals. We argue and compete and sometimes even vilify each other in our raucous public debates. But we have always had so much more in common with each other than in disagreement. If only we remember that and give each other the benefit of the presumption that we all love our country, we will get through these challenging times. We will come through them stronger than before. We always do. 7

Senator John McCain, "Farewell Statement" as released by McCain's office two days after his death.

Ten years ago, I had the privilege to concede defeat in the election for president.   8
I want to end my farewell to you with the heartfelt faith in Americans that I felt so
powerfully that evening.

I feel it powerfully still.   9

Do not despair of our present difficulties but believe always in the promise and   10
greatness of America, because nothing is inevitable here. Americans never quit. We
never surrender. We never hide from history. We make history.

Farewell, fellow Americans. God bless you, and God bless America.   11

Secretary of Defense James Mattis Pentagon, Washington, DC, December 20, 2018

Dear Mr. President: 1

I have been privileged to serve as our country's 26th Secretary of Defense which   2
has allowed me to serve alongside our men and women of the Department in defense
of our citizens and our ideals.

I am proud of the progress that has been made over the past two years on some of   3
the key goals articulated in our National Defense Strategy: putting the Department on
a more sound budgetary footing, improving readiness and lethality in our forces, and
reforming the Department's business practices for greater performance. Our troops
continue to provide the capabilities needed to prevail in conflict and sustain strong
U.S. global influence.

One core belief I have always held is that our strength as a nation is inextricably   4
linked to the strength of our unique and comprehensive system of alliances and
partnerships. While the US remains the indispensable nation in the free world, we
cannot protect our interests or serve that role effectively without maintaining strong
alliances and showing respect to those allies. Like you, I have said from the beginning
that the armed forces of the United States should not be the policeman of the world.
Instead, we must use all tools of American power to provide for the common defense,
including providing effective leadership to our alliances. NATO's 29 democracies
demonstrated that strength in their commitment to fighting alongside us following the
9-11 attack on America. The Defeat-ISIS coalition of 74 nations is further proof.

Similarly, I believe we must be resolute and unambiguous in our approach to those   5
countries whose strategic interests are increasingly in tension with ours. It is clear that
China and Russia, for example, want to shape a world consistent with their authoritarian
model - gaining veto authority over other nations' economic, diplomatic, and security
decisions - to promote their own interests at the expense of their neighbors, America
and our allies. That is why we must use all the tools of American power to provide for
the common defense.

My views on treating allies with respect and also being clear-eyed about both   6
malign actors and strategic competitors are strongly held and informed by over four
decades of immersion in these issues. We must do everything possible to advance
an international order that is most conducive to our security, prosperity and values,
and we are strengthened in this effort by the solidarity of our alliances.

Because you have the right to have a Secretary of Defense whose views are better   7
aligned with yours on these and other subjects, I believe it is right for me to step
down from my position. The end date for my tenure is February 28, 2019, a date that
should allow sufficient time for a successor to be nominated and confirmed as well
as to make sure the Department's interests are properly articulated and protected at
upcoming events to include Congressional posture hearings and the NATO Defense
Ministerial meeting in February. Further, that a full transition to a new Secretary of
Defense occurs well in advance of the transition of Chairman of the Joint Chiefs of
Staff in September in order to ensure stability within the Department.

I pledge my full effort to a smooth transition that ensures the needs and interests   8
of the 2.15 million Service Members and 732,079 DoD civilians receive undistracted
attention of the Department at all times so that they can fulfill their critical, round-the-
clock mission to protect the American people.

I very much appreciate this opportunity to serve the nation and our men and   9
women in uniform.

1   See Aristotle, *The Rhetoric* in *The Basic Works of Aristotle*, ed. Richard McKeon (New York: Random House, 1941), Book I, Ch. 2, p. 1329.

2   See Edwin P. Bettinighaus and Michael J. Cody, *Persuasive Communication*, 4th ed. (New York: Holt, Rinehart and Winston, 1987), p. 103.

3   See Kenneth Andersen and Theodore Clevenger Jr., "A Summary of Experimental Research in Ethos," in *The Process of Social Influence: Readings in Persuasion*, Thomas D. Beisecker and Donn W. Parson, eds. (Englewood Cliffs: Prentice Hall, 1972), p. 246.

4   Joel Aschenbach, "Did the news media, led by Walter Cronkite, lose the war in Vietnam?" *Washington Post*, May 25, 2018, https://www.washingtonpost.com/national/did-the-news-media-led-by-walter-cronkite-lose-the-war-in-vietnam/2018/05/25/a5b3e098-495e-11e8-827e-190efaf1f1ee_story.html?utm_term=.27beb4ff996a.

5   Aristotle, *The Rhetoric*, Book I, ch. 2, pp. 1329–1330.

6   Gleb Tsipursky, "(Dis)trust in Science: Can we cure the scourge of misinformation?" *Scientific American*, July 5, 2018, https://blogs.scientificamerican.com/observations/dis-trust-in-science/.

7   See for instance Kirk Victor, "The Lone Ranger," *National Journal* 12 April 1997, pp. 694–697.

8   See Wayne N. Thompson, "Barbara Jordan's Keynote Address: The Juxtaposition of Contradictory Values," *Southern Speech Communication Journal* 44 (1979), pp. 223–224.

9   Thompson, p. 223.

10   Thompson, p. 232.

11   Helene Cooper, "Jim Mattis, Defense Secretary, Resigns in Rebuke of Trump's Worldview," *New York Times*, December 20, 2018, https://www.nytimes.com/2018/12/20/us/politics/jim-mattis-defense-secretary-trump.htm.

CHAPTER 7
Aesthetic Strategies

Aesthetics is the study of beauty. How does aesthetics relate to rhetoric? The answer is that there is an aesthetic dimension to rhetoric. A short example may make this point clear. Former President Reagan often emphasized the greatness of America by saying that this nation had a "rendezvous with destiny," a phrase he borrowed from Franklin Roosevelt. Reagan used those words to highlight the history of the nation and to argue that we have a special role to play in the world.

Reagan's idea was important, but of equal importance was the way that he expressed the idea. One of our less articulate presidents might have expressed the same idea by saying that "America always has been on the way to an important destination." While the content is the same, the meaning is radically different because the second phrase lacks the aesthetic power of Reagan's usage.

The key point is that rhetoric persuades not merely with content, but also with the style of the presentation. The dominant means of expressing the aesthetic dimension of rhetoric is through language, but there are other possible devices as well. Film rhetoric might use particular camera angles or the picture itself to present a point. In his famous painting, "Guernica," Picasso used his artistic style to expose the horrors of the Spanish Civil War. There is also obviously an aesthetic dimension to works of persuasive music. While what is said is obviously most important in any work of rhetoric, how it is said matters as well.

TYPES OF AESTHETIC STRATEGIES

There are five main types of aesthetic strategies: language, graphic, objects, pictures, and sound.

Language

Language strategies are the most important type of aesthetic strategy and the bulk of the remainder of this chapter discusses types and functions of them. Linguistic strategies are more important than other aesthetic strategies because language is such a powerful vehicle for carrying both cognitive and artistic meaning. It is much harder to present a message about a complex topic, such as public policy, or an abstraction, like honor or duty, without language. Even in cases where nonlinguistic aesthetic strategies carry such meanings, as for example the national anthem sends a message of patriotism, this occurs through a kind of enthymematic translation. The melody is associated with patriotic moments in American history, with countless ceremonies where it has been played, and therefore the association with those memories sends the patriotic message. This could not happen without language, even if the anthem is played and not sung in a given case.

Graphic

Graphic aesthetic strategies include drawings, bullet points, charts, subheads, underlining, and other devices that are designed to make written rhetoric more persuasive. The primary functions of graphic strategies are to emphasize points and make the material easier to understand. While graphic strategies are important, they are more a supporting than a dominant form of persuasion. No one ever exclaimed after a presentation: "Wow, what bullet points. I'm persuaded!"

Objects

Objects can be used as an aesthetic strategy in a speech or other presentation. After 9/11, objects from ground zero in New York became associated with the heroism demonstrated by first responders. Thus, a chunk of steel from the site could be used to reflect both the terror of the day and the heroism of those who responded. Objects can be used for other purposes as well. A speaker may hold up an object to get the attention of the audience, to clarify the point, or to tap into values or needs. A grisly example of the last strategy occurs when a terrorist shows the media a body part such as a severed finger of a kidnapping victim. The terrorist is using the severed finger to make the point that he/she is willing to kill the hostages.

Pictures

The fourth type of aesthetic strategy is a picture. Still pictures, such as photographs, may be used to visually demonstrate a point. Alternatively, film or video may be used to reveal a situation, support an argument, or tell a story. Pictures, whether still or moving, are used to fulfill a variety of aesthetic functions. A picture may be cited as support for an argument. Since the Gulf War, we have gotten used to seeing footage of bombing raids. Those pictures demonstrate the success or failure of the raid. Alternatively, pictures may be used to tap into values or needs. Both pro-choice and pro-life advocates use pictures to create an emotional response. The pro-life activist uses a picture of a dead fetus to link to the value of life. In contrast, the pro-choice activist uses a picture of a woman in chains to support freedom of choice. Pictures also can be used to emphasize a point or clarify a position. The adage that a "picture is worth a thousand words," is often correct.

Paintings and other artwork also can function rhetorically. Much of the great art of the Western World, from the Middle Ages until at least the beginning of the 19th century, was focused on supporting Christianity. This art was both beautiful and highly rhetorical in that it used the power of aesthetics to link to both Christian narratives and values in support of Christian doctrine.

What should a critic look for in regard to the rhetorical use of pictures? This is a difficult question to answer because so much has been written about art, photography, film, and video. For example, entire books have been written discussing the use of different camera techniques in film and video. An example may make clear how complex film rhetoric can be. At the beginning of *Saving Private Ryan*, Steven Spielberg tries to make us feel as if we were there on Omaha beach on June 6, 1944. He uses a handheld camera and jumps back and forth among different images to give us the feel for the battle. This is only one example of how different camera techniques can influence the way that visual rhetoric functions. And of course, there are many other film and video strategies for producing persuasion.

From the perspective of rhetorical analysis, however, the important point is to describe how the visual strategy functions persuasively. The critic need not know every detail of film theory to make such a judgment. Instead, the key is simply to explain how the image relates to the other strategies in the rhetoric and how the image is likely to have been experienced by the audience. Here, it is important to recognize that there is a great deal more diversity in how people experience images than in how they understand words. The huge variability in the kinds of art or film that different people like is one sign of this point. One reason behind the variability in rhetorical interpretation of pictures (and this applies to the other nonlinguistic aesthetic strategies as well) is that for a picture to send a complex message it has to be translated at some point into words. There is no way to send a message about patriotism with pictures (or music and so forth) alone, because patriotism is a concept. Sometimes that translation process is provided by the dialogue in a movie or a voice-over. In other cases, it occurs internally within the viewer. The key point is that pictures and other nonlinguistic aesthetic devices require translation in order to send complex or abstract messages. That also means that there is a great deal more ground for varied interpretations of such messages than in verbal rhetoric.

Sound

The final type of aesthetic strategy is sound, primarily music. Sound can be used to add interest to a work of rhetoric in the same way that a soundtrack adds interest to a film or television. Sound also can be used to tap into values, needs, or symbols. If you want to get a crowd of alumni from a particular school excited, just play the fight song for their school. In some cases, sound also can be used to support an argument. For example, the "Ode to Joy" sequence in Beethoven's Ninth Symphony is associated with the United Nations. Playing that music could be a means of activating values associated with the UN. However, as this example indicates, music and other nonlinguistic aesthetic strategies are not as efficient at carrying content as are linguistic strategies. Linguistic aesthetic strategies can directly state a message. Nonlinguistic strategies rely on a process of translation to achieve that aim. If audience members don't know of the association between the "Ode to Joy" and the UN, they will not make the connection.

Summary of Types of Aesthetic Strategies

The four nonlanguage aesthetic strategies primarily are used to add interest to and clarify the meaning of a persuasive claim. In some instances, these aesthetic strategies also may be used to tap into one of the other main categories of persuasion. In particular, visual images are a powerful way of building supporting arguments, telling narratives, and tapping into values and needs. It is important to note, however, that visual rhetoric is not different in kind from other rhetoric. In fact, visual rhetoric works through the same strategy categories as do all other forms of rhetoric.

All five types of aesthetic strategies are important. There are cases in which each of these types of aesthetic strategy is the dominant form of persuasion in a given work of rhetoric. However, of the five types, language is far and away the most important. Language is the most important aesthetic strategy for two reasons. First, language is the dominant symbol system which humans use to communicate. Second, as I've explained, each of the other aesthetic strategies must be translated into language in the mind of the audience before it can function to produce persuasion. Take Spielberg's use of camera techniques in *Saving Private Ryan* as an example. Those film techniques give the viewer a sense of the horror and randomness of war and the great heroism of the men who landed in Normandy in June 1944. That visual sense of what they went through could be translated into support for a claim such as "we must never again have to fight such a war" or "we don't do enough for our veterans" or "we should not go to war unless the very security of the nation is at risk." The visual aesthetic strategy is very important, but to reach the level of a persuasive claim, it must be translated into language in the mind of the audience. While each of the messages I mentioned may have been drawn by members of the audience viewing the film, it also seems likely that many millions thought something like "wow, that was cool" and saw no larger implications in the film.

FUNCTIONS OF LANGUAGE STRATEGIES

Language strategies serve several important persuasive functions. First, language strategies may be used to make a point more vivid. A speaker might build an argument concerning genocide in Syria by citing various experts and other forms of support. Alternatively, he/she might combine that argument with a detailed description of one instance of murder. That detailed description might make the argument much more effective because it would hit home with the audience.

Second, language strategies can be used to make a conclusion more understandable and memorable. In this way, the language strategy both can clarify the claim being made and also make it more likely to be remembered. So, for example, a comparison might be used to clarify a complicated policy argument. That comparison could help the audience remember the argument at a later time.

Finally, language strategies can be used to add emphasis to any point. Politicians (and advertisers) use repetition to make their conclusion clear and to emphasize its importance. Think about how many times you have heard a given advertising slogan. Politicians do the same thing.

For example, the familiar chant "No New Taxes" is used by Republicans to distinguish themselves from Democrats and to emphasize their commitment to cutting taxes.

TYPES OF LANGUAGE STRATEGIES

Language strategies can be grouped into the following subcategories:

1 Metaphor and Other Forms of Comparison
2 Antithesis
3 Parallel Structure and Repetition
4 Rhetorical Questions
5 Depiction or Description
6 Personification
7 Rhythm and Rhyme
8 Definition
9 Alliteration and Assonance
10 Allusion
11 Labeling
12 Irony

Metaphor

The most important language strategy is clearly metaphorical usage, including metaphor itself and other forms of comparison such as analogies and similes. A somewhat more complex type of metaphor is a synecdoche in which a part of an object is used to refer to the entire object. In a statement referring to a fleet of ships as "fifty smokestacks on the horizon," the word smokestack is a synecdoche referring to the ships.

Reduced to its simplest form, a comparison says that two objects/ideas/people are similar in some way. When Martin Luther King, Jr. wanted to describe a harmonious future society, he called it a "dream." Both Republicans and Democrats often compare America to a family. In a speech considered in the next chapter, Jesse Jackson compares America to both a "rainbow" and a "quilt." In all of these examples, the speaker is relying on the power of metaphor to identify the inherent similarity between two things or people.

There are two important dimensions to metaphor: degree of development and a literal-figurative distinction. Some metaphors (or analogies or similes) are developed in more detail, while others are left as a single phrase. A politician might spend an entire speech developing an analogy between the economic problems facing the United States today and those that faced the nation on the eve of the Great Depression. On the other hand, a metaphor might simply be thrown out as I did the word "eve" in the previous sentence.

A distinction also can be drawn between figurative and literal forms of comparison. A literal comparison is drawn when the two objects being compared fall into the same category.

Comparisons of two presidents, two football players, two film stars, and so forth all would fall into the literal category because in each case the comparison is between two people from the same category of life. On the other hand, a comparison of Tom Hanks to President Obama would be a figurative comparison because the jobs of movie star and president of the United States are obviously different.

It should be clear that a continuum exists from the purely literal to the purely figurative. For example, a comparison of Meryl Streep to Katherine Hepburn would fall on the literal side of the continuum because both Streep and Hepburn acted in many films. But it would not be a purely literal comparison since the two acted in different eras. On the other hand, a statement such as "love is a rose" obviously falls on the figurative side of the continuum because roses are flowers and love is an emotional reaction. A good gardener sprays fungicide on his/her roses, but not on a significant other.

What are the functions of the various forms of metaphor? Metaphor usage serves two main functions. First, metaphors are often added to works of rhetoric very much as seasoning is added to a dish of food. In this way, the metaphor adds interest to the rhetoric. A speaker or writer might sprinkle a variety of metaphors in a work on pollution in order to make that rhetoric more interesting. Air pollution could be called "an invisible cloud of death." Pollution controls might be labeled "a sure-thing investment," rather than a business expense. In these examples, the comparison functions to make a topic more interesting and vivid.

Second, in some instances metaphor is used, not merely to make a work more interesting, but becomes the underlying core of the work. In these instances, metaphor functions as a worldview for understanding social conditions. For example, a number of United States Supreme Court cases have used a metaphor originally created by Thomas Jefferson to interpret the proper relationship between church and state in this nation. These cases have said that there should be a "wall" separating government from religion. The wall metaphor has functioned as more than a mere comparison.[1] To some extent it has shaped discussion in the courts. For example, some have argued that the wall should be high and wide. Others have argued that the wall should not provide absolute separation, but that there should be gates in it. In this example, the metaphor is functioning as a model for understanding the world.

Another example illustrates this same point. In the 1960s, some African American activists compared poor and mainly black sections of some cities to a colony.[2] With this comparison, they argued that America treated people of color the same way that colonial powers treated natives. The colony metaphor provided a framework for understanding racial conflict; it functioned as a "paradigm" for approaching the world.

In most instances, metaphors and other comparisons are used merely as spice to liven up a work of rhetoric. But it is important to recognize that in some cases comparisons are used as a model or paradigm to reveal the world. Used in this second sense, metaphors are powerful devices that shape human understanding. If you can change someone's metaphors, you can change how that person understands the world.[3]

Antithesis

Antithesis occurs when two opposing thoughts are juxtaposed in the same sentence or paragraph. Earlier I cited John Kennedy's famous statement "Ask not what your country can do for you. Ask what you can do for your country." In this comment, JFK relies on the "not this, but that" form which is common in antithesis to emphasize his point. Antithesis is also often used to draw distinctions between opposing ideas. It also can be a structural strategy, organizing paragraphs, rather than simply being part of a sentence.

Parallel Structure and Repetition

Parallel structure and repetition are closely related strategies that are used to emphasize the importance of a point and make it more memorable. Repetition occurs when a sentence, phrase, or even a single word is repeated. Advertisers do this with slogans. A Democrat might repeat the phrase "protect the elderly, no more cuts" to emphasize his/her commitment to programs like Social Security and Medicare.

Parallel structure is a special form of repetition. It occurs when a speaker/writer begins several paragraphs or sentences in a row with the same sentence structure. Imagine a Democrat defending a variety of social programs. He/she might begin a number of paragraphs by saying: "They say that we cannot afford adequate funding for Medicare, but I say we cannot afford not to fully fund that program." Succeeding paragraphs would begin with the same sentence, but a different program would be inserted in place of Medicare. In such an instance (which is also an example of antithesis), the speaker would be using parallel structure to defend current social programs. The parallel structure would both add interest and make the speech more memorable.

Rhetorical Question

A rhetorical question is a question asked by a speaker/writer which implies an answer. The point of the question is not to elicit information, but to get the audience involved in the presentation. At the end of the "New South" speech, which is included in the readings volume that goes with this book, Henry Grady uses a number of rhetorical questions to gain support from the audience. He asks "Now, what answer has New England to this message? Will she permit the prejudices of war to remain in the hearts of the conquerors, when it has died in the hearts of the conquered?" Grady uses these questions and others to pull the audience to his side. He obviously expects the audience to think or say "NO!" in response to the second rhetorical question. And that is exactly what they did. The questions both drew participation from the audience and also added interest to the speech. Rhetorical questions also often are used as transition devices.

It should be recognized, however, that rhetorical questions are most effective when the rhetor knows how the audience will react. If a speaker asks a rhetorical question expecting the audience to respond, "Yes, Yes, Yes," and instead they shout out "NO," that would be a major problem.

Depiction or Description

Depiction or description is used when the speaker/writer creates a vivid picture of some situation with language. Depiction is the equivalent of a verbal snapshot or a passage setting the scene in a story. It is used to add interest and make a conclusion more vivid. In a courtroom, for example, a prosecutor might use a portion of his/her opening statement to describe a murder in detail. There is no legal requirement to provide this detailed description. Under the law, the prosecutor would need to do no more than prove that the accused criminal had committed the murder. But the prosecutor might describe the crime in great detail in order to get the sympathy of the jury for the victim's family and make them hate the defendant. It may seem counterintuitive, but a skillful speaker or writer can create just as vivid a picture with words as can a filmmaker with images.

Personification

Personification is a strategy in which an inanimate object or concept is given human form. The "Jolly Green Giant" is not a real vegetable, but a personification of all vegetables transformed into a giant person. Personification is a kind of metaphor, which usually takes the form of a reference to some part of human anatomy. Thus, rhetors often refer to the "heart" or "backbone" of a nation. It is primarily a strategy of emphasis, although it is sometimes used to change the connotative meaning associated with a term. A conservative Republican might say, for instance, that "where once labor unions were America's muscle, they now are our beer belly."

Rhythm and Rhyme

Rhythm and rhyme work both to make rhetoric more interesting and also to aid the audience in remembering the point. Since the Greeks, humans have known that rhyme functions as a memory aid. In the era before writing, the power of rhyme was used to help people memorize epic poems and other literature and rhetoric. To some extent this function is still being fulfilled. Today, people find it much easier to remember song lyrics than passages from public speeches, largely because of the rhyme. One place that the power of rhyme is particularly evident is in contemporary rap music.

Rhyme or rhythm (when used in moderation) also can make a work of rhetoric more interesting. Johnny Cochran used a brief rhyme in his closing statement for the defense in the O.J. Simpson trial to bring home a point to the jury, "If the glove don't fit, you must acquit." There is, however, a danger that use of rhyme may seem hokey; that is why this language strategy should be used in moderation.

Definition and Redefinition

Definition works as a language strategy to define the terms under consideration. If you can control the subject of discussion, you often can control the discussion itself. For example, a definitional strategy might be used in a discussion of sexual harassment, either to magnify or minimize the problem. Using a very restrictive definition would reduce the amount of sexual harassment included in the category. On the other hand, use of a broad definition (any remark or action making any person feel uncomfortable) dramatically would expand the size of the problem.

As I explained in relation to the Kerry address considered in the previous chapter, redefinition is used literally to redefine an issue. It is a language strategy designed to get people to see a different reality than they previously had understood. In this way, definition and redefinition can be used to provide the audience with a new way of understanding the world. The strongest form of definition and redefinition is ultimate definition. Definitions or redefinitions can be presented as ideological arguments expressing a worldview. But a definition or redefinition also can be expressed through a narrative. A rhetor might use a story to redefine for the reader life in the Soviet Union as essentially life in a giant prison camp. Finally, definition or redefinition can be expressed in value terms. The strongest form of definition/redefinition is ultimate definition in which a coherent ideological definition of the world is combined with a narrative consonant with the ideological definition and a set of values consistent with the ideology and the narrative.[4]

Alliteration and Assonance

Alliteration is a strategy in which the speaker uses several words in a row all beginning with the same consonant. A liberal Democrat might refer to "callous, cruel, contemporary conservatism." Assonance is a similar strategy in which several words in a row contain the same vowel sound. In his Inaugural Address, which is included in the readings volume, John F. Kennedy refers to the "steady spread of the deadly atom," a phrase in which steady, spread, and deadly contain the same vowel sound.

Assonance is rarely used in contemporary rhetoric and when it is used might not even be noticed by the audience. Alliteration is somewhat more important. Both assonance and alliteration are strategies designed to make rhetoric more interesting. Obviously, no one will be persuaded merely through the use of alliteration or assonance.

Allusion

An allusion is an indirect reference to a work of rhetoric, literature, or history, not a direct quotation. In a speech following the assassination of John F. Kennedy, President Lyndon Johnson alluded to the Gettysburg Address when he said, "So let us here highly resolve that John Fitzgerald Kennedy did not live—or die—in vain."[5] Johnson was referring to a passage in the Gettysburg Address where Lincoln said, "that we here highly resolved that these dead shall not have died in vain"[6] Allusions also may be made to works of literature, history, or even figures in current events. In the 1950s and 1960s, some referred to the danger of aggressive communism in Asia as threatening to create a "bamboo curtain." This phrase combined metaphor with an allusion to the phrase that Winston Churchill used to describe Soviet tyranny in Eastern Europe, an "iron curtain."

Allusion works by tapping into the knowledge of the audience. The audience then fills in the reference. Again, it is a strategy to add interest to the rhetoric. In some instances, allusion also may function as an enthymeme. In that case, the allusion is used to support an implied argumentative judgment. Note that not all allusions are also enthymemes. Some allusions are simply references to other material and make no argument. One obvious weakness of allusion is that it will not work if people don't recognize that another work (or event) is being referenced.

Labeling

A label or slogan can be used to characterize a person, object, idea, or position. A liberal might refer, for example, to "Neanderthal Conservatism," as part of an attack on a budget proposal. The liberal would be using the word "Neanderthal," not as a reference to an earlier species in human evolution, but to label the particular conservative agenda as cruel or uncaring. Note that in this example a metaphor is used as part of the label. Such combination of language strategies in a sort of mix and match approach is common.

Labels are used to reduce a point to a phrase that encapsulates the concept. The label (or slogan) then can be used again and again to hammer the point home. British Prime Minister Margaret Thatcher often used the phrase "nanny state" as a way of encapsulating and critiquing what she saw as overreaching government regulation.

Irony

Irony is a language strategy in which the speaker explicitly says one thing, but means another altogether. A conservative might use irony in referring to a liberal senator as "that well known budget slasher." He/she would be implying that the senator was anything but a budget slasher; he/she was in fact a big spender.

In recent years, Jon Stewart probably has been the most skillful user of irony in the United States. Night after night, he skewered politicians of the left (and mostly) right with devastating ironic commentary. Irony is closely related to allusion and enthymematic argument since it relies on audience knowledge. But irony is somewhat different from these other strategies. Irony undercuts a position by poking fun at it. It is a strategy used primarily to add interest and depends upon audience knowledge in order to be successful. It is also important to recognize that irony is a risky strategy because it depends upon audience knowledge and also because it can produce backlash in the audience. Irony is also a limited strategy in that it is a powerful way of undercutting a position or politician, but not an effective way of building up support for action. Irony inherently subverts. It does not build up. There is a real danger that excessive reliance on irony creates a sense that nothing works, that the entire system is a failure. That perspective can be corrosive of a group or even nation's sense that productive change is possible. It is notable that when then-Senator Barack Obama created a huge national movement supporting his campaign for president he did it by tapping into "hope" for a better world. One cannot do that with irony.

ANALYSIS OF MARIO CUOMO'S 1984 KEYNOTE ADDRESS

To illustrate the various language strategies discussed in this chapter, a speech by former Governor Mario Cuomo of New York is included. The speech was presented at the 1984 Democratic National Convention in San Francisco and has been recognized as one of the most important convention speeches of the 20th century. Cuomo used a variety of language strategies to defend the Democratic ticket and attack the Reagan administration.

Keynote Address
1984 Democratic National Convention
Mario Cuomo

On behalf of the Empire State and the family of New York, I thank you for the great privilege of being allowed to address this convention.   1

Please allow me to skip the stories and the poetry and the temptation to deal in nice but vague rhetoric.   2

Let me instead use this valuable opportunity to deal with the questions that should determine this election and that are vital to the American people.   3

Ten days ago, President Reagan admitted that although some people in this country seemed to be doing well nowadays, others were unhappy, and even worried, about themselves, their families and their futures.   4

The President said he didn't understand that fear. He said, "Why, this country is a shining city on a hill."   5

The President is right. In many ways we are "a shining city on a hill."   6

But the hard truth is that not everyone is sharing in this city's splendor and glory.   7

A shining city is perhaps all the President sees from the portico of the White House and the veranda of his ranch, where everyone seems to be doing well.   8

But there's another part of the city, the part where some people can't pay their mortgages and most young people can't afford one, where students can't afford the education they need and middle-class parents watch the dreams they hold for their children evaporate.   9

In this part of the city there are more poor than ever, more families in trouble. More and more people who need help but can't find it.   10

Even worse: There are elderly people who tremble in the basements of the houses there.   11

There are people who sleep in the city's streets, in the gutter, where the glitter doesn't show.   12

Delivered in San Francisco, on July 17, 1984.

There are ghettos where thousands of young people, without an education or a job, give their lives away to drug dealers every day. 13

There is despair, Mr. President, in faces you never see, in the places you never visit in your shining city. 14

In fact, Mr. President, this nation is more a "Tale of Two Cities" than it is a "Shining City on a Hill." 15

Maybe if you visited more places, Mr. President, you'd understand. 16

Maybe if you went to Appalachia where some people still live in sheds and to Lackawanna where thousands of unemployed steel workers wonder why we subsidized foreign steel while we surrender their dignity to unemployment and to welfare checks; maybe if you stepped into a shelter in Chicago and talked with some of the homeless there; maybe, Mr. President if you asked a woman who'd been denied the help she needs to feed her children because you say we need the money to give a tax break to a millionaire or to build a missile we can't even afford to use—maybe then you'd understand. 17

Maybe, Mr. President. 18

But I'm afraid not. 19

Because, the truth is, this is how we were warned it would be. 20

President Reagan told us from the beginning that he believes in a kind of social Darwinism. Survival of the fittest. "Government can't do everything," we were told. "So it should settle for taking care of the strong and hope that economic ambition and charity will do the rest. Make the rich richer and what falls from their table will be enough for the middle class and those trying to make it into the middle class." 21

The Republicans called it trickle-down when Hoover tried it. Now they call it supply side. It is the same shining city for those relative few who are lucky enough to live in its good neighborhoods. 22

But for the people who are excluded—locked out—all they can do is to stare from a distance at the city's glimmering towers. 23

It's an old story, as old as our history. 24

The difference between Democrats and Republicans has always been measured in courage and confidence. The Republicans believe the wagon train will not make it to the frontier unless some of our old, some of our young and some of our weak are left behind by the side of the trail. 25

The strong will inherit the land! 26

We Democrats believe that we can make it all the way with the whole family intact. 27

We have. More than once. 28

Ever since Franklin Roosevelt lifted himself from his wheelchair to lift the nation from its knees. Wagon train after wagon train. To new frontiers of education, housing, peace. The whole family aboard. Constantly reaching out to extend and enlarge that family. Lifting them up into the wagon on the way. Blacks and Hispanics, people of 29 every ethnic group, and Native Americans—all those struggling to build their families claim some small share of America.

For nearly 50 years we carried them to new levels of comfort, security, dignity, even affluence.   30

Some of us are in this room today only because this nation had that confidence.   31

It would be wrong to forget that.   32

So, we are at this convention to remind ourselves where we come from and to claim the future for ourselves and for our children.   33

Today, our great Democratic Party, which has saved this nation from depression, from fascism, from racism, from corruption, is called upon to do it again—this time to save the nation from confusion and division, most of all from a fear of a nuclear holocaust.   34

In order to succeed, we must answer our opponent's polished and appealing rhetoric with a more telling reasonableness and rationality.   35

We must win this case on the merits.   36

We must get the American public to look past the glitter, beyond the showmanship—to reality, to the hard substance of things. And we will do that not so much with speeches that sound good as with speeches that are good and sound.   37

Not so much with speeches that bring people to their feet as with speeches that bring people to their senses.   38

We must make the American people hear our "tale of two cities."   39

We must convince them that we don't have to settle for two cities, that we can have one city, indivisible, shining for all its people.   40

We will have no chance to do that if what comes out of the convention, what is heard throughout the campaign, is a babel of arguing voices.   41

To succeed we will have to surrender small parts of our individual interests, to build a platform we can all stand on, at once, comfortably, proudly singing out the truth for the nation to hear, in chorus, its logic so clear and commanding that no slick commercial, no amount of geniality, no martial music will be able to muffle it.   42

We Democrats must unite so that the entire nation can. Surely the Republicans won't bring the convention together. Their policies divide the nation: into the lucky and the left-out, the royalty and the rabble.   43

The Republicans are willing to treat that division as victory. They would cut this nation in half, into those temporarily better off and those worse off than before, and call it recovery.   44

We should not be embarrassed or dismayed if the process of unifying is difficult, even at times wrenching.   45

Unlike any other party, we embrace men and women of every color, every creed, every orientation, every economic class. In our family are gathered everyone from the abject poor of Essex County in New York to the enlightened affluent of the gold   46 coasts of both ends of our nation. And in between is the heart of our constituency. The middle class, the people not rich enough to be worry-free but not poor enough to be on welfare, those who work for a living because they have to. White collar and blue collar. Young professionals. Men and women in small business desperate for the capital and contracts they need to prove their worth.

We speak for the minorities who have not yet entered the mainstream.   47

For ethnics who want to add their culture to the mosaic that is America.   48

For women indignant that we refuse to etch into our governmental commandments   49
the simple rule "thou shalt not sin against equality," a commandment so obvious it can be spelled in three letters: E.R.A.!

For young people demanding an education and a future.   50

For senior citizens terrorized by the idea that their only security, their Social   51
Security, is being threatened.

For millions of reasoning people fighting to preserve our environment from greed   52
and stupidity. And fighting to preserve our very existence from a macho intransigence that refuses to make intelligent attempts to discuss the possibility of nuclear holocaust with our enemy. Refusing because they believe we can pile missiles so high that they will pierce the clouds and the sight of them will frighten our enemies into submission.

We're proud of this diversity. Grateful we don't have to manufacture its appearance   53
the way the Republicans will next month in Dallas, by propping up mannequin delegates on the convention floor.

But we pay a price for it.   54

The different people we represent have many points of view. Sometimes they   55
compete and then we have debates, even arguments. That's what our primaries were.

But now the primaries are over, and it is time to lock arms and move into this   56
campaign together.

If we need any inspiration to make the effort to put aside our small differences, all   57
we need to do is to reflect on the Republican policy of divide and cajole and how it has injured our land since 1980.

The President has asked us to judge him on whether or not he's fulfilled the   58
promises he made four years ago. I accept that. Just consider what he said and what he's done.

Inflation is down since 1980. But not because of the supply-side miracle promoted   59
by the President. Inflation was reduced the old-fashioned way, with a recession, the worst since 1932. More then 55,000 bankruptcies. Two years of massive unemployment. Two-hundred-thousand farmers and ranchers forced off the land. More homeless than at any time since the Great Depression. More hungry, more poor—mostly women—and a nearly $200 billion deficit threatening our future.

The President's deficit is a direct and dramatic repudiation of his promise to   60
balance our budget by 1983.

That deficit is the largest in the history of this universe; more than three times larger than the deficit in President Carter's last year. 61

It is a deficit that, according to the President's own fiscal advisor, could grow as high as $300 billion a year, stretching "as far as the eye can see." 62

It is a debt so large that as much as one-half of our revenue from the income tax goes to pay the interest on it each year. 63

It is a mortgage on our children's futures that can only be paid in pain and that could eventually bring this nation to its knees. 64

Don't take my word for it—I'm a Democrat. 65

Ask the Republican investment bankers on Wall Street what they think the chances are this recovery will be permanent. If they're not too embarrassed to tell you the truth, they'll say they are appalled and frightened by the President's deficit. Ask them what they think of our economy, now that it has been driven by the distorted value of the dollar back to its colonial condition, exporting agricultural products and importing manufactured ones. 66

Ask those Republican investment bankers what they expect the interest rate to be a year from now. And ask them what they predict for the inflation rate then. 67

How important is this question of the deficit? 68

Think about it: What chance would the Republican candidate have had in 1980 if he had told the American people that he intended to pay for his so-called economic recovery with bankruptcies, unemployment and the largest Government debt known to humankind? Would American voters have signed the loan certificate for him on Election Day? Of course not! It was an election won with smoke and mirrors, with illusions. It is a recovery made of the same stuff. 69

And what about foreign policy? 70

They said they would make us and the whole world safer. They say they have. 71

By creating the largest defense budget in history, one even they now admit is excessive, failed to discuss peace with our enemies. By the loss of 279 young Americans in Lebanon in pursuit of a plan and a policy no one can find or describe. 72

We give monies to Latin American governments that murder nuns, and then lie about it. 73

We have been less than zealous in our support of the only real friend we have in the Middle East, the one democracy there, our flesh and blood ally, the state of Israel. 74

Our policy drifts with no real direction, other than an hysterical commitment to an arms race that leads nowhere, if we're lucky. If we're not—it could lead us to bankruptcy or war. 75

Of course we must have a strong defense! 76

Of course Democrats believe that there are times when we must stand and fight. And we have. Thousands of us have paid for freedom with our lives. But always, when we've been at our best, our purposes were clear. 77

Now they're not. Now our allies are as confused as our enemies. 78

Now we have no real commitment to our friends or our ideals to human rights, to 79
the refusenicks, to Sakharov, to Bishop Tutu and the others struggling for freedom in
South Africa.

We have spent more than we can afford. We have pounded our chest and made 80
bold speeches. But we lost 279 young Americans in Lebanon and we are forced to
live behind sand bags in Washington.

How can anyone believe that we are stronger, safer or better? 81

That's the Republican record. 82

That its disastrous quality is not more fully understood by the American people is 83
attributable, I think, to the President's amiability and the failure by some to separate
the salesman from the product.

It's now up to us to make the case to America. 84

And to remind Americans that if they are not happy with all the President has 85
done so far, they should consider how much worse it will be if he is left to his radical
proclivities for another four years unrestrained by the need once again to come before
the American people.

If July brings back Anne Gorsuch Burford, what can we expect of December? 86

Where would another four years take us? 87

How much larger will the deficit be? 88

How much deeper the cuts in programs for the struggling middle class and the 89
poor to limit that deficit? How high the interest rates? How much more acid rain killing
our forests and fouling our lakes?

What kind of Supreme Court? What kind of court and country will be fashioned by 90
the man who believes in having government mandate people's religion and morality?

The man who believes that trees pollute the environment, that the laws against 91
discrimination go too far. The man who threatens Social Security and Medicaid and
help for the disabled.

How high will we pile the missiles? 92

How much deeper will be the gulf between us and our enemies? 93

Will we make meaner the spirit of our people? 94

This election will measure the record of the past four years. But more than that, it 95
will answer the question of what kind of people we want to be.

We Democrats still have a dream. We still believe in this nation's future. 96

And this is our answer—our credo: 97

We believe in only the government we need, but we insist on all the government 98
we need.

We believe in a government characterized by fairness and reasonableness, a reasonableness that goes beyond labels, that doesn't distort or promise to do what it knows it can't do. 99

A government strong enough to use the words "love" and "compassion" and smart enough to convert our noblest aspirations. 100

We believe in encouraging the talented, but we believe that while survival of the fittest may be a good working description of the process of evolution, a government of humans should elevate itself to a higher order, one which fills the gaps left by chance or a wisdom we don't understand. 101

We would rather have laws written by the patron of this great city, the man called the "world's most sincere Democrat," St. Francis of Assisi, than laws written by Darwin. 102

We believe, as Democrats, that a society as blessed as ours, the most affluent democracy in the world's history, that can spend trillions on instruments of destruction, ought to be able to help the middle class in its struggle, ought to be able to find work for all who can do it, room at the table, shelter for the homeless, care for the elderly and infirm, hope for the destitute. 103

We proclaim as loudly as we can the utter insanity of nuclear proliferation and the need for a nuclear freeze, if only to affirm the simple truth that peace is better than war because life is better than death. 104

We believe in firm but fair law and order, in the union movement, in privacy for people, openness by government, civil rights, and human rights. 105

We believe in a single fundamental idea that describes better than most textbooks and any speech what a proper government should be. The idea of family. Mutuality. The sharing of benefits and burdens for the good of all. Feeling one another's pain. Sharing one another's blessings. Reasonably, honestly, fairly, without respect to race, or sex, or geography or political affiliation. 106

We believe we must be the family of America, recognizing that at the heart of the matter we are bound one to another, that the problems of a retired school teacher in Duluth are our problems. That the future of the child in Buffalo is our future. The struggle of a disabled man in Boston to survive, to live decently is our struggle. The hunger of a woman in Little Rock is our hunger. The failure anywhere to provide what reasonably we might, to avoid pain, is our failure. 107

For 50 years we Democrats created a better future for our children, using traditional democratic principles as a fixed beacon, giving us direction and purpose, but constantly innovating, adapting to new realities; Roosevelt's alphabet programs; Truman's NATO and the GI Bill of rights; Kennedy's intelligent tax incentives and the Alliance For Progress; Johnson's civil rights; Carter's human rights and the nearly miraculous Camp David peace accord. 108

Democrats did it—and Democrats can do it again. 109

We can build a future that deals with our deficit. 110

Remember, 50 years of progress never cost us what the last four years of stagnation have. We can deal with that deficit intelligently, by shared sacrifice, with all parts of the nation's family contributing, building partnerships with the private sector, providing a sound defense without depriving ourselves of what we need to feed our children and care for our people. 111

We can have a future that provides for all the young of the present by marrying common sense and compassion. 112

We know we can, because we did it for nearly 50 years before 1980. 113

We can do it again. If we do not forget. Forget that this entire nation has profited by these progressive principles. That they helped lift up generations to the middle class and higher: gave us a chance to work, to go to college, to raise a family, to own a house, to be secure in our old age and, before that, to reach heights that our own parents would not have dared dream of. 114

That struggle to live with dignity is the real story of the shining city. It's a story I didn't read in a book, or learn in a classroom. I saw it, and lived it. Like many of you. 115

I watched a small man with thick calluses on both hands work 15 and 16 hours a day. I saw him once literally bleed from the bottoms of his feet, a man who came here uneducated, alone, unable to speak the language, who taught me all I needed to know about faith and hard work by the simple eloquence of his example. I learned about our kind of democracy from my father. I learned about our obligation to each other from him and from my mother. They asked only for a chance to work and to make the world better for their children and to be protected in those moments when they would not be able to protect themselves. This nation and its government did that for them. 116

And that they were able to build a family and live in dignity and see one of their children go from behind their little grocery store on the other side of the tracks in south Jamaica where he was born, to occupy the highest seat in the greatest state of the greatest nation in the only world we know, is an ineffably beautiful tribute to the democratic process. 117

And on Jan. 20, 1985, it will happen again. Only on a much grander scale. We will have a new President of the United States, a Democrat born not to the blood of kings but to the blood of immigrants and pioneers. 118

We will have America's first woman Vice President, the child of immigrants, a New Yorker, opening with one magnificent stroke a whole new frontier for the United States. 119

It will happen, if we make it happen. 120

I ask you, ladies and gentlemen, brothers and sisters—for the good of all of us, for the love of this great nation, for the family of America, for the love of God. Please make this nation remember how futures are built. 121

Mario Cuomo's 1984 speech was a keynote address to the 1984 Democratic convention. A "keynote" address is designed to do exactly what its name implies—hit the key note for the convention. A convention keynote address is aimed at two audiences: the faithful and, to a lesser degree, undecided voters. In this case, Cuomo's primary task was to unify and energize the Democratic Party behind the presidential ticket of Walter Mondale and Geraldine Ferraro.

It is important to recognize that Cuomo definitely was not aiming at Republicans. From the second paragraph on, he sharply attacked the Reagan administration in general and President Reagan in particular. Republicans were unlikely to be persuaded by such approach.

What kind of barriers did Cuomo confront in his keynote address? One set of barriers facing Cuomo came from the nature of the occasion.[7] Traditionally, a convention keynote is designed to unify and energize the faithful supporters of a particular party. Therefore, these addresses generally have focused upon the history of the party, the basic values and other principles that unify supporters of the party, and points of commonality among all the groups that make up the party. In contrast, keynote addresses generally have not focused on public policy in any detail. Given the situation in which keynotes are presented, it is understandable that the style of such addresses has been relatively formal. In a formal setting we expect a formal style. The defining characteristics of previous keynote addresses are also important, because in order to succeed in his particular address, Cuomo had to adapt to the expectations of the audience about keynote addresses in general.[8]

The second set of barriers facing Cuomo came from the nature of the political situation in 1984. By the summer of 1984 when the Democratic convention occurred, it was obvious that the Democrats were facing a serious political problem. The economy had come out of recession and was beginning to pick up steam. And Ronald Reagan remained personally quite popular with the American people. Nor was there any foreign or domestic crisis that might aid the Democrats. A situation defined by a strong economy, a popular president, and a nation at peace gave an enormous political advantage to the incumbent president. It was this situation that Cuomo faced in 1984.

Cuomo's 1984 address to the Democratic convention is justly famous as one of the great speeches of the last half century. For example, a well known rhetorical critic, David Henry, concludes that Cuomo's address "received wide praise from the press and general public."[9] Even Republicans agreed that it was a great speech. Henry quotes Senator Barry Goldwater as rating it "one of the best speeches I've ever heard."[10]

In the address, Cuomo adapts to the demands of the keynote situation and brilliantly uses narrative, value-laden appeals, and language strategies to unify and energize the audience. Cuomo relies on three primary strategies in the speech. Given the length of the address and the many attacks on the Reagan administration contained within it, one might expect that the speech would be heavily argumentative. However, that is not the case. Cuomo does claim that Reagan's policies have been extremist, that his positions threaten the health of the economy, that they risk war, and so forth. But he does not so much build arguments as draw on ones that his primary audience of Democrats already accepts. For example, in a long introductory section, he mentions "elderly people who tremble in the basements" of their homes (paragraph 11). Here, he refers to the fear that many elderly had over potential cuts in Social Security. Note that

Cuomo simply asserts that the elderly are "trembling" in their homes. He references no evidence on this point. Clearly, statements like the one I cited are designed to appeal to an audience that already believes that Reagan's policies have gone too far. While Cuomo does build arguments, rational argument is not one of the primary strategies defining the speech.

Rather than argument, Cuomo uses appeals to values and needs, narrative, and language strategies. Throughout the address, he emphasizes the need for security and values such as equality and opportunity. In the opening section of the speech, Cuomo alludes to Charles Dickens' novel, *A Tale of Two Cities*. He claims that like the novel, Reagan's America is also "a tale of two cities." He then focuses on the part of the city where "there are more poor than ever, more families in trouble," where there "are people who sleep in the city's streets," and where there is "despair" (paragraphs 10, 12, 14). Clearly, Cuomo is drawing upon the basic human need for security and the necessities of life. He does this throughout the speech.

Cuomo uses appeals to basic values in all sections of the speech. For example, in paragraph 46, he links the Democrats to equality, opportunity, family, and diversity. Cuomo says:

> Unlike any other party, we embrace men and women of every color, every creed, every orientation, every economic class. In our family are gathered everyone from the abject poor of Essex County in New York to the enlightened affluent of the gold coasts of both ends of our nation. And in between is the heart of our constituency. The middle class, the people not rich enough to be worry-free but not poor enough to be on welfare, those who work for a living because they have to. White collar and blue collar.

In the following paragraphs, he claims that Democrats speak for minorities, for members of ethnic groups, for women, for the young, and for senior citizens (paragraphs 47–51).

Cuomo skillfully uses both basic needs and basic values to unify and energize his audience. By saying that basic needs are threatened, he hopes to motivate Democrats to act. By appealing to shared values, he pulls the party together.

Cuomo's second major strategy is narrative. He uses narrative in several different ways. First, he uses short anecdotes to support his larger theme that the Reagan administration had failed the nation. For example, in paragraph 86, he refers to Anne Gorsuch Burford. Burford had been forced out as head of the Environmental Protection Agency when allegations were made that the EPA was not adequately regulating polluters and in fact had maintained inappropriate contacts with some companies.[11] Cuomo does not tell this story in detail. He merely refers to Gorsuch, confident that his audience will recall the incident. Here he uses narrative to activate an enthymeme in the audience.

Second, and much more importantly, Cuomo tells a story of what might be called the "Democratic History of the United States." In that story, it is Democrats who have saved the country time and time again. Early in the speech, he uses a metaphor of the wagon train to lay out the theme of the Democratic history. He says that "Republicans believe the wagon train will not make it to the frontier unless some of our old, some of our young, and some of our weak are left behind by the side of the trail" (paragraph 25). In contrast, "We Democrats believe that we can make it all the way with the whole family intact" (paragraph 27). He then turns to a great hero in this Democratic history, Franklin Roosevelt, who, according to Cuomo, "lifted himself from his wheelchair to lift the nation from its knees" (paragraph 29). Roosevelt led this nation "To new frontiers of education, housing, peace" (paragraph 29).

And since FDR, the Democrats have continued to save the nation. It was Democrats who "saved this nation from depression, from fascism, from racism, from corruption" and, consequently, they are "called upon to do it again—this time to save the nation from confusion and division, most of all from fear of a nuclear holocaust" (paragraph 34). He returns to the Democratic history near the conclusion of his address when he talks about great Democratic leaders including Truman, Kennedy, and Carter (paragraph 108).

In the conclusion, Cuomo shifts the focus of his Democratic history from the heroes of the Democratic Party to the people they helped. He uses the story of his own father to reaffirm the importance of the values undergirding the party:

> I watched a small man with thick calluses on both hands work 15 and 16 hours a day. I saw him once literally bleed from the bottoms of his feet, a man who came here uneducated, alone, unable to speak the language, who taught me all I needed to know about faith and hard work by the simple eloquence of his example. I learned about our kind of democracy from my father. I learned about our obligation to each other from him and from my mother. They asked only for a chance to work and to make the world better for their children and to be protected in those moments when they would not be able to protect themselves. This nation and its government did that for them. (paragraph 116)

With the story of his father, Cuomo links together his appeals to values and needs with the Democratic history. The Democrats, in Cuomo's story, always have been the party that took care of people like his own father. The final story powerfully unifies the narrative and value appeals.

While Cuomo's appeals to values, needs, and his use of narrative were skillful, it was his language strategies that made the speech memorable. The content of the address can be summarized quite simply: Reagan and the Republicans are bad; Democrats are good. Cuomo is effective in the way he uses appeals to values and needs, narrative, and to a lesser degree argument to develop this simple dichotomy. But these strategies do not explain the reaction to the address. Cuomo's 1984 convention speech is justly famous primarily because of the way he uses language strategies to add interest, clarify his position, and excite his audience.

LANGUAGE STRATEGIES IN CUOMO'S ADDRESS

Cuomo uses each of the main language strategies discussed earlier in his address. He uses these strategies to illustrate the themes and add interest to the themes I have discussed.

Metaphor

Given the importance of metaphor and other forms of comparison, it is unsurprising that Cuomo's address is filled with examples of this language strategy. For example, in paragraph 53 he refers to "mannequin delegates" at the Republican convention as a way of attacking the Republican Party for representing only the rich and not the diverse nature of our entire society. In paragraph 56, he says that Democrats need to "lock arms and move into this campaign." The metaphor of "locking arms" is his way of calling for Democratic unity. In the following paragraph, he refers to the Republican policy of "divide and cajole" as a way of attacking Reagan. I picked these examples of metaphor from the middle of Cuomo's address at random to illustrate the point that nearly every paragraph has one or more metaphors or other comparisons. Clearly, Cuomo is quite skillful at using metaphor to add interest to his speech.

There is one metaphor, however, that potentially functions as a paradigm for distinguishing between Democrats and Republicans. With the "wagon train" comparison that I cited earlier, Cuomo claims that the basic difference between Republicans and Democrats is that Democrats care about all the people, while Republicans only care about the rich. This metaphor has the potential to inform his entire attack on Reaganism. However, Cuomo essentially drops the metaphor after using it in the first third of the address. The speech might have been even more powerful had he returned to it in the conclusion.

Antithesis

Cuomo uses antithesis throughout the speech to juxtapose caring and compassionate Democrats with uncaring and extreme Republicans. Early in the address, he uses antithesis as a structural strategy to organize a series of distinctions between Republicans and Democrats. After noting that Reagan often refers to the United States as a "shining city on a hill," he says that "this nation is more a 'Tale of Two Cities' than it is a 'Shining City on a Hill'" (paragraph 15). He then talks about the two cities, which reflect the Republican rich who are doing well and the rest of us, who are facing a variety of problems.

Cuomo also uses antithesis in individual sentences to contrast Democrats and Republicans. For example, in paragraph 35, he says that "In order to succeed, we must answer our opponent's polished and appealing rhetoric with a more telling reasonableness and rationality." Here, he combines metaphor with antithesis, as he does two paragraphs later when he calls for the people "to look past the glitter … to reality." He continues this theme, saying "And we will do that not so much with speeches that sound good as with speeches that are good and sound. Not so much with speeches that bring people to their feet as with speeches that bring people to their senses" (paragraphs 37, 38). With this extended series of antitheses, Cuomo casts Democrats as reasonable and Republicans as fundamentally unreasonable. Democrats are concerned with issues, while Republicans are concerned with style. Of course, the irony is that Cuomo is skillfully using the persuasive power of rhetoric to attack Reagan for doing exactly the same thing.

Parallel Structure and Repetition

Cuomo relies on parallel structure in a long passage toward the conclusion of his address. Beginning with paragraph 98 and continuing through paragraph 107, he emphasizes the commitment of the Democratic Party to a certain set of values and policies by beginning nearly every paragraph with "We believe." He calls this entire section the Democratic "credo" (paragraph 97). He varies this pattern slightly in paragraphs 102 and 104, where he uses a verb other than "believe" that better fits his message. For example, in paragraph 104, he uses "proclaim" rather than "believe" in order to state opposition to nuclear proliferation as strongly as possible. With this long "credo," Cuomo uses parallel structure to emphasize the basic Democratic message.

Rhetorical Questions

Cuomo uses rhetorical questions both as transition devices and to emphasize his conclusion that Republicans are extreme and represent special interests. In paragraph 68, he asks "How important is this question of the deficit?" as a transition device to an attack on the budget policies of the Reagan administration. In contrast, beginning with paragraph 86 and continuing through paragraph 94, he asks a series of questions to emphasize failures in the Reagan administration. Paragraph 93 is typical: "How much deeper will be the gulf between us and our enemies?" This question emphasizes Cuomo's claim that Reagan's defense policies risk war.

Depiction and Description

Cuomo focuses on the life of the poor throughout the address. In several of these passages, he uses depiction to give the audience a feel for the problems the poor face. For example, as I noted earlier, in paragraph 11 he refers to the "elderly people who tremble in the basements" to help us understand the problems facing older Americans. His use of the verb "tremble" makes this statement quite vivid.

The only extended use of depiction in Cuomo's address comes at the end when he describes his father. I cited this passage earlier, but a portion of it bears repeating. Cuomo says of his father, "I watched a small man with thick calluses on both hands work 15 and 16 hours a day. I saw him once literally bleed from the bottoms of his feet ..." (paragraph 116). With this description, Cuomo helps us picture his father as a hard-working immigrant who came to this nation to provide a better life for his family. Cuomo's vivid description of his father is a very important strategy in the address.

Personification

Cuomo does not rely on personification to any great extent, although he does refer to Roosevelt lifting "the nation from its knees" (paragraph 29). Except in rare cases, personification is a linguistic strategy of lesser importance.

Rhythm and Rhyme

As with personification, Cuomo does not rely heavily on rhythm or rhyme. There are, however, places in the address where there is a natural rhythm to the language that helps makes the speech flow. For example, very early in the speech he says "There is despair, Mr. President, in faces you never see, in the places you never visit in your shining city" (paragraph 14). The phrases "in faces you never see, in the places you never visit," have a natural rhythm that adds to the power of the passage.

Another example of rhythm is in the conclusion when he refers to the "highest seat in the greatest state of the greatest nation in the only world we know" (paragraph 117). The natural progression of "highest" to "greatest" to "highest" again is set off with the words "only world we know." In this statement, it isn't the content that matters, but the way the sentence works rhythmically. In both of the statements I have cited (and others), there is a natural rhythm to the phrasing that helps make the speech more interesting.

Definition and Redefinition

The most obvious use of redefinition in Cuomo's address is his statement that America is not "a shining city," but actually "A Tale of Two Cities." In this extended section, Cuomo redefines the social situation in America as one in which the vast majority of Americans are not doing well.

Alliteration and Assonance

Cuomo uses alliteration at several points in the address. For example, he says that the "President's deficit is a direct and dramatic repudiation of his promise to balance our budget by 1983" (paragraph 60). In paragraph 43, he says that Republican policies "divide the nation: into the lucky and the left-out, the royalty and the rabble." In this statement, Cuomo combines alliteration, metaphor, antithesis, and labeling to emphasize his characterization of the Reagan administration as fundamentally uncaring.

Allusion

Cuomo relies on allusion at a couple points in the address, most notably in the introduction with the reference to Dickens. He also alludes to a statement Reagan made that trees are a major source of pollution (paragraph 91) and to the scandal that led Anne Gorsuch Burford to be fired from the EPA (paragraph 86). Still, allusion is not a major aesthetic strategy in Cuomo's address.

Labeling

Cuomo uses labeling when he says that the poor have been "locked out" (paragraph 23). This statement functions as Cuomo's way of defining the essence of Reagan's social policy. He also labels support for an Equal Rights Amendment (ERA) for women as a "commandment": "thou shalt not sin against equality" (paragraph 49). It is somewhat surprising that Cuomo does not rely more heavily on labeling.

Irony

Cuomo relies primarily on direct attacks on the Reagan administration. This approach means that there is little room for irony. A rhetorical question concerning Anne Gorsuch Burford is the only important example of irony in the speech (paragraph 86).

SUMMARY OF CUOMO'S USE OF LANGUAGE STRATEGIES

As I noted in the discussion of antithesis, Cuomo sharply distinguishes the "reasonableness" of Democratic rhetoric, from what he labels the show and substance of Reagan. It is ironic, therefore, that the key element in the persuasiveness of Cuomo's address is his use of a wide variety of language strategies. Cuomo is every bit as showy as he accuses Reagan of being.

Cuomo uses language strategies as a way of making his narrative, value-laden, and argumentative strategies more interesting and memorable. With the exception of the "wagon train" metaphor and the "two cities" redefinition, the language strategies do not add to the content of his position. But the language strategies make that position quite memorable.

Was Cuomo successful? The 1984 elections were a disaster for Democrats. The Mondale-Ferraro ticket was crushed by Reagan-Bush at the polls. Judged from the perspective of ultimate political effect, the speech must be labeled a failure. However, judged as a work of rhetoric designed to unify and energize Democrats, the speech must be graded as near perfect. Cuomo did little if anything in the speech to broaden the base of the Democratic Party. But the combination of narrative, appeals to values/needs, and language strategies was very well-designed to do what he accused Reagan of doing, bringing "people to their feet" (paragraph 38).

STRENGTHS AND WEAKNESSES OF AESTHETIC STRATEGIES

There is no question that aesthetic strategies play a major role in successful rhetoric, whether in the form of a public speech, an essay, a film, or a music video. On the other hand, it is also easy to overestimate the importance of aesthetic strategies in general and language strategies in particular. How you say it is important, but you also need to have something to say. With this limitation in mind, the following generalizations can be made about aesthetic strategies.

First, aesthetic strategies do not, in general, work by themselves. Rather, their role is to make content more exciting, more memorable, and to provide emphasis. Second, the exception to this rule relates to metaphor. Unlike other language and aesthetic strategies, metaphor may form the very substance of a work of rhetoric. In most cases, metaphor functions as a rhetorical spice, but in some instances, metaphor works as a model for understanding the world. If a rhetor can change the metaphor through which an audience understands the world, the result may be to change their thinking and behavior.

Third, there is no single style that works for all people in all occasions. In fact, only very broad generalizations can be drawn about appropriate aesthetic strategies. As a rule the language or other aesthetic strategies used should be appropriate to the subject, the context, the speaker/writer/producer, and the audience. The rhetor should use language strategies to add interest to his/her rhetoric and to clarify complex or ambiguous information. These sensible generalizations help identify inappropriate use of language strategies, but they are not helpful in distinguishing between a powerful use of language strategies and the merely adequate. The truth is that people vary a great deal in what appeals to them aesthetically. Much modern art leaves me totally cold, but many highly educated informed observers love that art and find the Rembrandt and Monet paintings that I adore to be dated. Precisely the same point applies to aesthetic strategies in rhetoric.

Fourth, aesthetic strategies should be combined with other rhetorical strategies to produce the maximum effect. This is especially important when the dominant strategy is some form of rational argument. To be maximally effective, rational argument should be supported with a variety of aesthetic strategies that add interest or provide emphasis.

CONCLUSION

Aesthetic strategies in general and language strategies in particular play an important part in persuasion. The skillful use of aesthetic strategies can enliven a presentation or make any work of rhetoric more understandable. But it is also important to recognize that with the exception of metaphor and some visual strategies in film and video, aesthetic strategies mainly play a supporting role. They make the argument or value appeal more understandable and more powerful, but they don't function to produce persuasion by themselves.

An anecdote may make this point clear. There is a story that when a movie executive was told that Ronald Reagan was going to run for governor of California, the executive exclaimed, "No, Jimmy Stewart for governor; Ronald Reagan for best friend." The executive meant that Stewart was a far better actor than Reagan. The executive was wrong, however, because the essence of politics is not acting, but building a persuasive message. Reagan may not have been a great actor, but he was a great politician who was able to combine narrative and argument with strong appeals to values and needs. Reagan was skilled at using language and other aesthetic strategies, but in his rhetoric, as in the case of almost all successful persuaders, they played a supporting role.

FOR FURTHER DISCUSSION

On January 3, 2019, Nancy Pelosi became Speaker of the House for a second time, having also served in that role for four years from 2007 through 2011. She became the first person to serve nonconsecutive terms as Speaker in over half a century and of course is the only woman to have served in that role. In an address on the occasion of accepting the gavel as Speaker, Pelosi spoke of issues facing the nation and also of basic values. It was a situation that called for both a discussion of policy, but also for a ceremonial style enacting basic values. Carefully read and do an analysis outline of Pelosi's statement. Then consider the following questions:

1 What language strategies did Pelosi use to support her message?
2 What other strategies did Pelosi use in conjunction with the language strategies?

3 What barriers did she face? Was her rhetoric aimed at the audience in the House chamber or the American people as a whole?

4 Were her strategies well-designed to overcome the barriers she faced?

Pelosi Remarks upon Accepting the Gavel as Speaker of the House
Nancy Pelosi

Thank you very much, Leader McCarthy. I look forward to working with you in a bipartisan way for the good of our country, respecting our constituents, every one of you, I respect you and the constituents who sent each and every one of us here and deserve for us to find our common ground, and we must try to do that: stand our ground when we can't, but always extend a hand of friendship. 1

Thank you, Kevin McCarthy, for your leadership. I look forward to working with you. Congratulations on being the Leader of the party. 2

To each and every one of you, new Members of Congress, newly-elected Members of Congress, thank you for your courage to run for office and to serve in this distinguished body. 3

Every two years, we gather in this Chamber for a sacred ritual. Under the dome of this temple of our democracy, the Capitol of the United States, we renew the great American experiment. 4

I am particularly proud to be the woman Speaker of the House of this Congress, which marks 100 years of women having the right to vote. And that we all have the ability and privilege to serve with more than 100 women in Congress—the largest number in history. 5

As Leader McCarthy said, each of us comes to this Chamber strengthened by the trust of our constituents and the love of our families. Let us congratulate and welcome all your families who are with us today. Thank you to our families. 6

Let me take the privilege of thanking dear husband Paul and our five children. Our five children: Nancy Corinne, Christine, Jacqueline, Paul, and Alexandra. And our nine grandchildren: Madeleine, Alexander, Liam, Sean, Ryan, Thomas and Paul, Bella, and Octavio. We are so proud of all our grandchildren, and we're proud of everyone's grandchildren and children who are here today. We'll see more of them today. 7

I am also proud of my D'Alesandro family that is here from Baltimore too. 8

In that spirit, my mother and father and my brother Tommy, who was also Mayor of Baltimore, taught us through their example that public service is a noble calling, that we should serve with our hearts full of love—and that America's heart is full of love. 9

House Speaker Nancy Pelosi, Remarks Upon Accepting the Gavel as Speaker of the House, 2019

Singing that to us last night, my comrade as an Italian-American, with all that pride, I want to acknowledge Tony Bennett who is here with us today as well. Thank you Tony. He helped free the concentration camps in World War II. He marched with Martin Luther King. He is a true American patriot. Thank you, Tony.   10

And again, I want thank my constituents in San Francisco, who have entrusted me to represent them in Congress in the spirit of Saint Francis, the patron saint of San Francisco—and his song of Saint Francis is our anthem: "Make me a channel of thy peace." We heard that in church this morning, but it is our mission.   11

And let me thank our men and women in uniform, our veterans, and our military families and caregivers, whose service reminds us of our mission: to make the future worthy of their sacrifice. To our men and women in uniform.   12

We enter this new Congress with a sense of great hope and confidence for the future, and deep humility and prayerfulness in the face of the challenges ahead.   13

Our nation is at an historic moment. Two months ago, the American people spoke, and demanded a new dawn.   14

They called upon the beauty of our Constitution: our system of checks and balances that protects our democracy, remembering that the legislative branch is Article I: the first branch of government, coequal to the presidency and judiciary.   15

They want a Congress that delivers results for the people, opening up opportunity and lifting up their lives.   16

[Sound of child crying]

We are hearing the voice of the future there. Beautiful.   17

When our new Members take the oath, our Congress will be refreshed, and our democracy will be strengthened by their optimism, idealism, and patriotism of this transformative Freshman class. Congratulations to all of you in the Freshman class.   18

Working together, we will redeem the promise of the American Dream for every family, advancing progress for every community.   19

We must be pioneers of the future.   20

This Congress must accelerate a future that advances America's preeminence in the world, and opens up opportunities for all—building an economy that gives all Americans the tools they need to succeed in the 21st Century: public education, workforce development, good-paying jobs, and secure pensions.   21

We have heard from too many families who wonder, in this time of innovation and globalization, if they have a place in the economy of the future. We must remove all doubt that they do, and say to them individually: we will have an economy that works for you.   22

Let us declare that we will call upon the bold thinking to address the disparity of income in America—which is at the root of the crisis of confidence felt by so many Americans.   23

As Justice Brandeis said, "We may have democracy, or we may have wealth concentrated in the hands of a few, but we can't have both."   24

We must end that injustice and restore the public's faith in a better future for themselves and their children. 25

We must be champions of the middle class, and all those who aspire to it — because the middle class is the backbone of our democracy. It has been since the birth—it has been since the birth of democracy. 26

Aristotle said, "It is manifest that the best political community is formed by citizens of the middle class...in which the middle class is large and stronger than all of the other classes." 27

We must fight for the middle class that is fair and fiscally sound—protecting Medicare, Medicaid, and Social Security. 28

We must also face the existential threat of our time: the climate crisis—a crisis manifested in natural disasters of epic proportions. 29

The American people understand the urgency. The people are ahead of the Congress. The Congress must join them. 30

And that is why we have created the Select Committee on Climate Crisis. The entire Congress must work to put an end to the inaction and denial of science that threaten the planet and the future. 31

This is a public health decision about clean air, clean water for our children's health, it's a decision for America's global preeminence in green technologies, a security decision to keep us safe, and a moral decision to be good stewards of God's creation. 32

We have no illusions that our work will be easy and that all of us in this chamber will always agree. But let each of us pledge that when we disagree, we will respect each other and we will respect the truth. 33

We will debate and advance good ideas no matter where they come from. And in that spirit, Democrats will be offering the Senate Republican appropriations legislation to reopen government later today. We will do so to meet the needs of the American people, to protect our borders and to respect our workers. 34

And I pledge that this Congress will be transparent, bipartisan, and unifying; that we will seek to reach across the aisle in this Chamber and across the divisions across our great nation. 35

In the past two years, the American people have spoken. Tens of thousands of public events were held. Hundreds of thousands of people turned out. Millions of calls were made. Countless families—even sick little children, our Little Lobbyists, our Little Lobbyists—bravely came forward to tell their stories. And they made a big difference. 36

Now, the Floor of this House must be America's Town Hall: where the people will see our debates, and where their voices will be heard and affect our decisions. Transparency will be the order of the day. 37

And as Mr. [Hakeem] Jeffries, our distinguished Chairman, said, we will follow our mandate, For The People! And I thank you for the nomination and I accept those kind 38 remarks on behalf of the entire House Democratic Caucus who made all of those victories possible, some of them in a bipartisan way.

Empower our mandate, For The People: To lower health care costs and prescription drug prices, and protect people with pre-existing medical conditions. To increase paychecks by rebuilding America with green and modern infrastructure—from sea to shining sea. We look forward to working with the President on that. To pass H.R. 1 to restore integrity to government, so that people can have confidence that government works for the people, not the special interests, H.R. 1. 39

This House will take overdue legislation that has bipartisan support, bipartisan support, in the Congress and across the Country. We will make our communities safer and keep our sacred promise to the victims, survivors and families of gun violence by passing commonsense, bipartisan background check legislation. We will make America fairer by passing the Equality Act to end discrimination against the LGBTQ community. And we will make America more American by passing— protecting our patriotic, courageous Dreamers! 40

All three of those legislative initiatives have bipartisan support in this body. 41

And when we are talking about the Dreamers, let us remember what President Reagan said in his last speech as president of the United States. I urge you all to read it. It is a beautiful speech. He said, "If we ever close the door to new Americans, our leadership role in the world would soon be lost." Ronald Reagan. You're applauding for Ronald Reagan! 42

Our common cause is to find and forge a way forward for our country. Let us stand for the people—to promote liberty and justice for all as we pledge every day. And always, always keep our nation safe from threats old and new, from terrorism and cyberwarfare, overseas and here at home to protect and defend, that is the oath we all take to serve in this body. That is the oath we take: to protect and defend. 43

I close by remembering a cherished former Member of this body, who rose to become a beloved president of the United States, and who, last month, returned to the Capitol once more to lie in state. That week, we honored President George Herbert Walker Bush with eulogies, tributes, and tears. Today, I single out one of his great achievements: working with both Democrats and Republicans to write the Americans with Disabilities Act into the laws of our land. Thank you Steny Hoyer for being such a big part of that. 44

In 2010, we marked the 20th anniversary of the Act by making it possible for our colleagues with disabilities to preside over the House by changing the mechanics of this podium. In that same spirit of equality and justice, let me announce that, this afternoon, the first Speaker Pro Tempore, whom I will yield, of the 116th Congress will be: Congressman Jim Langevin of Rhode Island. 45

As we take the oath of office today, we accept responsibility as daunting and demanding as any that previous generations of leadership have faced. Guided by the vision and values of our Founders, the sacrifice of our men and women in uniform 46 and the aspirations that we have for our children, let us meet that responsibility with wisdom, with courage and with grace.

Together, we will let it be known: that this House will truly be the People's House!   47

Let us pray that God may bless our work, and crown our good with brotherhood—   48
and sisterhood—from sea to shining sea.

God bless you, and God bless the United States of America.   49

1   A discussion of how the "wall" metaphor has shaped Supreme Court analysis can be found in Benjamin Voth, "The Wall Separating Church and State," Doctoral Dissertation, University of Kansas, 1994.

2   See for instance "Stokely Carmichael Explains Black Power to a White Audience in Whitewater, Wisconsin," in Robert L. Scott and Wayne Brockriede, *The Rhetoric of Black Power* (New York: Harper and Row, 1969): 96–111. This article is a speech by Carmichael.

3   See George Lakoff and Mark Johnson, *Metaphors We Live By* (Chicago: University of Chicago Press, 1980).

4   This idea is developed in Robert C. Rowland and John M. Jones, *Reagan at Westminster: Foreshadowing the End of the Cold War* (College Station, TX: Texas A & M University Press, 2010).

5   Lyndon Baines Johnson, "Address Before a Joint Session of the Congress, November 27, 1963," *Public Papers of the Presidents of the United States: Lyndon Johnson, Book I* (Washington: Government Printing Office, 1965): 9.

6   Abraham Lincoln, "The Gettysburg Address," in *Three Centuries of American Rhetorical Discourse: An Anthology and Review*, ed. Ronald F. Reid (Prospect Heights: IL: Waveland, 1988): 463.

7   See David Henry, "The Rhetorical Dynamics of Mario Cuomo's 1984 Keynote Address: Situation, Speaker, Metaphor," *Southern Speech Communication Journal* 53 (1988), pp. 107–109.

8   Keynote addresses are one type of a rhetorical genre. In chapter ten, I discuss the way that genres influence rhetorical action.

9   Henry, p. 105.

10 Henry, p. 105.

11 For a description of the crisis, see Robert C. Rowland and Thea Rademacher, "The Passive Style of Rhetorical Crisis Management: A Case Study of the Superfund Controversy," *Communication Studies* 41 (1990), pp. 328–330.

CHAPTER 8
Generating an Emotional Response: Tapping into Values, Needs, and Symbols

It is common to hear the press speak of an emotional appeal in a politician's speech in negative terms. The comment "Senator X gave an emotional speech last night" nearly always contains an implied criticism of the address as not rational, but overly emotional. In some cases, this criticism may be well-taken. There certainly are many speeches, essays, films, and other works of rhetoric that are designed to provoke emotions, not thought. It is for that reason, among others, that the focus of chapter eleven is on developing a system to identify deceptive and irrational rhetoric. On the other hand, rhetoric that fails to produce an emotional response often fails to produce any response at all.

The main emphasis of this chapter is on identifying the characteristics of rhetoric that produce a strong emotional reaction. In the first section, I define the characteristics of emotion-producing rhetoric. I then consider dangers associated with such rhetoric and also the need for emotion-producing rhetoric as a means of generating action. In the next section, I outline nine sub-strategies for producing an emotional response and illustrate how they work by discussing an address by Jesse Jackson at the 1988 Democratic National Convention.

A DEFINITION OF EMOTION-PRODUCING RHETORIC

It has been traditional, since Aristotle wrote his classic rhetorical handbook, *The Rhetoric*, to distinguish among three modes of persuasion: logos, ethos, and pathos,[1] which correspond with argument, credibility, and emotional appeals, respectively. In earlier chapters, I have discussed credibility and argument as ways of persuading an audience. However, in relation to pathos or appeals to the emotions, the traditional label is not adequate.

While rhetoric producing an emotional response is quite important, it is not useful to talk about appeals to the emotions. The emotions are not an organ in the human body that one somehow addresses. Rather than *appealing* to the emotions, certain types of rhetoric *produce* a strong emotional response. For example, it is common for rhetoricians in the United States and around the world to use a nation's flag as a patriotic symbol representing the country. The rhetor refers to the flag in order to tap into the strong societal association between the flag and the particular nation. It is by tapping that association that the rhetor produces the emotional response in the audience. As this example indicates, rhetoric is not itself emotional or nonemotional.

Rather, some forms of rhetoric tap into values, needs, or symbols that have strong emotional associations and the result is an emotional response. The subtypes of rhetoric that produce a strong emotional response will be discussed later in this chapter.

DANGERS ASSOCIATED WITH EMOTION-PRODUCING RHETORIC

There are two major dangers associated with rhetoric that produces a strong emotional reaction. First, that form of rhetoric may lead people to make irrational decisions. We all know that strong emotion can cloud our thinking. The research that I summarized in chapter four on when rational argument fails certainly supports this judgment. Second, strong emotional reactions may lead to the creation of hate and societal conflict. Hitler used rhetoric to persuade the German people that the Jews had harmed Germany and must be destroyed. In the 1990s, Slobodan Milosevic, the leader of Serbia at the time, used rhetoric to persuade soldiers, police, and others to commit horrible acts, first in Bosnia and then in Kosovo. He tapped into Serbian history and nationalism to produce these strong reactions. Tragically, many other examples could be cited. Clearly, rhetoric that produces such strong reactions can be quite dangerous.

Given these dangers, one might think that the best solution would be to avoid rhetoric that produces a strong emotional response altogether. The judgment that emotion-producing rhetoric is always dangerous is, however, incorrect. Rhetoric may produce a strong emotional reaction and be quite rational. Two examples make this point clear. I have a friend whose father was a death camp survivor. My friend passionately hates the Nazis and bitterly criticizes so-called Holocaust Revisionists, who deny that the Holocaust happened. His reaction to the Holocaust Revisionists is both strongly emotional *and* highly rational. It makes sense that he hates the Nazis and those who defend them. Similarly, it is not irrational for a gunshot victim to be a passionate supporter of gun control. Some years ago, I had a student who strongly defended restrictions on gun ownership, largely based on a personal experience in which he was shot in a robbery of a convenience store. The student described in detail what it was like to have a gun pointed at you and then see the muzzle flash and feel the bullet hit your chest. This student's support for gun control was based on emotion and equally on reason.

In both the cases I have described, the beliefs of the individual were both strongly emotional and perfectly reasonable. The point is that oftentimes emotional reactions are completely rational. Aristotle himself made this exact point almost 2,500 years ago, when he argued that emotions are often rational reactions to a given situation.[2] Of course, not all emotional reactions are rational. Some are quite irrational and extremely dangerous. But in other cases, an emotional reaction and a rational evaluation of the situation may be quite consistent.

Moreover, humans are by their very nature emotional beings. It is unreasonable to think that an emotionless "Spock-like" rhetoric ever could be effective. Very few, if any, people are motivated by pure reason. It is for this reason that politicians who cannot use rhetoric to produce strong emotional responses are often referred to as wooden.[3] The politician is not an oak, but the media is onto something, even if the metaphor is misleading. It is not the stiffness of the politician that is the problem, but his/her inability to utilize strategies that produce strong human emotions.

Finally, if one is to combat immoral emotional rhetoric, one has no choice but to rely on rhetoric that can produce a strong countervailing emotional response. It is very common for historians to argue that Franklin Roosevelt saved the United States from demagogues such as former Louisiana Senator Huey Long.[4] In this view, Roosevelt was all that stood in the way of a turn toward extremism during the Great Depression. Of course, not everyone agrees that U.S. democracy was threatened or even that Long was a demagogue. But they do agree that Roosevelt was successful because he used all of the available rhetorical strategies, not just rational argument. His First Inaugural Address, in which he reassured the country that "the only thing we have to fear is fear itself,"[5] is a magnificent example of how a politician can use strategies that tap into human emotion in order to calm an audience.

For all of the reasons I have developed, rhetoric that produces a strong emotional response plays a crucial role in public persuasion and any skilled rhetorician must be able to utilize it effectively.

STRATEGIES FOR PRODUCING A STRONG EMOTIONAL RESPONSE

There are nine main sub-strategies for producing a strong emotional response in an audience, and one important notation concerning language usage and emotional response. In regard to language, the rule of thumb is that concrete descriptive language is more adapted to producing a strong emotional reaction than other forms of language. Here, it is important to distinguish between graphic description and abstract language. Abstract language is used to deal with complex issues in a purely rational framework. It also allows humans to talk about ideas that have no direct real-world referent, including scientific theories. Abstract language plays an essential role in human civilization; it is one key to the ability of people to use conceptual thought.

On the other hand, graphic description is better adapted to producing a strong emotional reaction than is the use of abstract language. A detailed description of what happened to a victim massacred by the government in Syria might produce a very powerful emotional reaction in an audience. Through describing the life and then murder of this person in detail, the speaker would bring home the horror of his/her death. Graphic or concrete language is used to tap into the emotional content of an issue, while ambiguous or abstract language avoids that content.

It is important to recognize, however, that use of graphic descriptive language is not itself a sub-strategy for producing a strong emotional reaction. A detailed description of a wiring diagram will not produce a strong emotional reaction in anyone. Thus, graphic language will produce a strong emotional reaction only if it links to one of the sub-strategies discussed in the following section.

In relation to emotional reaction, the subtypes of strategies for producing that effect are:

1   Appeals to Basic Needs
2   Appeals to Basic Values
3   Appeals to Self-interest
4   Appeals to Guilt

Appeals to Basic Needs

An appeal to basic needs is aimed at a "need" that is inherent in human psychology. Basic needs include life itself, security, the resources of life (food, water, housing, and similar needs), sex, social support, and so forth. Maslow's hierarchy of needs is one common analysis of basic needs shared by humans. A rhetor appeals to needs by pointing to a need that is not being met or that could be threatened in the future. He/she then either draws on audience fear of the need not being fulfilled or promises a better means of fulfilling it in the future.

In political rhetoric, for instance, it is common for politicians to focus on the need for security in relation to crime, the death penalty, gun control, and social support programs. The power of an appeal to basic needs is most easily illustrated in relation to Social Security, which has been called the "third rail" of American politics. The "third rail" metaphor is a reference to the "third rail" in a subway, which is electrified. A person who touches the third rail in a subway is electrocuted. Similarly, according to the metaphor, a politician who threatens Social Security will be defeated. Why is Social Security the "third rail" of American politics? The answer is that people fear being old and unable to take care of themselves. Social Security has guaranteed at least a minimum level of income and people don't want to lose that guarantee.

In appealing to needs, it is important to keep in mind the following rules of thumb. First, it doesn't make sense to appeal to the needs of the audience if those needs are both being met currently and do not seem threatened in the future. If people feel secure in relation to crime, then a scare rhetoric about the threat of crime will not have much impact. Before 9/11, rhetoric focused on the danger of terrorism often failed to produce much reaction, precisely because people didn't really think that a major terrorist attack could occur. After 9/11, the situation was very different. Thus, the "need" being appealed to must be one that credibly could be threatened in the world of the audience. Second, an appeal to needs should be strong enough to elicit a response, but not so strong that it loses credibility. Persuasion research in the area of fear appeals indicates that if a fear appeal seems excessive, the result will be to produce audience backlash instead of persuasion.[6] Too strong a fear appeal may seem incredible to the audience. But a weak fear appeal will not generate action. The same point applies when the rhetor is promising a better future. That better future must be a significant improvement or no one will care. But when someone promises us a perfect future, we are likely to be skeptical.

Third, familiar risks may be seen as less threatening than unfamiliar ones, especially if the unfamiliar risk seems to pose a particularly unpleasant result. The dangers of texting while driving are well-known and clearly many people ignore them. On the other hand, in the fall of 2014 millions of Americans were terrified of the dangers of an Ebola epidemic, despite the fact that there was extremely low risk of such an epidemic and standard medical procedures worked well both to treat patients and isolate them from the public. Ebola was an unfamiliar disease that came from a place that was scary for many Americans, the jungles of Africa, and it killed in a particularly grotesque way, by causing bodily organs to bleed massively. That made it far scarier to Americans than diseases like the flu that actually kill many Americans. The gap between the actual risk and the perceived risk led the organization *Politifact* to conclude that the "lie of the year" in 2014 was "Exaggerations About Ebola."[7]

Finally, fear appeals and other messages tapping basic needs work most effectively when there is some direct action that the audience can take to reduce whatever risk is at issue or otherwise achieve the basic need. This makes perfect sense. If you tell a group that there is a problem facing them that threatens their existence, but that there is nothing that can be done about it, the likely reaction of the audience will be to throw up their hands and ignore the issue.

In summary, appeals to needs, either positive or negative, are most powerful when four conditions are present: 1) basic needs are not being met or are threatened; 2) the rhetor can show the existence of a significant problem or potential benefit, but not one so large that it lacks credibility; 3) unfamiliar risks are scarier than familiar ones, especially if the unfamiliar risk presents a particularly grotesque danger; 4) it is possible to take relatively simple steps either to protect the individual or to fulfill the need in the future.

Appeals to Basic Values

An appeal to basic values taps into the value structure of a given society. The contrast between values and needs can be thought of as similar to the distinction between hardware and software in the context of computers. Needs are the equivalent of hardware; they apparently are inherent in human psychology. We all need food, water, shelter, love, and so forth. Values, by contrast, are like software; they differ across culture. For example, Americans tend to value "progress" very highly. Consequently, there is a great deal of focus on creating a better country, improving the quality of our infrastructure, and so forth. By contrast, in many societies progress is valued less and stability is more highly valued.

Values, therefore, are basic statements of good and bad in a society or a subset of that society. The most basic values in the United States include freedom, peace, equality, justice, opportunity, and progress. In subsets of the society, other values are important. For example, in the culture of an American research university, values such as diversity, knowledge, and intellectual rigor are important, along with the basic values of American society as a whole.

The essential point is that a skilled rhetorician can tap into the dominant values that undergird any society (or part of a society). The rhetorician either cites the values in support or opposition to an idea or says that the values are threatened in order to motivate action. For example, conservatives often use the values of freedom and opportunity in opposing affirmative action programs. In contrast, Democrats cite the values of diversity and equality in defending those programs. As this example indicates, the values that define a given society may not be completely consistent. For example, U.S. culture tends to value both equality and freedom, but at a certain point, such as in regard to affirmative action programs that establish quotas to increase the representation of a particular racial or ethnic group in a given institution, those values may come into conflict.

One other point is important in regard to appeals to basic values. It obviously is essential to identify the dominant values that energize any particular culture or subculture, in order to explain how this strategy functions in a particular work of rhetoric for a particular audience. Values vary across culture. What is valued in one culture (or subculture) may not be valued in another.

Appeal to Self-Interest

In an appeal to self-interest, the rhetor essentially offers the audience something that they want. Since the 1980s, as the budget deficit of the United States increased and increased, both Democrats and especially Republicans have continued to advocate tax cuts. Tax cuts remained popular throughout this period, despite the rising deficit, because everyone prefers low taxes. It is true that some conservatives believed that a tax cut would stimulate the economy, producing enough new growth to offset lost revenues (this did not happen in Reagan's two terms or in either term of the second President Bush or in response to the Trump tax cut). And liberals advocated tax increases for the wealthy, but not for anyone making less than $250,000, a quite high figure. In rhetorical terms, the appeal of the tax cut proposals was not based on complex economic arguments, but on the simple fact that people wanted their taxes to go down. The obvious conclusion is that people generally react favorably to positions that help them. This point is generalizable and applies more broadly than to just taxes.

It is also important to understand that people don't tend to see themselves as selfish. Instead, they often perceive that their self-interest is the interest of the entire community. It would not be inaccurate, for example, to say that people define a "tax loophole" as a tax provision that helps "someone else." For instance, ordinary people do not tend to perceive the home mortgage deduction as a tax loophole, but of course in a technical sense, that is precisely what it is. Instead, they see it as a sensible government policy that recognizes the importance of home ownership. Truthfully, the home mortgage deduction is both a loophole and a government policy that supports home ownership. The important conclusion is that people often interpret policies that aid them personally as principled attempts to accomplish a valid public purpose.

From the perspective of understanding how rhetoric produces a strong emotional response, the key judgment is that appeals to self-interest are a very powerful way of motivating people. For example, in the 1988 election, Vice President Bush appealed to self-interest by promising "No New Taxes." The ability of Bush and other Republicans to make Democrats look like supporters of high taxes with the slogan "Tax and Spend Democrats" played a part in his victory in that election and the victories of many Republicans in campaigns for other offices. However, when Bush later signed a tax increase, this undercut his position with some conservative Republicans. This action encouraged conservative commentator Pat Buchanan to mount a primary challenge to Bush in 1992, a challenge that undoubtedly weakened Bush's position in the general election that was won by Bill Clinton.

Appeal to Guilt

Guilt is a powerful motivating force in human society. It is easy to think of many instances in which someone felt guilt over some action (or inaction) and could not rest until that guilt was purged. On the other hand, there are many people who seem to be able to commit horrible acts and not feel the least bit guilty. It might seem that the fact that some feel guilt so strongly and others apparently not at all would make it difficult to predict how guilt will function as a factor in any given work of rhetoric.

While it may not be possible to explain why some people don't feel guilt, despite lying, cheating, or committing other terrible acts, in rhetorical terms there are general principles that explain when guilt-producing rhetoric will be effective. How is guilt created in rhetoric? One appeals to guilt in a speech or essay by pointing to a gap between the values and the actions of an individual or a group. Thus, for an audience that values opportunity for all, an advocate of civil rights might point to the gap between their economic situation and that of youths in the central city. Implicitly, the speaker would be saying the following: "You have enormous wealth and claim to value opportunity for all. But you aren't giving to this community in need. Either you are hypocrites or you should start giving now." Appeals using this strategy are found in a great deal of rhetoric. For example, advertisements asking for support for children in the third world are another example of this strategy.

In relation to when appeals to guilt are likely to be successful, there are two key points to recognize. First, the strategy will not be successful unless the value is strongly held by the audience. It will not work to appeal to the sense of fairness of a racist. Second, the strategy is best applied via an enthymematic argument. A direct attempt to tap guilt in an audience may produce denial or backlash. In most situations, a stronger approach is to make the appeal indirect, as in the examples cited earlier. Appeals to guilt are also more likely to work over the long term, rather than the short term. In the short term, denial can be an effective response to guilt; in the long term that is much less true.

Appeal to History

An appeal to history is a means of tapping into the basic stories that undergird any society. In a speech in the same church where Martin Luther King, Jr. gave his final speech,[8] President Clinton tapped into the history of the civil rights movement as a means of motivating his audience. He also assumed the persona of King as a means of motivating his audience. Clinton actually told the audience what King would say to them if he were there. The same strategy is present any time a rhetor uses the history of the larger society or a particular subset of the society as a means of tapping into strong emotion.

For an appeal to history to produce a strong emotional reaction, three conditions must be present. First, the history must be shared by the group members. If the story doesn't connect with the audience, there will be no emotional response. This is why stories about World War II work much more effectively with an older audience than those who are under thirty. Second, there must be a strong emotional resonance to the story. People feel strongly about history that made a difference for the group. A recounting of the efforts to pass the 1986 Tax Reform Act is unlikely to strongly motivate any group, but a recounting of the events leading up to Martin Luther King's "I Have a Dream" speech may produce very strong reactions.

Third, the historical reference must be relevant to whatever issue is being discussed. For example, many have used the history of U.S. involvement in Vietnam to oppose sending American troops into a foreign war. Clearly, this historical analogy has influenced several American presidents to be quite careful about sending ground troops into a conflict. And the analogy had great resonance after the war in Iraq became a quagmire. But the same historical analogy would have no relevance to the use of troops in purely humanitarian missions. No one would have accepted the "No More Vietnams" position as a reason to stop U.S. Marines from helping hurricane victims. This point became quite evident when anti-war efforts focused on U.S. support of rebel groups in Libya failed to generate much public response.

In summary, shared history can be used in any society, organization, or group to produce an emotional reaction. By citing the history of the group, the rhetor draws on the way that history unifies the group. That is just as true of a social organization as it is of the United States.

Appeal to Religion

An appeal to religion utilizes the power of religious dogma. The rhetor uses the principles at the heart of the faith as a means of energizing the audience. Alternatively, the rhetoric may cite heroes within the religion, such as saints or martyrs, in order to tap the emotional power of faith.

The power of religion in producing a strong emotional reaction is obvious in history and the world today. For example, religion obviously plays a strong role in the conflict between Israelis and Arabs over Jerusalem. That city is not just real estate; it is a sacred religious site for Muslims, Jews, and Christians. As this example indicates, when people feel that their religion is threatened, they may both have a strong emotional reaction and be motivated to act to protect their religious heritage. A similar point can be made about the controversy over building an Islamic Center near ground zero in New York City. Religion also may be a powerful motivating force in cases where there is no threat to the group. For example, strong religious beliefs encourage many people to do volunteer work for the poor. In summary, appeals to religion are a powerful specific type of value appeal and also may be a means of producing a sense of guilt in an audience.

Appeal to Myth

When most people think of myth, they think of a false story. It is common to read articles with titles like "The Myth of Gun Control." From a rhetorical perspective, however, this interpretation of myth is inadequate. In fact, the better argument is that myths are not false stories at all. Rather, myths are the most basic stories told in any society, stories believed to be absolutely true by the people who tell them.[9] In the United States, our most basic myths are the stories of the pioneers and of the founding of this nation, stories that may be grouped together as the American Dream.

Why are these stories so important? Myths in general, and the stories I mentioned, in particular, serve a definitional function. The stories of the pioneers and the Founding Fathers tell us what it means to be an American. In this way, the American Dream tells us that ordinary people can through hard work and continued effort build a better nation. More broadly, humans tell myths to answer big questions about the meaning of life, the nature of a good life or a good society, the chance for eternal life, and so forth. In this way, myths are anything but false stories. They are instead the most powerful stories that are perceived as true in any society.

It is important to recognize, however, that not all myths are understood by the people who tell them as literally true. Instead, they may be interpreted as embodying a fundamental truth of some kind. In this way, a story about the pioneers may not literally have happened, but it still may contain a "truth" about what it means to be an American.

How are myths different from other stories? Myths possess a special rhetorical form that allows them to fulfill the functions I have mentioned.[10] Initially, before treating a story as a myth, the critic should make certain that the story is taken seriously by the people who tell it. Tales about Paul Bunyan, for instance, are not myths in the sense developed here, because they are stories told for fun. No one believes that Paul Bunyan and his ox, Babe, really existed. After making certain that the story is a serious one, it is important to identify the following characteristics. Myths tell the stories of larger-than-life heroes, operating outside of normal space and time, and involve a theme that in some way answers a crucial question for the people telling the story.

The heroes in myth must be larger than life (Washington or Jefferson, for instance or the extraordinary ordinary Americans in the American Dream), because their function is to provide a model for action. The hero solves the problem facing the society because he/she is greater than we are. And by solving the problem, the hero provides us with a model for how we should act in life. This is precisely how stories about both the pioneers and the founding of the nation continue to function in U.S. culture. The pioneer and revolutionary periods are long gone. But people who tell stories about these events link them to contemporary life. The late President Ronald Reagan was a master at using our basic mythology to convince the American people that they could overcome whatever problem was confronting them at a given point in time.[11]

In relation to geography, myths occur in special places, places like Valley Forge, Gettysburg, Ellis Island, the site where the two towers of the World Trade Center stood, and so forth. These places are the proper site for a mythic narrative because of the crucial events that have occurred there. In essence, the function of the place is to add power to the story. For example, because of the heroic acts that occurred at Gettysburg, the place has great meaning in American history. The perfect example of proper mythic geography would be to place the story in Jerusalem, which as I noted earlier is sacred for three religions.

In terms of time, myths generally occur at the beginning or end of a society.[12] We tend to think of the beginning of anything as possessing special power. That is why the Supreme Court continues to consult the writings of the Founders in relation to Constitutional interpretation. It seems unlikely that James Madison had much to say about the application of the First Amendment to the Internet. However, the Supreme Court still consults his writing because he was the primary author of both the Constitution and the Bill of Rights. A similar point can be made about the end of any society. We tend to think of endings as particularly important and meaningful. That is one reason why so many religious myths focus on the "end times." In this country, our basic myths tell of the beginning of the nation and of the new beginning provided by the frontier, and of the constant recreation of a new America in the American Dream.

Finally, in relation to theme, myths speak to essential issues facing the group telling the story. In the cases of the Founding Fathers, the pioneers, and the American Dream, the myths provide the basic American story. They tell of a nation created out of many different cultures, drawing strength from both unity and diversity, which faces terrible obstacles and overcomes them through grit and determination. A rhetor can tap into that mythology by retelling a portion of it and in so doing draw on the power associated with the story.

Appeals to myth are related to the two previous strategies. Mythic stories are the most central stories told in a society. They are therefore even more basic than appeals to history. And myths also are tied to religion, although not all myths are religious. It is the mythic narratives of the Old and New Testament which undergird Christian and Jewish theology. A similar point can be made about all the great religions in the world.

Elemental and Societal Symbols

The final two subtypes of strategies that can be used to produce an emotional response relate to the "symbols" used by the rhetorician. Symbols are words or objects that represent an idea, need, value, or other principle. Elemental and societal symbols produce an emotional reaction by linking into one or more of the other categories for producing an emotional response. For example, a speaker can tap the value of patriotism, as well as both history and myth, by using the American flag as a symbol. Other examples of symbols include the Statue of Liberty, the Golden Gate Bridge, and blood as a means of representing

© ELLA_K./SHUTTERSTOCK.COM

sacrifice. By citing these symbols, the rhetor draws on the emotional power associated with them.

There are two essential types of symbols: elemental (or natural) and societal. An elemental symbol (sometimes called an archetypal symbol)[13] has a single meaning regardless of culture. The best example of an elemental symbol is "blood," which represents life and sacrifice, but also the threat of pollution. To "shed your blood" is to risk death. On the other hand, bad blood will kill you, a threat that became a reality early in the AIDS epidemic. Other elemental symbols include "fire," which represents both warmth and the threat of destruction, excrement, the sea, and so forth.

It should be clear that there are not very many truly elemental symbols. Even in the case of some that I have mentioned, there may be some variation in usage. The "sea" seemed a lot more terrifying a thousand years ago than it does today.[14] Elemental symbols are tied to the basic structure of human existence on this earth. Since there are few universals across the planet, there are not many elemental symbols.

The use of societal symbols, symbols which have a particular meaning for a group or society, is far more common than the use of elemental symbols. For example, U.S. politicians often "wrap themselves in the flag" or make announcements concerning veterans benefits at the Tomb of the Unknown Soldier as ways of tapping into the power of societal symbols. In so doing, the rhetor uses the symbol as a means of getting at basic values, history, myth, or another substrategy for producing an emotional response. Societal symbols are also present in regions and for various organizations. At my university, the University of Kansas, the Jayhawk is a powerful symbol, but that symbol will not resonate at all at neighboring universities.

SUMMARY OF STRATEGY CATEGORIES

In the previous section, I identified the nine main sub-strategies for producing an emotional response in an audience. These nine sub-strategies are often found in combination. In some cases, such as appeals to history, myth, and religion, it may be difficult to distinguish between the subcategories. The important principle to keep in mind is that the subcategories are a starting point for analysis. They should be used to identify the specific way that a speaker/writer attempts to create an emotional reaction in a given instance.

In the next section, I illustrate how the subcategories can be used to produce a strong emotional response via an analysis of the "Common Ground" address which Jesse Jackson presented at the 1988 Democratic National Convention. Jackson had been a candidate for the Democratic nomination and had won more votes than anyone other than the eventual nominee, Governor Michael Dukakis of Massachusetts. In his address, Jackson appealed to both his constituency, the Rainbow Coalition, and also to the entire party. Jackson's 1988 address was one of the most discussed and influential speeches of the decade of the 1980s. It is a fine example of how a rhetor can tap values, needs, and symbols representing those values and needs in order to produce a strong emotional response.

Common Ground Address
1988 Democratic National Convention
Jesse Jackson

Tonight we pause and give praise and honor to God for being good enough to 1
allow us to be at this place at this time. When I look out at this convention, I see the
face of America, red, yellow, brown, black and white, we're all precious in God's
sight—the real rainbow coalition. All of us, all of us who are here and think that we are
seated. But we're really standing on someone's shoulders. Ladies and gentlemen,
Mrs. Rosa Parks.

The mother of the civil rights movement. 2

I want to express my deep love and appreciation for the support my family has 3
given me over these past months.

They have endured pain, anxiety, threat and fear. 4

But they have been strengthened and made secure by a faith in God, in America 5
and in you.

Your love has protected us and made us strong. 6

To my wife Jackie, the foundation of our family; to our five children whom you 7
met tonight; to my mother Mrs. Helen Jackson, who is present tonight; and to my
grandmother, Mrs. Matilda Burns; my brother Chuck and his family; my mother-in-
law, Mrs. Gertrude Brown, who just last month at age 61 graduated from Hampton
Institute, a marvelous achievement; I offer my appreciation to [Atlanta] Mayor Andrew
Young who has provided such gracious hospitality to all of us this week.

And a special salute to President Jimmy Carter. 8

President Carter restored honor to the White House after Watergate. He gave 9
many of us a special opportunity to grow. For his kind words, for his unwavering
commitment to peace in the world and the voters that came from his family, every
member of his family, led by Billy and Amy, I offer him my special thanks, special
thanks to the Carter family.

My right and my privilege to stand here before you has been won—in my lifetime— 10
by the blood and the sweat of the innocent.

Twenty-four years ago, the late Fanny Lou Hamer and Aaron Henry—who sits here 11
tonight from Mississippi—were locked out on the streets of Atlantic City, the head of
the Mississippi Freedom Democratic Party.

But tonight, a black and white delegation from Mississippi is headed by [state 12
party Chairman] Ed Cole, a black man, from Mississippi, 24 years later.

Many were lost in the struggle for the right to vote. Jimmy Lee Jackson, a young student, gave his life. Viola Liuzzo, a white mother from Detroit, called nigger lover, and brains blown out at point blank range.   13

[Michael] Schwerner, [Andrew] Goodman and [James] Chaney—two Jews and a black—found in common grave, bodies riddled with bullets in Mississippi. The four darling little girls in the church in Birmingham, Ala. They died so that we might have a right to live.   14

Dr. Martin Luther King Jr. lies only a few miles from us tonight.   15

Tonight he must feel good as he looks down upon us. We sit here together, a rainbow, a coalition—the sons and daughters of slaves sitting together around a common table, to decide the direction of our party and our country. His heart would be full tonight.   16

As a testament to the struggles of those who have gone before; as a legacy for those who will come after; as a tribute to the endurance, the patience, the courage of our forefathers and mothers; as an assurance that their prayers are being answered, their work has not been in vain, and hope is eternal; tomorrow night my name will go into nomination for the presidency of the United States of America.   17

We meet tonight at a crossroads, a point of decision.   18

Shall we expand, be inclusive, find unity and power; or suffer division and impotence?   19

We come to Atlanta, the cradle of the old South, the crucible of the new South.   20

Tonight there is a sense of celebration because we are moved, fundamentally moved, from racial battlegrounds by law, to economic common ground. Tomorrow we will challenge to move to higher ground.   21

Common ground!   22

Think of Jerusalem—the intersection where many trails met. A small village that became the birthplace for three great religions—Judaism, Christianity and Islam.   23

Why was this village so blessed? Because it provided a crossroads where different people met, different cultures, and different civilizations could meet and find common ground.   24

When people come together, flowers always flourish and the air is rich with the aroma of a new spring.   25

Take New York, the dynamic metropolis. What makes New York so special?   26

It is the invitation of the Statue of Liberty—give me your tired, your poor, your huddled masses who yearn to breathe free.   27

Not restricted to English only.   28

Many people, many cultures, many languages—with one thing in common, they yearn to breathe free.   29

Common ground!   30

Tonight in Atlanta, for the first time in this century we convene in the South.   31

A state where governors once stood in school house doors. Where [former Georgia state Sen.] Julian Bond was denied his seat in the state legislature because of his conscientious objection to the Vietnam War. 32

A city that, through its five black universities, has graduated more black students than any city in the world. 33

Atlanta, now a modern intersection of the new South. 34

Common ground! 35

That is the challenge to our party tonight. 36

Left wing. Right wing. Progress will not come through boundless liberalism nor static conservatism, but at the critical mass of mutual survival. It takes two wings to fly. 37

Whether you're a hawk or a dove, you're just a bird living in the same environment, in the same world. 38

The Bible teaches that when lions and lambs lie down together, none will be afraid and there will be peace in the valley. It sounds impossible. Lions eat lambs. Lambs sensibly flee from lions. But even lions and lambs find common ground. Why? 39

Because neither lions nor lambs want the forest to catch on fire. Neither lions nor lambs want acid rain to fall. Neither lions nor lambs can survive nuclear war. If lions and lambs can find common ground, surely, we can as well, as civilized people. 40

The only time that we win is when we come together. In 1960, John Kennedy, the late John Kennedy, beat Richard Nixon by only 112,000 votes—less than one vote per precinct. He won by the margin of our hope. He brought us together. He reached out. He had the courage to defy his advisors and inquire about Dr. King's jailing in Albany, Georgia. We won by the margin of our hope, inspired by courageous leadership. 41

In 1964, Lyndon Johnson brought both wings together. The thesis, the antithesis and to create a synthesis and together we won. 42

In 1976, Jimmy Carter unified us again and we won. When we do not come together, we never win. 43

In 1968, division and despair in July led to our defeat in November. 44

In 1980, rancor in the spring and the summer led to [President Ronald] Reagan in the fall. When we divide, we cannot win. We must find common ground as a basis for survival and development and change and growth. 45

Today when we debated, differed, deliberated, agreed to agree, agreed to disagree, when we had the good judgment to argue our case and then not self-destruct, George Bush was just a little further away from the White House and a little closer to private life. 46

Tonight, I salute Governor Michael Dukakis. 47

He has run a well-managed and a dignified campaign. No matter how tired or how tried, he always resisted the temptation to stoop to demagoguery. 48

I've watched a good mind fast at work, with steel nerves, guiding his campaign out   49
of the crowded field without appeal to the worst in us. I've watched his perspective
grow as his environment has expanded. I've seen his toughness and tenacity close
up. I know his commitment to public service.

Mike Dukakis' parents were a doctor and a teacher; my parents, a maid, a   50
beautician and a janitor.

There's a great gap between Brookline, Massachusetts, and Haney Street, the   51
Fieldcrest Village housing projects in Greenville, South Carolina.

He studied law; I studied theology. There are differences of religion, region, and   52
race; differences in experiences and perspectives. But the genius of America is that
out of the many, we become one.

Providence has enabled our paths to intersect. His foreparents came to America   53
on immigrant ships; my foreparents came to America on slave ships. But whatever
the original ships, we're in the same boat tonight.

Our ships could pass in the night if we have a false sense of independence, or they   54
could collide and crash. We would lose our passengers. But we can seek a higher
reality and a greater good apart. We can drift on the broken pieces of Reaganomics,
satisfy our baser instincts, and exploit the fears of our people. At our highest, we can
call upon noble instincts and navigate this vessel to safety. The greater good is the
common good.

As Jesus said, "Not my will, but thine be done." It was his way of saying there's   55
higher good beyond personal comfort or position.

The good of our nation is at stake—its commitment to working men and women, to   56
the poor and the vulnerable, to the many in the world. With so many guided missiles,
and so much misguided leadership, the stakes are exceedingly high. Our choice,
full participation in a democratic government, or more abandonment and neglect.
And so this night, we choose not a false sense of independence, but our capacity to
survive and endure.

Tonight we choose interdependency in our capacity to act and unite for the greater   57
good. The common good is finding commitment to new priorities, to expansion
and inclusion. A commitment to expanded participation in the Democratic Party at
every level. A commitment to a shared national campaign strategy and involvement
at every level. A commitment to new priorities that ensure that hope will be kept
alive. A common ground commitment for a legislative agenda by empowerment
for the [Michigan Rep.] John Conyers bill, universal, on-site, same-day registration
everywhere—and commitment to D.C. statehood and empowerment—D.C. deserves
statehood. A commitment to economic set-asides, a commitment to the [California
Rep. Ronald V.] Dellums bill for comprehensive sanctions against South Africa, a
shared commitment to a common direction.

Common ground. Easier said than done. Where do you find common ground at   58
the point of challenge? This campaign has shown that politics need not be marketed

by politicians, packaged by pollsters and pundits. Politics can be a marvelous arena where people come together, define common ground.

We find common ground at the plant gate that closes on workers without notice. We find common ground at the farm auction where a good farmer loses his or her land to bad loans or diminishing markets. Common ground at the schoolyard where teachers cannot get adequate pay, and students cannot get a scholarship and can't make a loan. Common ground at the hospital admitting room where somebody tonight is dying because they cannot afford to go upstairs to a bed that's empty, waiting for someone with insurance to get sick. We are a better nation than that. We must do better.   59

Common ground. What is leadership if not present help in a time of crisis? And so I met you at the point of challenge in Jay, Maine, where paper workers were striking for fair wages; in Greenfield, Iowa, where family farmers struggle for a fair price; in Cleveland, Ohio, where working women seek comparable worth; in McFarland, Calif., where the children of Hispanic farm workers may be dying from poison land, dying in clusters with cancer; in the AIDS hospice in Houston, Texas, where the sick support one another, 12 are rejected by their own parents and friends.   60

Common ground.   61

America's not a blanket woven from one thread, one color, one cloth. When I was a child growing up in Greenville, S.C., and grandmother could not afford a blanket, she didn't complain and we did not freeze. Instead, she took pieces of old cloth—patches, wool, silk, gabardine, crockersack on the patches—barely good enough to wipe off your shoes with.   62

But they didn't stay that way very long. With sturdy hands and strong cord, she sewed them together into a quilt, a thing of beauty and power and culture.   63

Now, Democrats, we must build such a quilt. Farmers, you seek fair prices and you are right, but you cannot stand alone. Your patch is not big enough. Workers, you fight for fair wages. You are right. But your patch labor is not big enough. Women, you seek comparable worth and pay equity. You are right. But your patch is not big enough. Women, mothers, who see Head Start and day care and pre-natal care on the front side of life, rather than jail care and welfare on the back side of life, you're right, but your patch is not big enough.   64

Students, you seek scholarships. You are right. But your patch is not big enough. Blacks and Hispanics, when we fight for civil rights, we are right, but our patch is not big enough. Gays and lesbians, when you fight against discrimination and a cure for AIDS, you are right, but your patch is not big enough. Conservatives and progressives, when you fight for what you believe, right-wing, left-wing, hawk, dove—you are right, from your point of view, but your point of view is not enough.   65

We the people can win. We stand at the end of a long dark night of reaction. We stand tonight united in a commitment to a new direction. For almost eight years, we've been led by those who view social good coming from private interest, who viewed public life as a means to increase private wealth. They have been prepared to   66 sacrifice the common good of the many to satisfy the private interest and the wealth of a few. We believe in a government that's a tool of our democracy in service to the public, not an instrument of the aristocracy in search of private wealth.

We believe in government with the consent of the governed of, for, and by the people. We must emerge into a new day with a new direction. Reaganomics, based on the belief that the rich had too much money—too little money, and the poor had too much.   67

That's classic Reaganomics. It believes that the poor had too much money and the rich had too little money.   68

So, they engaged in reverse Robin Hood—took from the poor, gave to the rich, paid for by the middle class. We cannot stand four more years of Reaganomics in any version, in any disguise.   69

How do I document that case? Seven years later, the richest 1 percent of our society pays 20 percent less in taxes; the poorest 10 percent pay 20 percent more. Reaganomics.   70

Reagan gave the rich and the powerful a multibillion-dollar party. Now, the party is over. He expects the people to pay for the damage. I take this principled position—convention, let us not raise taxes on the poor and the middle class, but those who had the party, the rich and the powerful, must pay for the party!   71

I just want to take common sense to high places. We're spending $150 billion a year defending Europe and Japan 43 years after the war is over. We have more troops in Europe tonight than we had seven years ago, yet the threat of war is ever more remote. Germany and Japan are now creditor nations—that means they've got a surplus. We are a debtor nation—it means we are in debt.   72

Let them share more of the burden of their own defense—use some of that money to build decent housing!   73

Use some of that money to educate our children!   74

Use some of that money for long-term health care!   75

Use some of that money to wipe out these slums and put America back to work!   76

I just want to take common sense to high places. If we can bail out Europe and Japan, if we can bail out Continental Bank and Chrysler—and Mr. Iacocca makes $8,000 an hour—we can bail out the family farmer.   77

I just want to make common sense. It does not make sense to close down 650,000 family farms in this country while importing food from abroad subsidized by the U.S. government.   78

Let's make sense. It does not make sense to be escorting oil tankers up and down the Persian Gulf paying $2.50 for every $1.00 worth of oil we bring out while oil wells are capped in Texas, Oklahoma and Louisiana. I just want to make sense.   79

Leadership must meet the moral challenge of its day. What's the moral challenge of our day? We have public accommodations. We have the right to vote. We have open housing.   80

What's the fundamental challenge of our day? It is to end economic violence. Plant closing without notice, economic violence. Even the greedy do not profit long from greed. Economic violence. Most poor people are not lazy. They're not black. They're not brown. They're mostly white, and female and young.   81

But whether white, black or brown, the hungry baby's belly turned inside out is the same color. Call it pain. Call it hurt. Call it agony. Most poor people are not on welfare.   82

Some of them are illiterate and can't read the want-ad sections. And when they can, they can't find a job that matches their address. They work hard every day, I know. I live amongst them. I'm one of them.   83

I know they work. I'm a witness. They catch the early bus. They work every day. They raise other people's children. They work every day. They clean the streets. They work every day. They drive vans with cabs. They work every day. They change the beds you slept in these hotels last night and can't get a union contract. They work every day.   84

No more. They're not lazy. Someone must defend them because it's right, and they cannot speak for themselves. They work in hospitals. I know they do. They wipe the bodies of those who are sick with fever and pain. They empty their bedpans. They clean out their commode. No job is beneath them, and yet when they get sick, they cannot lie in the bed they made up every day. America, that is not right. We are a better nation than that. We are a better nation than that.   85

We need a real war on drugs. You can't just say no. It's deeper than that. You can't just get a palm reader or an astrologer; it's more profound than that. We're spending $150 billion on drugs a year. We've gone from ignoring it to focusing on the children. Children cannot buy $150 billion worth of drugs a year. A few high profile athletes—athletes are not laundering $150 billion a year—bankers are.   86

I met the children in Watts who are unfortunate in their despair. Their grapes of hope have become raisins of despair, and they're turning to each other and they're self-destructing—but I stayed with them all night long. I wanted to hear their case. They said, "Jesse Jackson, as you challenge us to say no to drugs, you're right. And to not sell them, you're right. And to not use these guns, you're right."   87

And, by the way, the promise of CETA [Comprehensive Employment and Training Act]—they displaced CETA. They did not replace CETA. We have neither jobs nor houses nor services nor training—no way out. Some of us take drugs as anesthesia for our pain. Some take drugs as a way of pleasure—both short-term pleasure and long-term pain. Some sell drugs to make money. It's wrong, we know. But you need to know that we know. We can go and buy the drugs by the boxes at the port. If we can buy the drugs at the port, don't you believe the federal government can stop it if they want to?   88

They say, "We don't have Saturday night specials any more." They say, "We buy AK-47s and Uzis, the latest lethal weapons. We buy them across the counter on Long Beach Boulevard." You cannot fight a war on drugs unless and until you are going to challenge the bankers and the gun sellers and those who grow them. Don't just focus   89 on the children, let's stop drugs at the level of supply and demand. We must end the scourge on the American culture.

Leadership. What difference will we make? Leadership cannot just go along to get along. We must do more than change presidents. We must change direction. Leadership must face the moral challenge of our day. The nuclear war build-up is irrational. Strong leadership cannot desire to look tough, and let that stand in the way of the pursuit of peace. Leadership must reverse the arms race. 90

At least we should pledge no first use. Why? Because first use begat first retaliation, and that's mutual annihilation. That's not a rational way out. No use at all—let's think it out, and not fight it out, because it's an unwinnable fight. Why hold a card that you can never drop? Let's give peace a chance. 91

Leadership—we now have this marvelous opportunity to have a breakthrough with the Soviets. Last year, 200,000 Americans visited the Soviet Union. There's a chance for joint ventures into space, not Star Wars and the war arms escalation, but a space defense initiative. Let's build in space together, and demilitarize the heavens. There's a way out. 92

American, let us expand. When Mr. Reagan and Mr. [Mikhail S.] Gorbachev met, there was a big meeting. The represented together one-eighth of the human race. Seven-eighths of the human race was locked out of that room. Most people in the world tonight—half are Asian, one-half of them are Chinese. There are 22 nations in the Middle East. There's Europe; 40 million Latin Americans next door to us; the Caribbean; Africa—a half-billion people. Most people in the world today are yellow or brown or black, non-Christian, poor, female, young, and don't speak English—in the real world. 93

This generation must offer leadership to the real world. We're losing ground in Latin America, the Middle East, South Africa, because we're not focusing on the real world, that real world. We must use basic principles, support international law. We stand the most to gain from it. Support human rights; we believe in that. Support self-determination; we'll build on that. Support economic development; you know it's right. Be consistent, and gain our moral authority in the world. 94

I challenge you tonight, my friends, let's be bigger and better as a nation and as a party. We have basic challenges. Freedom in South Africa—we've already agreed as Democrats to declare South Africa to be a terrorist state. But don't just stop there. Get South Africa out of Angola. Free Namibia. Support the front-line states. We must have a new, humane human rights assistance policy in Africa. 95

I'm often asked, "Jesse, why do you take on these tough issues? They're not very political. We can't win that way." 96

If an issue is morally right, it will eventually be political. It may be political and never be right. Fannie Lou Hamer didn't have the most votes in Atlantic City, but her principles have outlasted every delegate who voted to lock her out. Rosa Parks did not have the most votes, but she was morally right. Dr. King didn't have the most votes 97 about the Vietnam war, but he was morally right. If we're principles first, our politics will fall in place.

"Jesse, why did you take these big bold initiatives?" A poem by an unknown author went something like this: We mastered the air, we've conquered the sea, and annihilated distance and prolonged life, we were not wise enough to live on this earth without war and without hate.   98

As for Jesse Jackson, I'm tired of sailing my little boat, far inside the harbor bar. I want to go out where the big ships float, out on the deep where the great ones are. And should my frail craft prove too slight, the waves that sweep those billows o'er, I'd rather go down in a stirring fight than drown to death in the sheltered shore.   99

We've got to go out, my friends, where the big boats are.   100

And then, for our children, young America, hold your head high now. We can win. We must not lose you to drugs and violence, premature pregnancy, suicide, cynicism, pessimism and despair. We can win.   101

Wherever you are tonight, I challenge you to hope and to dream. Don't submerge your dreams. Exercise above all else, even on drugs, dream of the day you're drug-free. Even in the gutter, dream of the day that you'll be upon your feet again. You must never stop dreaming. Face reality, yes. But don't stop with the way things are: dream of things as they ought to be. Dream. Face pain, but love, hope, faith, and dreams will help you rise above the pain.   102

Use hope and imagination as weapons of survival and progress, but you keep on dreaming, young America. Dream of peace. Peace is rational and reasonable. War is irrational in this age and unwinnable.   103

Dream of teachers who teach for life and not for living. Dream of doctors who are concerned more about public health than private wealth. Dream of lawyers more concerned about justice than a judgeship. Dream of preachers who are concerned more about prophecy than profiteering. Dream on the high road of sound values.   104

And in America, as we go forth to September, October and November and then beyond, America must never surrender to a high moral challenge.   105

Do not surrender to drugs. The best drug policy is a no first use. Don't surrender with needles and cynicism. Let's have no first use on the one hand, or clinics on the other. Never surrender, young America.   106

Go forward. America must never surrender to malnutrition. We can feed the hungry and clothe the naked. We must never surrender. We must go forward. We must never surrender to illiteracy. Invest in our children. Never surrender; and go forward.   107

We must never surrender to inequality. Women cannot compromise ERA [Equal Rights Amendment] or comparable worth. Women are making 60 cents on the dollar to what a man makes. Women cannot buy milk cheaper. Women deserve to get paid for the work that you do. It's right and it's fair.   108

Don't surrender, my friends. Those who have AIDS tonight, you deserve our compassion. Even with AIDS you must not surrender in your wheelchairs. I see you   109 sitting here tonight in those wheelchairs. I've stayed with you. I've reached out to you across our nation. Don't you give up. I know it's tough sometimes. People look down on you. It took you a little more effort to get here tonight.

And no one should look down on you, but sometimes mean people do. The only justification we have for looking down on someone is that we're going to stop and pick them up. But even in your wheelchairs, don't you give up. We cannot forget 50 years ago when our backs were against the wall, [Franklin D.] Roosevelt was in a wheelchair. I would rather have Roosevelt in a wheelchair than Reagan and [George] Bush on a horse. Don't you surrender and don't you give up. 110

Don't surrender and don't you give up. Why can I challenge you this way? "Jesse Jackson, you don't understand my situation. You be on television. You don't understand. I see you with the big people. You don't understand my situation." I understand. You're seeing me on TV but you don't know the me that makes me, me. They wonder why does Jesse run, because they see me running for the White House. They don't see the house I'm running from. 111

I have a story. I wasn't always on television. Writers were not always outside my door. When I was born late one afternoon, October 8th, in Greenville, S.C., no writers asked my mother her name. Nobody chose to write down her address. My mama was not supposed to make it. And I was not supposed to make it. You see, I was born to a teen-age mother who was born to a teen-age mother. 112

I understand. I know abandonment and people being mean to you, and saying you're nothing and nobody, and can never be anything. I understand. Jesse Jackson is my third name. I'm adopted. When I had no name, my grandmother gave me her name. My name was Jesse Burns until I was 12. So I wouldn't have a blank space, she gave me a name to hold me over. I understand when nobody knows your name. I understand when you have no name. I understand. 113

I wasn't born in a hospital. Mama didn't have insurance. I was born in the bed at the house. I really do understand. Born in a three-room house, bathroom in the backyard, slop jar by the bed, no hot and cold running water. I understand. Wallpaper used for decoration? No. For a windbreaker. I understand. I'm a working person's person, that's why I understand you whether you're black or white. 114

I understand work. I was not born with a silver spoon in my mouth. I had a shovel programmed for my hand. My mother, a working woman. So many days she went to work with runs in her stockings. She knew better, but she wore runs in her stockings so that my brother and I could have matching socks and not be laughed at at school. 115

I understand. At 3 o'clock on Thanksgiving Day we couldn't eat turkey because mama was preparing someone else's turkey at 3 o'clock. We had to play football to entertain ourselves and then around 6 o'clock she would get off the Alta Vista bus when we would bring up the leftovers and eat our turkey—leftovers, the carcass, the cranberries around 8 o'clock at night. I really do understand. 116

Every one of these funny labels they put on you, those of you who are watching this broadcast tonight in the projects, on the corners. I understand. Call you outcast, low 117

down, you can't make it, you're nothing, you're from nobody, subclass, underclass—
when you see Jesse Jackson, when my name goes in nomination, your name goes
in nomination.

I was born in the slum, but the slum was not born in me. And it wasn't born in you,   118
and you can make it. Wherever you are tonight you can make it. Hold your head high,
stick your chest out. You can make it. It gets dark sometimes, but the morning comes.
Don't you surrender. Suffering breeds character. Character breeds faith. In the end
faith will not disappoint.

You must not surrender. You may or may not get there, but just know that you're   119
qualified and you hold on and hold out. We must never surrender. America will get
better and better. Keep hope alive. Keep hope alive. Keep hope alive. On tomorrow
night and beyond, keep hope alive.

I love you very much. I love you very much.   120

ANALYSIS OF JESSE JACKSON, COMMON GROUND: ADDRESS TO THE 1988 DEMOCRATIC NATIONAL CONVENTION

Jackson's 1988 Democratic Convention Address might be labeled a "dissident keynote" address. Jackson's speech was not the official keynote address of the 1988 convention, but it served much the same function as a keynote address. As I noted in reference to Cuomo's 1984 address, keynotes are primarily aimed at unifying and energizing the party faithful. To some extent, they also aim at pulling undecided voters into the fold. I label Jackson's address a "dissident" keynote because Jackson had been a candidate for the nomination and clearly was representing the liberal wing of the party. His purposes, therefore, included not only the general goals of any keynote, but also the aim of pulling the party to the political left so that it would better represent the interests for which Jackson had fought. Jackson also may have been using the address to set the stage for a possible run for the Democratic nomination in 1992. Of course, he later decided not to run for the nomination in that year.

The "dissident" nature of the speech is most evident in paragraphs 65 and 66, where he compares various interest groups within the Democratic party to the patches on a quilt. He begins the section by focusing on farmers, workers, women, students, African Americans, and then Hispanics. In each case he calls for unity by saying "You are right. But your patch is not big enough." Then Jackson turns to what he calls "conservatives and progressives," (the moderate wing of the party represented by people like Bill Clinton). In relation to this group he says: "when you fight for what you believe, right-wing, left-wing, hawk, dove—you are right, from your point of view, but your point of view is not enough" (65). While every other group in the party is simply "right," the moderate wing is only right "from your point of view." Of course, when someone says that you are right "from your point of view," what they really mean is that you are wrong.

Jackson did desire to unify and energize the party, but he also represented the agenda of his organization, the Rainbow Coalition, and supported other liberal groups as well. Clearly, his address was concerned with defending their position within the party.

Jackson faced significant rhetorical barriers and possessed one major rhetorical advantage in this address. His rhetorical advantage was that he was the second largest vote getter in the primaries and represented some of the largest constituencies in the Democratic Party. In particular, Jackson was the most prominent Democrat who was associated with civil rights organizations and the African American community.

In relation to barriers, Jackson faced problems similar to those faced by Cuomo. Like Cuomo (see chapter six), he had to adapt to the constraints associated with a keynote address. In addition, Jackson faced barriers associated with his role as the most important spokesperson for the Rainbow Coalition. Any time the representative of a particular group calls for national action that helps his/her group, there is the potential that the person may be perceived as self-interested. Jackson, as the leader of the Rainbow Coalition, supported initiatives that would aid people of color, women, gays, etc. Some, therefore, could perceive his remarks as self-interested.

Since Jackson is an African American, one might expect that racism would be a barrier. However, given his message, racists are simply not in the implied audience. Jackson spoke to the Democratic Party, which already was committed to strong support for civil rights for all Americans. As a consequence, outright racists or others who might feel some bias against Jackson because he is an African American simply were not in his audience.

STRATEGIES IN JACKSON'S COMMON GROUND ADDRESS

Jackson relies on four major strategies in his 1988 address: narrative, credibility, language strategies, and various sub-strategies for producing an emotional response. Before discussing these strategies, it is important to note that Jackson does not rely heavily on rational argument. Jackson is, as the saying goes, "preaching to the saved." This religious metaphor expresses the fact that Jackson was talking to people who already agreed with him. In that context, argument, especially evidence-oriented argument, is not necessary. This explains why in most cases in his 100-plus paragraph address, Jackson simply asserts claims. For example, in paragraphs 72–76 he calls for cutting defense spending in Europe and spending the money on education, health care, and slum redevelopment. In no case does he support the effectiveness of the increased expenditures. For his audience, it was an article of faith that such expenditures were valuable, while defense spending was not. Rational argument is not a core strategy in Jackson's address.

Narrative, Credibility, and Language Strategies

Instead of argument, Jackson relies on narrative, credibility appeals, language strategies, and all of the main sub-strategies for producing an emotional response.

The narrative strategy takes two forms. Throughout the address he briefly cites characters, each of whose story will be well-known to the audience. This strategy is used most extensively in the introduction, where he cites any number of heroes of the civil rights movement including Rosa Parks, Fanny Lou Hamer, Aaron Henry, and of course his mentor, Dr. Martin Luther King, Jr. (paragraphs 11–16). Here, he positions himself as a successor to these great heroes of the civil rights movement.

The second narrative strategy and Jackson's attempts to develop internal credibility are related. To some extent throughout the address, but most noticeably in the conclusion, Jackson uses his own life history as a model for others to emulate. From paragraph 112 to the conclusion of the address, he develops this narrative/credibility strategy. In paragraph 112, he establishes his "credentials" as someone born into poverty. He concludes the paragraph by saying "I was not supposed to make it. You see, I was born to a teenage mother who was born to a teenage mother." In the following paragraph, he talks about how he did not live in a traditional nuclear family, but instead lived with his grandmother.

He continues with the theme that he was born into poverty in paragraph 114, where he notes that he was not born in a hospital, but at home in a house where wallpaper was not for decoration, but "for a wind breaker." In the next paragraph, he says that he "was not born with a silver spoon in my mouth. I had a shovel programmed for my hand." He then describes the sacrifices that his mother made for him and his brothers.

Paragraph 116 continues the theme that his mother sacrificed for him, but that the family still lived in utter poverty:

> I understand. At 3 o'clock on Thanksgiving Day we couldn't eat turkey because mama was preparing someone else's turkey at 3 o'clock. We had to play football to entertain ourselves and then around 6 o'clock she would get off the Alta Vista bus when we would bring up the leftovers and eat our turkey—leftovers, the carcass, the cranberries around 8 o'clock at night. I really do understand.

It is the details in Jackson's description that make the passage so vivid. He remembers the specific bus his mother took and how she brought home the carcass of the rich folks' turkey.

Jackson uses the narrative to build his credibility, both as someone who can identify with the poor, and as someone who proved his mettle by escaping from poverty. He then uses both the credibility and the narrative to pound home his point that others can do what he has done. In the final four paragraphs of the address, he hits this theme again and again. In paragraph 117, he casts himself as a representative of all the downtrodden in our society: "Call you outcast, low down, you can't make it, you're nothing, you're from nobody, subclass, underclass—when you see Jesse Jackson, when my name goes in nomination, your name goes in nomination." Jackson then calls on these groups to reject the labels that others apply to them: "I was born in the slum, but the slum was not born in me. And it wasn't born in you." Instead of accepting that label, they must fight: "Don't surrender. Suffering breeds character. Character breeds faith. In the end faith will not disappoint." In the next paragraph, he continues with this theme, almost screaming "Keep hope alive," before he concludes by again expressing his shared identity with the audience, "I love you very much."

In the final paragraphs of his speech, Jackson builds his credibility as a poor kid who made it out of poverty, but still knows his roots. He then uses his personal narrative and credibility both to reaffirm identity with the groups within the Rainbow Coalition and to call on them to emulate his example. It is an extremely powerful passage.

In addition to his use of narrative and credibility, the Jackson address contains numerous language strategies. Jackson is a skilled rhetorician who relies primarily on language strategies to add interest to whatever specific point he is making. For example, in the concluding passages which I just cited, Jackson uses antithesis when he says, "I was born in the slum, but the slum was not born in me." His statement, "Suffering breeds character. Character breeds faith. In the end faith will not disappoint" has a natural rhythm that makes it memorable. "Never surrender" is a slogan that encapsulates a good portion of Jackson's message. He relies on parallel structure when he begins several passages in this section by saying "I understand."

The key point is that throughout the address Jackson relies on a wide variety of language strategies to invigorate his message. Jackson's use of multiple language strategies in combination with narrative, credibility, and various sub-strategies for creating an emotional response, which I will discuss in the next section, illustrates the point made in chapter seven that aesthetic strategies can be integrated into any work of rhetoric to add power to other strategies.

While Jackson primarily uses language strategies to make his message more vivid, there are four metaphors in the address that serve a more important function. At various points in the address, he compares the Democratic Party to a "crossroads," to "common ground," to a "quilt," and of course to a "rainbow." The point of each of these metaphors is to define the party as composed of a number of different interest groups. The Democrats in Jackson's view are a diverse party including many groups in our society. Note that for Jackson the party is not a "melting pot" in which various groups are transformed and strengthened into a single group—Americans. Nor is the party, to borrow a phrase that Ronald Reagan borrowed in turn from James Madison, an "empire of ideas." Instead, the party is a place (crossroads or common ground), an object (a quilt), or an image (a rainbow), in which different people come together to work in common cause, but maintain their group affiliations.

Of these metaphors, Jackson develops the quilt theme in the most depth. He introduces the metaphor with a story about his grandmother:

> America's not a blanket woven from one thread, one color, one cloth. When I was a child growing up in Greenville, S.C., and grandmother could not afford a blanket, she didn't complain, and we did not freeze. Instead, she took pieces of old cloth—patches, wool, silk, gabardine, crockersack on the patches—barely good enough to wipe off your shoes with.
>
> But they didn't stay that way very long. With sturdy hands and strong cord, she sewed them together into a quilt, a thing of beauty and power and culture. (paragraphs 62, 63)

In the following passage, which I cited earlier, he then compares the quilt to the various interest groups in the party. Jackson's powerful metaphor both adds interest to the address and provides a vision of the fundamental purpose of the Democratic Party.

Jackson's 1988 convention address includes powerful narrative, credibility, and aesthetic strategies. It would have been an important speech with just these strategies, but the dominant strategy in the address is Jackson's use of various sub-strategies to produce a strong emotional response.

Emotion Producing Strategies in Jackson's Address

Jackson's address is literally a textbook example of how a rhetor can use various strategies to produce an emotional response from his audience. He also clearly recognizes the association between emotional response and vivid descriptive language. As I noted in the previous section, it is the detail that Jackson provides which makes the short narrative in the conclusion so powerful. We can imagine what it must have been like to wait until 8 p.m. to eat someone else's turkey carcass. Jackson clearly understands that graphic language is better adapted to producing an emotional response than abstract language.

Appeals to Basic Needs

Jackson cites basic human needs at several points in the address. For example, in paragraphs 81 and 82, he talks about the "Plant closings without notice, economic violence." He then refers to the effects of those plant closings. "But whether white, black, or brown, the hungry baby's belly turned inside out is the same color. Call it pain. Call it hurt. Call it agony." Here, Jackson shows the effect of the relocation of manufacturing plants outside of the United States on ordinary people, in this case babies. He is arguing that basic human needs are threatened by what he calls "economic violence." This same strategy is found in other forms at several other points in the address.

Appeals to Basic Values

Throughout the address, Jackson draws on basic values including equality, opportunity, and diversity. For example, in paragraph 57, he says:

> Tonight we choose interdependency in our capacity to act and unite for the greater good. The common good is finding commitment to new priorities, to expression and inclusion. A commitment to expanded participation in the Democratic Party at every level.

He then uses the "common ground" metaphor to apply his call for inclusion to workers, teachers, hospital admissions, farmers, and others (paragraphs 59, 60).

Jackson also appeals to basic values in the conclusion. In this section, he taps into American values such as hard work, responsibility, and opportunity. For example, in a long passage, he calls on kids to reject drugs. He says "Do not surrender to drugs. The best drug policy is no first use" (paragraph 106). He then moves into the concluding narrative, which I cited earlier. The key point in relation to the values that come out of this narrative is that hard work and continued effort can produce opportunity. In essence, Jackson uses himself as the example proving that the American Dream can be achieved.

Throughout the address, Jackson attacks Ronald Reagan and the values for which he says Reagan stands. The irony is that in the conclusion, Jackson endorses basic values very similar to the values at the core of Reagan's rhetoric—values like opportunity, hard work, and personal responsibility. His rejection of drug use sounds very much like Nancy Reagan's anti-drug slogan—"just say no." I am not saying that Jackson is a hypocrite. My point is that basic American values, such as the ones Jackson draws on in the conclusion, are shared by nearly everyone in our culture. Those values are quite consistent with the messages of both Jackson and Reagan.

Appeals to Self-interest

Jackson clearly appeals to the self-interest of the Democratic constituencies, which he represents. His appeal to self-interest is most obvious in paragraph 64, where he uses the quilt metaphor to describe the party. "Farmers, you seek fair prices and you are right, but you cannot stand alone. Your patch is not big enough. Workers, you fight for fair wages. You are right. But your patch labor is not big enough. Women, you seek comparable worth and pay equity. You are right. But your patch is not big enough." He continues with this same theme in the following paragraph. The important point is that Jackson is appealing to the self-interest of each of the groups he references. He supports higher prices for farmers, better wages for labor, pay equity for women, and so forth. Note that in each case, he justifies an increased benefit for the group in terms of a universal principle, such as justice or equity.

Appeals to Guilt

Jackson's appeal to guilt is found most prominently in the section where he discusses the 1988 Democratic nominee for president, Michael Dukakis. After praising Dukakis for running a good campaign, Jackson comments on differences in their backgrounds. In four short paragraphs (50–53), he reminds the audience that unlike Dukakis, Jackson grew up in poverty and continues to suffer from the fact that his ancestors were slaves. In paragraph 53, he draws these themes together: "His foreparents came to America on immigrant ships; my foreparents came to America on slave ships. But whatever the original ships, we're in the same boat tonight." Here, and in several other passages, Jackson reminds the audience of the terrible treatment that African Americans received in the past and implicitly says to his audience, "Past treatment mandates action today."

In my earlier discussion of appeals to guilt, I noted that the strategy is best used when the guilt is implicit, rather than explicit. Jackson clearly understands this point. He does not come out and say, "past injustice mandates action today." Instead, he uses statements such as his reference to "the sons and daughters of slaves sitting together around a common table" (paragraph 16) to implicitly make that point to the audience.

Appeals to History

Jackson uses the history of the civil rights movement to tap the emotions of his audience. In the very first paragraph he uses antithesis to set up his historical reference. He says that the audience is not really seated, "we're standing on someone's shoulders." He then introduces Rosa Parks, who was famous for starting a protest against unequal treatment in transportation by refusing to go to the back of a segregated bus. Parks is used as a symbol of the civil rights movement as a whole. A little later in the address, but still in the introduction, Jackson refers to a number of heroes and martyrs of the civil rights movement. He speaks of Fanny Lou Hamer and Aaron Henry, who attempted to send an integrated delegation from Mississippi to the 1964 Democratic National Convention (paragraph 11). He then references martyrs of the civil rights movement including "[Michael] Schwerner, [Andrew] Goodman, and [James] Chaney—two Jews and a black—found in a common grave, bodies riddled with bullets in Mississippi. The four darling little girls in the church in Birmingham, Alabama.[15] They died so that we might have a right to live" (paragraph 14).

Jackson's purpose in citing the history of the civil rights movement, especially the sacrifices of the innocent, is to draw on the emotion associated with the movement in order to support his cause. He makes that purpose clear in paragraph 10, immediately prior to his discussion of heroes and martyrs of the movement, when he says, "My right and my privilege to stand here before you has been won—in my lifetime—by the blood and sweat of the innocent."

Jackson also appeals to the history of the Democratic Party. In paragraphs 41–46, he discusses past elections. His ultimate point is that Democrats can succeed if they are unified. In 1960 they were unified behind John Kennedy and they won "by the margin of our hope, inspired by courageous leadership" (paragraph 42). They also won in 1964 and 1976 (paragraphs 42, 43), but in 1968 and 1980 "division and despair" led to defeat (paragraphs 44, 45). "Today when we debated, differed, deliberated, agreed to agree, agreed to disagree, when we had the good judgment to argue our case and then not self-destruct, George Bush was just a little further away from the White House and a little closer to private life" (paragraph 46). In this section, Jackson uses history to support his call for Democratic unity. Of course, as I noted earlier, he wanted unity on his terms. It is also important to recognize how he integrates the appeal to history with language strategies. In paragraph 46, which I cited earlier, he uses alliteration and antithesis in combination with the history.

Appeals to Religion

Jackson draws on Christian dogma at several points in the address. In paragraph 39, he notes that "The Bible teaches that when lions and lambs lie down together, none will be afraid and there will be peace in the valley." He then uses this biblical passage to call for common ground among Democrats. Even though "Lions eat lambs" and "Lambs sensibly flee from lions," "Neither lions nor lamb can survive nuclear war. If lions and lambs can find common ground, surely, we can as well, as civilized people" (paragraphs 39, 40). A little later, Jackson quotes Jesus, "Not my will, but thine be done" (paragraph 55) as support for his cause. Jackson is saying that in his own way, he is trying to do Christ's will.

Appeals to Myth

Jackson appeals to myth in conjunction with his historical narrative of the civil rights movement. At the end of the section in which he talks of martyrs of the civil rights movement, he says:

> Dr. Martin Luther King, Jr., lies only a few miles from us tonight.
> Tonight he must feel good as he looks down upon us. We sit here together, a rainbow, a coalition—the sons and daughters of slavemasters and the sons and daughters of slaves sitting together around a common table, to decide the direction of our party and our country. His heart would be full tonight. (paragraphs 15, 16)

King is a mythic figure, who in Jackson's description is looking down on the convention from heaven. Jackson draws upon the power associated with King as a hero to support his Rainbow Coalition. A similar point can be made about his reference to other heroes of the civil rights movement and the Democratic Party and to his citation of the heroes of religious myths, especially Christ.

Appeals to Elemental Symbols

Jackson uses several elemental symbols in his address. In a passage I cited when discussing his appeals to history, Jackson refers to the "blood and the sweat of the innocent" (paragraph 10). Similarly, at the end of the main body of the address, Jackson uses elemental symbols as a way of showing that ordinary people are being harmed in this country. In discussing the effects of what he calls the "economic violence" brought on by the Reagan presidency, Jackson speaks of people who "work in hospitals" and "wipe the bodies of those who are sick with fever and pain. They empty their bedpans. They clean out their commode. No job is beneath them, and yet when they get sick, they cannot lie in the bed they made up every day. America, that is not right. We are a better nation than that" (paragraph 85).

In these passages, Jackson draws on symbols that are cultural universals. Blood means sacrifice. Sweat means effort. And in referencing those who wipe the bodies of the sick and clean out commodes, he is implicitly using "excrement" as a negative symbol. His point is that people who work so hard that they are willing to clean out excrement ought to have access to health care.

Appeals to Societal Symbols

In addition to his use of elemental symbols, Jackson cites any number of societal symbols, which in turn link to one of the other sub-strategies for producing an emotional response. For example, in paragraph 27 Jackson cites the inscription on the Statue of Liberty—"give me your tired, your poor, your huddled masses who yearn to breathe free." In this passage, Jackson links the values of the Democratic Party to the Statue of Liberty as a cultural symbol representing freedom and opportunity. The various heroes and martyrs of the civil rights movement and the Democratic Party also function as societal symbols in Jackson's speech. They are symbols that represent values such as equality, justice, unity, and sacrifice.

SUMMARY OF JACKSON'S USE OF EMOTION-CREATING STRATEGIES

Jackson masterfully draws upon all of the sub-strategies for producing an emotional response in the audience. Throughout the address, he combines these sub-strategies with language devices, narratives, and appeals to his own credibility. In so doing, Jackson brilliantly responds to the demands of the rhetorical situation. He unifies and energizes the Democratic party, but on his terms.

Jackson also implicitly responds to those who label him as the self-interested representative of a set of Democratic constituencies. Jackson both ties his message to fundamental values that unify the party and also shows that those core constituencies are essential to the party. In this way, he tries to have it both ways by saying on the one hand that he represents not special interests, but "justice," and on the other hand that his policies would help the very constituencies that he linked to universal values.

While Jackson's address brilliantly adapted to the rhetorical constraints that he faced, his message had one weakness. The combination of universal values with appeals to specific constituencies works very well for unifying the "quilt" of groups that Jackson believes make up the Democratic Party. But a strategy that works well for appealing to a number of interest groups might not be as strong a strategy for appealing to an entire nation.

Jackson's quilt metaphor can be used to illustrate this point. The metaphor masks the fact that the interests of each of the patches in the quilt are not fully consistent with those of the other patches. Higher prices for farmers mean higher food prices for the poor. More money for one group inevitably means less for another. The metaphor itself also has a weakness. A skillful moderate or conservative could argue that America is not a quilt of interest groups tied together. Nor is the nation a blanket of one color, as Jackson suggests that conservatives believe. Rather, it is a multi-colored tapestry in which each of the groups that came to the nation has become Americans. Although he did not use this metaphor, Ronald Reagan used essentially this strategy in two election victories in the 1980s and of course George H.W. Bush relied on Reagan's narrative vision to defeat Dukakis in 1988.

CONCLUSION

An effective rhetor needs to do more than simply present a strong argument. He/she also needs strategies for energizing the audience to whom the argument is presented. This means that in order to motivate an audience to take action, it almost always will be necessary to utilize strategies that produce a strong emotional reaction. These strategies are not inherently inconsistent with also building a strong case. In the Declaration of Independence, Thomas Jefferson both built a strong case that Britain has usurped American liberty and also linked that case to basic values and needs, societal symbols, history, and so forth.

At the same time, not all strategies producing an emotional response are ethical. Hitler relied on unethical means of producing an emotional reaction to take control of Germany. In discussion of The Informed Citizen, I will develop criteria for distinguishing between ethical and unethical use of strategies that are aimed at producing an emotional response.

FOR FURTHER DISCUSSION

No question of value has produced more controversy over the last decade than gay rights. In a Congressional hearing on July 20, 2011 before the Committee on the Judiciary of the United States Senate, Tracey L. Cooper-Harris argued that the Defense of Marriage Act, a Federal law limiting marriage to heterosexual couples, should be overturned. Cooper-Harris, a U.S. Army veteran, used a variety of value-oriented and other strategies to defend her perspective. The law was later struck down by the Supreme Court. Carefully read and do an analysis outline on Cooper-Harris's testimony. Then consider the following questions:

1   What appeals to values, needs, or symbols does Cooper-Harris use to persuade the Congressional committee?

2   What other strategies does Cooper-Harris develop? Are the non-value laden strategies consistent with the value appeals? Which set of strategies is more important?

3   What barriers would Cooper-Harris face if her testimony were presented to the general public in a magazine article or a television show such as *60 Minutes*?

4   If Cooper-Harris's testimony were presented to the general public, would her combined use of strategies be successful?

5   One of the difficulties that Cooper-Harris faced was that many members of the general public reject values that she believes are basic to the American Dream. How can Cooper-Harris (or anyone) develop value appeals for an audience that fundamentally disagrees with some aspects of her views?

Statement of Tracey L. Cooper-Harris Before the Committee on the Judiciary United States Senate

Submitted for the Record of a Hearing Entitled "S.598,
The Respect for Marriage Act: Assessing the Impact of
DOMA on American Families"

July 20, 2011

My name is Tracey Cooper-Harris. I am a U.S. Army Veteran of Operation Enduring 1
Freedom & Operation Iraqi Freedom. I served with honor for a total of 12 yrs as
an Animal Care Specialist in all 3 components of the Army: Active, South Carolina
National Guard, & Army Reserves. While in my Reserve unit in California, I deployed
to the Middle East for 11 months in 2002. I was stoplossed during my deployment,
and I did not reenlist after I came home. Although I loved my job and the Army
wanted me to stay because of my hard work and exemplary service, I was tired of
having to live a lie under Don't Ask, Don't Tell as a gay soldier.

When I returned home in 2003, it took me a bit of time to readjust back to civilian 2
life. I struggled with the invisible wounds of war, the 5-year relationship I had prior
to deployment, the subsequent breakup of that relationship, steady employment, &
housing. I couch-surfed for weeks while I was trying to get myself back on track with
housing, work, & eventually school. The person who helped me through all that was
my then teammate, Maggie. Maggie & I played rugby together. She was known for
her compassion, warm & gregarious nature, and dominance in moving people on the
rugby pitch.

As our friendship grew romantic & into a committed relationship, I knew that this 3
is the woman I wanted to marry. After 3 years together, that opportunity came. We
married on November 1, 2008, days before Prop 8 passed. Even though we were
able to marry, it was bittersweet to have fellow citizens in our state vote to stop other
same-sex couples from making the ultimate commitment to each other in marriage
as we had done. We knew that there would continue to be uncertainty if something
happened to either one of us outside of California, or within the scope of the federal
government's jurisdiction because of the Defense of Marriage Act (DOMA).

The one thing on our side was time, and since the tide started to change favorably 4
in the acceptance of gays and same-sex marriage throughout the country, we figured
that laws would change before we became old or sick.

Well, I've had a reality check that is part of me now. A disease that I saw devastate 5
the life of one of the most important people in my life is now affecting me. I have
Multiple Sclerosis (MS), which is a chronic, often disabling disease that attacks the
central nervous system (CNS). Myelin, a fatty substance that protects/insulates the
nerve fibers and conducts electric impulse to get signals between the brain and

CNS to make them move faster, is damaged/destroyed. When this happens, nerve impulses traveling to and from the brain and spinal cord are distorted or interrupted, producing the variety of symptoms that can occur. Symptoms may be mild, such as numbness in the limbs, or severe, such as paralysis or loss of vision. The progress, severity, and specific symptoms of MS are unpredictable and vary from one person to another.

I saw this disease ravage my Mom for 20 years, and the news that I had it was pretty hard to bear. There's no cure for MS, only medication to slow down the progression of the disease. Although I am on weekly medication that I take through injection, the future continues to be uncertain.   6

I can't help but remember how fast my Mom's health declined with this disease, causing her to be bedridden within three years after I joined the Army in 1991. I remember how she was no longer able to perform simple activities of daily living like feeding herself, bathing, or using the bathroom on her own. She needed a nurse to help her with all these tasks. I remember how much pain she was in, and I remember my Pop staying by her side through it all, because of his love & commitment to his wife.   7

Like my Mom, I am blessed to have a spouse by my side to help me through this difficult time.   8

All this emotion and coming to grips with having this disease has made me focus on making sure that my wife, Maggie, has every benefit that any spouse of an honorably discharged veteran should have. Unfortunately, because we are a same sex couple, she would not be afforded the benefits and protections the federal government automatically bestows on other legally married couples.   9

To break it down, although the State of California recognizes our marriage (as do the states of New York, Rhode Island, Maryland, Connecticut, Vermont, Massachusetts, New Hampshire, Iowa, and Washington, DC), the federal government: 10

- does not allow us to file our taxes jointly (we lost out on thousands the 1st year we were married alone);
- can have us testify against each other in federal court, even though straight spouses enjoy the protection of a "spousal privilege";
- will tax the surviving spouse on any joint property we owned together;
- will not allow the surviving spouse to access social security survivors' benefits;
- will not allow my spouse to be buried with me at any veterans cemetery which has received federal funding;
- will not consider my wife as my dependent for any of my veterans benefits I earned through 12 years of honorable service in the U.S. Army; and
- taxes us on my portion of health insurance benefits provided by Maggie's employer that they don't charge to heterosexual married couples.

The only way that we can get the things I mentioned above (plus more than 1,100 other protections at the federal level) is through the repeal of the Defense of Marriage Act.

11

Right now, same-sex couples who are married and have followed the marriage laws of their states are left out in the cold by the federal government. No attorney, no legal documents can ensure that federal benefits go to the surviving spouse should the other spouse die or become incapacitated.

12

Many of these federal benefits come up for the surviving spouse when their spouse dies or becomes incapacitated. I've seen this first hand with my Pop after my Mom died in 2001, as he is able to use her social security benefits, was not subject to any inheritance tax on the home they bought together in 1989, and was not taxed on health insurance provided by her employer. This is in stark contrast to what my wife or I will experience should something happen to either one of us.

13

My family will be left out in the cold at one of the most difficult times in life in the very real event that I start to become more affected by MS or should I die.

14

Even my final wishes after I die are affected by DOMA, since I want my wife to be buried with me at a state/federal veterans' cemetery. As long as that cemetery has taken federal monies, my final wishes can't be fulfilled. Yet a straight veteran, even one who is in a common-law marriage, is allowed to have their spouse buried with them in a cemetery that has received federal monies.

15

Marriage equality isn't a gay thing. It's a family thing. There are thousands of families out there that are affected by DOMA and are forced to experience the turmoil that comes with not being able to protect their loved ones.

16

I am married to an amazing woman. We married for the same reason as many others have and continue to do: to show our commitment and love to each other in the presence of our Creator, our families, our friends, and our community. We married to ensure that our future children would grow in a home that has stability, love, and helps them become productive, contributing members of society.

17

We married to ensure that if one of us becomes incapacitated, we could visit our better half and make medical decisions based on the wishes of our spouse. And, we married to make sure if one of us dies, the surviving spouse would have the benefits earned at the state and federal level by the deceased. That's it. We're in this for better or worse, in sickness & in health, until parted by death. We want our marriage to be treated like any other marriage-nothing less.

18

After all the trials and tribulations this country has been through with discrimination & unequal treatment of its citizens based on religion, race/skin color, nationality, gender, veteran status, disability, or social status, we should have learned from our past.

19

Marriage equality should be a non-issue, but the fear of the unknown is creating challenges for families like mine. It is time to correct this inequity and grant all people who have taken the commitment to marriage the protections offered by the federal

20

government. I can't stand the thought of burdening my wife with the frustrations of DOMA when I start to get sicker.

My wife should not have to worry about all of these DOMA-related issues when my MS starts to get worse. It's just not right. I served this country honorably for 12 years. It is time for Congress to behave honorably and repeal DOMA.   21

Thank you.   22

1   See Aristotle, *The Rhetoric* in *The Basic Works of Aristotle*, ed. Richard McKeon (New York: Random House, 1941), Book 1, Ch. 2, p. 1329.

2   Aristotle's analysis of the emotions is detailed in Robert C. Rowland and Deanna, Womack, "Aristotle's View of Ethical Rhetoric," *Rhetoric Society Quarterly*, 15 (1985): 13–31.

3   For example, an article in *The New Republic* referred to both former Senator Bill Bradley and then Vice President Al Gore as "wooden orators." See, John B. Judis, "Journey Man," *The New Republic* 5 April 1999, p. 27.

4   See for example James MacGregor Burns, *Roosevelt: The Lion and the Fox* (New York: Harcourt, Brace & World, 1956), p. 477.

5   Franklin Delano Roosevelt, "First Inaugural Address," in Halford Ross Ryan, *Contemporary American Public Discourse*, 3rd edition (Prospect Heights, Illinois, Waveland, 1992), p. 13.

6   The classic essay on this point is Irving L. Janis, "Effects of Fear Arousal on Attitude Change: Recent Developments in Theory and Experimental Research," in *The Process of Social Influence: Readings in Persuasion*, Ed. Thomas Beisecker and Donn W. Parson (Englewood Cliffs, NJ: Prentice-Hall, 1972): 277–317.

7   Angie Drobnic Holan, Aaron Sharockman , "2014 Lie of the Year: Exaggerations about Ebola," *Politifact*, December 15, 2014, https://www.politifact.com/truth-o-meter/article/2014/dec/15/2014-lie-year-exaggerations-about-ebola.

8   William J. Clinton, "Remarks to the Convocation of the Church of God in Christ in Memphis," *Weekly Compilation of Presidential Documents* 13 November 1993: 2357–2362. This rhetoric is included in the Workbook associated with this text.

9   See Mircea Eliade, *Myth and Reality*, Trans. Willard R. Trask (New York: Harper & Row, 1963): 1.

10   A detailed analysis of how myth functions in rhetoric is developed in Robert C. Rowland, "On Mythic Criticism," *Communication Studies* 41 (1990): 101–116.

11   William Lewis, "Telling America's Story: Narrative Form and the Reagan Presidency," *Quarterly Journal of Speech* 73 (1987): 280–302.

12   See Eliade, especially pp. 71-78.

13   See Shirley Park Lowry, *Familiar Mysteries: The Truth in Myth* (New York: Oxford University Press, 1982).

14   See Michael Osborn, "The Evolution of the Archetypal Sea in Rhetoric and Poetic," *Quarterly Journal of Speech* 63 (1977): 347–363.

15   Jackson is referring to a church bombing that killed the four girls.

CHAPTER 9
Confrontative Rhetoric and Social Movements

Perhaps the most basic rule for judging the persuasiveness of any work of rhetoric is that strategies should be adapted to the views of the particular audience. This basic rule is almost, but not always, right. In this chapter, the focus of discussion is on two related subjects: the final strategy category, confrontative rhetoric, and a context area in which confrontation is often used, the advocacy of social movements. Confrontation is a rhetorical strategy in which the rhetor refuses to adapt to his/her audience, but instead intentionally attacks or offends them. Social movements advocate change on such subjects as the environment, civil rights, animal rights, and so forth, and include mainstream organizations such as the Sierra Club, the National Organization of Women, and more radical organizations that may utilize civil disobedience or other strategies that are very different from adaptive rhetoric.

Why combine the discussion of confrontation and social movements into a single chapter? The short answer to this question is that confrontation is a strategy most appropriately used by those who cannot use adaptive rhetorical strategies and lack the power to change society directly. While confrontation is used in a variety of contexts, it is most commonly associated with the rhetoric of social movements. In addition, it is appropriate to include a discussion of confrontation along with a consideration of social movements because use of confrontation creates certain rhetorical problems to which a movement must respond.

In the remainder of this chapter, I first define the nature of confrontative rhetoric. The next section considers when confrontation is an appropriate strategy and lays out the quite rare situation in which confrontation is likely to be effective. In the third main section, I discuss confrontation as it relates to social movement rhetoric and develop a typology of confrontative sub-strategies. Finally, I illustrate the use of confrontation in the context of a social movement by discussing an excerpt from one of the most famous speeches given by an American, Frederic Douglass' oration "What to the Slave Is The Fourth of July." It is important to note that while the focus of this chapter is on confrontation as it is used in social movements, the chapter is not intended to provide a complete theory of social movement rhetoric.[1] Rather, the goal is to provide an introduction to how social movements and others rely on confrontation as a rhetorical strategy.

USE OF CONFRONTATION AS A RHETORICAL STRATEGY

Going back to Aristotle, rhetorical critics and theorists have recognized that the most basic principle of rhetorical strategy is that the rhetor must begin with where the audience is.[2] In other words, to be successful, rhetoric must be adapted to the attitudes, values, and beliefs of the audience. This principle lies behind the standards for intrinsic evaluation of rhetorical effectiveness that I discussed earlier and also was assumed in the analysis of the first five strategy categories.

There is an old saying, however, that it "is the exception that proves the rule." The exception that proves the general rule that rhetoric should be adapted to an audience relates to the sixth strategy category, confrontation. There are rare circumstances in which the speaker or writer should not adapt to the audience, but confront that audience, sometimes offending or even attacking them. Confrontation is necessary in those instances to create the preconditions for successful rhetoric.

Traditional adaptive rhetorical strategies will not work in two particular situations. First, adaptive strategies generally will be ineffective if the position being supported would result in radical change in the society. Take the example of radical advocates of animal rights who believe it is fundamentally unethical to use animals for food or clothing. Support for legislation in support of this view or even simple advocacy for it would require a major change in diet in the United States, eliminate or drastically reduce the use of leather, wool, and other products derived from animals, and devastate sectors of agriculture that work with animals, as well as the fishing industry. Normal adaptive strategies will not work on this subject because the public as a whole simply will reject the idea.

Second, adaptive strategies also may fail for groups that are outside of the system. In the 1950s, gay rights activists either were ignored or persecuted in our society. Writing letters to the editor or giving public speeches that adapted to dominant values was not going to accomplish much, because society labeled gays as deviant. This explains why gay activists beginning in the 1960s often relied upon confrontation.

Therefore, confrontation may be a viable rhetorical option for groups calling for radical change or for groups that have been excluded from society. While I have focused on examples from the social movement context, there are other instances where confrontation may be the only option. Some therapists advocate use of what is essentially confrontative rhetoric to get the attention of a loved one or friend who has become addicted to drugs or alcohol or become a member of a cult. The cult member or addict cannot be reached through normal adaptive strategies because the person will deny that there is any problem. The alcoholic will say that he/she can quit at any time. The cult member will say that he/she is there of their own free will. In such a context, some psychologists believe that radical intervention by friends or family is needed to get the addict or cult member to change their life. While psychologists do not label that intervention as "confrontative rhetoric," in fact, that is what it is.

The hypothetical example of the use of confrontation to deal with addiction or membership in a cult highlights an additional point, the risks associated with confrontation. When dealing with a drug addict or a cult member, there may come a time when there is no other alternative but to use radical confrontation to attempt to shake the person out of their lifestyle. However, there are obviously enormous risks associated with this choice. If you use confrontation with a friend who you believe has become an alcoholic, you may wake your friend up to the dangers of alcohol abuse, but you may lose the friendship. And you could spark a violent reaction from your former friend. In the next section, I consider the dangers associated with confrontation and the circumstances in which confrontation is an appropriate strategic choice.

RISKS ASSOCIATED WITH CONFRONTATION

There are two primary risks associated with confrontation as a rhetorical strategy. First, the strategy may offend the audience and result in loss of credibility. By offending the audience, whether in an interpersonal context or in the larger society, the individual or the group may lose whatever credibility they had with the audience. For example, an environmental group that puts spikes in the tires of trash trucks as protest against the expansion of a landfill may be perceived as a bunch of common criminals. In the mind of the public, this one act of confrontation may wipe out memory of a host of good works. In the interpersonal context, use of confrontation may lead a friend to simply shut you out of his/her life.

Second, use of confrontation can produce audience backlash and, in the case of social movements, societal repression. Remember, no one likes to be attacked. Throughout the history of this nation, groups that have used strong rhetoric to attack the system often have faced police investigations, legislative restrictions, and even outright repression. For example, the FBI and other federal agencies spent large sums to investigate both the peace and civil rights movements in the 1960s. There were news reports of similar investigations of those who have opposed the war in Iraq. In the interpersonal context, use of confrontation could provoke a (former) friend to respond in kind or even use violence.

Since confrontation can produce backlash and make things much worse, even if the issue falls into one of the two categories where adaptive strategies generally fail, confrontation may not be the proper option. This suggests that confrontation should be used only in the most serious situations and only if backlash seems unlikely.

As a general rule, confrontation is only an appropriate strategy in the following circumstances. First, confrontation should never be used if traditionally adaptive rhetoric is an option. It always makes sense to rely on a mixture of the first five strategy categories if it is possible that they could be used to achieve a particular rhetorical goal. Adaptation is much less risky than confrontation and generally more effective. Second, confrontation should be utilized only as a last resort. Even if it seems unlikely that adaptive strategies could work, the attempt should be made because the risks associated with confrontation are quite high. And over time, the combination of rational argument, especially involving new data, narrative to personalize the argument, and value-laden appeals can be very powerful. In the case of the gay rights movement, for example, after confrontation successfully got the attention of many, the three adaptive strategies of rational argument, narrative, and value appeals over time produced a vast change in public attitudes and now a clear majority of the American people support gay rights and gay marriage.

Third, confrontation should not be utilized except on crucial issues. It is one thing to hold a sit-down strike over a fundamental issue of civil rights and quite another to hold the same protest because you don't like the landscaping in front of a building. In the interpersonal context, an intervention of some kind may be required if you fear that a roommate or close friend is about to harm themselves or someone else. But it would be silly to use confrontation because someone didn't put their dirty socks in the clothes hamper.

Fourth, confrontation only works in a certain kind of society. Confrontative rhetorical strategies could not work in Hitler's Germany, Stalin's Soviet Union, or in Iran, Libya, Syria, China, North Korea, and many other places today. As these examples indicate, confrontation as a rhetorical strategy only works in a democratic society, where rights are protected and a strong media exists that can cover the confrontative rhetoric. It is for this reason that confrontation has been so much more effective in Israel than it has been in other nations in the Middle East. Regardless of the wisdom of its policies, Israel is a democratic society with strong protections of rights and a very active media. In such a society, confrontation can be a powerful rhetorical option. If the result of the Arab spring had been to create a group of democratic states that protect human rights, confrontation might have become just as important a strategy in these nations as in Israel, Europe, or the United States. With the failure of the Arab Spring to produce lasting democratic change in the region except for Tunisia, confrontation remains an extremely hazardous strategy in the remaining nations, a strategy that is more likely to produce repression than change. In a nondemocratic society, use of a confrontative strategy simply results in punishment. For example, a sit-down strike in Stalin's Soviet Union likely would have led to execution or, at best, a long sentence to the Gulag prison system. In such a society, only war or revolution can bring about fundamental change. The nonviolent revolution that ended the Soviet Union illustrates the long-term power of the primary triad of strategies—rational argument, narrative, and value appeals. But those strategies never would have worked in earlier periods in the Soviet Union.

In addition to democratic rights, a strong media or access to powerful new communication technologies is necessary for confrontation to be effective. Dr. Martin Luther King, Jr. and others were able to use civil disobedience and other forms of confrontation to great effect in the United States in part because their acts generated great media coverage. The major television networks took pictures of the civil disobedience and, in many cases, of police violence against peaceful protesters. These pictures, along with written accounts, did a lot to convince millions of Americans of the morality of King's cause. Without the media coverage, the protests would have been much less effective.

In summary, rhetorical confrontation only works in a society which provides basic protection of human rights and which has a strong media. A similar point can be made about small group settings. Confrontative strategies would not work within a cult because there is no rhetorical space for them to function. In that context, rather than protest the cult's practices, the dissident cult member should simply leave and then go after the cult from the outside.

Finally, confrontation should be used only if there is nothing to lose. The dangers associated with confrontation are so high that it is too risky to use unless the rhetor *cannot* be in a worse situation if the confrontation fails. In chapter three, I explained how Booker T. Washington adapted to Southern attitudes in the "Atlanta Exposition Address." Given the many lynchings of innocent black people in that period, Washington was wise to make that choice. Confrontative rhetoric might have caused white backlash, which could have resulted in violence against African Americans. Washington had something to lose; confrontation would not have been a good option for him.

A BRIEF INTRODUCTION TO SOCIAL MOVEMENT RHETORIC

There is an enormous literature discussing the ways that social movements use rhetoric to achieve their aims.[3] Most of that literature is not relevant to this book, which introduces the ways in which rhetoric is used in a democratic society. However, a brief discussion of the role of social movements and the importance of confrontation in social movement rhetoric is needed.

Rhetorical theorists have proposed a number of different perspectives on social movements. In the original essay on rhetoric and social movements, Leland Griffin took a largely historical perspective. Later theorists used other approaches including an emphasis upon the sociological constraints groups lacking power face in calling for change in the larger society,[4] a treatment of movements as defined by rhetorical conflict with society,[5] and an analysis of movements as similar to drama.[6] Others have argued that social movement rhetoric is not always that different from the rhetorical practices of the establishment, noting that in many cases, establishment leaders lack the power to simply implement an agenda and must rely on persuasion to accomplish their aims.[7]

In relation to the primary focus of this chapter, confrontation as a rhetorical strategy, there are two points about social movements that are important. First, in many instances, social movements support radical actions, lack the power to implement change directly, and cannot adapt to dominant societal attitudes and values. This situation is not always the case. For example, Herbert Simons argues that social movements "are struggles on behalf of a cause by groups whose core organizations, modes of action, and/or guiding idea are not fully legitimated by the larger society."[8] Clearly, there are many social movements that fall within Simons' definition (those that are partially legitimated by society), which can rely on the five main adaptive rhetorical strategies.

However, there are also instances in which the movement has no real option other than confrontation. After presenting the definition cited above, Simons goes on to note that "the paradigm case of social movements continues to be an antiestablishment grassroots group spouting radical ideas in a manner calculated to get the attention but not necessarily the approval of those it opposes."[9] These groups cannot adapt to the dominant values of the society, because it is those very values that they are trying to change. For example, Martin Luther King, Jr. could not adapt to racist attitudes and values; he was trying to transform a segregationist system into a system defined by equality and justice. Thus, the first key point to understand about social movement rhetoric is that there are some movements which are essentially forced into confrontation in order to have any chance of ultimate success.

The second essential point to understand about social movements relates to the two primary audiences of social movement rhetoric. Many rhetors speak to both an internal audience within the organization and an external audience composed of the larger society. To some extent both Jesse Jackson and Mario Cuomo, in the convention addresses considered earlier, spoke to an internal audience of Democratic loyalists and an external audience of undecided voters. The same is true in the area of organizational rhetoric. Any organization, whether a business, a governmental entity, a charitable group, or a social movement, speaks both to members of the organization and also to those outside the organization. The important point is that it is often difficult to satisfy both the internal and the external audiences. Adapting to the larger public audience may offend the internal audience and vice versa.

It is important to recognize that the internal/external audience problem is generally more difficult for the leaders of social movements that lack power and are forced to use confrontation than it is for other organizations. In such cases, movement leaders may have to overcome not only barriers present in the larger society, but also severe barriers associated with the group. In particular, social movement rhetoric often must change the very way that members of the movement see themselves. In the discussion of metaphor in chapter seven, I mentioned the negative effects that labels can have on the self-concept of an individual. If a person is consistently told by society that he/she is inferior, it is inevitable that this labeling will have an effect.

This point applies most strongly to movements that attempt to gain rights for groups that previously have been labeled as inferior by the larger society. It is easily illustrated in relation to the civil rights movement, the feminist movement, and the gay rights movement. In each case, the larger society used words that "put down" members of the group. African American men often were called "boy," a label which denied their manhood. On many occasions, both black men and women were called still worse names. Similarly, grown successful women were referred to as "one of the girls" or by some other demeaning term. And gays were labeled as deviant. In each case, the effect of this labeling was to threaten the self-worth of the individual. Social movements that fight for the rights of oppressed groups face a particularly difficult "two audience" problem because they must confront the negative labels applied by society and reinforce a positive image for group members.

And after that self-definition has been reinforced or changed, social movement leaders may be forced to deal with a radicalized internal audience that demands extreme action. For this audience, action on the problem must be both immediate and significant, characteristics that will be difficult to justify for the mass audience. Consequently, balancing the internal and external audiences in social movements that must rely on confrontation can be a very difficult task.

The movement leader must speak to the larger society in a way that does not produce backlash, but also help members of the group discover and express their own identity. This was precisely what happened in the civil rights movement with the focus on "black" power, "black" history, "black" studies, and so forth. Exactly the same point could be made about the feminist and gay rights movements. After identity has been reinforced, the movement leader must support action that is radical enough to satisfy the internal audience, but not so radical that it produces backlash from the external audience. All three of the identity movements I've mentioned dealt with this issue.

Much of the advocacy of social movements looks very similar to the persuasion of government officials, business lobbyists, and so forth. For example, the pro-environment rhetoric of the Sierra Club relies on a host of adaptive strategies including narrative, rational argument, credibility, and appeals to basic values and needs. In opposing the position of the Sierra Club, an oil company public relations campaign would rely on similar adaptive strategies, although from the opposite position.

However, there are two cases in which social movement rhetoric is quite different from other advocacy. Social movements sometimes have so little power and favor such radical action that confrontation is the only available primary rhetorical strategy. And movements that seek to liberate oppressed groups often face an extremely difficult "two audience" problem because of the negative effects of societal labeling on the self-worth of group members or because of demands on movement leaders to support radical action to satisfy members, but action that is not so radical that it offends the larger national audience.

The next section fleshes out the two ways in which some social movement rhetoric differs from other advocacy by focusing on the functions fulfilled by confrontative rhetoric.

FUNCTIONS OF CONFRONTATIVE RHETORIC

Confrontative rhetoric, as I've explained, is often is aimed at two audiences: an internal audience within a social movement or organization and an external audience composed of the larger society. Confrontative rhetoric does somewhat different work for the internal and external audiences.

For the internal audience, confrontative rhetoric serves two primary functions. First, confrontation can be used to create the perception that change is possible. Given the horrible oppression of people of color in this nation in the first half of the 20th century, why was there not a more developed civil rights movement prior to the 1950s? One part of the answer is that people of color did not believe that change was possible. They saw a system in which African Americans were lynched every year, a system in which they lacked significant political power, and a system in which segregation seemed to be totally entrenched, and concluded that protest was impossible. In this context, one of the key aims of the civil rights movement was to create the understanding that change could occur. Confrontative rhetoric often fulfills this function.

Second, confrontation may work for the internal audience as part of what might be called the rhetorical redefinition of self.[10] As I explained earlier, one of the terrible effects of oppression is to deny the selfhood of the individuals who are being oppressed. Through confrontative rhetoric, however, the oppressed people can assert their own independent identity. One of the most important aspects of the civil rights movement was that it fulfilled this identity reinforcement function. Slogans like "Black is Beautiful," "Black Power," or "Black History" served both as language strategies and also as a means of redefining what it meant to be black and American. Something similar happened within both the gay rights and feminist movements.

It is important to recognize that not all social movements advocating major change (and therefore using confrontation) confront the barrier faced by movement members who have been labeled as inferior by society. Radical environmentalists face immense problems in convincing fellow citizens that major restructuring of the economy is necessary, but they do not need to confront denied identity and reinforce a sense of self.

For the external audience, confrontation serves two different functions. First, confrontative rhetoric is a means of getting the attention of the larger society. Without popular attention, the social movement can accomplish little. Gaining public attention usually requires use of strategies that make people mad. For example, animal rights activists spray-paint women in mink coats as a way of bringing media attention to their cause. Other strategies may serve this function in an even more radical way. For example, in Great Britain, the Irish Republican Army (IRA) used bomb threats (and real bombs) to bring attention to their cause. In this regard, terrorism is by its very nature a rhetorical act designed "not to defeat the enemy but to send a message."[11] For example, the fundamental aim of the 9/11 terror-

© KEN TANNEBAUM/SHUTTERSTOCK.COM

ists was to attack iconic symbols of American power, what Jenkins called "the heart of the power and wealth in the Western world."[12] The attacks were aimed at representations of American capitalism (the twin towers), American military power (the Pentagon), and American political power (the Capitol). Osama bin Laden himself made this point quite clear when he commented in an interview published on November 12, 2001, that "The main targets were the symbol of the United States: their economic and military power."[13] While terrorism is the most radical confrontative strategy for gaining the attention of the audience (and an immoral one, at least in a democratic society), all confrontative rhetoric must fulfill the same function, although in a less radical way, in order to get the attention of the external audience.

In general, confrontative rhetoric gets the attention of the audience by doing or saying things that make the audience angry. It is the anger that focuses attention on the issue. But this also illustrates the risk associated with confrontation. It is a dangerous thing to make your audience angry at you.

Second, confrontative rhetoric may be used to both create guilt and threaten the external audience. Oftentimes, different leaders of a social movement may utilize a sort of "good cop-bad cop" rhetorical strategy. In the 1960s, some radical black nationalists threatened to use violence unless society changed. At the same time, people like Martin Luther King, Jr. drew on the Bible and the non-violent philosophies of Henry David Thoreau and Mahatma Gandhi to argue for civil disobedience in support of civil rights for all Americans. King and his followers called for radical action but did so in a less confrontative and more inclusive fashion than did the radical black nationalists of the time. It is shameful, but the initial reaction of many Americans was to label King a radical; he was often called a communist. However, when white Americans heard the rhetoric of the radical nationalists, one result was to make King's approach seem much more reasonable. In that way, the black nationalist message strengthened King's approach within the civil rights movement.

In summary, to be effective, confrontative rhetoric must fulfill two functions for each of the internal and external audiences. For the internal audience, it must create the sense that change is possible and in many cases assist in the rhetorical redefinition of the self. For the external audience, it must gain public attention and both threaten and create guilt in the larger audience.

STRATEGIES OF CONFRONTATIVE RHETORIC

There are eight sub-strategies for achieving the four functions of confrontative rhetoric, six of which deal primarily with the functions for the external audience and two of which relate to the internal audience.

Strategies for Confronting the External Audience

The first strategy for confronting the external audience is for the rhetor consciously to speak/write/act in order to shock or offend the audience. During the Vietnam era, anti-war protesters burned the American flag to achieve this effect. Groups opposed to the war in Iraq avoided flag burning because they did not want to appear unpatriotic, but used other tactics to shock the audience. As in the Vietnam era, their efforts garnered a great deal of public attention. Again, by shocking the audience, the rhetor at least gets the attention of the external public.

A second strategy is to attack the audience. Rather than adapt to them, the rhetor actually lashes out at them. Attacking an audience almost always will get their attention. It may seem odd, but this strategy is most appropriate when a rhetor is speaking to an audience that is in some sense sympathetic to the cause being advocated. The rhetor attacks this audience as a way of arguing that they really are not doing enough. If used against an audience that is unfriendly, the likely result is severe audience backlash. In the 1960s, for example, an advocate for civil rights might have attacked a group of liberals for being insufficiently supportive of real reform. This strategy might activate the audience to do more. However, it would not have been successful with an audience opposed to civil rights for all Americans. Racists probably would have responded to the verbal attacks with real violence.

The third strategy is closely related to the second. Oftentimes, movement leaders will attempt to create guilt in the larger audience. In essence, the speaker/writer says, "You claim to support our values, but you do nothing. That makes you worse than our opponents, who are at least honest in their views." As with explicit attacks on the audience, guilt creation only works with an audience that is already strongly sympathetic to the cause. For example, guilt creation might be used to shame a group of religious liberals into doing more to help the homeless or oppose military action in the Middle East or Africa. But guilt creation would not work on a group that supported that military action, precisely because no guilt would be created.

A fourth confrontative strategy is to threaten the audience. One effect of a threat to the audience may be to make more conservative advocates of a similar position seem more reasonable. Once again, in the 1960s, threats of violence from radical black nationalists had the effect in the dominant white society of making Dr. Martin Luther King, Jr. seem quite reasonable. Threats may also be a way of convincing the larger society that change is needed. Explicit threats generally will be perceived as quite radical and, therefore, risk serious backlash, even violent repression. To avoid this problem, the threat may be made implicit. In the "Atlanta Exposition Address," Booker T. Washington made the point that investment in the South would create jobs for black Americans and, therefore, avoid all of the dangers associated with a large impoverished population. He did not explicitly threaten his audience, for to have done so would have been very foolish, but he used an implicit threat to argue for investment that would produce jobs for black Americans.

The fifth confrontative strategy is civil disobedience. Civil disobedience occurs when an individual breaks a law in order to draw attention to a problem. The individual does not attempt to escape responsibility, but accepts his/her punishment as a means of proving moral superiority. From Thoreau to Gandhi to King, civil disobedience has been advocated as a means of opposing a repressive society. In rhetorical terms, civil disobedience works best if the society responds by punishing, even beating, the protesters. The willingness of people to suffer for their cause then, in a sense, proves the morality of the cause. And the repression also may bring media attention to the dispute. The point that civil disobedience works best when it provokes repression illustrates why the civil rights movement could not have used the strategy in the first part of the 20th century. At that point, use of civil disobedience might have produced an even more violent response than occurred in the 1950s and 1960, and the absence of television networks covering the issue, as well as federal law enforcement concern with the issue by the FBI and Department of Justice, would have meant that the tactic likely would not have been rhetorically successful.

The sixth confrontative strategy for dealing with the external audience is terrorism. As I noted earlier in relation to the 9/11 attacks, terrorism (or violence or disruption) is primarily a rhetorical strategy. The terrorist attacks the system in order to draw attention to whatever problem is at issue. For decades, one goal of the IRA was to focus as much world attention on Northern Ireland as possible. Terrorism also may be used as a kind of rhetorical threat to induce societal action. In essence, the terrorists use violence to send a symbolic message that even greater violence will occur unless their demands are met.

While terrorism inevitably gets public attention, this does not mean that it is morally acceptable. Terrorism is never justified in a democratic society that protects rights because alternative rhetorical approaches are available. In most cases, terrorism is also an ineffective strategy because democracies generally respond with pure fury to violent attacks on their institutions. The response of the United States to 9/11 is one example of this phenomenon, as is the special forces raid that killed Osama bin Laden in 2011. The fact that the United States never stopped looking for the terrorist mastermind of 9/11 even after nearly a decade had passed is a strong indication of efforts that democratic nations will take to find and punish terrorists.

CONFRONTATIVE STRATEGIES FOR APPEALING TO AN EXTERNAL AUDIENCE

1 Shock or offend the audience
2 Attack the audience
3 Create guilt in the audience
4 Threaten the audience
5 Use civil disobedience
6 Use terrorism or other violence to draw attention to the cause
  Note: This strategy is never appropriate in a democratic society that protects rights.

Strategies for Appealing to an Internal Audience

In addition to the six confrontative strategies for dealing with the external audience, there are two primary rhetorical strategies that are used for the internal audience of people within a movement or group. These two strategies are to draw on myth as a means of creating identity and to use rhetorical redefinition in order to create a strong sense of selfhood for members of the movement.

Movement leaders often draw on myth in order to energize their followers. In chapter eight, I explained that societal myths are not perceived as false, but as fundamentally true stories. By telling or retelling a myth, movement leaders can connect a movement to great heroes and transcendent events. This explains why today, members of militia movements cast themselves as the heirs of the soldiers of the American Revolution, which they sometimes rather ominously call the "First" Revolution. The Tea Party movement also claims to want to take the nation back to the values present at the founding of the republic. Mythic definition can create the sense that change is possible by linking the present movement to the heroic myth.

Mythic definition is especially important for movements representing those who perceive themselves to be oppressed. Via the myth, the individual no longer sees himself/herself as powerless, but rather as powerful. The myth also ties the goal of the movement to a higher ideal. In the case of religious myths, the movement can claim to be doing God's work. For example, in the civil rights movement, some leaders tied the movement to stories of great heroism in Africa, prior to the time when their ancestors were seized and sold into slavery. In this narrative, contemporary black Americans were metaphorically the sons and daughters of kings and queens. At a pragmatic level, this mythic story had little import since the members of the movement continued to face a bleak political and economic situation in the United States of the time. In another way, however, it provided both a sense of identity and a model of past heroism, two very powerful rhetorical messages.

The second primarily internal movement strategy is to use rhetoric to redefine the role of members of the movement. As I noted earlier, it was this process of rhetorical redefinition that was operating in the focus on Black Pride, Black History, and so forth in the 1960s and 1970s. By redefining what it meant to be a black American, leaders of the movement sought to change all of the associations that went along with Black, Negro, and other terms. Such redefinition also has been a prominent strategy in the feminist and gay movements. An example from popular culture clarifies this point. In her song "I Am Woman," Helen Reddy precisely states a message of rhetorical redefinition. Reddy redefines women from weak to strong in lines such as "I am woman, hear me roar." Such a message is needed before a social movement can take off because movement leaders and members must be able to overcome how a society defines their proper role. A similar strategy is apparent in the work of gay rights leaders who have redefined the word "queer" from an offensive slur to a statement of power and identity.

This redefinition strategy also can be important for movements that do not face the need to create a strong identity for movement members. Radical environmentalists, for example, might define themselves as emergency technicians for the planet as a way of reinforcing the importance of the movement.

SUMMARY OF CONFRONTATION AND SOCIAL MOVEMENTS

Confrontation is a dangerous rhetorical strategy, both from the perspective of the rhetor and the society. It is dangerous for the rhetor because it may produce backlash. It is dangerous for society because it may result in increased conflict. Therefore, confrontation should be used as a last resort only.

To illustrate the dangers and sometime necessity of confrontation, in the next section I focus on extended excerpts from one of the greatest speeches ever delivered by an American, Frederick Douglass' "What to the Slave Is the Fourth of July," which was presented on July 5, 1852, in Rochester, New York. Douglass, who was born into slavery and escaped from it, was the foremost American black leader for almost half a century. The distinguished historian James M. McPherson has written of Douglass that he "strode across the stage of American history with a commanding presence equaled by few of his countrymen." Douglass, who based on his "gift of oratory, rose to international fame as a champion of freedom and equal rights" was a counselor to eight presidents.[14] There is no question about the influence of Douglass or the fact that the influence can be traced to what McPherson called "the moral force of his language."[15] In a web page commemorating the 100th anniversary of Douglass' death, the Smithsonian Institution labeled him "the father of the civil rights movement," and noted that of his more than 1,000 speeches opposing slavery, the most "powerful" was "What to the Slave Is the Fourth of July."[16] In this address, he confronts the difficulty of motivating anti-slavery white Northerners to take radical action in order to end slavery.

Excerpt from "What to the Slave Is the Fourth of July"

Frederick Douglass

Fellow citizens: Pardon me, and allow me to ask, why am I called upon to speak here today? What have I or those I represent to do with your national independence? Are the great principles of political freedom and of natural justice, embodied in that Declaration of Independence, extended to us? And am I, therefore, called upon to bring our humble offering to the national altar, and to confess the benefits, and express devout gratitude for the blessings resulting from your independence to us? 1

Would to God, both for your sakes and ours, that an affirmative answer could be truthfully returned to these questions. Then would my task be light, and my burden easy and delightful. For who is there so cold that a nation's sympathy could not warm him? Who so obdurate and dead to the claims of gratitude, that would not thankfully acknowledge such priceless benefits? Who so stolid and selfish that would not give his voice to swell the hallelujahs of a nation's jubilee, when the chains of servitude had been torn from his limbs? I am not that man. In a case like that, the dumb might eloquently speak, and the "lame man leap as an hart." 2

But such is not the state of the case, I say it with a sad sense of disparity between us. I am not included within the pale of this glorious anniversary! Your high independence only reveals the immeasurable distance between us. The blessings in which you this day rejoice are not enjoyed in common. The rich inheritance of justice, liberty, prosperity, and independence bequeathed by your fathers is shared by you, not by me. The sunlight that brought life and healing to you has brought stripes and death to me. This Fourth of July is *yours*, not *mine*. You may rejoice, I must mourn. To drag a man in fetters into the grand illuminated temple of liberty, and call upon him to join you in joyous anthems, were inhuman mockery and sacrilegious irony. Do you mean, citizens, to mock me, by asking me to speak today? If so, there is a parallel to your conduct. And let me warn you, that it is dangerous to copy the example of a nation whose crimes, towering up to heaven, were thrown down by the breath of the 3

Presented in Rochester, NY, July 5, 1852.

Almighty, burying that nation in irrecoverable ruin. I can today take up the lament of a peeled and woe-smitten people.

"By the rivers of Baylon, there we sat down. Yes! We wept when we remembered Zion. We hanged our harps upon the willows in the midst thereof. For there they that carried us away captive, required of us a song; and they who wasted us, required of us mirth, saying, Sing us one of the songs of Zion. How can we sing the Lord's song in a strange land? If I forget thee, O Jerusalem, let my right hand forget her cunning. If I do not remember thee, let my tongue cleave to the roof of my mouth."

Fellow citizens, above your national, tumultuous joy, I hear the mournful wail of millions, whose chains, heavy and grievous yesterday, are today rendered more intolerable by the jubilant shouts that reach them. If I do forget, if I do not remember these bleeding children of sorrow this day, "may my right hand forget her cunning, and may my tongue cleave to the roof of my mouth!" To forget them, to pass lightly over their wrongs, and to chime in with the popular theme, would be treason most scandalous and shocking, and would make me a reproach before God and the world. My subject, then, fellow citizens, is "American Slavery." I shall see this day and its popular characteristics from the slave's point of view. Standing here, identified with the American bondman, making his wrongs mine, I do not hesitate to declare, with all my soul, that the character and conduct of this nation never looked blacker to me than on this Fourth of July. Whether we turn to the declarations of the past, or to the professions of the present, the conduct of the nation seems equally hideous and revolting. America is false to the past, false to the present, and solemnly binds herself to be false to the future. Standing with God and the crushed and bleeding slave on this occasion, I will, in the name of humanity, which is outraged, in the name of liberty, which is fettered, in the name of the Constitution and the Bible, which are disregarded and trampled upon, dare to call in question and to denounce, with all the emphasis I can command, everything that serves to perpetuate slavery—the great sin and shame of America! "I will not equivocate; I will not excuse"; I will use the severest language I can command, and yet not one word shall escape me that any man, whose judgment is not blinded by prejudice, or who is not at heart a slave-holder, shall not confess to be right and just.

But I fancy I hear some of my audience say it is just in this circumstance that you and your brother Abolitionists fail to make a favorable impression on the public mind. Would you argue more and denounce less, would you persuade more and rebuke less, your cause would be much more likely to succeed. But, I submit, where all is plain there is nothing to be argued. What point in the anti-slavery creed would you have me argue? On what branch of the subject do the people of this country need light? Must I undertake to prove that the slave is a man? That point is conceded already. Nobody doubts it. The slave-holders themselves acknowledge it in the enactment of laws for their government. They acknowledge it when they punish disobedience on the part of the slave. There are seventy-two crimes in the State of Virginia, which, if committed by a black man (no matter how ignorant he be), subject him to the punishment of death; while only two of these same crimes will subject a white man to like punishment.

What is this but the acknowledgement that the slave is a moral, intellectual, and responsible being? The manhood of the slave is conceded. It is admitted in the fact that Southern statute-books are covered with enactments, forbidding, under severe fines and penalties, the teaching of the slave to read and write. When you can point to any such laws in reference to the beasts of the field, then I may consent to argue the manhood of the slave. When the dogs in your streets, when the fowls of the air, when the cattle on your hills, when the fish of the sea, and the reptiles that crawl, shall be unable to distinguish the slave from a brute, then I will argue with you that the slave is a man!

For the present it is enough to affirm the equal manhood of the Negro race. It is not astonishing that, while we are plowing, planting, and reaping, using all kinds of mechanical tools, erecting houses, constructing bridges, building ships, working in metals of brass, iron, copper, silver, and gold; that while we are reading, writing, and cyphering, acting as clerks, merchants, and secretaries, having among us lawyers, doctors, ministers, poets, authors, editors, orators, and teachers; that while we are engaged in all the enterprises common to other men—digging gold in California, capturing the whale in the Pacific, feeding sheep and cattle on the hillside, living, moving, acting, thinking, planning, living in families as husbands, wives, and children, and above all, confessing and worshipping the Christian God, and looking hopefully for life and immortality beyond the grave—we are called upon to prove that we are men? 7

Would you have me argue that man is entitled to liberty? That he is the rightful owner of his own body? You have already declared it. Must I argue the wrongfulness of slavery? Is that a question for republicans? Is it to be settled by the rules of logic and argumentation, as a matter beset with great difficulty, involving a doubtful application of the principle of justice, hard to understand? How should I look today in the presence of Americans, dividing and subdividing a discourse, to show that men have a natural right to freedom, speaking of it relatively and positively, negatively and affirmatively? To do so would be to make myself ridiculous, and to offer an insult to your understanding. There is not a man beneath the canopy of heaven who does not know that slavery is wrong *for him*. 8

What! Am I to argue that it is wrong to make men brutes, to rob them of their liberty, to work them without wages, to keep them ignorant of their relations to their fellow men, to beat them with sticks, to flay their flesh with the lash, to load their limbs with irons, to hunt them with dogs, to sell them at auction, to sunder their families, to knock out their teeth, to burn their flesh, to starve them into obedience and submission to their masters? Must I argue that a system thus marked with blood and stained with pollution is wrong? No; I will not. I have better employment for my time and strength than such arguments would imply. 9

What, then, remains to be argued? Is it that slavery is not divine; that God did not establish it; that our doctors of divinity are mistaken? There is blasphemy in the thought. That which is inhuman cannot be divine. Who can reason on such a proposition? They that can, may; I cannot. The time for such argument is past. 10

At a time like this, scorching irony, not convincing argument, is needed. Oh! Had   11
I the ability, and could I reach the nation's ear, I would today pour out a fiery stream
of biting ridicule, blasting reproach, withering sarcasm, and stern rebuke. For it is
not light that is needed, but fire; it is not the gentle shower, but thunder. We need the
storm, the whirlwind, and the earthquake. The feeling of the nation must be quickened;
the conscience of the nation must be exposed; and its crimes against God and man
must be denounced.

What to the American slave is your Fourth of July? I answer, a day that reveals to   12
him more than all other days of the year, the gross injustice and cruelty to which he is
the constant victim. To him your celebration is a sham; your boasted liberty an unholy
license; your national greatness, swelling vanity; your sounds of rejoicing are empty
and heartless; your denunciation of tyrants, brass-fronted impudence; your shouts
of liberty and equality, hollow mockery; your prayers and hymns, your sermons and
thanksgivings, with all your religious parade and solemnity, are to him mere bombast,
fraud, deception, impiety, and hypocrisy—a thick veil to cover up crimes which would
disgrace a nation of savages. There is not a nation of the earth guilty of practices
more shocking and bloody than are the people of these United Sates at this very
hour.

Go where you may, search where you will, roam through all the monarchies and   13
despotisms of the Old World, travel through South America, search out every abuse
and when you have found the last, lay your facts by the side of the every-day practices
of this nation, and you will say with me that, for revolting barbarity and shameless
hypocrisy, America reigns without a rival.

ANALYSIS OF FREDERICK DOUGLASS, WHAT TO THE SLAVE IS THE FOURTH OF JULY

In "What to the Slave Is the Fourth of July," Douglass clearly identifies his ultimate purpose
as the elimination of slavery. But unlike some abolitionists who believed that slavery could be
ended via political action, without a major crisis, Douglass recognized that major conflict was
quite likely. Near the conclusion of the address, he essentially lays out the case for the necessity
of radical confrontation. According to Douglass:

> At a time like this, scorching irony, not convincing argument, is needed. Oh! Had I
> the ability, and could I reach the nation's ear, I would today pour out a fiery stream
> of biting ridicule, blasting reproach, withering sarcasm, and stern rebuke. For it is
> not light that is needed, but fire; it is not the gentle shower, but thunder. We need
> the storm, the whirlwind, and the earthquake. The feeling of the nation must be
> quickened; the conscience of the nation must be exposed; and its crimes against God
> and man must be denounced. (paragraph 11)

Douglass clearly understood that radical action would be needed to eliminate slavery from
American life. In paragraph 11, he justifies radical confrontation, what he calls "the storm, the

whirlwind, and the earthquake," as the proper rhetorical approach to "quicken" the conscience of the nation.

Why was such a radical rhetoric needed? To answer this question it is important to consider the audience to whom Douglass spoke. Douglass gave the address at a meeting of an anti-slavery society in Rochester, New York, on July 5, 1852. In one sense, he clearly was preaching to the "saved," to a group that already agreed with him that slavery was an abomination. But in another sense, he was trying to convince them that truly radical action, such as support for violence, even terrorism,[17] against slavery was needed.

In persuading the anti-slavery group that radical action would be needed, Douglass faced several barriers. First, he was speaking to a group in Rochester, New York, almost on the Canadian border. They were separated from slavery by a great distance, bore no personal responsibility for slavery, and could do little directly to attack slavery. Second, direct action against slavery clearly would require violence. It was obvious by 1852 that the South was not going to give up slavery in the near term without being made to do so. Thus, radical action clearly risked conflict and war, a point that later was demonstrated by the Civil War.

Third, Douglass faced the expectations of the audience in regard to a speech on the Fourth of July. In the 19th century, Fourth of July orations played a prominent role in American culture. Probably because the nation was so much closer to the first Fourth of July and because of the absence of an electronic media, public celebrations of the Fourth were far more important than they have become today.[18] Typically, speeches on the Fourth followed a very strict pattern. These addresses included an affirmation of basic American values, a discussion of the importance and meaning of patriotism, a reflection on the American Revolution and the history of the nation, and a prediction of greatness to come. These aspects of content were combined with a formal, serious, and sentimental style.[19] Audiences were familiar with a typical Fourth of July oration and had strong expectations about what they would hear in any given speech.[20]

Audience expectations were a particular problem for Douglass because, given his purpose, he could not simply praise the nation and talk in a reverential tone about American history. In order to rouse his audience to take radical action, Douglass had to convince them that there were serious evils that had to be confronted, even if it risked war. Praise for America and patriotic sentiments would not do the trick and in all likelihood would be counterproductive, because they risked creating a sense of self-satisfaction in the audience.

Finally, Douglass faced the problem of racism. Even in Rochester, New York, Douglass confronted racist attitudes. For example, McPherson notes that Douglass' children were not allowed to attend the white public schools.[21] Racism created a double-barreled problem for Douglass. He had to overcome racist attitudes in order to persuade his audience of the justice of his cause. But he also had to be careful that he did not simply reinforce that sense of self-satisfaction that I mentioned as a potential problem in those who had chosen to come listen to a black man talk. It would have been easy for Douglass to have given a speech in which he thanked the audience members for all that they had done and praised their work in the abolitionist movement. If he had taken this approach, his audience would not have been motivated to act. Instead, they would have had an increased sense of self-satisfaction. Thus, Douglass had little choice but to attack the audience.

Strategies in Douglass' Address

Clearly, the dominant strategy in Douglass' address was confrontation. He utilizes four of the sub-strategies for appealing to an external audience and both of the sub-strategies for dealing with the internal audience. In this case, of course, the external and the internal audiences are somewhat mixed together. Opponents of slavery are in one sense an internal audience for Douglass. In another sense, the white abolitionists are part of Douglass' external audience.

Throughout the address, Douglass both offends and directly attacks his audience. He begins the address with a rhetorical question, "why am I called upon to speak here today?" (paragraph 1). He then states that the "great principles of freedom and of natural justice, embodied in that Declaration of Independence" (paragraph 1) are not guaranteed to "us" (slaves and other black Americans). From this introductory device, Douglass then notes "the immeasurable distance between us" (paragraph 2) and moves to a direct attack on "the Fourth of July" that must have seemed shocking to his audience. "This Fourth of July is *yours*, not *mine*. You may rejoice, I must mourn" (paragraph 3).

The pattern of both offending and attacking his audience that is evident in the first three paragraphs continues throughout the address. In paragraph 5, he says that he hears "the mournful wail of millions whose chains, heavy and grievous yesterday, are today rendered more intolerable by the jubilant shouts that reach them." He goes on to say "that the character and conduct of this nation never looked blacker to me than on this Fourth of July." Later in the same paragraph he says that "America is false to the past, false to the present, and solemnly binds herself to be false to the future."

And despite the sharpness of the language that I have quoted from the first half of the speech, Douglass is far harsher in the conclusion. In the final two sentences of the address, Douglass makes his position quite clear:

> There is not a nation of the earth guilty of practices more shocking and bloody than are the people of these United States at this very hour.
>
> Go where you may, search where you will, roam through all the monarchies and despotisms of the Old World, travel through South America, search out every abuse and when you have found the last, lay your facts by the side of the every-day practices of this nation, and you will say with me that, for revolting barbarity and shameless hypocrisy, America reigns without a rival. (paragraphs 12, 13)

Saying on the Fourth of July that the United States leads the world in "revolting barbarity and shameless hypocrisy" is not exactly audience adaptation.

Douglass also is adept at both creating guilt and implicitly threatening his audience. The guilt creation is obvious throughout the speech, but is most evident in the introduction. It is easy to imagine the audience settling into their chairs with the expectation that Douglass will praise them for their commitment to the anti-slavery cause. Instead, he speaks of the "sad sense of disparity between us. I am not included within the pale of this glorious anniversary! Your high independence only reveals the immeasurable distance between us" (paragraph 3). He continues that "You may rejoice, I must mourn. To drag a man in fetters into this grand illuminated temple of liberty, and call upon him to join you in joyous anthems, were inhuman mockery and sacrilegious irony?" Douglass then asks his audience, "Do you mean, citizens, to mock me, by asking me to speak today?"

Rather than the praise that they undoubtedly expected, Douglass points directly to the gap between them and him. In so doing, he also points to the gap between their values (opposition to slavery) and their actions. In this passage and at many other places, he attempts to create guilt in order to motivate truly radical action.

Douglass also threatens his audience. Here, he shows considerable rhetorical ingenuity. As part of a very small African American community in Rochester, Douglass has no way to threaten the audience directly. So, he invokes the threat of God's vengeance on them. At the end of paragraph 3, he warns his audience "that it is dangerous to copy the example of a nation whose crimes, towering up to heaven, were thrown down by the breath of the Almighty, burying that nation in irrecoverable ruin. I can today take up the lament of a peeled and woe-smitten people." Here, Douglass is alluding to the fate of the Babylonian Empire, after that nation forced the Jews of the Old Testament into exile. He drives the point home in the following paragraph by quoting directly from the Old Testament to make certain that no one in his audience misses his allusion and argument.

It is important to recognize that in the 19th century, it is likely that every member of his audience immediately would have recognized this reference to the Bible and Douglass' implicit threat of divine retribution for the "sin" of slavery. In some ways, his comments foreshadow a similar statement in Abraham Lincoln's Second Inaugural Address.

While Douglass used four of the sub-strategies of confrontation for dealing with an external audience, he did not use civil disobedience or threaten violence. Of course, civil disobedience was not needed in the North and would have been counterproductive in the South. Slaves could not use civil disobedience; that would only get them beaten. In a sense, Douglass advocates violence, not against his audience, but against slavery. That was the implication of the paragraph in which he called for "the storm, the whirlwind, and the earthquake" (paragraph 11). In summary, Douglass either uses or suggests the importance of using all of the sub-strategies of confrontation for dealing with an external audience, save civil disobedience, which does not fit the context.

I said earlier that terrorism is never a legitimate rhetorical strategy in a democratic society that protects rights. Does that mean that suggesting the need for violence was an unethical strategy for Douglass? The unpleasant truth is that at the time when Douglass spoke, the United States not only did not protect the rights of African Americans, but guaranteed the rights of slave owners in the South to own human beings. In confronting this enormous human evil, Douglass' speech must be viewed as an example of great moral courage.

Douglass also uses both sub-strategies for speaking to an internal audience. Abolitionists always faced the problem of race. It is important to recognize that even many committed abolitionists were racists, at least by the standards of our time. Thus, it was important that Douglass both draw on myth to support the cause and redefine what it means to be a black American.

In relation to myth, Douglass casts the slaves in the role of the Jews in the Old Testament. That is evident in the comparison of America to Babylon. Douglass' message goes like this. Babylon kept the Jews in chains. The United States keeps slaves in chains. Babylon was destroyed by God for harming his Chosen People. Therefore, the United States must either recognize that the slaves are the Chosen People of God or suffer the same fate as Babylon. As this example indicates, Douglass skillfully draws on religious myth in advocating radical action for abolition.

He also redefines what it means to be a slave. Douglass' redefinition is quite simple. Slaves are human. In five powerful paragraphs beginning at the mid-point of the speech, Douglass makes this point. In the first, he builds an argument for the personhood of slaves by noting that in Virginia there are 72 crimes that subject the slave to the death penalty. Douglass then says, "When you can point to any such laws in reference to the beasts of the field, then I may consent to argue the manhood of the slave" (6). Here, Douglass is essentially saying that slave states can't have it both ways. If they treat slaves as human by punishing them for wrongdoing, then they cannot deny that slaves are in fact human beings.

The following paragraph reinforces this theme. Although it is a long paragraph, it merits consideration in its entirety:

> For the present it is enough to affirm the equal manhood of the Negro race. Is it not astonishing that, while we are plowing, planting, and reaping, using all kinds of mechanical tools, erecting houses, constructing bridges, building ships, working in metals of brass, iron, copper, silver, and gold; that while we are reading, writing, and cyphering, acting as clerks, merchants, and secretaries, having among us lawyers, doctors, ministers, poets, authors, editors, orators, and teachers; that while we are engaged in all the enterprises common to other men—digging gold in California, capturing the whale in the Pacific, feeding sheep and cattle on the hillside, living, moving, acting, thinking, planning, living in families as husbands, wives, and children, and above all, confessing and worshipping the Christian God, and looking hopefully for life and immortality beyond the grave—we are called to prove that we are men?

The first sentence in this paragraph clearly states the theme: We are human. The second proves it argumentatively by citing all the things that black people are doing. But even more importantly, Douglass proves the equality of black people with the sentence itself, which is more than 130 words long. Douglass' statement is filled with language strategies including rhythm, alliteration, assonance, parallel structure, repetition, and of course functions as a rhetorical question. The ultimate point is to prove that a person who could utter such a sentence must be a human being. It is difficult to think of a contemporary political figure who could write such a sentence. This one sentence by itself demonstrates both Douglass' genius as a speaker and the essential insanity in the view of black Americans as inherently inferior.

Douglass completes the redefinition in paragraphs 8, 9, and 10 with a series of rhetorical questions. "Would you have me argue that man is entitled to liberty?" "Must I argue the wrongfulness of slavery?" "Is that a question for republicans?" (paragraph 8). He continues with questions in paragraphs 9 and 10, asking his audience if he should have to prove that slavery is wrong or prove that it is "not divine" (paragraph 10). The rhetorical questions are meant to drive home the point that he has established in paragraphs 6 and 7. If slaves are human then all morality demands that slavery be eliminated immediately. His redefinition of slaves as human leads him to conclude in paragraph 10, "The time for such argument is past."

In "What to the Slave Is the Fourth of July," Frederick Douglass brilliantly uses confrontation both to demand action from the external audience and to fulfill the needs of the internal audience for self-definition. Douglass clearly understood that given the South's economic and cultural commitment to slavery, the system was not going to simply wither away in the short term. Radical action was needed. History clearly proves that he was right. Thus, Douglass knew that he needed to shock his audience out of its lethargy. He also knew that he could not adapt to the constraints associated with a traditional Fourth of July address and achieve his purpose. In this rhetorical situation, Douglass correctly chose confrontation as the only sensible rhetorical option.

There is no evidence of the immediate reaction of his audience to the address. But we do know that the speech was widely reprinted and continues to speak to the American experience with race. Clearly, Douglass did a magnificent job of adapting to a difficult set of rhetorical barriers. He not only uses confrontation, but even explains why that strategy must be used. It is a wonderful speech, one of the most important defenses of real democracy and freedom ever uttered.

One other point is relevant about Douglass' address. It is important to recognize that a similar speech would not have been appropriate in the South. For even a white abolitionist to give such a speech in the South would have been foolhardy. Given the Southern commitment to slavery, the likely effect would have been immediate backlash against the speaker and possibly violence. Douglass could rely on confrontation in Rochester, New York, but in Atlanta or Charleston such a choice would have been counterproductive.

CONCLUSION

The focus of this chapter has been on the relationship between confrontative rhetoric and social movements. I identified the characteristics of confrontative rhetoric, explained the risks associated with the strategy, discussed the situations in which confrontation is an appropriate strategic option, laid out the relationship between social movements and confrontation, specified the functions served by rhetorical confrontation, identified sub-strategies of confrontation, and applied this system to Frederick Douglass' famous speech, "What to the Slave Is the Fourth of July."

Confrontation is a powerful, but extremely dangerous rhetorical strategy. In most situations, it should be rejected as a strategy, but in a few limited situations it is the only reasonable strategic response.

FOR FURTHER DISCUSSION

In an op-ed commentary published in *The New York Times* in August 2001, Nikolay Palchikoff criticizes the U.S. bombing of Japan with nuclear weapons at the conclusion of World War II. His clear goal was to shock Americans into thinking again about this event of more than a half-century ago. Carefully read and do an analysis outline of Palchikoff's commentary. Then consider the following questions.

1   What confrontative strategies does Palchikoff rely on to present his message?
2   What other strategies does he use?
3   What barriers did he confront in the commentary?
4   Could he have confronted these barriers without relying on confrontation?
5   Was Palchikoff successful in persuading the audience of readers in *The New York Times*?

The Nuclear August of 1945
Nikolay Palchikoff

I was one of the first American soldiers to visit Hiroshima after its destruction by the   1
atomic bomb 56 years ago today. Until recently, it was not something I talked about. Still now, at 77, it's hard not to cry when I picture walking into that city more than half a century ago. But it's important to remember. There are few of us around who do.

I went to Hiroshima some three weeks after the fatal day. I had been born and   2
raised there and was going home to search for my family. My father was a member of the Russian nobility and had been an officer in the White Army. He fled Russia with my mother during the Russian Revolution and settled in Japan. I grew up eating piroshki and sushi, speaking Russian and Japanese. Before the war, when I was 16, I left Japan to go to school in the United States. The rest of my family stayed behind.

After Pearl Harbor, like many 18-year old boys, I yearned to become a soldier. With   3
my Slavic ethnicity and Japanese language fluency, I became a member of United States Army intelligence, working in translation and interrogation.

I first heard about the bombing of Hiroshima the day it happened. I was 21 at the 4
time, translating Japanese radio in the Philippines. No one believed my reports. My
Army superiors ridiculed my translation skills. The next day, President Harry Truman
announced to the world that, indeed, the United States had dropped an atomic bomb
on Hiroshima.

Soon afterward I was sent to Japan to help make sure the Japanese were living up 5
to the conditions of the surrender agreement, and I traveled to Hiroshima. It was the
worst moment of my life. Although I had seen wartime atrocities, I wasn't prepared
for what I saw now: nothing. No birds. No people. No buildings. No trees. No life.
Outlines of human bodies burned like negatives in cement.

The house I had grown up in was gone. The city had vaporized. 6

Fortunately, just a few days before Hiroshima was attacked, my family had moved 7
to a house far enough away from the bomb's epicenter so that they survived. When
I found them, there was a moment of joy, until they described the bomb's aftermath:
People walking and dropping dead in their tracks. People running for the river, seeking
escape from the scorching heat. Skin falling off bodies. Everyone desperate for water.

My family and I left for Tokyo and then went to America. I vowed never to return. 8
What does one do after walking into a nuclear dust bowl? Like many, I believed that
peace could come only from having a strong defense. I decided to remain in the
Army while the United States prepared for its newest enemies, the Russians. During
the Cuban missile crisis I built an elaborate bomb shelter under my house, complete
with water, septic tank and canned food. I was ready for an attack.

One day the reserves called me away from work to participate in an "emergency" 9
drill. But when I discovered they were simulating a nuclear war in the drill, and that
my job was to keep the "contaminated" people away from the "noncontaminated"
people, something suddenly didn't seem right. I knew that in a real nuclear war there
would be few people standing around, contamination would affect everyone and most
people would be dead. I began to rethink the Army's mission and soon resigned.

For a long time, despite what I had seen in Hiroshima, I thought dropping the bomb 10
had been the right thing to do. I believed what Truman had said, that the bomb had
saved lives. But as we entered the arms race with the Soviet Union, my mind began
to change. I had seen the destruction that was felt for generations to come. I feared
for the future of my grandchildren. Often, I envisioned my classmates, evaporated by
the bomb. Why couldn't the United States have dropped the bomb on an island with
no inhabitants to show Japan what a powerful weapon it had?

I have returned to Hiroshima twice since 1945, once in 1986 and once in 1995 on 11
the 50th anniversary of the bombing. On that second trip, I walked for one month, in
the scorching heat of Japan's summer, from Kobe to Hiroshima, talking to Japanese
people about my experiences. I spoke at a conference in Hiroshima commemorating
the anniversary, begging forgiveness for any part I might have played in what I now
consider a heinous crime. It was a speech I couldn't finish. But I had come to realize
that remembering and talking about such atrocities is the only way we can prevent
them from happening again.

1   A good introduction to how rhetoric functions in social movements can be found in Charles J. Stewart, Craig Allen Smith, and Robert E. Denton, *Persuasion and Social Movements*, 6th ed. (Long Grove, IL: Waveland, 2012).

2   In *Rhetoric*, Aristotle focuses on multiple means of adapting to the preconceptions of the audience. *The Rhetoric* is contained in *The Basic Works of Aristotle*, Ed. Richard McKeon (New York: Random House, 1941): 1325–1451.

3   A rhetorical approach to the study of social movements was first suggested by Leland Griffin in his essay "The Rhetoric of Historical Movements," *Quarterly Journal of Speech* 37 (1953): 184–188.

4   See Herbert W. Simons, Elizabeth A. Mechling, and Howard N. Schreier, "The Functions of Human Communication in Mobilizing for Collective Action from the Bottom Up: The Rhetoric of Social Movements," in *Handbook of Rhetorical and Communication Theory*, ed. Carroll C. Arnold and John Waite Bowers (Boston: Allyn and Bacon, 1984), 792–868.

5   See for example Robert Cathcart, "New Approaches to the Study of Movements: Defining Movements Rhetorically," *Western Journal of Speech Communication* 36 (1972): 82–89.

6   Leland Griffin, "A Dramatistic Theory of the Rhetoric of Movements," in *Critical Responses to Kenneth Burke*, ed. William Rueckert (Minneapolis: University of Minnesota Press, 1969), 456–478.

7   One perspective on this position is found in David Zarefsky, "A Skeptical View of Movement Studies," *Central States Speech Journal* 31 (1980): 245–254.

8   Herbert Simons, "On the Rhetoric of Social Movements, Historical Movements, and 'Top-Down' Movements: A Commentary," *Communication Studies* 42 (1991), p. 100.

9   Simons, "On the Rhetoric of Social Movements, Historical Movements, and 'Top-Down' Movements: A Commentary," p. 100.

10   For a similar argument see Robert L. Scott and Donald K. Smith, "The Rhetoric of Confrontation," *Quarterly Journal of Speech* 55 (1969): 1–8.

11   Louise, Richardson, *What Terrorists Want: Understanding the Enemy, Containing the Threat* (New York: Random House, 2006), p. 4. I've written in some detail about terrorism as rhetoric. See Robert C. Rowland and Kirsten Theye, "The Symbolic DNA of Terrorism," *Communication Monographs*, 75, (2008): 52–85.

12   P. Jenkins, *Images of Terror: What We Can and Can't Know about Terrorism* (New York: Aldine de Gruyter, 2003), p. 83.

13   Bin Laden's statements to the world have over the last dozen years have been collected in a very useful book, *Messages to the World: The Statements of Osama Bin Laden*, Ed. Bruce Lawrence (London: Verso, 2005). The quotation cited here is from p. 140.

14   James M. McPherson, "The Agitator," *The New Republic* 11 March 1991, p. 37.

15   McPherson, p. 37.

16   "Historians commemorate political reformer Frederick Douglass," http://www.si.edu/resour...ics/ research/african.html.

17   McPherson notes that Douglass "counseled violent resistance" to the Fugitive Slave Law and "supported John Brown's guerrilla warfare against slavery," p. 37.

18   See Howard H. Martin, "The Fourth of July Oration," *Quarterly Journal of Speech* 44 (1958), p. 398.

19   Klaus Lubbers, "Reinventing Native Americans in Fourth of July Orations," *Studies in the Literary Imagination* 27 (Spring 1994), p. 48.

20   See Martin p. 399.

21   McPherson, p. 37.

CHAPTER 10
Generic Analysis

A genre is a category. In every area of human endeavor, categorization plays an important role in explaining and evaluating the object or concept. A good pop song will not meet the same standards as a symphony and vice versa. As this example indicates, it is almost impossible to judge anything without some knowledge of the larger category in which it fits.

There are many ways to categorize works of rhetoric. One could categorize a work based on its subject, the time or place where it was presented, the type of occasion, the situation, and so forth. Given the variety of possible categorical approaches, clearly there is need for guidance concerning appropriate and inappropriate categorization. For example, the category "Midwest" rhetoric would not seem to be very useful. Nor is it especially helpful to discuss a topic like foreign policy rhetoric, because of the wide diversity of approaches taken to so broad a subject.

Why is it important to place a work of rhetoric in a category? The short answer is that in some cases knowing the category of the rhetoric helps the critic both describe and evaluate the rhetoric. There is, for example, a category of rhetoric called "the employment interview." In this situation, the job applicant wants to make a good impression and find out as much about the company or organization as possible. Given these purposes, most job applicants dress formally, try to present a positive demeanor, emphasize their skills and experience, and downplay weaknesses in their record. Knowing that these characteristics typify the employment interview, employers also know where to probe. For example, a two-year gap on a resume is a red flag that demands explanation.

Knowledge of the general characteristics of a typical employment interview also provides the employer with general standards for evaluating the interview. If the potential employee comes to the interview dressed for the beach and continually refers to the interviewer as "dude," there are good reasons to doubt whether he/she will fit into the culture of a big accounting or law firm. On the other hand, if the potential employee is applying for a job at a surf shop, he/she may fit in beautifully.

What does this example have to do with rhetoric? An employment interview is itself rhetorical. Both the interviewer and the potential employee rely on rhetoric in the interview. Knowledge of the category—employment interview—helps the rhetorical critic (a role played by both the interviewer and the interviewee) analyze and evaluate the exchange.

At this point, it should be clear that in some contexts ("Midwest" and foreign policy rhetoric), analysis of the category in which the rhetoric fits doesn't provide much assistance in analyzing that rhetoric. On the other hand, in some contexts (the employment interview), knowledge of the norms of that category of rhetoric is very helpful for both interviewers and interviewees. It would seem that sometimes generic analysis is quite useful and sometimes it is almost useless. In the remainder of this chapter, I untangle this confusing situation. In the first section, I lay out the functions of generic analysis and more fully develop the potential problems with the approach. I then discuss a model for identifying useful rhetorical genres. In the final sections, I apply that model to two common rhetorical genres, the eulogy and the inaugural address.

FUNCTIONS AND PROBLEMS OF GENERIC ANALYSIS

The two primary functions of generic analysis are to reveal the nature of the category in order to: 1) aid in the description or analysis of the rhetoric and 2) provide standards for evaluating the rhetoric.

In many cases, an understanding of the category in which a given work of rhetoric falls can aid in explaining the nature of that rhetoric. Knowing the genre of the rhetoric can provide a shortcut in the analysis process. For example, later in this chapter, I identify seven characteristics that typically are found in eulogies. This list of the form, content, substance, and style that defines eulogies assists in the analysis process, because it gives the critic a place to start in analyzing any given eulogy.

The typical list of characteristics found in a eulogy essentially functions as a "recipe" for the normal eulogy. The analyst can use that list as a kind of "check-off" sheet to see if a given speech does what normal eulogies do. In that way, knowledge of the genre simplifies the analysis stage. It is important to note, however, that the analyst does not stop with identifying the recipe for the eulogy or any other genre. After that recipe is identified, the analyst checks both for what is there and what isn't there in a given speech or other work of rhetoric. In that way the generic recipe can help the analyst identify both typical characteristics and unique aspects of a work of rhetoric. In some cases, it may be the unique characteristics of the work, those that are not typically found in the genre, that make it important or persuasive. And in other cases, the failure to fulfill a normal generic element may point the analyst toward a specific aspect of the given rhetorical situation that makes the normal generic characteristic inapplicable in that instance.

The second function of generic analysis is to provide a shortcut in evaluating a work of rhetoric. Once the characteristics that define the genre have been identified, the critic can use that list as the first step in evaluating the effectiveness of rhetoric falling in the category. For example, in relation to eulogies, the critic would ask: "Does this speech do everything that a eulogy is supposed to do?" If one of the defining characteristics of the eulogy is absent, that is a sign that the speech probably won't be successful. A second question is even more useful: "Does the speech violate any of the normal characteristics found in the eulogy?" For example, a good eulogy is personal in that it focuses on the human dimensions of the deceased and the relationship between the deceased and the person giving the eulogy. A eulogy that violates this principle by presenting a resume of the person's accomplishments is unlikely to achieve the general purposes served by all eulogies.

The two evaluative questions provide the analyst with a shortcut to evaluation. They do not, however, eliminate the need to consider the specific audience and other aspects of the situation that the rhetor faced. For example, despite the general principle that a eulogy should be somber, there are some eulogies that must include humor. A eulogy for David Letterman, for example, would not be complete without humor, because of Letterman's long career in comedy.

In summary, knowledge of a genre can aid the analyst in both explaining and evaluating a work of rhetoric. That knowledge also can assist the practitioner in constructing a speech or essay. For example, it is much easier to create a good eulogy if you understand the characteristics of eulogies as a category of rhetoric.

While a generic approach is quite useful in many cases, there are other instances in which it is not useful at all. Take the category called "lecture." While all lectures serve the purpose of presenting information to an audience, many different tactics can be used. Some lectures are built around presentation of material in outline form. Others use audio-visual devices to add to the presentation. Some lecturers use various tricks to get the participation of the audience. Other lecturers take questions only at the end. Still others pepper the audience with questions as the lecture proceeds. And a few use questions to humiliate members of the audience. In relation to strategy types, some lecturers rely on argument. Others rely on narrative, credibility, aesthetic strategies, and so forth. It is difficult to think of a single characteristic that applies to all lectures.

The key point is that while generic analysis is often useful, in many instances it is not useful at all. In those cases, application of a generic approach would be quite problematic. What are the problems associated with generic analysis? In the case of the lecture, the problem is that the category is too vague to tell us anything useful. Generic analysis also may fail if the critic tries to make the category too specific. A critic might argue that all lectures have X and Y characteristics. The problem is that there are no universal characteristics found in all lectures.

A third problem occurs if the critic misidentifies the category. I once attended a presentation which the speaker thought was supposed to be a detailed, highly academic lecture for graduate students. The problem was that it in fact was designed to be a lecture for the general public. The speech was a disaster because the academic lecture did not fit the public audience. This example supports the point that misidentification of the category may lead to a radical misunderstanding of the rhetoric.

At this point, we are faced with a problem. It is clear that in some cases generic analysis is quite useful. It is equally clear that in many other instances generic analysis is not only not useful, but is positively misleading. The problem is to distinguish between the two cases. The answer to the difficulty is to develop a model for understanding generic constraints that helps the critic distinguish between the *useful* and the *useless* generic categories.

A MODEL FOR GENERIC ANALYSIS[1]

The place to start in building a model for generic analysis is with the factor that makes a category like "employment interview" useful and the category "lecture" so useless. What factor is that? The obvious answer is that for a variety of reasons there are strict limitations on what is acceptable in an employment interview, but no such limitations on the lecture. It is important to consider how these limitations work and from where they come.

In a useful genre, the rhetor will feel constrained to choose from a narrow range of strategies, themes, and so forth. The characteristics defining the content, form, strategy, theme, and so on of the genre will be limited by his/her perception (and that of the audience) that the rhetoric has to be done in a given way or it will fail. That is why job interviewees behave as they do; they know that other rhetorical choices will prevent them from getting the job.

At this point, two thirds of a model for identifying useful genres can be described. The characteristics of the rhetoric—the form, content, style, and substance of a useful genre—are produced because the rhetor perceives strategic constraints that limit what he/she can say. So far the model looks like this:

The problem is to determine what brings into existence the perceived strategic constraints.

The perceived strategic constraints are created by the interaction of three forces that operate broadly in the situation in which the rhetoric is presented. The first of these forces is the recurrent problem confronted by the rhetoric. The recurrent problem faced in a job interview is the need to get a job. The recurrent problem faced by a speaker giving a eulogy is the death of someone close to the audience. If a given type of rhetoric does not respond to an easily definable recurrent problem, that type of rhetoric probably cannot be defined as a useful genre. This explains why the category "Midwest" rhetoric is valueless. There is no limiting problem associated with being in the Midwest and thus no force that limits what rhetors can say about the subject. Nor is the situation of being in the Midwest necessarily different in kind from being in the East or South. Similarly, foreign policy rhetoric is not limited to confronting any particular foreign policy issue or problem.

The second force is the purpose of the rhetor. In the job interview situation, the potential employee wants to get the job. That purpose constrains what the interviewee can say. Occasionally, someone will go on a job interview just because they are curious about the firm. They already have a good job and just want to check things out. That person may behave quite differently from a normal interviewee because his/her purpose is different.

The same point can be made about any useful genre. In a useful genre, rhetors will share a purpose that constrains what they can say. An example of a speech type that is related to, but is not the same as a eulogy, may make this point clear. If a terrible dictator were to die, a given senator might comment on the event, but he/she would not present a eulogy. The senator would not give a eulogy because his/her purpose would not be to honor the dictator's memory. Because his/her purposes would not be those which are found in a normal eulogy, the senator would not present a eulogy at all.

The third force creating the perceived strategic constraints is the limitation on acceptable rhetoric established by the society in which the rhetoric is presented. Societal limitations define what is appropriate in a given context. For example, in a job interview, formal business clothes are appropriate; shorts and a T-shirt are not. In recent years, there has been movement toward much greater informality than in the past. Today, it is not expected that job interviewers wear a suit for men or similarly formal clothes for women, when that would have been expected even 15 years ago. Thus, societal limitations evolve over time. Social forces limit other types of rhetorical action as well, but they are also constantly evolving. In the 19th century, it was common for politicians to speak for hours at a time. Today, audiences would not accept such long-winded speakers.

The combination of the recurrent problem, the purpose of the rhetor, and the societal constraints facing the rhetor together create the perceived strategic constraints that in turn produce the characteristics of form, content, substance, and style that define the rhetoric in a useful genre. The complete model looks like this:

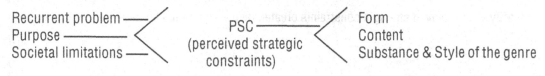

Recurrent problem —
Purpose —
Societal limitations —
< PSC —
(perceived strategic constraints)
< Form
Content
Substance & Style of the genre

At this point, it is possible to distinguish between useful and useless generic analysis. It will be useful to identify the genre in which a work of rhetoric is operating if the combination of recurrent problem, purpose, and societal limitations is stable across rhetoric in the category *and* those characteristics produce narrow perceived strategic constraints to which the rhetor must adapt if he/she is to successfully persuade an audience.

If these conditions are met, then the critic can use the characteristics of form, content, substance, and style that define the category as a starting point for analyzing any particular work of rhetoric in the category. As I noted earlier in this section, the characteristics of form, content, substance, and style also can be used to evaluate rhetoric. A speech or essay that does not contain the required characteristics in all likelihood will be an ineffective work. One other point is important in application of the system. If a work that appears to fall in a particular category does not share the same recurrent problem, purpose, or societal constraints with other works in the category, there is good reason to doubt that the work in fact falls into the genre. This aspect of the model provides a check against inappropriate application of generic analysis.

In summary, in order to identify a useful rhetorical genre, the critic should identify the recurrent problem, purpose(s), and societal constraints influencing works in the category. From those characteristics, the critic can infer the perceived strategic constraints and identify the form, content, substance, and style that define a given category of rhetoric. Using this approach, the critic also can discover whether the perceived strategic constraints are narrow or broad. It is only when the perceived strategic constraints are both consistent across the category and quite narrow that generic analysis is likely to be extremely useful. A summary of the process of generic analysis is included below.

GENRE ANALYSIS

Identify the following situational factors

    Recurring Problem

    Constraining Purpose

    Societal Constraints

Identify the perceived strategic constraints created by the situational factors

Identify the characteristics of form, content, substance, and style required by the perceived strategic constraints

Generic evaluation:

1 Does the rhetoric contain all of the defining characteristics of the genre?
2 Does the rhetoric violate any of the defining characteristics of the genre?
3 Are there specific circumstances or purposes that demand adaptation of the genre?

A CASE STUDY OF GENERIC ANALYSIS: THE EULOGY

To illustrate the value of generic analysis, it is helpful to apply the system to perhaps the most limited and unfortunately all too common category of rhetoric, the eulogy. The recurrent problem faced in a eulogy is the death of a person close to us. When someone important to us dies, grief is created. In addition, the death also reminds us that we are going to die. And death also may shock the

© DAVID KAY/SHUTTERSTOCK.COM

organization or community in which the deceased lived. For example, the assassination of President Kennedy brought this nation to a standstill. Almost anyone who was alive at the time of his death can tell you where they were and what they were doing when they heard the news. For an older generation, the same was true when President Franklin Roosevelt died.

There are four purposes fulfilled by an effective eulogy, all of which are closely related to the recurrent problem. The first purpose of a eulogy is to directly confront the death of the person. There is a psychological principle that healing cannot begin until the pain has been confronted. A good eulogy forces us to deal with the death of someone important in our lives. Second, eulogies fulfill the purpose of bringing closure to our relationship with the deceased. The eulogy tells us the meaning of the person's life in relation to our own. Third, eulogies help the audience confront the inevitability of their own mortality. The death of someone close to us always reminds each of us that someday we will die. The eulogy may help us cope with that unpleasant truth. Finally, an effective eulogy pulls the community back together. Just as individual healing cannot occur until the death has been confronted, the organization cannot move on until the community has been reestablished.

In terms of societal limitations, eulogies are governed by the culture of today's society. In the 19th century, religious references would have been mandatory. Today, they aren't. Similarly, in an earlier era, a longer and more flowery address would have been the norm. Today, the style is more subdued. While eulogies are not nearly as constrained by societal factors as they once were, one particular societal limitation remains in effect, the rule that one does not speak ill of the dead.

In the case of the eulogy, the combination of recurrent problem, purpose, and societal limitations creates extremely narrow perceived strategic constraints. In essence, there is only one way to give a good eulogy, at least in Western culture.

An effective eulogy is defined by seven characteristics of form, content, style, and substance. First, in an effective eulogy the rhetor begins by acknowledging and confronting the death, usually by stating what a sad day it is. Again, the pain must be confronted before it can be transformed. The second and third characteristics of an effective eulogy are both related to linguistic tone. A good eulogy possesses a somber tone, especially at the beginning. The somber tone is demanded by the occasion of the eulogy, the death of someone close to us. At the same time, a good eulogy is personal. It tells the audience about the relationship between the deceased and the living. It isn't a recital of accomplishments, but a reflection on the person who has died.

The fourth characteristic of a good eulogy is closely related to the third. An effective eulogy tells us who the deceased was. A eulogy is not a resume. Rather, it is a description of the essence of the person. Oftentimes, the eulogist will pick out two or three qualities of the deceased and illustrate those qualities with personal examples. In so doing, he/she tells us the meaning of the life of the person who has died.

Fifth, a good eulogy can be thought of as a kind of rhetorical journey. It begins in darkest night with the pain of the person's death. It then gives us an understanding of the person's life and ends with emotional catharsis. The eulogy has brought closure to the crisis created for the community by the death; that community now can go on. In that way, the journey is from pain to emotional release. That same rhetorical journey helps us all confront the inevitability of our own deaths.

Sixth, a good eulogy comforts the living by telling us that the deceased lives on in some way. One can live on in heaven, in the memory of the audience, or in the work of the audience. Many effective eulogies hit all three possibilities. The fact that the deceased lives on helps us face the loss of the individual and our own future mortality.

Finally, a good eulogy is shaped around the character of the person who has died. As I noted earlier, when David Letterman dies, the person giving the eulogy will need to use humor to make the eulogy effective, despite the fact that humor is not normally used in eulogies. Why? Letterman has been one of our very best comedians for decades and the message of his life is that humor can help us deal with even the most difficult situation. An appropriate eulogy for Letterman will have to use humor as a way of paying tribute to his life. This point can be generalized. Effective eulogies must be adapted to the specifics of the person's life. This can be especially tricky given the norm that one does not speak ill of the dead when someone dies who is well known for some wrongdoing.

1 The eulogy must confront the death of the person.

2 The tone of the eulogy should be somber, especially at the beginning of the speech.

3 The content of the eulogy should be personal.

4 The eulogist should tell us the meaning of the life of the person who has died and not give us a résumé of their life.

5 A good eulogy is a rhetorical journey from pain to catharsis.

6 In a good eulogy, the deceased lives on in some way.

7 The eulogy must be adapted to the specifics of the person's life.

The important point is that the eulogy must meet the general characteristics I have outlined, but also be adapted to the particular individual. So, for example, all of the eulogies for Richard Nixon that were presented after his death in some way had to deal with the Watergate scandal, but do so in a way that did not explicitly criticize Nixon.

The critic can apply the system I have developed to analyze and evaluate any eulogy. The first step is to identify the recurrent problem, purpose, and societal limitations to make certain the work falls into the category of eulogy. Recall that I noted earlier that a speech by a senator following the death of a brutal dictator would not be a eulogy. At this point, the reason should be obvious. An American senator would not be fulfilling the four eulogistic purposes in speaking of the death of a tyrant. For example, there were many speeches in the United States after the deaths of Saddam Hussein and Osama bin Laden, but the overwhelming majority of them were not eulogies.

The second step is to compare the speech to the seven characteristics of an effective eulogy. This should help in breaking the speech down into analysis categories. A comparison of the speech to the seven characteristics also can be used to evaluate the eulogy. If the eulogy met all seven characteristics, that is a strong indication that it was a good speech. If it violated one or more of the seven characteristics, it probably

© JOSE ANTONIO PEREZ/SHUTTERSTOCK.COM

failed as a work of rhetoric, but it is important to consider whether some aspect of the specific situation called for an alteration in normal eulogistic form. After asking these questions, a final judgment about the eulogy can be made recognizing that language and style are also important, although not nearly as important as fulfilling the generic norms.

In order to illustrate application of the system, I next use it in judging a eulogy presented by President Ronald Reagan. Reagan spoke following the terrible tragedy in which the NASA space shuttle *Challenger* was destroyed shortly after being launched, killing all of the astronauts on board.

REAGAN'S *CHALLENGER* EULOGY IN HOUSTON, TEXAS

The Houston eulogy was presented a few days after the tragic death of the *Challenger* Seven in the explosion of the space shuttle. President Reagan spoke to the families of the astronauts and also to workers at NASA.

Memorial Service for the Crew of the Space Shuttle *Challenger*
Ronald Wilson Reagan

1 We come together today to mourn the loss of seven brave Americans, to share the grief that we all feel, and perhaps in that sharing, to find the strength to bear our sorrow and the courage to look for the seeds of hope.

2 Our nation's loss is first a profound personal loss to the family and the friends and the loved ones of our shuttle astronauts. To those they left behind—the mothers, the fathers, the husbands and wives, brothers and sisters, yes, and especially the children—all of America stands beside you in your time of sorrow.

3 What we say today is only an inadequate expression of what we carry in our hearts. Words pale in the shadow of grief; they seem insufficient even to measure the brave sacrifice of those you loved and we so admired. Their truest testimony will not be in the words we speak, but in the way they led their lives and in the way they lost their lives—with dedication, honor, and an unquenchable desire to explore this mysterious and beautiful universe.

4 The best we can do is remember our seven astronauts, our *Challenger* Seven, remember them as they lived, bringing life and love and joy to those who knew them and pride to a nation.

5 They came from all parts of this great country—from South Carolina to Washington State; Ohio to Mohawk, New York; Hawaii to North Carolina to Concord, New Hampshire. They were so different; yet in their mission, their quest, they held so much in common.

President Ronald Reagan, Eulogy for Crew of Challenger, *January 31, 1986*

We remember Dick Scobee, the commander who spoke the last words we heard   6
from the space shuttle *Challenger*. He served as a fighter pilot in Vietnam earning
many medals for bravery and later as a test pilot of advanced aircraft before joining
the space program. Danger was a familiar companion to Commander Scobee.

We remember Michael Smith, who earned enough medals as a combat pilot to   7
cover his chest, including the Navy Distinguished Flying Cross, three Air Medals, and
the Vietnamese Cross of Gallantry with Silver Star in gratitude from a nation he fought
to keep free.

We remember Judith Resnik, known as J.R. to her friends, always smiling, always   8
eager to make a contribution, finding beauty in the music she played on her piano in
her off-hours.

We remember Ellison Onizuka, who as a child running barefoot through the coffee   9
fields and macadamia groves of Hawaii dreamed of someday traveling to the Moon.
Being an Eagle Scout, he said, had helped him soar to the impressive achievements
of his career.

We remember Ronald McNair, who said that he learned perseverance in the cotton   10
fields of South Carolina. His dream was to live aboard the space station, performing
experiments and playing his saxophone in the weightlessness of space. Well, Ron,
we will miss your saxophone; and we will build your space station.

We remember Gregory Jarvis. On that ill-fated flight he was carrying with him a   11
flag of his university in Buffalo, New York—a small token, he said, to the people who
unlocked his future.

We remember Christa McAuliffe, who captured the imagination of the entire nation,   12
inspiring us with her pluck, her restless spirit of discovery; a teacher, not just to her
students, but to an entire people, instilling us all with the excitement of this journey we
ride into the future.

We will always remember them, these skilled professionals, scientists, and   13
adventurers, these artists and teachers and family men and women; and we will
cherish each of their stories, stories of triumph and bravery, stories of true American
heroes.

On the day of the disaster, our nation held a vigil by our television sets. In one   14
cruel moment our exhilaration turned to horror; we waited and watched and tried
to make sense of what we had seen. That night I listened to a call-in program on
the radio; people of every age spoke of their sadness and the pride they felt in our
astronauts. Across America we are reaching out, holding hands, and finding comfort
in one another.

The sacrifice of your loved ones has stirred the soul of our nation and through the   15
pain our hearts have been opened to a profound truth: The future is not free; the story
of all human progress is one of a struggle against all odds. We learned again that this
America, which Abraham Lincoln called the last, best hope of man on Earth, was built
on heroism and noble sacrifice. It was built by men and women like our seven star

voyagers, who answered a call beyond duty, who gave more than was expected or required, and who gave little thought to a worldly reward.

We think back to the pioneers of an earlier century, the sturdy souls who took their families and their belongings and set out into the frontier of the American West. Often they met with terrible hardship. Along the Oregon Trail, you can still see the grave markers of those who fell on the way. But grief only steeled them to the journey ahead. 16

Today the frontier is space and the boundaries of human knowledge. Sometimes when we reach for the stars, we fall short. But we must pick ourselves up again and press on despite the pain. Our nation is indeed fortunate that we can still draw on immense reservoirs of courage, character, and fortitude; that we're still blessed with heroes like those of the space shuttle Challenger. 17

Dick Scobee knew that every launching of a space shuttle is a technological miracle. And he said, "If something ever does go wrong, I hope that doesn't mean the end to the space shuttle program." Every family member I talked to asked specifically that we continue the program, that is what their departed loved one would want above all else. We will not disappoint them. 18

Today we promise Dick Scobee and his crew that their dream lives on, that the dream lives on, that the future they worked so hard to build will become reality. The dedicated men and women of NASA have lost seven members of their family. Still, they, too, must forge ahead with a space program that is effective, safe, and efficient, but bold and committed. 19

Man will continue his conquest of space. To reach out for new goals and ever greater achievements—that is the way we shall commemorate our seven Challenger heroes. 20

Dick, Mike, Judy, El, Ron, Greg, and Christa—your families and your country mourn your passing. We bid you goodbye: we will never forget you. For those who knew you well and loved you, the pain will be deep and enduring. A nation, too, will long feel the loss of her seven sons and daughters, her seven good friends. We can find consolation only in faith, for we know in our hearts that you who flew so high and so proud now make your home beyond the stars, safe in God's promise of eternal life. 21

May God bless you all and give you comfort in this difficult time. 22

Since Reagan's speech clearly responded to the situational factors that define a eulogy (recurrent problem, purpose, and societal limitation), there is no question that it was a eulogy. The next step in the generic analysis is to consider whether it possesses the characteristics of form, content, style, and substance of an effective eulogy. A brief description of the organization of the speech will aid in this effort.

In the first paragraph, Reagan confronts the death of the astronauts. He says that "We come together today to mourn the loss of seven brave Americans." This theme is continued in the second paragraph where he refers to "Our nation's loss" and then talks of the "personal loss to the family and the friends and the loved ones of our shuttle astronauts." The somber tone continues in the third paragraph where he says that "Words pale in the shadow of grief."

At the end of the third paragraph, Reagan begins a transition to a personal discussion of the character of the astronauts. He refers to "the way they led their lives," which was "with dedication, honor, and an unquenchable desire to explore this mysterious and beautiful universe."

The following paragraphs then tell us who they were. Reagan begins by emphasizing that they came from all over this nation. In so doing, he features their character as Americans, a theme he will return to a few paragraphs later. He then devotes one paragraph to each of the *Challenger* Seven (paragraphs 6 through 12). In so doing, he tries both to give the audience a personal detail about each individual and also to put the person's life into perspective. At the end of this section, he pulls together the description of the *Challenger* Seven and labels them "American heroes" (paragraph 13). Throughout this section, Reagan emphasizes that the crew members of the *Challenger* were both different and the same. They had individual characteristics, but they all were typical American heroes.

In the following paragraphs, Reagan puts their heroism into perspective. He labels the astronauts as pioneers who sacrificed in order to pull this nation into the future. Reagan says that "The future is not free" (paragraph 15). It has to be earned with hard work and sacrifice. And that sacrifice will not have been in vain. Reagan promises that the dream of the *Challenger* Seven "lives on" (paragraph 19). He adds that "the future they worked so hard to build will become a reality" (paragraph 19).

In the final paragraphs, Reagan calls for this nation to "commemorate" the astronauts by continuing the "conquest of space" (paragraph 20). He then adds that the nation "will never forget you" and concludes by stating that those "who flew so high and so proud now make your home beyond the stars, safe in God's promise of eternal life" (paragraph 21).

Reagan's Houston eulogy is a near perfect example of what a eulogy is supposed to do. Reagan begins by directly confronting the death of the astronauts. He uses a somber tone in the introduction, a tone that will gradually change as the eulogy progresses. He next provides a personal detail relating to each of the *Challenger* Seven, giving us a sense of each individual and the meaning of each of their lives, before he pulls them back together labeling them as heroes and pioneers. In this section, he makes particular reference to Christa McAuliffe, the teacher who was on the mission. In the conclusion, Reagan states that the *Challenger* Seven live on in the space program, in our memory, and in heaven.

Reagan's speech clearly contains all seven characteristics of form, content, style, and substance that define an effective eulogy. He does an especially good job of adapting to the specifics of the situation, in this case the fact that he is eulogizing seven people in one speech. Reagan adapts to this problem by discussing each astronaut in turn, but also treating them as a group. It is a brilliant speech that effectively fulfills the characteristics that define the eulogy.

REAGAN'S COMMEMORATION OF THE *CHALLENGER* SEVEN ON THE NIGHT OF THE ACCIDENT

Reagan's eulogy for the *Challenger* astronauts in Houston did a terrific job of doing everything that a eulogy is supposed to do. But it isn't the speech that we remember Reagan giving about the explosion of the space shuttle. On the night of the accident, President Reagan made a very moving five-minute speech about the shuttle accident. The primary author of that speech, Peggy Noonan, reports that there was an outpouring of public response to Reagan's brief comments, and that Reagan himself called the next day to thank her for her "wonderful remarks."[2] If this is the famous "eulogy," the generic system that I have developed should explain its success as well.

Address to the Nation on the Explosion of the Space Shuttle *Challenger*
Ronald Wilson Reagan

Ladies and gentlemen, I'd planned to speak to you tonight to report on the state of the Union, but the events of earlier today have led me to change those plans. Today is a day for mourning and remembering. Nancy and I are pained to the core by the tragedy of the shuttle Challenger. We know we share this pain with all of the people of our country. This is truly a national loss. 1

Nineteen years ago, almost to the day, we lost three astronauts in a terrible accident on the ground. But we've never lost an astronaut in flight; we've never had a tragedy like this. And perhaps we've forgotten the courage it took for the crew of the shuttle. But they, the Challenger Seven, were aware of the dangers, but overcame them and did their jobs brilliantly. We mourn seven heroes: Michael Smith, Dick Scobee, Judith Resnik, Ronald McNair, Ellison Onizuka, Gregory Jarvis, and Christa McAuliffe. We morn their loss as a nation together. 2

For the families of the seven, we cannot bear, as you do, the full impact of this tragedy. But we feel the loss, and we're thinking about you so very much. Your loved ones were daring and brave, and they had that special grace, that special spirit that says, "Give me a challenge, and I'll meet it with joy." They had a hunger to explore the universe and discover its truths. They wished to serve, and they did. They served all of us. We've grown used to wonders in this country. It's hard to dazzle us. But for 25 years the United States space program has been doing just that. We've grown used to the idea of space, and perhaps we forget that we've only just begun. We're still pioneers. They, the members of the Challenger crew, were pioneers. 3

And I want to say something to the schoolchildren of America who were watching the live coverage of the shuttle's takeoff. I know it is hard to understand, but sometimes 4

President Ronald Reagan, Address to the Nation on the Explosion of the Space Shuttle Challenger, *January 28, 1986* painful things like this happen. It's all part of the process of exploration and discovery. It's all part of taking a chance and expanding man's horizons. The future doesn't belong to the fainthearted; it belongs to the brave. The Challenger crew was pulling us into the future, and we'll continue to follow them.

I've always had great faith in and respect for our space program, and what happened today does nothing to diminish it. We don't hide our space program. We don't keep secrets and cover things up. We do it all up front and in public. That's the way freedom is, and we wouldn't change it for a minute. We'll continue our quest in space. There will be more shuttle flights and more shuttle crews and, yes, more volunteers, more civilians, more teachers in space. Nothing ends here; our hopes and our journeys continue. I want to add that I wish I could talk to every man and woman who works for NASA or who worked on this mission and tell them: "Your dedication and professionalism have moved and impressed us for decades. And we know of your anguish. We share it."

There's a coincidence today. On this day 390 years ago, the great explorer Francis Drake died aboard ship off the coast of Panama. In his lifetime the great frontiers were the oceans, and an historian later said, "He lived by the sea, died on it, and was buried in it." Well, today we can say of the Challenger crew: Their dedication was, like Drake's, complete.

The crew of the space shuttle Challenger honored us by the manner in which they lived their lives. We will never forget them, nor the last time we saw them, this morning, as they prepared for their journey and waved goodbye and "slipped the surly bonds of earth" to "touch the face of God."

5

6

7

Reagan begins his commemoration of the *Challenger* Seven on the night of the accident by explaining to the national audience that the State of the Union Address had been postponed. As in any good eulogy, he expresses his grief over the loss, stating that "Nancy and I are pained to the core by the tragedy" (paragraph 1).

In the second paragraph, he puts the accident in a larger frame, noting that while astronauts had been killed before, "we've never had a tragedy like this." He then labels the *Challenger* astronauts as "heroes" and adds that "We mourn their loss as a nation together."

The theme of mourning is continued in the third paragraph, where he speaks to the families of the astronauts. At the end of this paragraph, he labels the *Challenger* astronauts as "pioneers." In paragraphs four and five, he shifts his focus to schoolchildren and NASA. Paragraph four speaks to the many schoolchildren who had been watching the shuttle launch live because of the teacher, Christa McAuliffe, who was a member of the shuttle crew. He explains that "sometimes painful things like this happen" but that "It's all part of the process of exploration and discovery." According to Reagan, "The *Challenger* crew was pulling us into the future, and we'll continue to follow them."

Paragraph five shifts the focus to NASA. Reagan expresses his admiration for the space program and inserts a jab at the Russians by saying "We don't keep secrets and cover things up.

We do it all up front and in public. That's the way freedom is, and we wouldn't change it for a minute." Here, he implicitly reminds his audience that the Soviet Union does keep secrets and does cover things up. Then, Reagan promises "more shuttle flights and more shuttle crews" and praises the "dedication and professionalism" of those who work at NASA.

In paragraph six, Reagan compares the shuttle crew to the famed explorer Sir Francis Drake, who died 390 years before on the same day. He concludes in paragraph seven by quoting a selection from the poem "High Flight." "We will never forget them, nor the last time we saw them, this morning, as they prepared for their journey and waved goodbye and 'slipped the surly bonds of earth' to 'touch the face of God.'"

There is no question that the speech is one of the most famous and admired of Reagan's presidency. Reagan himself chose to include it, and not the Houston eulogy, in the collection of speeches that he published after the conclusion of his presidency.[3] However, the speech raises questions about using a generic system to evaluate a work of rhetoric. The problem is that in many ways this highly praised speech doesn't look like a normal eulogy.

In some ways the speech does possess the characteristics of a typical eulogy. Reagan begins by confronting the deaths of the astronauts and he uses a somber tone throughout. He certainly adapts to the unique characteristics of the situation by explaining why the State of the Union had been delayed and speaking directly to schoolchildren and NASA.

In other ways, however, the speech is not a typical eulogy. For example, Reagan says little about the *Challenger* astronauts themselves. He labels them heroes and pioneers, but gives us no personal details. In fact, he focuses more on NASA than on the astronauts. And it is decidedly odd to see an attack on the Soviets in a eulogy. Nor does Reagan clearly say that the *Challenger* astronauts will live on in our memory, our work, or heaven. In the last line, he does say that they touched the "face of God," but he certainly does not develop the theme that the astronauts live on, as he would do in Houston a few days later.

Finally, the speech lacks the emotional progression typically found in eulogies. Reagan does not move us from pain to catharsis. Instead, he talks about the nation's pain in virtually every paragraph. And the touching concluding quotation reinforces that point. In a way, he begins and ends in pain, a pattern that is not at all typical of effective eulogies.

The clear conclusion is that the speech that Reagan gave on the night of the *Challenger* accident isn't a very good eulogy. But both public reaction and expert commentary label it as one of his most successful speeches. One might think that this contradictory state of affairs undercuts generic analysis of rhetoric, but there is a clear explanation.

The reason that Reagan's first *Challenger* speech could be so successful, while not fulfilling the requirements of a typical eulogy, is that it wasn't a eulogy at all. This point is obvious when the speech is analyzed from the perspective of the generic model I discussed earlier in this chapter. While the speech had the same recurrent problem and cultural constraints of a typical eulogy, it did not have the same purposes. It is obvious from the address that two of Reagan's main purposes were to help school kids cope with their grief and to protect NASA from political fallout from the accident. That is why he spends roughly one third of the address dealing with these subjects. In addition, it is clear that Reagan's purpose was not to move the nation to catharsis, but to hold the pain in. On the night of the accident, it was too soon to give a normal eulogy that moves us to acceptance and almost joyful remembrance of the deceased. It was still time to feel the pain of the accident. Reagan's speech was designed to help us feel that pain, but to make certain that the anguish did not overcome school kids or create a political backlash that harmed NASA.

When the real purposes served by the speech are considered, it is immediately obvious that the address was not a traditional eulogy. It thus makes no sense to evaluate it by applying the defining characteristics of the eulogy. In addition, a consideration of the purpose of the speech helps make clear why the public found it so comforting. Reagan did exactly what he needed to do on the night of the accident. He was comforting and eloquent about the sacrifice of the astronauts. And he spoke directly to America's schoolchildren and NASA. The speech did exactly what was needed, but that didn't fulfill the purposes of a traditional eulogy.

In a memoir of her time as a speech writer for Reagan, Peggy Noonan reports that she sensed that President Reagan was dissatisfied with the *Challenger* speech that he gave on the night of the accident. She quotes him as saying, "And I got off the air and I thought, well, not so good. But then I got these calls and telegrams…"[4] Although it is impossible to know for sure, it seems likely that Reagan's disquiet with the speech draft was because he knew it wasn't a good eulogy. However, Noonan's draft was right on target, because she correctly realized that a eulogy was not what was needed so soon after the accident. That was why the public responded with those calls and telegrams.

THE INAUGURAL ADDRESS

A number of the most famous speeches in American history are inaugural addresses. The inaugural addresses by Washington, Jefferson, both of Lincoln's, Franklin Roosevelt, Kennedy, and others are justly famous. Why is it that inaugurals have had such an important influence in American history? The answer can be seen in the word inaugural itself. Inaugural addresses "inaugurate" the new administration. They lay out both the general policy of the administration and also give the nation a feel for the style of the new president. While I will focus on presidential inaugurals, it is important to recognize that many other leaders give what are essentially inaugural addresses. Governors, mayors, and other political leaders often present inaugural addresses. Major corporate leaders may do so as well. If the inaugural address is understood as rhetoric presenting the agenda of a new leader, then it immediately becomes clear that many leaders in public and private life present what are essentially inaugural addresses. The new president of a university or the new chair of the school board may give a talk that serves the same functions and fulfills nearly all of the formal elements of an inaugural address.

Inaugural addresses are really about organizational change. They represent the first attempt by a new leader (or a leader who has been reelected or reselected) to lay out his/her agenda in both substance and style. They are particularly important rhetorical acts both because of the importance of first impressions in any communication context and also because of the tendency for organizational stakeholders to give a new leader a "honeymoon" period. A "honeymoon" period is the time in which the stakeholders in a given organization (other elected officials, the media, and the public for a president) avoid criticism of the new leader and give him/her support in the new position. As should be apparent, inaugural addresses at all levels are crucially important works of rhetoric.

In the following section, I lay out the characteristics of presidential inaugurals. I then explain how the critic can use those characteristics both to describe and evaluate any given speech. I then illustrate those principles by applying them to the first inaugural address of President George W. Bush.

In order to describe the characteristics of inaugurals, the first step is to consider the recurring problem and purposes served by the addresses. At that point, the characteristics of form, content, substance, and style that define the characteristics of the genre can be identified.[5] The recurring problem that inaugurals confront is the election of a new president or the reelection of a sitting president. When a person takes over a position of responsibility, that situation calls for a statement of his/her goals, aims, and so forth. This is true whether the office is chairman of the board of a corporation, dean of a college, minister of a church, or president of the United States. The point is that the moment of transition to new (or renewed) leadership calls for an assessment of where the organization is. As I noted earlier, inaugural addresses can be found in many contexts. Presidential inaugurals are simply the most important type of the genre.

What purposes are served by inaugurals? Inaugural addresses serve three primary purposes: expressing the essence of the new administration, reunification of the organization, and energizing the population. A new leader in any organization (and especially a president of the United States) needs to tell his/her constituents what he/she wants to do. Presidents would give inaugural addresses to achieve this aim even if there were no ritual associated with taking the oath of office. On occasion, events make the purpose of expressing the essence of the new administration especially important. In their first inaugurals, both FDR and Barack Obama confronted an economic crisis. To a lesser degree, Reagan faced a similar problem in 1981. In such a situation, the new president must lay out an agenda that will be perceived as sufficient to confront the national crisis.

In addition, the inaugural provides the president with an opportunity to reunify the nation. This purpose may be fulfilled to a lesser degree in any organization where leadership changeovers may result in division of the organization into groups supporting different candidates. For a president, the inaugural provides a chance for the new leader to say "I am now president of all the people and not just of my political supporters." The reunification purpose of inaugurals will be more important when the previous presidential campaign has been extremely divisive and less important if an incumbent president is easily reelected. In the case of the Bush inaugural that I will consider in a moment, the reunification purpose was very important. The 2000 election campaign was quite divisive and of course dragged on for weeks after election day due to the controversy about counting votes in Florida. In that rhetorical situation, it was crucial for Bush to reunify the people. In other recent elections this purpose has been less important. In 1984, for instance, Ronald Reagan won a crushing victory over Walter Mondale. The reunification purpose was much less important on January 20, 1985, when Reagan presented his second inaugural, than it was on January 20, 2001, because the country had not been split apart by the election to any significant degree. The people knew who Reagan was and largely approved of his presidency.

The third purpose of the inaugural address is to energize the nation. A president may be able to use the inaugural to energize the public behind a legislative agenda. Two of the most successful presidents (in terms of getting their agendas passed) in the 20th century, Franklin Roosevelt and Ronald Reagan, used their inaugurals to gain public support for their initiatives. A similar point is true in any organization. The new president of a company might use a first talk to the board of directors to build support for his/her plans to expand the firm.

It should be obvious that the importance of each of these purposes will vary to some degree with the particular situation. As noted, the reunification purpose will be less important when there has not been much division. In second inaugural addresses, all three purposes are likely to be less important than in first inaugural addresses. In a second inaugural, the people already know who the president is and the principles for which he/she stands. Apparently, they like the person enough to reelect him or her, so reunification is unlikely to be a crucial need. And second honeymoons in a presidency are unlikely to be as passionate as first honeymoons. The point is that there is less at stake in second inaugurals because the country already knows a great deal about the president. The fact that there is less at stake for second inaugurals may help explain why as a general rule they have been both less important and not as memorable as first inaugurals.[6]

In relation to societal constraints, the nature of the inaugural ceremony restricts the style of a presidential inaugural. The simple rule is that the more formal the ceremony and the more serious the purpose, the more formal the style should be. Since the inaugural ceremony is quite formal and the purposes served by it very important, this demands a quite formal style. The same rule would apply to a lesser degree in other inaugural-like settings.

The second constraint on presidential inaugurals relates to the position of the United States in the world. The United States has been the most powerful nation in the world since the end of the Second World War. Moreover, the United States has responsibilities across the globe and is, of course, a nuclear power. The role of the United States as the leader of the "free world" essentially requires that a president of the United States comment on our relations with both our allies and our enemies. Clearly, this second constraint is unique to the presidential inaugural. We would not expect the new chairperson of Ford to comment about world affairs. And if he/she did so, we might think the speech quite odd. The degree to which the role of world leader constrains the president also will be shaped by the world situation. At the height of the Cold War, it was crucial that the new president tell the nation where he stood on our relations with the Soviet Union. After the end of the Soviet Union, it became less important to make such comments. No one would say today that an inaugural missed the mark because it didn't sketch U.S./Russian relations. On the other hand, in the post September 11 climate, a new president will need to comment on United States policy in the war on terrorism. That was not true before September 11, 2001.

The combination of the recurrent problem (the election campaign and the transition to a new or renewed presidency), the three purposes, and the societal constraints imposes strong perceived strategic constraints on presidential inaugurals. To a lesser degree this is true of all inaugural-like rhetoric. A consideration of these constraints indicates that a presidential inaugural should contain the following characteristics of form, content, substance, and style.

First, the inaugural should state the political principles that will guide the administration. Under this requirement, the president needs to tell the country what he/she hopes to accomplish in general terms. However, the inaugural is not the time to lay out a specific legislative agenda. The nation is looking for a broad vision, not the nuts and bolts of public policy. If the speech is too specific, it may lose the audience. But if it is too vague, it will not help the president achieve his/her agenda. The inaugural is a time to present grand themes, not specific policy proposals. The same is true in similar settings.

Second, the inaugural should speak to all of the people and not merely to partisans of one party. This is the president's chance to reunify the nation behind his/her leadership. To achieve that goal, the president needs to put aside partisanship in favor of representing the entire nation. Once again, the same principle applies to inaugurals given by leaders other than a president, if the process of picking that leader has split the organization. One can imagine a situation in which the new chair of a particular committee in a large church would need to reach out to all of the membership of the committee in order to reunify the group. While we tend to think of political campaigns as much more partisan than real life, that is not always the case.

Third, the inaugural should restate the president's commitment to the basic values of the nation. An inauguration is a time for the United States to celebrate what it means to be an American. To accomplish this aim requires a recommitment to the nation's basic values. Thus, a new president will often talk about key values such as freedom, equality, justice, and so forth. The same would be true in any organization. However, it is important to recognize that the more serious the ceremony, the more that such value reaffirmation is needed. The presidential inaugural ceremony is held on the steps of the Capitol building and occurs with much pomp and celebration. It definitely calls for a reaffirmation of basic values.

It might seem that value affirmation serves a purely ceremonial function. If all inaugurals have such value statements, then perhaps they don't mean much. While all presidential inaugurals affirm basic values to one degree or another, the values which are affirmed and their relationship to each other will vary. A Democrat is much more likely to focus on equality and justice, while a Republican might emphasize freedom and opportunity. Value affirmation is important both because it is a way of recommitting the organization (the United States for a president) to those values and because the specific values that are affirmed may undergird the policies of the administration.

Fourth, because the inaugural is a point of transition for the nation, it calls for the president to tell the people where the nation is in relation to American history. The inaugural is a time to reflect on where the nation has been and where it is going. A good inaugural treats the present day as only one moment in the life of the nation. It shows the country how a better future can be produced by following the vision of the president. This same point could be made about any rhetoric created at a key transition point for an organization.

Fifth, the importance of the occasion demands a serious and ceremonial style. The people expect the president to explain his/her agenda in words that move us. We expect a ceremonial style that reflects the importance of the ceremony and what it reflects. Over the last quarter century, millions of people have laughed at the parodies of presidential rhetoric on *Saturday Night Live*. Various members of the cast of the show have used a decidedly non-ceremonial style to make fun of the sitting president. While we laugh at the comics, we would be aghast if a real president violated the stylistic assumptions associated with a ceremonial occasion such as the inaugural. It is funny on television, but it would be decidedly unfunny in real life. President Trump often used a decidedly non-ceremonial style, but in his inaugural address, which is included in the Workbook associated with this volume, he relied on a ceremonial style similar to other presidents. The constraints of the situation pushed him to use a style quite dissimilar from his normal approach.

Sixth, because of the role of the United States in the world and our possession of a large nuclear weapons arsenal, the president needs to "reassure" our allies and "warn" our adversaries about general U.S. policy. Since other nations make policy decisions in relation to what they perceive U.S. policy to be, it is very important that the president send the right message. As I noted earlier, this aspect of presidential inaugurals was most important during the Cold War, when the Soviet Union still existed as a second superpower. Today, the changed circumstances demand a focus on the War on Terror. Clearly, non-presidential inaugurals will not possess this characteristic.

Finally, the president, and any new leader, should try to come across as a strong, but not arrogant, leader. The saying goes that you "only have one chance to make a first impression." The inaugural is the president's chance to make that "first impression" on the people as a new president. It is important that he/she come across as a strong leader, but not a vain or arrogant one. The American people want a president to be both a strong leader and, in a different sense, one of us. Thus, U.S. presidents often have stated their position quite strongly, but then said that the success or failure of the agenda depends upon the people. A very similar point applies to a new leader in any context.

The seven characteristics that define the form, content, style, and substance of inaugurals obviously vary to some degree in their importance in a given speech. As a general rule, for instance, it is less important in a second inaugural than a first that the president explain the political principles of the administration (presumably we already know what those principles are from the first term), reunify the nation, and express the strength of his/her leadership. Even these generalizations are not universal. In a wartime context, it might be more important that the president express the strength of his/her leadership in a second inaugural than it had been when he/she presented the first inaugural. The key point is that the degree to which the seven characteristics are important will vary somewhat in relation to the specific political situation facing the president and also in relation to how important each of the three normal purposes served by inaugurals is in the particular case. Precisely the same point can be made about non-presidential inaugurals. The six characteristics that remain after the expression of foreign policy principles is excluded should be present to one degree or another, but how they are present will vary with the specifics of situation and purpose.

CHARACTERISTICS THAT DEFINE THE FORM, CONTENT, SUBSTANCE, AND STYLE OF PRESIDENTIAL INAUGURALS

1 The inaugural should state political principles of the administration, but not enunciate specific policy.
2 The inaugural should speak to all the people to reunify the public.
3 The inaugural should restate basic values.
4 The inaugural should place the administration within the story of the nation by telling where we have been and where we are going.
5 The inaugural should be presented in a formal, ceremonial style.
6 The inaugural should reassure our allies and warn our enemies.
7 The president should come across as a strong, but not a vain leader.

The characteristics that define presidential inaugurals can be used to describe and evaluate an inaugural address. The first step is for the analyst to carefully consider whether the inaugural fulfills all seven characteristics of form, content, substance, and style or whether it violates some of them. As a second step, the critic should consider whether the specifics of the situation in which a given president was inaugurated may have made one or more of the characteristics more or less important than is the norm. There may be something in the situation that demands a specific focus in the inaugural, such as the impending Civil War in the case of Lincoln's First Inaugural. Thus, the absence of a given characteristic may not indicate that an inaugural failed to fulfill the genre, but instead may indicate that the normal characteristics that define the genre were not required in that specific situation. Still, as a general rule, failure to fulfill a characteristic or violation of the characteristic in all likelihood mean that in some way the speech missed the mark.

Finally, it is important to remember that style plays an important role in the effectiveness of rhetoric in a highly ceremonial situation, such as an inaugural. This means that in addition to the seven defining characteristics, it is important that the president make the address stylistically satisfying. An inaugural which is stylistically interesting is more likely to be remembered as a great inaugural than an address which fulfills all of the requirements of an inaugural, but does so in pedestrian language. As Karlyn Kohrs Campbell and Kathleen Jamieson note, "Great inaugurals capture complex, situationally resonant ideas in memorable phrases."[7] Of course, great style by itself will matter little if the president doesn't fulfill the norms of the genre.

SUMMARY OF THE STAGES IN EVALUATING AN INAUGURAL ADDRESS

1 Consider whether the inaugural possesses the seven characteristics of form, content, substance, and style that typify the inaugural address. As a double-check, consider whether it violates any of those standards.

2 Ask whether the specific situation or a particular purpose in that situation either de-emphasizes the importance of one or more of the seven characteristics or requires a different rhetorical pattern.

3 Evaluate the degree to which the style of the address is memorable.

THE FIRST INAUGURAL OF GEORGE W. BUSH

Given the terrible events of September 11, 2001, it may be difficult to remember that George W. Bush faced a very difficult situation in persuading the nation to follow his leadership in his First Inaugural Address. After September 11, 2001, the country strongly supported the president in his war on terrorism and for many months his personal popularity soared to the 80 percent range, an unheard of figure for a president. However, on January 20, 2001, Bush was definitely not a universally admired figure. The 2000 presidential election had been quite divisive and, of course, ended in a political crisis that persisted for many weeks about counting ballots in Florida. When the issue was resolved by Supreme Court edict stopping the ballot counting process, many Democrats were outraged by what they saw as the "theft" of the presidency by Florida officials and the Supreme Court. They believed that the Democratic nominee for president, Al Gore, had in fact won the most votes in Florida, which would have given him enough electoral votes to win the election, but that Republican officials had rigged the process so that not every vote was counted. As a consequence, "Unlike most of his 41 precursors, Mr. Bush entered the White House without an unchallenged universally accepted title to office."[8] No recent president had faced a situation in which "Thousands of naysayers took to the streets of Washington...in angry protest"[9] of his election. President Bush also faced a situation in which many Americans doubted his ability to lead the country. Throughout the campaign, it was common to hear jokes suggesting that Bush lacked the requisite ability to be president. Because of the election dispute in Florida and public doubts about his capacity, Bush's overwhelming purpose in the inaugural was "to unify the nation after one of the most disputed elections in American history."[10]

The First Inaugural Address of George W. Bush—January 20, 2001

1   Thank you all. Chief Justice Rehnquist, President Carter, President Bush, President Clinton, distinguished guests and my fellow citizens. The peaceful transfer of authority is rare in history, yet common in our country. With a simple oath, we affirm old traditions and make new beginnings. As I begin, I thank President Clinton for his service to our nation. And I thank Vice President Gore for a contest conducted with spirit and ended with grace.

2   I am honored and humbled to stand here, where so many of America's leaders have come before me, and so many will follow.

3   We have a place, all of us, in a long story, a story we continue, but whose end we will not see. It is the story of a new world that became a friend and liberator of the old. The story of a slave-holding society that became a servant of freedom. The story of a power that went into the world to protect but not possess, to defend but not to conquer. It is the American story, a story of flawed and fallible people, united across the generations by grand and enduring ideals.

4   The grandest of these ideals is an unfolding American promise: that everyone belongs, that everyone deserves a chance, that no insignificant person was ever born. Americans are called to enact this promise in our lives and in our laws. And though our nation has sometimes halted, and sometimes delayed, we must follow no other course.

5   Through much of the last century, America's faith in freedom and democracy was a rock in a raging sea. Now it is a seed upon the wind, taking root in many nations. Our democratic faith is more than the creed of our country, it is the inborn hope of our humanity, an ideal we carry but do not own, a trust we bear and pass along. And even after nearly 225 years, we have a long way yet to travel.

6   While many of our citizens prosper, others doubt the promise—even the justice—of our own country. The ambitions of some Americans are limited by failing schools, and hidden prejudice and the circumstances of their birth. And sometimes our differences run so deep, it seems we share a continent, but not a country.

7   We do not accept this, and we will not allow it. Our unity, our union, is the serious work of leaders and citizens in every generation. And this is my solemn pledge: I will work to build a single nation of justice and opportunity. I know this is in our reach, because we are guided by a power larger than ourselves, who creates us equal in his image. And we are confident in principles that unite and lead us onward.

President George W. Bush, First Inaugural Address, January 20, 2001

America has never been united by blood or birth or soil. We are bound by ideals   8
that move us beyond our backgrouds, lift us above our interests and teach us what it
means to be citizens. Every child must be taught these principles. Every citizen must
uphold them. And every immigrant, by embracing these ideals, makes our country
more, not less, American.

Today we affirm a new commitment to live out our nation's promise through civility,   9
courage, compassion and character.

America, at its best, matches a commitment to principle with a concern for civility.   10
A civil society demands from each of us good will and respect, fair dealing and
forgiveness.

Some seem to believe that our politics can afford to be petty because in a time of   11
peace the stakes of our debates appear small. But the stakes for America are never
small. If our country does not lead the cause of freedom, it will not be led. If we do
not turn the hearts of children toward knowledge and character, we will lose their
gifts and undermine their idealism. If we permit our economy to drift and decline, the
vulnerable will suffer most.

We must live up to the calling we share. Civility is not a tactic or a sentiment. It   12
is the determined choice of trust over cynicism, of community over chaos. And this
commitment, if [we] keep it, is a way to shared accomplishment.

America at its best is also courageous. Our national courage has been clear in   13
times of depression and war, when defeating common dangers defined our common
good. Now we must choose if the example of our fathers and mothers will inspire
us or condemn us. We must show courage in a time of blessing, by confronting
problems instead of passing them on to future generations.

Together, we will reclaim America's schools before ignorance and apathy claim   14
more young lives. We will reform Social Security and Medicare, sparing our children
from struggles we have the power to prevent. And we will reduce taxes to recover the
momentum of our economy and reward the effort and enterprise of working Americans.
We will build our defenses beyond challenge, lest weakness invite challenge. We will
confront weapons of mass destruction, so that a new century is spared new horrors.

The enemies of liberty and our country should make no mistake, America remains   15
engaged, in the world, by history and by choice, shaping a balance of power that
favors freedom. We will defend our allies and our interests. We will show purpose
without arrogance. We will meet aggression and bad faith with resolve and strength.
And to all nations, we will speak for the values that gave our nation birth.

America at its best is compassionate.   16

In the quiet of American conscience, we know that deep, persistent poverty is   17
unworthy of our nation's promise. And whatever our views of its cause, we can agree
that children at risk are not at fault. Abandonment and abuse are not acts of God,
they are failures of love. And the proliferation of prisons, however necessary, is no
substitute for hope and order in our souls.

Where there is suffering, there is duty. Americans in need are not strangers, they are citizens; not problems, but priorities; and all of us are diminished when any are hopeless. 18

Government has great responsibilities, for public safety and public health, for civil rights and common schools. Yet compassion is the work of a nation, not just a government. And some needs and hurts are so deep they will only respond to a mentor's touch or a pastor's prayer. Church and charity, synagogue and mosque, lend our communities their humanity and they will have an honored place in our plans and in our laws. 19

Many in our country do not know the pain of poverty. But we can listen to those who do. And I can pledge our nation to a goal: When we see that wounded traveler on the road to Jericho, we will not pass to the other side. 20

America at its best is a place where personal responsibility is valued and expected. Encouraging responsibility is not a search for scapegoats, it is a call to conscience. And though it requires sacrifice, it brings a deeper fulfillment. We find the fullness of life, not only in options, but in commitments. And we find that children and community are the commitments that set us free. 21

Our public interest depends on private character, on civic duty and family bonds and basic fairness, on uncounted, unhonored acts of decency which give direction to our freedom. 22

Sometimes in life we are called to do great things. But as a saint of our times has said, every day we are called to do small things with great love. The most important tasks of a democracy are done by everyone. 23

I will live and lead by these principles: to advance my convictions with civility, to pursue the public interest with courage, to speak for greater justice and compassion, to call for responsibility and try to live it as well. In all these days—ways—I will bring the values of our history to the care of our times. 24

What you do is as important as anything government does. I ask you to seek a common good beyond your comfort, to defend needed reforms against easy attacks, to serve your nation, beginning with your neighbor. I ask you to be citizens. Citizens, not spectators. Citizens, not subjects. Responsible citizens, building communities of service and a nation of character. 25

Americans are generous and strong and decent, not because we believe in ourselves, but because we hold beliefs beyond ourselves. When this spirit of citizenship is missing, no government program can replace it. When this spirit is present, no wrong can stand against it. 26

After the Declaration of Independence was signed, Virginia statesman John Page wrote to Thomas Jefferson: "We know the race is not to the swift, nor the battle to the strong. Do you not think an angel rides in the whirlwind and directs this storm?" 27

Much time has passed since Jefferson arrived for his inauguration. The years and changes accumulate. But the themes of this day he would know: our nation's grand story of courage, and its simple dream of dignity. We are not this story's author, who 28 fills time and eternity with his purpose. Yet his purpose is achieved in our duty and our duty is fulfilled in service to one another.

Never tiring, never yielding, never finishing, we renew that purpose today: to make   29
our country more just and generous, to affirm the dignity of our lives and every life.

This work continues. This story goes on. And an angel still rides in the whirlwind   30
and directs this storm.

God bless you all, and God bless America.   31

AN EVALUATION OF BUSH'S INAUGURAL

The Bush inaugural clearly contains all of the defining characteristics that are typically found in the inaugural address, although one of those characteristics is not adequately fulfilled. The address does an excellent job at the second through seventh characteristic; in relation to the political principles of the new administration, it was less successful. In order to make this analysis clear, I will treat each characteristic in turn, concluding with a consideration of the political principles in the speech.

Bush clearly attempts to reunify the nation. In the very first paragraph he thanks "President Clinton for his service to our nation." Bush then praises Vice President Gore "for a contest conducted with spirit and ended with grace." With these gracious words, the president reached out to his opponents. But the address does more than praise Clinton and Gore. Bush clearly reaches out to all Americans. He makes a number of efforts to appeal to the poor and to members of minority groups who had disproportionately supported his opponent. In the seventh paragraph, for example, he states a "solemn pledge: I will work to build a single nation of justice and opportunity." He follows that pledge in the next paragraph by arguing that Americans "are bound by ideals that move us beyond our backgrounds, lift us above our interests, and teach us what it means to be citizens." Later in the speech, he returns to this theme when he pledges to "listen to those who" know the pain of poverty (paragraph 18).

Bush also uses reaffirmation of basic values as a means of unifying the people. Value affirmation is found throughout the address. For example, in the fifth paragraph he refers to "America's faith in freedom and democracy." Similar comments are found throughout the middle third of the speech, where Bush speaks eloquently about basic values such as civility, courage, compassion, and character. He uses these value statements both to show his own commitment to values shared by all Americans and also to reunify the nation around those values. The strategy of seeking unity around value affirmation is exemplified in paragraph 26 where Bush states, "Our public interest depends on private character, on civic duty and family bonds and basic fairness, on uncounted, unhonored acts of decency which give direction to our freedom." Here, Bush implicitly argues that the values of the nation are more important than the actions of government.

Bush's inaugural is also quite successful in telling the nation where the country is in the long history of the nation. Bush tells a story that includes continuity in basic values, but adaptation and accomplishment in a changing world. Early in the speech, he emphasizes the continuity when he notes that "The peaceful transfer of authority is rare in history, yet common in our country" (paragraph 1). Two paragraphs later, he refers explicitly to "a long story, a story we continue, but whose end we will not see." What is that story?

> It is the story of a new world that became a friend and liberator of the old. The story of a slave-holding society that became a servant of freedom. The story of a power that went into the world to protect but not to possess, to defend but not to conquer. It is the American story, a story of flawed and fallible people, united across the generations by grand and enduring ideals. (paragraph 4)

He returns to this theme in the last two paragraphs of the speech when he calls for renewal of our basic national "purpose," "to make our country more just and generous, to affirm the dignity of our lives and every life." He adds that "This work continues. This story goes on" (paragraph 27).

In these passages, Bush argues that the American story is one of continuity in terms of basic values, but progress in relation to the obstacles facing the nation. In the conclusion of the address, he draws on religious values and also a sense of American destiny to reinforce these themes. He quotes John Page as writing to Thomas Jefferson at the time of the American Revolution, "We know the race is not to the swift, nor the battle to the strong. Do you not think that an angel rides in the whirlwind and directs this storm?" (paragraph 25). In the final paragraph of the speech, he returns to this theme and confidently states "And an angel still rides in the whirlwind and directs this storm." With this statement, Bush appeals not only to the religious values of many of his supporters, but also draws on a theme of American exceptionalism and destiny that has been common in inaugural addresses. In essence, he argues that America is destined for greatness because of our commitment to basic values of freedom and democracy.

From the discussion of the address to this point, it should be clear that Bush uses an appropriate formal and ceremonial style. The address is serious and at times quite eloquent. For example, in the fourth paragraph, Bush expresses the essence of American "ideals" as "an unfolding promise: that everyone belongs, that everyone deserves a chance, that no insignificant person was ever born." At the very end of the address, he restates his commitment to this promise, "Never tiring, never yielding, never finishing, we renew that purpose today: to make our country more just and generous, to affirm the dignity of our lives and every life" (paragraph 27). While comics on *Saturday Night Live* and other shows had ridiculed Bush's syntax, in his inaugural address, his style was appropriate, formal, ceremonial, and sometimes moving.

The address also successfully speaks to the foreign audience. In the 14th paragraph, Bush clearly expresses support for our allies and warns our enemies. Bush states:

> The enemies of liberty and our country should make no mistake. America remains engaged in the world, by history and by choice, shaping a balance of power that favors freedom. We will defend our allies and our interests. We will show purpose without arrogance. We will meet aggression and bad faith with resolve and strength. And to all nations, we will speak for the values that gave our nation birth.

This statement completely fulfills the sixth defining characteristic of an inaugural address and also ties foreign policy to the basic values that he emphasizes throughout the speech.

Bush comes across as both a strong leader and also as someone who recognizes the limitations of the office. As I have noted, he confidently predicts that the nation will continue to prosper. There is not a hint of personal doubt in the speech. In the statement to our allies and enemies that I just quoted, for example, Bush strongly states his administration's policy. On the other hand, Bush does not come across as vain or arrogant. For example, late in the speech he speaks of the limitations of government action:

> Government has great responsibilities, for public safety and public health, for civil rights and common schools. Yet compassion is the work of a nation, not just a government. And some needs and hurts are so deep they will only respond to a mentor's touch or a pastor's prayer. Church and charity, synagogue and mosque, lend our communities their humanity and they will have an honored place in our plans and in our laws. (paragraph 17)

In this passage and others, Bush argues that the defining character of the nation is found in our values. Implicitly he argues that those values are more important than the policies or leadership or any president. Thus, Bush uses his commitment to basic values as a way of demonstrating both his strength and also that he recognizes the limitations of government.

While Bush's inaugural is completely successful in fulfilling the second through seventh characteristics of form, content, substance, and style that define inaugural addresses, it is less successful in relation to the first characteristic. The most important thing that an inaugural address must do is state the political principles of the administration. Great inaugural addresses reveal the political principles that will guide the new administration and do so in a way that produces strong public support. For example, Franklin Roosevelt promised the nation a "New Deal" to confront the Depression. Ronald Reagan told the nation that less government and more marketplace reforms were needed in domestic policy. In the Roosevelt and Reagan inaugurals, the political principles that guided each administration were clearly established. Those political principles then energized the new administration.

In respect to political principles, the Bush address is somewhat deficient. Bush does lay out political principles, but it is difficult to see how they fit together. Early in the speech, he speaks of the problems of "failing schools and hidden prejudices" (paragraph 6). A little later, in the single paragraph devoted exclusively to laying out the general political principles of the administration, he promises:

> Together, we will reclaim America's schools before ignorance and apathy claim more young lives. We will reform Social Security and Medicare, sparing our children from struggles we have the power to prevent. And we will reduce taxes to recover the momentum of our economy and reward the effort and enterprise of working Americans. We will build our defenses beyond challenge, lest weakness invite

challenge. We will confront weapons of mass destruction, so that a new century is spared new horrors. (paragraph 13)

Two paragraphs later, he promises the nation a "compassionate" administration and then assures the country that "Where there is suffering, there is duty" (paragraph 16). But he follows this statement by emphasizing the limitations of government action stating, "compassion is the work of a nation, not just a government" (paragraph 17).

It would seem that Bush is promising an activist government that will reform education, fix Social Security and Medicare, and help the disadvantaged, while also cutting taxes, building up defenses, and emphasizing private instead of government action. The problem is that it is not at all clear how these policy statements fit together, if it is even possible to combine them, or how he can accomplish all of these goals. Some of the policy principles in his inaugural seem to emphasize compassionate government action to help people in need. But other policy principles seem to emphasize cuts in government and greater reliance on private charitable action. It is hard to see how these principles are consistent. It is also hard to see how a dramatic cut in taxes and a major increase in defense spending could be combined with compassionate social programs. In his discussion of problems facing the poor, Bush sounds very much like a traditional liberal, but it is difficult to understand how the policy principles he enunciates will produce the compassionate result he discusses.

Another way of making this point is to note that Bush discusses policy goals and policy principles that are to some extent incompatible. His goals are to reform Social Security and Medicare, improve education, help the poor and so forth. While Bush does not clearly state the policy principles that he will use to achieve those goals, he does imply that he believes in less government action and more private and individual action. The only place he is at all clear about policy principles is when he calls for more defense spending and significant tax cuts. Clearly, these two actions will leave little left to deal with the social problems he describes so eloquently. It would seem that the policy goals and implied policy principles in the address are at least somewhat inconsistent. Bush obscures this conflict between his goals and the implicit policy principles of his administration by only hinting at the policy principles and using vague terms like "reform" to describe his agenda. Reform is one of those words that can mean very different things to different people.

In summary, Bush does not clearly lay out the policy principles that will guide his administration. In his discussion of social problems, he sometimes sounds like a "bleeding heart liberal," who is very concerned with the poor and disadvantaged. But he does not clearly enunciate the principles that his administration will follow to achieve the goals he describes. And the principles that are hinted at in the speech seem inconsistent with many of the policy goals that he lays out.

How should the Bush inaugural be evaluated? The first step is to consider the degree to which the speech fulfills the seven characteristics of form, content, substance, and style that define a normal inaugural address. As I have explained, Bush completely fulfills six of the seven characteristics, but does not clearly lay out the policy principles that will guide his administration. In fact, there is a strong argument that he attempts to obscure the strongly conservative agenda of his administration with compassionate rhetoric. Overall, it would be fair to grade the speech as mostly successful in fulfilling the generic characteristics of inaugurals. The second step in evaluation is to consider the degree to which the speech adapts to specifics of the situation. Here, Bush's speech is quite successful, especially in his graceful words about Clinton and Gore and his use of basic American values as a unification device. The final step is to consider the degree to which the style is memorable. Here, Bush must be given relatively high marks. I have quoted any number of passages that eloquently appeal to basic values or that memorably retell what might be called the American narrative.

And yet, overall the speech cannot be graded as highly as the great inaugurals by presidents such as Roosevelt and Reagan. Roosevelt and Reagan were eloquent on behalf of basic principles that guided each of their administrations. At the end of their first inaugurals, you knew that Roosevelt stood for an activist government to confront the Depression and that Reagan stood for less government in domestic policy and a firm anti-Soviet foreign policy. Style and substance were quite consistent. While Bush's inaugural is in most ways quite successful, the lack of clarity or even consistency about political principles must impact the evaluation of the address.

CONCLUSION

The analysis of Reagan's two *Challenger* speeches and the Bush Inaugural Address indicates both the value of generic analysis and the difficulty of carrying it out. When a work of rhetoric fits clearly into a narrow genre, as Reagan's Houston eulogy and Bush's inaugural do, generic analysis is very useful for explaining the functioning of the work and evaluating it. But there are also severe dangers associated with generic analysis. Incorrect categorization of Reagan's speech on the night of the *Challenger* accident as a eulogy would produce a wildly inaccurate evaluation of the speech. The best way to minimize the problems associated with generic analysis and to maximize the benefits is to utilize the system for identifying narrow, limiting genres, which I laid out earlier in this chapter.

FOR FURTHER DISCUSSION

After the terrible shooting of twenty young school kids and six teachers and other staff members at the Sandy Hook Elementary School in Newtown, Connecticut, President Obama presented a powerful eulogy for those lost that also honored first responders. Carefully read the eulogy and do a genre analysis outline. Then consider the following questions.

1   Does Obama fulfill all of the characteristics that define a eulogy?
2   Are there unique characteristics in Obama's eulogy that are tied to the specific events involved in the mass murder of young children and teachers bravely trying to protect them?
3   Was Obama successful in leading his audience on the rhetorical journey from pain to catharsis or were the events so horrible that no words could help?

President Barack Obama, Remarks at Prayer Vigil for Victims of Sandy Hook Elementary School in Newtown, CT

Thank you, Governor. To all the families, first responders, to the community of Newtown, clergy, guests, scripture tells us, "Do not lose heart. Though outwardly we are wasting away, inwardly, we are being renewed day by day. 1

"For light and momentary troubles are achieving for us an eternal glory that far outweighs them all, so we fix our eyes not on what is seen, but on what is unseen, since what is seen is temporary, but what is unseen is eternal. 2

"For we know that if the earthly tent we live in is destroyed, we have a building from God, an eternal house in heaven not built by human hands." 3

We gather here in memory of 20 beautiful children and six remarkable adults. They lost their lives in a school that could have been any school in a quiet town full of good and decent people that could be any town in America. 4

Here in Newtown, I come to offer the love and prayers of a nation. I am very mindful that mere words cannot match the depths of your sorrow, nor can they heal your wounded hearts. 5

I can only hope it helps for you to know that you're not alone in your grief, that our world, too, has been torn apart, that all across this land of ours, we have wept with you. We've pulled our children tight. 6

And you must know that whatever measure of comfort we can provide, we will provide. Whatever portion of sadness that we can share with you to ease this heavy load, we will gladly bear it. Newtown, you are not alone. 7

As these difficult days have unfolded, you've also inspired us with stories of strength and resolve and sacrifice. We know that when danger arrived in the halls of Sandy Hook Elementary, the school's staff did not flinch. They did not hesitate. 8

Dawn Hochsprung and Mary Sherlach, Vicki Soto, Lauren Rousseau, Rachel D'Avino and Anne Marie Murphy, they responded as we all hope we might respond in such terrifying circumstances, with courage and with love, giving their lives to protect the children in their care. 9

We know that there were other teachers who barricaded themselves inside classrooms and kept steady through it all and reassured their students by saying, "Wait for the good guys, they are coming. Show me your smile." 10

And we know that good guys came, the first responders who raced to the scene helping to guide those in harm's way to safety and comfort those in need, holding at 11

President Barack Obama, Remarks at Prayer Vigil for Victims of Sandy Hook Elementary School in Newtown, CT, December 16, 2012 bay their own shock and their own trauma, because they had a job to do and others needed them more.

And then there were the scenes of the schoolchildren helping one another, holding 12 each other, dutifully following instructions in the way that young children sometimes do, one child even trying to encourage a grown-up by saying, "I know karate, so it's OK; I'll lead the way out."

As a community, you've inspired us, Newtown. In the face of indescribable 13 violence, in the face of unconscionable evil, you've looked out for each other. You've cared for one another. And you've loved one another. This is how Newtown will be remembered, and with time and God's grace, that love will see you through.

But we as a nation, we are left with some hard questions. You know, someone once 14 described the joy and anxiety of parenthood as the equivalent of having your heart outside of your body all the time, walking around.

With their very first cry, this most precious, vital part of ourselves, our child, is 15 suddenly exposed to the world, to possible mishap or malice, and every parent knows there's nothing we will not do to shield our children from harm. And yet we also know that with that child's very first step and each step after that, they are separating from us, that we won't—that we can't always be there for them.

They will suffer sickness and setbacks and broken hearts and disappointments, 16 and we learn that our most important job is to give them what they need to become self-reliant and capable and resilient, ready to face the world without fear. And we know we can't do this by ourselves.

It comes as a shock at a certain point where you realize no matter how much you 17 love these kids, you can't do it by yourself, that this job of keeping our children safe and teaching them well is something we can only do together, with the help of friends and neighbors, the help of a community and the help of a nation.

And in that way we come to realize that we bear responsibility for every child, 19 because we're counting on everybody else to help look after ours, that we're all parents, that they are all our children.

This is our first task, caring for our children. It's our first job. If we don't get that 20 right, we don't get anything right. That's how, as a society, we will be judged.

And by that measure, can we truly say, as a nation, that we're meeting our 21 obligations?

Can we honestly say that we're doing enough to keep our children, all of them, safe 22 from harm?

Can we claim, as a nation, that we're all together there, letting them know they are 23 loved and teaching them to love in return?

Can we say that we're truly doing enough to give all the children of this country the 24 chance they deserve to live out their lives in happiness and with purpose?

I've been reflecting on this the last few days, and if we're honest with ourselves, 25 the answer's no. We're not doing enough. And we will have to change. Since I've been president, this is the fourth time we have come together to comfort a grieving community torn apart by mass shootings, fourth time we've hugged survivors, the fourth time we've consoled the families of victims.

And in between, there have been an endless series of deadly shootings across the country, almost daily reports of victims, many of them children, in small towns and in big cities all across America, victims whose—much of the time their only fault was being at the wrong place at the wrong time. 26

We can't tolerate this anymore. These tragedies must end. And to end them, we must change. 27

We will be told that the causes of such violence are complex, and that is true. No single law, no set of laws can eliminate evil from the world or prevent every senseless act of violence in our society, but that can't be an excuse for inaction. Surely we can do better than this. 28

If there's even one step we can take to save another child or another parent or another town from the grief that's visited Tucson and Aurora and Oak Creek and Newtown and communities from Columbine to Blacksburg before that, then surely we have an obligation to try. 29

In the coming weeks, I'll use whatever power this office holds to engage my fellow citizens, from law enforcement, to mental health professionals, to parents and educators, in an effort aimed at preventing more tragedies like this, because what choice do we have? We can't accept events like this as routine. 30

Are we really prepared to say that we're powerless in the face of such carnage, that the politics are too hard? 31

Are we prepared to say that such violence visited on our children year after year after year is somehow the price of our freedom? 32

You know, all the world's religions, so many of them represented here today, start with a simple question. 33

Why are we here? What gives our life meaning? What gives our acts purpose? 34

We know our time on this Earth is fleeting. We know that we will each have our share of pleasure and pain, that even after we chase after some earthly goal, whether it's wealth or power or fame or just simple comfort, we will, in some fashion, fall short of what we had hoped. We know that, no matter how good our intentions, we'll all stumble sometimes in some way. 35

We'll make mistakes, we'll experience hardships and even when we're trying to do the right thing, we know that much of our time will be spent groping through the darkness, so often unable to discern God's heavenly plans. 36

There's only one thing we can be sure of, and that is the love that we have for our children, for our families, for each other. The warmth of a small child's embrace, that is true. 37

The memories we have of them, the joy that they bring, the wonder we see through their eyes, that fierce and boundless love we feel for them, a love that takes us out of ourselves and binds us to something larger, we know that's what matters. 38

We know we're always doing right when we're taking care of them, when we're teaching them well, when we're showing acts of kindness. We don't go wrong when we do that. 39

That's what we can be sure of, and that's what you, the people of Newtown, have reminded us. That's how you've inspired us. You remind us what matters. And that's what should drive us forward in everything we do for as long as God sees fit to keep us on this Earth. 40

"Let the little children come to me," Jesus said, "and do not hinder them, for to such belongs the kingdom of heaven." 41

Charlotte, Daniel, Olivia, Josephine, Ana, Dylan, Madeline, Catherine, Chase, Jesse, James, Grace, Emilie, Jack, Noah, Caroline, Jessica, Benjamin, Avielle, Allison, God has called them all home. 42

For those of us who remain, let us find the strength to carry on and make our country worthy of their memory. May God bless and keep those we've lost in His heavenly place. May He grace those we still have with His holy comfort, and may He bless and watch over this community and the United States of America. 43

1 The analysis of genres and the model for applying generic analysis was developed in my essay "On Generic Categorization," *Communication Theory* 1 (1991): 128–144.

2 Peggy Noonan, *What I Saw At the Revolution: A Political Life in the Reagan Era* (New York: Random House, 1990), p. 258.

3 Ronald Reagan, *Speaking My Mind: Selected Speeches* (New York: Simon and Schuster, 1989), pp. 290–293.

4 Noonan quoting Reagan, p. 258.

5 Seminal research on inaugural addresses has been done by Karlyn Kohrs Campbell and Kathleen Hall Jamieson. Although my analysis of inaugurals is somewhat different from theirs, I have been influenced by their groundbreaking research. See "Inaugurating the Presidency," in *Form, Genre and the Study of Political Discourse*, ed. Herbert W. Simons and Aram A. Aghazarian (Columbia: University of South Carolina Press, 1986), pp. 203–225. Also see their analysis of inaugurals in their excellent book *Presidents Creating the Presidency: Deeds Done in Words* (Chicago: University of Chicago Press, 2008).

6 The exception as they say proves the rule. Perhaps the most famous inaugural address in American history and many believe the greatest speech by an American was Abraham Lincoln's Second Inaugural. In fact, the special circumstances of speaking during the Civil War, at a time when the nation was beginning to consider what the soon to be reunified nation would look like, play a large role in explaining why Lincoln's Second Inaugural could have so much impact. Lincoln's brilliant ability to use language to express the most fundamental principles behind the American republic also was evident in the speech. There is also a strong argument that Barack Obama's Second Inaugural was more important and a better speech than his First Inaugural.

7   Campbell and Jamieson, "Inaugurating the Presidency," p. 217.

8   R. W. Apple, Jr., "In the Television Age, Power by Image," *The New York Times* 21 January 2001, A1.

9   Apple, A1.

10   Frank Bruni and David E. Sanger, "Bush, Sworn In, Asks Citizens to Seek 'A Common Good Beyond Your Comfort'" *The New York Times* 21 January 2001, A1.

CHAPTER 11
The Informed Citizen

Rhetoric is often viewed as something fundamentally inconsequential, mere deceptive pandering, and of course in many cases, rhetoric is used in order to deceive and manipulate. But rhetoric also has the capacity to inspire a nation. We remember Dr. Martin Luther King, Jr., Abraham Lincoln, Ronald Reagan, Barack Obama, and many other figures in politics and public life not merely for their actions, but also for their words. Those words continue to resonate in American life. And it is also through rhetoric that any democratic society works through how it is going to address problems. Healthy and effective rhetoric is essential to a democracy. In a very real sense, rhetoric plays the same role in democratic institutions that blood does in human life. It is through the rhetorical circulation of ideas that decisions get made. Just as a disease of the bloodstream can harm the body, so can sickness in rhetoric harm the body politic. If the rhetorical blood does not circulate properly, the result inevitably will be poor decisions, decisions that ignore the wishes of many citizens, or both.

Unfortunately, leaders at every level in society have tremendous incentives to mislead and deceive us. If they don't have good reasons for their proposals, deceptive rhetoric may allow them to get their way. This means that effective democracy depends upon the ability of citizens to distinguish between good reasons and bunk, and between honest appeals to basic values and needs and deceptive attempts to irrationally manipulate our emotions. In the following section, I develop a system, which I call the Informed Citizen, that a truly Informed Citizen can use to protect him or herself from such unethical rhetoric.

The Informed Citizen provides a means of *rhetorical self-protection*. Through its use, people can identify manipulative or deceptive rhetoric. The Informed Citizen can be understood as similar to virus protection software on a computer. It operates in the background to protect the most important and powerful computer on the planet (the human mind) from the virus of manipulative and deceptive rhetoric. There are four stages in the Informed Citizen.

STAGE ONE: DETERMINING THE NEED FOR CRITICAL SELF-PROTECTION

The first stage in becoming an Informed Citizen is to determine the need for self-protection. While it is important that citizens be critical thinkers, not all situations call for application of rigorous standards testing the strength of every statement. For example, most family gatherings do not call for application of stringent standards of critical analysis. When Uncle Charlie says at the Thanksgiving table that as a child he walked four miles uphill both ways going to school and coming home, it isn't the time to test the claim, but to ask him to pass the stuffing. Therefore, before moving to the following stages of the Informed Citizen, the critic (all of us are critics when we are exposed to rhetoric) should ask two questions:

1 Is a major claim on beliefs/attitudes/values or actions being made?

2 Is the person merely relaying information or is he/she strategically presenting the material?

If no claim is being made or if the rhetoric is merely informational, there is probably no reason to apply rigorous analytical standards to it. But if the rhetoric asks you to change your actions or beliefs or if the material is being presented in a persuasive fashion, there may be a very good reason to apply the further tests in the Informed Citizen system. And if the rhetoric both calls for action and presents material strategically, then it certainly makes sense to apply the remaining steps in the system.

STAGE TWO: IDENTIFYING THE CLAIM BEING MADE

The second stage in the Informed Citizen is to identify the claim on action/belief/attitude that is being made and to lay out the strategies that are used in support of that claim. Data for this stage comes from the application of the analysis categories discussed in chapter two. This stage is necessary because one cannot fairly evaluate a position without knowing exactly what has been said. In this stage, the individual should make a list of the claims and requested actions in the rhetoric, the supporting evidence and reasoning, and other rhetorical strategies that were presented. The focus is on laying out what was said in order to later test whether a strong case was presented.

STAGE THREE: TESTING THE CLAIM

The third stage in the Informed Citizen is to evaluate the case made in the rhetoric. The essence of this stage is to consider whether the rhetor provides strong supporting materials to back up his/her conclusion. Of course, it is not possible to know or check every fact in the world. But it is possible to test the evidence and reasoning cited in support of a claim by applying pragmatic standards for testing argument. The key point is that an Informed Citizen can demand that those who want us to do something provide strong argument in support of their positions.

By demanding strong evidence and good reasoning before a claim is accepted, a person can increase the chance that he/she will not be deceived and also that he/she will be able to make good and sensible decisions. There undoubtedly are instances in which the better arguments are on one side, but truth on the other side. No one expected the U.S. Olympic hockey team to beat the Russians in 1980. But in almost all circumstances, testing the case being made gives you a good chance to uncover the stronger position and therefore the best option for addressing a given problem.

In the third stage, the critic should apply five main questions to test the case being made.

1 Does the rhetor provide evidence and reasoning for every claim?

2 Does the support material meet the tests of evidence?

3 Is the reasoning consistent?

4   Does the reasoning lead to the conclusion directly or could there be alternative factors that invalidate the conclusion?

5   Are there counterarguments or facts that invalidate the conclusion?

These substages are important for identifying strengths and weaknesses in the position being advocated.

Presence of Evidence and Reasoning

If the rhetor does not back up every claim with evidence and reasoning, then he/she is asking the audience to accept that claim on faith. Thus, it is very important to see if every claim in a given work is supported. Without support, a claim is merely a statement of personal opinion, not a rational argument. If the analyst discovers that a given claim or set of claims is not supported with evidence and reasoning, he or she then should ask if the rhetor is himself/herself an expert on the subject. If that is not the case, then the claim should be treated as merely an unsubstantiated personal opinion. There is no reason to give significant credibility to such opinions.

Tests of Evidence

Even if evidence is presented, that does not mean that the data is adequate. Fortunately, there are general questions that can be applied to test each of the four main types of evidence: examples, statistics, comparisons, and authoritative material. The general tests of evidence are not perfect. In exceptional cases, evidence may not meet the general tests of evidence, but still be useful. And in specialized fields, there may be more specific tests for data. With these limitations in mind, however, the general tests of evidence are still quite useful for distinguishing between strong and weak evidentiary support. Earlier, I cited strengths and weaknesses of each evidence type as a form of persuasion. It is important to recognize, however, that in applying the Informed Citizen to test claims, the concern is not with persuasiveness, but with strength of rational support.

Examples

In relation to examples, it is important to consider the following:

1   Are there enough examples to support the conclusion?
2   Are the examples from a relevant time/place/culture?
3   Are the examples typical?
4   Are there counterexamples?

Each of the four questions gets at an important point. First, it is important that there are sufficient examples to support a given claim. Sports provides an excellent example of the importance of this principle. On any given day in baseball, for instance, an average player may hit three home runs. One good day, however, does not make a season. Over time, the average player is likely to return to his/her normal performance.

The second, third, and fourth questions all get at the degree to which an example is typical. The second question forces the critic to think about whether the example comes from a relevant place and time. For instance, an example of how college students behave at an extremely conservative religious school would not necessarily reveal how students behave at a secular, liberal place like the University of California, Berkeley. The third question also tests representativeness, in this case by asking whether the example is typical of the factual situation. Finally, it is important to ask about counterexamples. One occurrence of a given problem may not prove much if there are many counterexamples indicating that the problem happens only very rarely.

Taken together, these questions allow the critic to determine whether there are enough relevant examples supporting a conclusion and to judge whether those examples are typical.

Statistics

In relation to statistics, it is important to consider the following:

1   Is the sample large enough in order to draw a conclusion?
2   Is the sample representative of the population being studied?
3   Are alternative variables allowed for in the statistics?
4   Did the research follow appropriate statistical procedures?

The first question is a way of considering whether the results might be accidental. Early in an NBA season, for example, some obscure player may well be averaging 20 points a game. But by season's end, however, it is quite likely that the player will be down near his historical average. It is likely that he had such a high average at the beginning of the season simply because of random factors. Over time, the player almost certainly will return to his normal level of success.

The second question is a way of making certain that the sample in the statistics is representative of the larger society. For example, if one were interested in how average Americans were coping with inflation, it would not make sense to survey Lexus owners. Since the Lexus is an extremely expensive car, almost all owners are (at minimum) upper middle class. In this case, the sample of Lexus owners clearly would not be representative of all U.S. citizens.

The third question notes that in some cases a statistical finding may relate more to alternative factors than to the main point being claimed. For example, it might not be sensible to make national policy toward teen pregnancy based on the experience of the State of Utah. Utah is one of the most conservative places in America and many residents of the state are Mormons, a conservative religious group. A public policy that worked in Utah might not work at all elsewhere.

The fourth question focuses on the statistical procedures followed in the study. It is important, for example, that researchers consistently apply the same definition of terms in all aspects of a study. If the procedures followed in doing the research are not proper ones, the findings of the study may well be invalid. There is one problem with applying this test, however. In many cases, the details concerning the statistics may not be presented. If this is the case, the Informed Citizen carefully should test the credentials of the source of the research against the standards for authoritativeness, which will be discussed in a moment.

The four tests of statistics provide a means of distinguishing between statistics that powerfully support a point and misleading statistical data.

Comparisons

In relation to comparisons of all types, it is important to consider the following questions:

1   Are there enough points of similarity to back up the conclusion?
2   Are the similarities relevant to the issue being considered?
3   Are there important differences between the two objects, people, or ideas being compared?

Comparisons are generally believed to be the weakest form of proof. Through application of the above questions, it is possible to test whether a comparison is adequate to support a point.

Obviously, if the two objects/ideas/people being compared are not similar in important ways, the comparison probably isn't valid. That is why it is important to check a comparison for points of similarity between the items being compared. A comparison of Michael Jordan and Larry Bird would contain many points of similarity. They were, after all, both great basketball players who dominated the sport and led their teams to NBA titles. A comparison of Michael Jordan to Michael Dukakis, on the other hand, would seem to be based only on one point of similarity: each has the same first name. In other ways, the great basketball player and the former Massachusetts Governor and failed Democratic presidential candidate appear to have little in common.

The Jordan versus Dukakis comparison illustrates the other questions as well. Clearly, the similarity in first names is unlikely to be important; it isn't a relevant point of similarity. And there are obviously many differences between Jordan and Dukakis. One is probably the greatest basketball player of all time; the other is a failed Democratic nominee for president. Many other differences could be cited. Thus, it is important to consider the points of similarity between two objects, people, or ideas being compared, the relevance of those points of similarity, and relevant differences. By applying these three tests, it should be possible to distinguish between strong and weak comparisons as a form of rational support.

Authoritative Evidence

In relation to authoritative evidence, there are three important questions to consider:

1   Does the source have expertise or experience in the area under consideration?
2   Is the source in a position to know the conclusion being developed?
3   Is the source biased?

The first question tests whether the person is actually an authority. If he/she does not have either special expertise or relevant experience on the subject, then there is little reason to treat his/her views with any special deference. If a famous actor or actress talks about acting, I listen. When he/she testifies about foreign policy, I say "pass the popcorn." The key point is that we should value the opinion of experts precisely because they have expertise either in the form of training or personal experience in the area. A wise patient with heart disease goes to a cardiologist, but it would not necessarily be wise for that patient to accept the views of his/her cardiologist on immigration policy. As this example illustrates, it is foolish to ignore the opinion of real experts on a topic relevant to their expertise and equally foolish to pay great attention to the opinions of the same experts when speaking outside their area of expertise.

The second question relates to the degree to which the source could know the conclusion being drawn. During the Cold War, both liberals and conservatives sometimes speculated about the motivations of the leaders of the Soviet Union. But these sources were not in a good position to know Soviet goals. The Soviet Union was a closed society in which no one had direct access to the views of the leadership. Rather than expert opinion, a statement about the motives of Soviet leaders more accurately could be considered to be an informed guess.

The third question gets at the motivation of the source. The key point to consider is whether the source is in any way self-interested. For example, it makes sense to doubt testimony of a scientist employed by the tobacco industry that smoking is not that harmful. There is good reason to believe that the scientist takes that position because he/she is paid to defend it. On the other hand, not all strong advocates for a position are biased. On global warming, for example, some see scientists employed by the energy industry, who attack global warming, and scientists working at universities or think tanks, who support global warming theory, as equally biased. In this view, all advocates are biased. But there is a difference between having a strong opinion and being biased. The anti-global warming scientist who works for a big oil company is biased because his/her paycheck comes from the energy industry, which could be impacted by regulation of global warming. But the scientist on the other side has no financial self-interest in global warming theory. He/she is a strong advocate for the theory based on a consideration of the balance of evidence about the growing problem of global warming and possible solutions to it. The second scientist has strong views, but is not biased. The key issue in testing for bias is to ask whether the person has a financial or other self-interest that could influence their judgment.

The three questions for testing authoritative evidence provide simple rule of thumb standards for distinguishing between real authorities and those who either lack the proper credentials to be considered an authority or who possess a substantial bias that makes their comments untrustworthy.

Summary of Testing Evidence

In sum, in the second substage of stage three, the Informed Citizen should check the adequacy of the evidence presented. This may seem a daunting task, but in fact it is simply a matter of considering each individual bit of evidence in relation to the specific tests of evidence that have been discussed. At the end of this substage, the critic would have a list of strong and weak evidence presented for a given claim. If there is a wealth of strong evidence, that is an obvious strength of the rhetoric, but by the same token if there are many weaknesses to the cited evidence, that casts significant doubt about the claim or claims being made.

Testing Consistency

The third substage asks whether the reasoning presented in support of the claim is consistent. An example may make clear the importance of testing the reasoning for consistency. Many conservatives oppose social programs as handouts that destroy personal initiative. At the same time, some of them favor government programs that provide support for business development. But the business development program and the social program would seem to have very similar goals. They both support development by providing government support either directly or indirectly by lessening taxes. It is hard to see why it is OK to support rich companies, but not OK to provide a training program for a poor person. The existence of this inconsistency suggests that one or the other position may not be sensible. If it is appropriate to support big companies, then maybe some programs for the poor can be justified. On the other hand, if programs aiding the poor are wasteful, then perhaps big companies don't need the support either.

Of course, it is possible that the inconsistency is only apparent, that there is a relevant distinction that can be drawn between the two situations. Still, the presence of an apparent inconsistency is important. If you see smoke billowing out of your house, it makes sense to investigate. It may be nothing, steam from a drier vent, but it would be wise to check. The presence of a major inconsistency is a lot like that smoke. It may mean nothing, but it would be wise to check—and quickly.

Testing Reasoning

In the fourth substage, the Informed Citizen considers whether the reasoning leads to the conclusion directly. Recall that it is reasoning which "links" the evidence to the conclusion. In some cases, however, the reasoning does not perform that linking function adequately. The best way to test the adequacy of the linkage is to mentally test whether the reasoning present in the argument *necessarily* leads to the conclusion.

Consider the following example: "Joe Jones has friends who have been convicted of drunk driving. Therefore, he should not be elected to the City Council." In this example, the conclusion is that Jones should not be elected to the City Council. The data is that he has friends who have been convicted of drunk driving. The implied reasoning is that someone who has friends who drink and drive is not an appropriate member of the Council. More specifically, the thinking appears to be that someone who associates with a convicted drunk driver must be either immoral or a drunk him or herself. This reasoning seems obviously specious. The fact that a friend drove drunk says little about the behavior of the candidate. In fact, remaining loyal to a friend might be a sign of strong personal morality.

Note that the conclusion drawn in relation to the above example could have been quite different had the data been different. If the friends had been convicted of multiple acts of racist violence, our judgment would have been changed. Someone who remains friends with an individual who commits racially motivated violent acts is not an appropriate representative of the people.

It is traditional in books on argument and logic to label the flaw in reasoning in the above example as "guilt by association." In guilt by association, a person is judged guilty of some act based on his/her association with someone else. This is generally a fallacious form of reasoning as I have explained. Along with guilt by association, these books tend to list a host of other fallacies including the following: ad hominem (a personal attack), slippery slope (some action will push us down the slippery slope to a disastrous result), and many others. The question then is why not use these specific fallacies, rather than a general focus on whether the reason links directly the claim and the conclusion.

The answer to this question is that the specific fallacies are not fallacious in all cases. For example, personal attacks are often irrelevant to a claim being made, but not always. If the issue is the person, then the personal attack may be completely relevant. Rather than applying a list of fallacies that are not always failures in reasoning, it makes more sense to apply the principle underlying the fallacies. The underlying point behind each of the fallacies I have mentioned is the principle that reasons must directly link the evidence to the conclusion. It is for this reason that I focus on the linkage itself. The key point, therefore, is that the Informed Citizen should ask whether the reasoning leads to the conclusion directly or whether there might be an exception that would invalidate the reasoning in this case. Thus, the problem with the argument that a person is unqualified for the city council if he/she has friends who have been convicted of drunk driving is that it is perfectly possible to be a well-qualified and ethical candidate for city council, while also loyally standing by friends who have committed some wrongdoing. A person could both stick by a friend and criticize their decision to drive after drinking. The key to the fourth question is to consider whether the evidence cited necessarily leads to the conclusion or whether there might be alternative reasons that invalidate the conclusion.

Considering Alternative Data and Counter Arguments

In the fifth substage, the Informed Citizen considers whether there are counterarguments or conflicting data that might deny the conclusion. No work of rhetoric can present the entire story. It, therefore, makes sense both to weigh counter evidence before accepting a claim and consider counterarguments against those presented by the rhetor.

For example, at the end of the 1990s, both President Clinton and some Republicans talked a great deal about the new budget surplus for the United States. Predictably, they disagreed about what to do with that surplus. The Republicans wanted tax cuts and Clinton wanted to save most of it to strengthen Social Security and Medicare. In considering the arguments of both sides, however, one of the most important points is that the United States, in fact, did not have a real budget surplus at all. Rather, the United States had a net surplus when you took into account revenues paid into the Social Security system.[1] Without the Social Security surplus, there was a net deficit on the federal books. But the Social Security money will be needed someday to pay for the retirement of baby boomers. The upshot is that in fact the United States had no surplus at all.

The discovery that the United States was not, in fact, running a surplus in turn casts doubt on the proposals of both the Congressional Republicans and President Clinton. Since there was no real surplus, there would seem to be little reason to cut taxes. And President Clinton's call to hold the majority of the money for Social Security must be seen as politically self-serving since that is where the money already was going. If the counterargument that there in fact was no real surplus had been considered carefully, the United States might not have passed the Bush tax cuts and the nation's current fiscal situation might be much better than it is today.

As the budget surplus example makes clear, it is important to consider counterarguments and counterevidence to whatever claim has been presented. By considering this material, the analyst can make a better judgment concerning whatever claim has been made. Clearly, the fifth substage often will require the analyst to investigate the claims made in the rhetoric, often by doing substantial research. On trivial issues (where to go to dinner on Tuesday), it may not be sensible to spend the time on the research. On more important issues, however, the research is essential. Surely it would have been better for the country if the arguments of those who said that an invasion of Iraq could produce chaos had been considered more carefully prior to the invasion of that country in 2003. The nation might still have decided to go to war, but the military would have been better prepared for the conditions in Iraq. Just as early detection is essential in medicine it is also essential in argument analysis, and as a consequence, the Informed Citizen should consider counterarguments before making any decision.

Summary of Stage Three

At the end of the third main stage in the Informed Citizen system, the critic should be in a good position to evaluate the strength of the claim being made. In drawing this judgment, it makes sense to list the strengths and weaknesses of the case being presented and then make an on-balance conclusion about the quality of the argument. The strengths or weaknesses would include a list of claims where there was no evidence or reasoning, a list of weaknesses and/or strengths in the evidence cited, a list of places where the reasoning was not consistent or where it did not necessarily lead to the claimed conclusion, and a list of possible counterarguments or conflicting evidence. Alternatively, the list might include strengths related to each of these substages, including supporting arguments or evidence that were not cited. The critic then should make an overall judgment based on the balance of strengths and weaknesses of the argument presented.

It is important to remember that when applying the Informed Citizen system, persuasiveness is not at issue. A position can be a strong argument, but not persuasive for an audience. Or an argument can be persuasive for a given audience, but still a weak argument. Persuasive but weak arguments are particularly dangerous because they can cause an individual, organization, or government to make a popular but ultimately disastrous choice. At the end of applying the five substages, the critic should consider the balance of strengths and weaknesses of the argument. Possible conclusions include the following:

1 There are good reasons to accept the claim.
2 There may be something in the claim, but there isn't enough support without more data.
3 The claim is totally flawed. I am being deceived.

One makes this judgment after carefully considering the balance of strengths and weaknesses in the claim that was presented.

STAGE FOUR: TESTING RHETORIC FOR MANIPULATION

Rhetoric may be used to unify and motivate us, but it also can be used to divide society and create hate. In the fourth stage, the critical analyst asks questions to protect himself/herself and society from divisive and hateful rhetoric.

There are three important questions to be considered:

1 Does the rhetoric attempt to prevent other voices from being heard?
2 Does the rhetoric attempt to overwhelm our reason?
3 Does the rhetoric attack groups or individual people, rather than their ideas or actions?

These questions are tied to the function of rhetoric in a democratic society. Rhetoric is the vehicle through which various groups in society negotiate their disagreements and work to solve problems. Rhetoric that violates one of these three principles cannot fulfill its function and in fact can harm the society.

First, rhetoric that denies someone the right to speak is unethical because it prevents the democratic society from functioning. For any democracy to work, the people must be able to speak both directly to each other and via their representatives. If that opportunity to speak is denied, the democracy has failed. Moreover, when we fail to listen to all voices on an issue, the result may be that we ignore crucial data. Thus, rhetoric that attempts to cut off debate is unethical both because it denies a fellow citizen the right to participate and because it may cause society to ignore an important position on an issue.

It is important to understand, however, that people rarely say explicitly "Don't listen to X." At the same time, they often do that implicitly by labeling the other side as immoral. When someone says that X group should be excluded from the debate because of their extreme views on some issue, this claim can have the effect of cutting that group out of the democratic dialogue. When President Trump labeled a given story or news organization as "Fake News," without backing up that claim with strong documentary evidence, he was telling his supporters to not listen to the news outlet, individual political commentator, or other political figure. It is dangerous to close your ears to the views of others. Rhetoric that excludes groups of people from democratic discussion is also dangerous because it denies a group of citizens the right to participate in the democratic dialogue about some issue. In addition, such rhetoric makes it more likely that an unwise decision will be made. If we don't listen to the other side, we will never hear their views and there is a greater chance of making an inappropriate decision. For example, opponents of the war in Iraq sometimes were labeled as unpatriotic, a strategy aimed at convincing the rest of us to ignore their views. Of course, opponents of the war in fact viewed themselves as true patriots in the sense that they were standing up for what they believed was correct and trying to prevent the nation from making a dangerous political decision. It would have been perfectly acceptable for a proponent of invading Iraq to argue that those on the other side were wrong, but labeling them as unpatriotic was unethical. Similarly, it would not be appropriate to attempt to silence a strong supporter of the war, someone like the late Senator John McCain, by labeling him as a warmonger.

Of course, there are exceptions to the rule that rhetoric which limits debate is unethical. It makes sense to prevent someone from putting directions for making a nuclear bomb on the Internet. But the exception, in a sense, proves the rule. As a rule, rhetoric which implicitly or explicitly labels an individual or group as illegitimate in order to limit their capacity to express their views is quite dangerous.

Second, some rhetoric is unethical because it is dominated by strategies that are designed to overwhelm our reason. The problem is not emotion-producing rhetoric per se. As I explained earlier, on occasion rhetoric can produce a strong emotional reaction *and* also build a powerful rational case for a position. On the other hand, the strategies for producing an emotional response may be used to distract us from the best case that can be made for a position. When anti-abortion advocates show pictures of aborted fetuses or pro-choice advocates show pictures of "women in chains," both sides are trying to overwhelm rational thought. The issue is not whether a fetus had blood; the question is whether the fetus had a soul. The picture cannot speak to that issue. Nor does the picture of a "woman in chains" relate to an issue such as whether a regulation requiring a 24-hour waiting period following consultation with a physician prior to having an abortion is reasonable. The waiting period in fact may be a bad idea, but it hardly places a woman in "chains" to require her to think for a day before having an abortion.

In both cases, the point of the rhetoric is to overwhelm the reason of the audience with emotional reactions. On an issue such as abortion, we need the power of "sweet reason" in order to talk to each other. An overly emotional rhetoric drowns out rational discussion. Some might respond that I am privileging reason over emotion, a charge that is in part true and in part false. There are many issues where reason cannot provide an answer. On fundamental value conflicts, for example, reason cannot tell us whether freedom or equality is more important. On the other hand, in the world of facts, reason is our most valuable resource. One may not like a diagnosis or the bottom line in a bank account, but our dislike will not change the situation. It is for this reason that rhetoric that overwhelms our reason is so dangerous. We ignore the best available arguments on any topic at great peril.

Third, rhetoric which attacks groups or individuals, rather than their ideas, is extremely dangerous in a democratic society. Rhetoric is a powerful force for unification. Many presidents and others have used rhetoric to pull together the people of this nation. Dr. Martin Luther King, Jr. sometimes has been called a "saint" of our time because of the eloquent vision of a color-blind society that he presented. Similarly, Presidents Reagan and Franklin Roosevelt before him were beloved because of their inclusive rhetoric. For millions of Americans, the same was true of President Obama, although it is obvious that millions strongly disagreed with this view. On the other hand, rhetoric also can be used to divide us and create hate. Hitler and Stalin did that. Extremist and cult leaders do it every day. Tragically, Osama bin Laden was very effective in creating hate aimed at this nation. Rhetoric that creates hate or divides society into the just and unjust, the moral and the evil, threatens the very fiber of democratic action.

In the 1996 presidential campaign, ultra-conservative Pat Buchanan presented several speeches in which he referred to illegal immigrants to the United States with the name "Jose."[2] Buchanan's reference implicitly devalued all Americans of Hispanic origin. What difference would it make whether the illegal immigrant was named Sven or Olaf or any other name? In using the name Jose, Buchanan drew on racist stereotypes of Hispanic Americans. Such rhetoric threatens our democratic system both because it risks creating hate and because it says that some citizens of this nation are "real" Americans and some are not. Tragically, many similar examples could be cited.

Through the application of the three questions in stage four, the Informed Citizen can protect all of us from unethical rhetorical practice. The first question reminds us of the importance of listening to all voices in a dispute and not devaluing or ignoring someone simply because we disagree with them. The second question reminds us that in confronting any problem it is essential to consider all of the available arguments and supporting evidence and very foolish to ignore those arguments or evidence for emotional reasons. The third question reminds us that rhetoric can be a force for unity and empowerment, but also for division and hate and that it is essential to reject the latter rhetorical practice.

SUMMARY OF STAGES IN THE INFORMED CITIZEN

I. Determine the need for critical self-protection by asking:

  1. Is a major claim on beliefs/attitudes/values or actions being made?

  2. Is the person merely relaying information or is he/she strategically presenting the material?

II. Identify the claims that are being made, the supporting evidence and reasoning, and other strategies in the rhetoric.

III. Test the Quality of the Case for the Claims

  1. Does the rhetor provide evidence and reasoning for every claim?

  2. Does the support material meet the tests of evidence?

  3. Is the reasoning consistent?

  4. Does the reasoning lead to the conclusion directly or could there be alternative factors that invalidate the conclusion?

  5. Are there counterarguments or conflicting data points that invalidate the conclusion? Or are there additional supporting arguments and additional evidence that backs up the position?

IV. Test the Rhetoric for Manipulation

  1. Does the rhetoric in any way prevent other voices from being heard?

  2. Does the rhetoric do something to overwhelm our reason?

  3. Does the rhetoric attack groups or individual people, rather than their ideas or actions?

APPLICATION OF THE INFORMED CITIZEN

As I explained earlier, the Informed Citizen system should be applied in the same way that a virus protection program operates on a hard drive. A good virus protection program is always running in the background. It doesn't impact the computer user until a virus is detected. At that point, the program identifies and destroys the virus. The Informed Citizen system can serve a similar function. It can be running in the mental background, always ready to help the individual identify poor arguments or deceptive or manipulative rhetoric.

In what follows, I apply the Informed Citizen system to two important works of rhetoric. The first is a brief speech by President Donald Trump justifying his veto of a Congressional resolution that would have blocked his use of emergency powers to shift funding from other government agencies to support building a border wall. Both the House and the Senate had passed resolutions blocking Trump's shift of funds from agencies to which they had been appropriated to fund the wall. Trump's statement justifying his veto included similar themes to the speech on immigration I discussed in chapter two. I also analyze brief remarks made by President Reagan when he announced the firing of air traffic controllers after this group called a strike against the Federal Government in order to pressure the government to provide a large raise in pay.

Remarks by President Trump on the National Security and Humanitarian Crisis on Our Southern Border, March 15, 2019

Note, the president began his remarks by commenting on a massacre of people of Islamic faith by a white supremacist in New Zealand.

THE PRESIDENT: Thank you very much. Earlier today, I spoke with Prime Minister Ardern of New Zealand to express the sorrow of our entire nation following the monstrous terror attacks at two mosques. These sacred places of worship were turned into scenes of evil killing. You've all been seeing what went on. It's a horrible, horrible thing. I told the Prime Minister that the United States is with them all the way, a hundred percent. Whatever they need, we will be there. New Zealand has been a great friend and partner for many years. Our relationship has never been better. And what they're going through is absolutely terrible. 1

So our hearts are with them, and whatever we can do. 2

We're grateful to be joined today by the Vice President—thank you very much, Mike, for being here—members of my Cabinet, devoted public servants, and Angel parents—very important people to me and to a lot of other people. I want to thank you all for being here. Thank you so much for being here, and we appreciate it. Thank you. You've gone through a lot. As we take action to restore our national sovereignty and defend this nation from criminal cartels, human traffickers, and drug smugglers. Crime of all kinds coming through our southern border and other places. But this is the place. This is the place. We have the biggest problem by far. 3

And I want to also compliment the incredible people at Border Patrol and ICE and law enforcement for the job they have done. They've apprehended so many thousands and thousands of people that, if we had the proper protection, we wouldn't even have to apprehend. They wouldn't be coming in. 4

As president, the protection of the nation is my highest duty. Yesterday, Congress passed a dangerous resolution that, if signed into law, would put countless Americans in danger—very grave danger. The Democrat-sponsored resolution would terminate vital border security operations by revoking the national emergency issued last month. It is definitely a national emergency. Rarely have we had such a national emergency. 5

President Donald Trump, Remarks on the National Security and Humanitarian Crisis on Southern Border, March 15, 2019

Therefore, to defend the safety and security of all Americans, I will be signing and issuing a formal veto of this reckless resolution—and that's what it was. And I have to, in particular, thank the Republican—strong, wonderful people—the Republican senators that were on our side and on the side of border security and on the side of doing what they have to keep our nation safe. They were very courageous yesterday, and I appreciate that very much.

6

Congress's vote to deny the crisis on the southern border is a vote against reality. It's against reality. It is a tremendous national emergency. It is a tremendous crisis.

7

Last month, more than 76,000 illegal migrants arrived at our border. We're on track for a million illegal aliens to rush our borders. People hate the word "invasion," but that's what it is. It's an invasion of drugs and criminals and people. We have no idea who they are, but we capture them because border security is so good. But they're put in a very bad position, and we're bursting at the seams. Literally, bursting at the seams. What Border Patrol is able to do is incredible.

8

I also, by the way, want to thank our military, because our military has been very much involved, as you know. And they're putting up walls, in some cases temporary; in some cases, they were supposed to be temporary. They're so good that they're better than the permanent. So we're leaving them.

9

We've really nowhere left to hold all of the people that were captured. And we're at a point where we're just going to have to say, with these horrible decisions that we've been handed by people that aren't living in reality, that there's nothing we can do. There's absolutely nothing we can do. We're bursting at the seams. You can only do so much. And the only option then is to release them, but we can't do that either. Because when you release them, they come into our society, and in many cases they're stone-cold criminals. And in many cases, and in some cases, you have killers coming in and murderers coming in, and we're not going to allow that to happen. Just not going to allow it to happen.

10

There has been a nearly 2,000 percent increase in border-related asylum claims over the last decade. Part of the reason is because our country is doing so well economically that people are coming up in droves. The vast majority are rejected, but smuggling organizations—making a tremendous amount of money, like they've never made before—are using these people to crash the system. Our immigration system is stretched beyond the breaking point.

11

And as I said, nothing much we can do. We can just do our job and do it well. But there's a point at which, if the Democrats would—we'd get in, we'd be able to make a deal. Literally, in 15 minutes, we could make a deal on changing catch and release; changing the horrible asylum laws that are so unfair; changing visa lottery, chain migration. These laws are just horrendous. I won't explain them, but everybody standing behind me knows exactly what they are: They're dangerous for our country, and they're inspired by Democrats who have to change.

12

One in three migrant women is sexually assaulted on the journey north. The border crisis is driving the drug crisis. Seventy thousand Americans a year are killed by

13

drugs, including meth, heroin, cocaine, and fentanyl. And the 70,000 people is a number that's so low that it probably shouldn't even be used anymore.

The mass incursion of illegal aliens, deadly drugs, dangerous weapons, and criminal gang members across our borders has to end.   14

We are bringing out thousands and thousands a year of MS-13 gang members, and other gang members that are just as bad, where they come into our country, they're able to skirt the border, come through areas where we don't have proper wall, where we don't have any wall at all. And they get into the country and they do a lot of damage, in many cases. But we get them out by the thousands, and we bring them back or we incarcerate them.   15

The national emergency I declared last month was authorized by Congress under the 1976 National Emergencies Act. And there haven't been too many that are a bigger emergency than we have right at our own border.   16

Consistent with the law and the legislative process designed by our Founders, today I am vetoing this resolution. Congress has the freedom to pass this resolution, and I have the duty to veto it. And I'm very proud to veto it. And I'm very proud, as I said, of a lot of Republican senators that were with me. And I'm also very proud of the House. The Republicans in the House voted overwhelmingly in favor of a secure border.   17

Since 1976, presidents have declared 59 national emergencies. They often involved protecting foreign citizens in far-off lands, yet Congress has not terminated any of them. Every single one of them is still in existence. And yet, we don't worry about our land; we worry about other people's lands. That's why I say "America first." If that's okay: "America first."   18

The only emergency Congress voted to revoke was the one to protect our own country. So, think of that: With all of the national emergencies, this was the one they don't want to do. And this is the one, perhaps, they should most do.   19

We're joined today by many brave law enforcement officers, including sheriffs and just people that have been just tremendous, tremendous backers of law and order, which we have to have.   20

We're also joined by friends of mine, Mary Ann Mendoza, Kent Terry, Laura Wilkerson, Sabine Durden, and Steve Ronnebeck. And I'm going to ask Steve to say a few words. And I'm going to ask some of the folks behind me to say, also, a few words as to the importance of what we're doing. There's nothing more important.   21

As I said, I was elected on a very—by a very, very great group of American people—millions and millions of people—because they want security for our country. And that's what we're going to have.   22

Note: President Trump then allowed several officials in his administration to make statements. At the end of those statements, he concluded his remarks.

THE PRESIDENT: And that's true. I say it today with even more meaning. It was a big step.   23

(The veto is signed.) (Applause.) 24

Thank you very much. Thank you. That's a big—a big step. We're building a lot 25
of wall right now. It's started. A lot of people are saying, "Well, gee, you took down
wall and you're building new." Well, we took down wall that almost didn't exist. It was
like paper. And we're replacing it with, in many cases, 30-foot bollards. And, in many
cases, we're replacing it with 18-foot wall.

But we have a lot of—we have many miles under construction right now, and we're 26
going to be signing contracts over the next couple of days for literally hundreds of
miles of wall. And it's being built in the right places, and it's doing the job. It's doing
the job.

And it's interesting—it's like a little bit like water. As we do—we did San Diego. 27
You know, California is very interesting because they keep talking in California—"We
don't want wall." I see a new candidate who is in the mix; he wants to take down the
walls. Try that sometime. You'll see what will happen. You'd have tens of millions of
people coming in.

You see—take a look at Tijuana. Take down that wall. You want to see a mess? 28
Take down that wall; you'll see what will happen. Right now, we have thousands of
people who are in Tijuana trying to get in. They're not getting in.

So as we build it, it gets better and better. But it gets really to a point, and they 29
come through a point. But you can control that point. And this is serious stuff. This
is—we're able to do it cheaper, better. It's better wall. It's different from what you've
been watching going up. We had to take the old plans. We didn't want to stop, so we
took the old plans. We didn't like it.

This wall is a beautiful-looking structure. It's much stronger. And you can build it 30
faster and cheaper. Other than that, what can I say, right?

It's a—it's going to be great, and it's going to have a tremendous impact. 31

And on top of that, I have to thank the Secretary and all the people that have 32
worked so hard, because what you do on the Border Patrol—what you do, what those
patrol agents and what the ICE folks do, and taking people out of the country that
nobody wants to talk to. Even some of the sheriffs there—you know, if you can get
ICE to do it, you don't mind if they do it. Right, Sheriff? As tough as you are.

These are tough people and they're great people. These are people that—the ICE 33
folks take such abuse from Democrats and some others. They love our country as
much as anybody loves our country.

So we're building a lot of wall and we're taking good care of our people. And we're 34
doing, at point of entry, a tremendous amount of work. We're already in contract to
buy—they make pretty incredible new equipment for drug detection where you can
find out what's in the wheel of a car, where it is, where it's in the engine, where it's in
the hubcaps. I mean, we have some incredible stuff.

Plus, we have—also, we're getting dogs. More dogs, believe it or not. I still say—is 35
that still true? There's nothing that replaces a good dog. Is that right?

PARTICIPANT: Absolutely.   36

THE PRESIDENT: Buying this equipment for very expensive. But we haven't been able—it's true. We haven't been able to match the dog.

I've seen out at Secret Service, where they showed me the dogs, certain types of   37
German Shepherd—very specific types of dog. But what they do is they'll run by 15 boxes, all empty except one. And they'll be very, very strongly sealed boxes. And they'll coming running full speed and stop like on a dime. They know the drugs are in that box. It's the most incredible thing.

So, we're spending hundreds of millions of dollars on equipment, but I will say this: 38
It's not as good as the dogs. (Laughter.) But, as you know, we're getting you—so you're going to have the best equipment, but we're getting a lot of dogs for the various entry points also.

So with that, I just want to thank everybody for being here. In particular, I want   39
to thank you, folks, because you have been—and please say "hello" to all of your friends that have been with us, really, from day one. What you've gone through is unthinkable, and I appreciate it.

And you're strong people. You're strong and you're proud. And your kids are, you   40
know, looking down on you right now and they're—they're very proud of their moms and their dads. You know that, right? They're very proud. (Applause.) Thank you very much.

And, again, to those Republican senators that did what they had to do yesterday,   41
I want to thank them. They're very special friends and very special people. And they want to see borders that are strong, where we don't allow drugs and crime and all of the problems coming into our country.

Thank you all very much. Thank you.   42

He then took questions. The first question asked: 43

Q: Do you see, today, white nationalism as a rising threat around the world?   44

THE PRESIDENT: I don't really. I think it's a small group of people that have   45
very, very serious problems. I guess if you look at what happened in New Zealand, perhaps that's the case. I don't know enough about it yet. They're just learning about the person and the people involved. But it's certainly a terrible thing. Terrible thing.

APPLICATION OF THE INFORMED CITIZEN SYSTEM TO TRUMP'S SPEECH ON MARCH 15, 2019

The first step in applying the Informed Citizen is to determine whether application of the system is needed. In this case, it is obvious that President Trump is asking the audience to support his administration's immigration policies and his veto of the Congressional resolution. It is also clear that he is not simply relaying information, but making a case for his view. Consequently, it makes sense to apply the remaining stages of the system.

The second step is to lay out the primary claims developed in the rhetoric. The most important claim is that undocumented immigration is a crisis that justifies his declaration of a national emergency. In the 3rd paragraph, he says that his actions were necessary "to restore our national sovereignty and defend this nation from criminal cartels, human traffickers, and drug smugglers." In paragraph 8 (note that paragraph citations are made in parentheses in the remainder of the analysis), he labels the undocumented immigrants coming across the border as "an invasion of drugs and criminals and people." He also claims that many of those who cross the border are "stone-cold criminals" and "killers" (10), including "thousands and thousands a year of MS-13 gang members, and other gang members that are just as bad" (15), and adds that these undocumented immigrants are "driving the drug crisis" that kills 70,000 Americans a year (13).

A second claim focuses on the large number of undocumented immigrants who claim asylum when they reach the border. The asylum seekers often explain that conditions are so terrible in their home country that they need to be offered sanctuary in the U.S. Trump argues that a "2,000 percent increase in border-related asylum claims" (11) has created a situation in which facilities for holding these people are "bursting at the seams" (8). He also claims that one third of "migrant women . . . [are] sexually assaulted on the journey north" (13). Trump's third claim is that the declaration of a national emergency is entirely legitimate. He argues that it is authorized by "the 1976 National Emergencies Act" and adds that "presidents have declared 59 national emergencies" (18). He also notes that "there haven't been too many that are a bigger emergency than we have right at our border" (16).

Finally, he claims that because of his declaration of a national emergency, "We're building a lot of wall right now" (25). By implication, he is also claiming that building a wall will solve the problems that he identified related to immigration. He claims of the wall "it's going to have a tremendous impact" (31). He also briefly expresses condolences to the people of New Zealand for a terrorist attack carried out by a white supremacist and suggests that there is not a major problem involving violence by white supremacists, saying "I think it's a small group of people that have very, very serious problems" (45).

The third step in the Informed Citizen is to system is to systematically apply the five questions for testing the strength of the claims that are made. Here, there are numerous problems related to the first question that asks whether evidence and reasoning are presented in support of every claim. Notably, Trump cites almost no evidence that undocumented immigration is in any way an "invasion." He makes claims about crimes committed by undocumented immigrants including murders and gang activity, but cites no support of any kind. He does document that a great many undocumented immigrants arrived at the border in the previous month, but does not prove that these individuals in any way threaten the nation. Trump also fails to cite any evidence demonstrating that a border wall would solve any of the problems that he describes. He is on stronger ground for his claim that a declaration of a national emergency is justified. He cites previous examples and refers to the statute that allows for such declarations. Similarly, he cites evidence on the increase in asylum claims. On the other hand, he cites no evidence that the nation is in fact "bursting at the seams" and thus unable to take additional asylum seekers. In summary, in relation to what appear to be the two most important claims in the remarks—the claims that undocumented immigrants constitute an invasion and that a wall would solve the problem—there is essentially no supporting evidence and reasoning. Of course, it is possible that the evidence exists and he simply neglected to present it. I will deal with that possibility when I discuss the fifth sub-question of stage three.

In relation to the second sub-question, which tests the quality of the evidence presented, there are fewer problems. In part, that is the case because there is so little evidence presented in the speech. There is no apparent reason to doubt the statistics that are presented on the rise in undocumented immigrant in general and asylum claims in particular. Nor is there a reason to doubt the statistic indicating that many women are assaulted on the journey to the United States. Moreover, there isn't a problem in relation to the third sub-question. Trump is quite consistent in viewing undocumented immigration as a danger to the nation and claiming that building a wall is a solution. In relation to the fourth sub-question of stage three, there is a significant problem only on the justification for the declaration of a national emergency. Trump's reasoning is that since presidents have declared 59 prior national emergencies, this emergency must also be justified. However, this claim would not be valid if the previous national emergencies were different in kind from the claimed national immigration emergency. For example, many of the previous national emergencies have related to destruction caused by tornadoes, floods, and hurricanes. These weather related emergency declarations would seem to be different from the declaration of emergency on the border both in the scope of the emergency and also in that destruction referenced in the emergencies tied to extreme weather was tangible and obvious. In this case, however, the "invasion" referenced by President Trump was more metaphorical than real. The asylum seekers from Central America did not come on tanks. In addition, in the 59 previous national emergencies, both houses of Congress did not pass a resolution attempting to overturn the declaration of emergency.

The final sub-question in stage three asks if there are counterarguments or conflicting evidence or additional supporting arguments and evidence. In this case, there are major problems. First, the experts are agreed that undocumented immigrants do not commit more crimes than American citizens. In fact, on average they commit fewer crimes than citizens commit.[3] Second, the available research demonstrates that President Trump dramatically overstates the problem of gang members crossing the border to enter the U.S.[4] Third, there is also strong evidence that undocumented immigration is not driving drug overdose deaths. In fact, there is evidence that "increased undocumented immigration was significantly associated with reductions in drug arrests, drug overdose deaths, and drunk driving arrests."[5] While opioids and other drugs are shipped across the border, the cause is not undocumented immigration, but demand for the drugs in the U.S. Fourth, there is strong evidence that expanding existing walls and fences would not either substantially reduce undocumented immigration or drug shipments.[6] Fifth, there is strong evidence that the increase in those seeking asylum is driven by crime, corruption, and government dysfunction in Central America. A fact check found that "The majority have valid claims of fear in their home countries."[7] This means that blocking asylum seekers from coming to the U.S. might mean that they were abused or even killed in their home countries. The asylum system exists to protect such people and in the past the U.S. often welcomed asylum seekers as part of the nation's mission as expressed on the Statue of Liberty to "Give me your tired, your poor, Your huddled masses yearning to breathe free."[8] Finally, it is not true that the asylum system is "bursting at the seams." In fact, the Trump administration has continued the policy of releasing asylum seekers into the community.[9] Moreover, most undocumented immigrants show up for court hearings about their immigration status and asylum keepers in particular show up at high rates.[10] Thus, the claim that the system is "bursting at the seams" is not supported because the asylum seekers can be released into the community until their hearing occurs.

The application of stage three reveals a number of major problems in the argument presented by President Trump. He cites little to no evidence for two primary claims and his reasoning justifying a national emergency is quite questionable. Moreover, research done to answer subquestion 5 reveals both counterevidence and a number of important counterarguments and it does not reveal additional supporting evidence or arguments.

The last step in the Informed Citizen is to apply the three sub-questions of stage four. Again, there are problems. The first sub-question considers whether the rhetoric in any way acts to limit full debate of the issue. While President Trump does not call for silencing critics, he does label opposition to his proposal "a vote against reality" (7). In this way, he implies that his critics are not operating in the real world. In relation to the second sub-question, the problems are much more serious. Trump attempts to overwhelm the reason of the audience with emotion throughout the speech. He does so by labeling the increase in asylum seekers and other undocumented immigrants coming to the border an "invasion" (8) and by describing immigrants as "stone-cold criminals" and "killers" (10). I've noted that statistical comparisons of crime committed by undocumented immigrants and American citizens do not support these claims. The key point is that the speech is designed to scare Americans into supporting his policies, rather than thinking them through. Finally, in relation to the third sub-question of stage four, President Trump clearly demonizes undocumented immigrants and his opponents in Congress. For example, he says that Republicans are "strong, wonderful people" who are "on the side of doing what they have to keep our nation safe" (6). The implication is obvious that Democrats are not concerned with guaranteeing the safety of the nation. It is also notable that President Trump goes out of his way to minimize the threat of white supremacist violence, claiming that "It's a small group of people" (45). In fact, white supremacists have committed a large number of terror attacks in the U.S. and in the world.[11] The point that is notable is that Trump goes out of his way to minimize the threat posed by white supremacists, many of whom have self-identified as supporters of the Trump administration,[12] while claiming that Democrats are unconcerned with protecting the nation.

In summary, the application of the Informed Citizen system to President Trump's statement justifying his veto of the Congressional resolution blocking his emergency declaration identifies major problems in both the argument developed in the statement and the way that it appeals to the American people. In the next section, I apply the same system to the brief statement by President Reagan explaining his decision to fire air traffic controllers who had gone on strike against the government in 1981.

Remarks and a Question-and-Answer Session with Reporters on the Air Traffic Controllers Strike— Ronald Reagan, August 3, 1981

This morning at 7 a.m. the union representing those who man America's air traffic control facilities called a strike. This was the culmination of seven months of negotiations between the Federal Aviation Administration and the union. At one point in these negotiations agreement was reached and signed by both sides, granting a $40 million increase in salaries and benefits. This is twice what other government employees can expect. It was granted in recognition of the difficulties inherent in the work these people perform. Now, however, the union demands are 17 times what had been agreed to—$681 million. This would impose a tax burden on their fellow citizens which is unacceptable. 1

I would like to thank the supervisors and controllers who are on the job today, helping to get the nation's air system operating safely. In the New York area, for example, four supervisors were scheduled to report for work, and 17 additionally volunteered. At National Airport a traffic controller told a newsperson he had resigned from the union and reported to work because, "How can I ask my kids to obey the law if I don't?" This is a great tribute to America. 2

Let me make one thing plain. I respect the right of workers in the private sector to strike. Indeed, as president of my own union, I led the first strike ever called by that union. I guess I'm maybe the first one to ever hold this office who is a lifetime member of an AFL-CIO union. But we cannot compare labor-management relations in the private sector with government. Government cannot close down the assembly line. It has to provide without interruption the protective services which are government's reason for being. 3

It was in recognition of this that the Congress passed a law forbidding strikes by government employees against the public safety. Let me read the solemn oath taken by each of these employees, a sworn affidavit, when they accepted their jobs: "I am not participating in any strike against the Government of the United States or any agency thereof, and I will not so participate while an employee of the Government of the United States or any agency thereof." 4

It is for this reason that I must tell those who fail to report for duty this morning they are in violation of the law, and if they do not report for work within 48 hours, they have forfeited their jobs and will be terminated. 5

President Ronald Reagan, Remarks on the Air Traffic Controllers Strike, August 3, 1981

APPLICATION OF THE INFORMED CITIZEN TO REAGAN'S STATEMENT

The first step in the Informed Citizen is to consider whether it is necessary to apply the system at all. In this case, President Reagan is clearly trying to persuade the national audience to support his decision to fire air traffic controllers unless they come back to work. He also is making a case for his policy, rather than simply providing a list of possible arguments on each side.

The second step is to identify the claims and supporting evidence in the statement. Reagan claims that the demands of the controllers were unreasonable since they had originally agreed to accept a $40 million salary increase and were now demanding $681 million. He also claims that the strike was not justified and explains that in contrast to the private sector, "Government cannot close down the assembly line. It has to provide without interruption the protective services which are government's reason for being" (3). He also quotes from the oath that that the controllers signed when they accepted a job in which they promised not to go on strike. Finally, the president denies that he is anti-union. He notes that he "is a lifetime member of an AFL-CIO union," and as president of that union, "led the first strike ever called by that union" (3).

The third step in the Informed Citizen is to test the argument by applying the five sub-questions in stage three. Reagan is so clear about developing his claims and providing supporting evidence that the application of stage three can be quite brief. He clearly presents evidence and reasoning for all of the claims and there is no apparent problem in any of the evidence. In addition, his reasoning is consistent. He makes it evident that he supports the rights of workers to strike in the private sector, but draws a clear distinction between public and private sector strikes, both by noting that the work of the government is needed at all times and also that the controllers had signed an oath promising not to go on strike. The argument that government workers are needed at all times seems particularly strong in the case of air traffic controllers since the risk of air travel would rise dramatically without appropriate air traffic control.

In relation to sub-question four, the reasoning seems to clearly link the evidence he cites to the claims that he makes. In relation to sub-question 5, one could argue that it was dangerous to fire the air traffic controllers because it could have created a crisis in the system. In fact, although air traffic was slowed for a period, no crisis occurred.[13] It also could be argued that Reagan's policies weakened labor unions. This claim may well be true, but it would seem to have little relationship to Reagan's statement about the air traffic controllers. Reagan made it quite clear that he supported the right of private-sector unions to strike and even mentioned that he had led such a strike himself. Other Reagan policies may have harmed labor, but the statement explicitly endorsed the right to strike by those in the private-sector. Thus, Reagan's statement holds up quite well when the sub-questions of stage three are applied to it.

Nor is there a problem when the three questions of stage four are applied to the system. Reagan says nothing in the statement that is aimed at limiting debate. He simply makes an argument for his view and accounts for the likely objection that he is anti-union. Nor does he attempt to overwhelm the audience's reason. He could have discussed dangers to the nation's aviation system or even described a potential air disaster. In fact, he simply lays out the apparently sensible argument that the nation needs an operating air traffic control system at all times.

Reagan does not attack any individuals or groups as opposed to their arguments. Note that he does not attack the patriotism of the controllers, but makes the argument that they are not living up to their oath and are endangering their fellow citizens. He does attack their actions, but not them as individuals or as members of a group. In summary, Reagan not only makes a strong argument, but also an ethical one. He does what a president is supposed to do. He lays out a rationale for his administration's policies and even accounts for the most obvious objection. In other words, he treats the people as citizens who deserve to know why he favors a given policy.

In the two applications of the Informed Citizen, I have shown how the system can be used to uncover weak arguments, as well as manipulative and deceptive rhetoric. Those flaws were quite evident in the speech by President Trump. But I also have shown that the system will reveal virtues as well as flaws. President Reagan presented a strong and ethical argument in support of firing the air traffic controllers. Implicitly, I also have shown that the system is not ideologically biased. President Trump and President Reagan are both conservative Republicans, but the application of the system revealed weak and deceptive arguments in one case and strong and ethical ones in the other. The Informed Citizen system can be used to test the claims and ethics of rhetoric regardless of the political views of the rhetor.

The principles developed in this chapter are both among the most important and the most complex in this book. In order to provide additional guidance on how the analyst should apply the Informed Citizen system, at the end of this chapter, I have included two sample essays illustrating the application of the system.

CONCLUSION

President Abraham Lincoln is reported to have said that "You can fool all the people some of the time, and some of the people all the time, but you cannot fool all the people all of the time."[14] For Lincoln's aphorism to remain true in an age where there are hundreds of channels of mass media and an infinite amount of rhetoric on social media and the Internet, people need to become Informed Citizens. Through the use of the system I have described they can do that.

At the beginning of this chapter, I noted the importance of being able to distinguish between strong ethical argument and utter bunk. The four stages of the Informed Citizen system can be thought of as a sort of "bunk detector" to aid in this process. By

© PANDA PAW/SHUTTERSTOCK.COM

systematically testing claims, evidence, and reasoning, people can distinguish between strong argument and utter deception, between honest appeals to our values and attempts to mislead or deceive us.

FOR FURTHER DISCUSSION

In the summer of 2002 the stock market took a major nose dive after it became clear that a number of major corporations had not been accurately reporting their corporate books. In the aftermath of scandals involving Enron, WorldCom, Arthur Anderson, and other companies, President Bush called for reform of corporate accounting practices. Some argued that President Bush lacked credibility on the issue because of his close ties to the corporate world, and also because questions had been raised about business deals that he had made when he was an oil executive. Carefully read Bush's speech on corporate responsibility and do an Informed Citizen analysis outline of it. Then consider the following questions:

1 Does the speech merit analysis via the Informed Citizen system?

2 Does the speech make a strong case for Bush's corporate reform proposals? Does he demonstrate that the reform proposals are strong enough to deal with the problem?

3 Does the speech meet the standards for ethics in the Informed Citizen system?

President Announces Tough New Enforcement Initiatives for Reform

Thank you all. Thank you very much for that warm welcome. I'm pleased to be back in New York City. New York City is a unique symbol of America's creativity and character and resilience. In the last 10 months, New Yorkers have shown a watching world the true spirit of your city. (Applause.) A spirit that honors the loss, remembers its heroes, and goes forward with determination and with confidence.   1

People of this city are writing one of the greatest chapters in our nation's history, and all Americans are proud of New York. (Applause.)   2

I've come to the financial capital of the world to speak of a serious challenge to our financial markets, and to the confidence on which they rest. The misdeeds now being uncovered in some quarters of corporate America are threatening the financial well-being of many workers and many investors. At this moment, America's greatest economic need is higher ethical standards—standards enforced by strict laws and upheld by responsible business leaders.   3

President George W. Bush, Announcement of Enforcement Initiatives for Economic Reform, July 9, 2002

The lure of heady profits of the late 1990s spawned abuses and excesses. With strict enforcement and higher ethical standards, we must usher in a new era of integrity in corporate America.   4

I want to thank Bill for his introduction. There's nothing like being recycled. (Laughter and applause.) But thanks for having me. I'm honored to meet your family and Uncle Jack. (Laughter and applause.)   5

I appreciate very much Secretary O'Neill and Secretary Evans traveling with me today. I want to thank the members of the New York delegation, Senators Schumer and Clinton, as well as Congressman Fossella and Congressman Rangel. I appreciate so very much the Mayor—my friend, the Mayor, for being here to greet me as I came in on the chopper. Thank you, Mr. Mayor, and thanks for the great job you're doing for New York. (Applause.)   6

I'm honored that Cardinal Egan is here. And I appreciate so very much seeing John Whitehead, the Chairman of the Lower Manhattan Development Corporation. And thank you all for coming, as well.   7

The American economy—our economy—is built on confidence. The conviction that our free enterprise system will continue to be the most powerful and most promising in the world. That confidence is well-placed. After all, American technology is the most advanced in the world. Our universities attract the talent of the world. Our workers and ranchers and farmers can compete with anyone in the world. Our society rewards hard work and honest ambition, bringing people to our shores from all around the world who share those values. The American economy is the most creative and enterprising and productive system ever devised. (Applause.)   8

We can be confident because America is taking every necessary step to fight and win the war on terror. We are reorganizing the federal government to protect the homeland. We are hunting down the terrorists who seek to sow chaos. My commitment, and the commitment of our government, is total. We will not relent until the cold-blooded killers are found, disrupted, and defeated. (Applause.)   9

We can be confident because of the amazing achievements of American workers and entrepreneurs. In spite of all that happened last year, from the economic slowdown to the terrorist attack, worker productivity has grown by 4.2 percent over the last four quarters. In the first quarter of 2002, the economy grew at an annual rate exceeding six percent. Though there's much work left to do, American workers have defied the pessimists and laid the foundation for a sustained recovery.   12

We can be confident because we're pursuing pro-growth reforms in Washington, D.C. Last year we passed the biggest tax cut in a generation, which encouraged job creation and boosted consumer spending at just the right time. For the sake of long-term growth, I'm asking Congress to make the tax reductions permanent. I'm asking Congress to join me to promote free trade, which will open new markets and create better jobs and spur innovation. I ask Congress to work with me to pass a terrorism insurance bill, to give companies the security they need to expand and to build. (Applause.) And I will insist on—and, if need be, enforce—discipline in federal spending, so we can meet our national priorities without undermining our economy.   13

We have much to be confident about in America. Yet our economy and our country   14
need one more kind of confidence—confidence in the character and conduct of
all of our business leaders. The American economy today is rising, while faith in
the fundamental integrity of American business leaders is being undermined. Nearly
every week brings better economic news, and a discovery of fraud and scandal—
problems long in the making, but now coming to light.

We've learned of some business leaders obstructing justice, and misleading   15
clients, falsifying records, business executives breaching the trust and abusing
power. We've learned of CEOs earning tens of millions of dollars in bonuses just
before their companies go bankrupt, leaving employees and retirees and investors to
suffer. The business pages of American newspapers should not read like a scandal
sheet.

The vast majority of businessmen and women are honest. They do right by their   16
employees and their shareholders. They do not cut ethical corners, and their work
helps create an economy which is the envy of the world.

Yet high-profile acts of deception have shaken people's trust. Too many corporations   17
seem disconnected from the values of our country. These scandals have hurt the
reputations of many good and honest companies. They have hurt the stock market.
And worst of all, they are hurting millions of people who depend on the integrity of
businesses for their livelihood and their retirement, for their peace of mind and their
financial well-being.

When abuses like this begin to surface in the corporate world, it is time to reaffirm   18
the basic principles and rules that make capitalism work: truthful books and honest
people, and well-enforced laws against fraud and corruption. All investment is an act
of faith, and faith is earned by integrity. In the long run, there's no capitalism without
conscience; there is no wealth without character.

And so again today I'm calling for a new ethic of personal responsibility in the   19
business community; an ethic that will increase investor confidence, will make
employees proud of their companies, and again, regain the trust of the American
people.

Our nation's most respected business leaders—including many gathered here   20
today—take this ethic very seriously. The Business Roundtable, the New York
Stock Exchange, the NASDAQ have all proposed guidelines to improve corporate
conduct and transparency. These include requirements that independent directors
compose a majority of a company's board; that all members of audit, nominating,
and compensation committees be independent; and that all stock option plans be
approved by the shareholders. I call on all the stock markets to adopt these sensible
reforms—these common-sense reforms—as soon as possible.

Self-regulation is important, but it's not enough. Government cannot remove risk   21
from investment—I know that—or chance from the market. But government can do
more to promote transparency and ensure that risks are honest. And government can
ensure that those who breach the trust of the American people are punished.

Bold, well-considered reforms should demand integrity, without stifling innovation   22
and economic growth. From the antitrust laws of the 19th century to the S&L reforms
of recent times, America has tackled financial problems when they appeared. The
actions I'm proposing follow in this tradition, and should be welcomed by every
honest company in America.

First, we will use the full weight of the law to expose and root out corruption. My   23
administration will do everything in our power to end the days of cooking the books,
shading the truth, and breaking our laws.

Today, by executive order, I create a new Corporate Fraud Task Force, headed   24
by the Deputy Attorney General, which will target major accounting fraud and other
criminal activity in corporate finance. The task force will function as a financial crimes
SWAT team, overseeing the investigation of corporate abusers and bringing them to
account.

I'm also proposing tough new criminal penalties for corporate fraud. This legislation   25
would double the maximum prison terms for those convicted of financial fraud from
five to 10 years. Defrauding investors is a serious offense, and the punishment must be
as serious as the crime. I ask Congress to strengthen the ability of SEC investigators
to temporarily freeze improper payments to corporate executives, and to strengthen
laws that prevent the destruction of corporate documents in order to hide crimes.

Second, we're moving corporate accounting out of the shadows, so the investing   26
public will have a true and fair and timely picture of assets and liabilities and income
of publicly traded companies. Greater transparency will expose bad companies and,
just as importantly, protect the reputations of the good ones.

To expose corporate corruption, I asked Congress four months ago for funding   27
to place 100 new enforcement personnel in the SEC. And I call on Congress to act
quickly on this request. Today I announce my administration is asking Congress
for an additional $100 million in the coming year to give the SEC the officers and
the technology it needs to enforce the law. If more scandals are hiding in corporate
America, we must find and expose them now, so we can begin rebuilding the
confidence of our people and the momentum of our markets.

I've also proposed a 10-point Accountability Plan for American Business, designed   28
to provide better information to shareholders, set clear responsibility for corporate
officers, and develop a stronger, more independent auditing system. This plan is
ensuring that the SEC takes aggressive and affirmative action.

Corporate officers who benefit from false accounting statements should forfeit   29
all money gained by their fraud. An executive whose compensation is tied to his
company's performance makes more money when his company does well—that's
fine, and that's fair when the accounting is above-board. Yet when a company uses
deception—deception accounting to hide reality, executives should lose all their
compensation—all their compensation—gained by the deceit.

Corporate leaders who violate the public trust should never be given that trust   30
again. The SEC should be able to punish corporate leaders who are convicted of

abusing their powers by banning them from ever serving again as officers or directors of a publicly-held corporation. If an executive is guilty of outright fraud, resignation is not enough. Only a ban on serving at the top of another company will protect other shareholders and employees.

My accountability plan also requires CEOs to personally vouch for their firms' annual financial statements. Currently, a CEO signs a nominal certificate, and does so merely on behalf of the company. In the future, the signature of the CEO should also be his or her personal certification of the veracity and fairness of the financial disclosures. When you sign a statement, you're pledging your word, and you should stand behind it. 31

And because the shareholders of America need confidence in financial disclosures right away, the SEC has ordered the leaders of nearly a thousand large public companies to certify that the financial information they submitted in the last year was fair and it was accurate. 32

I've also called on the SEC to adopt new rules to ensure that auditors will be independent and not compromised by conflicts of interest. 33

The House of Representatives has passed needed legislation to encourage transparency and accountability in American businesses. The Senate also needs to act quickly and responsibly, so I can sign a good bill into law. 34

Third, my administration will guard the interests of small investor and pension holders. More than 80 million Americans own stock, and many of them are new to the market. Buying stock gives them an opportunity to build wealth over the long-term, and this is the very kind of responsible investment we must promote in America. To encourage stock ownership, we must make sure that analysts give honest advice, and pension plans treat workers fairly. 35

Stock analysts should be trusted advisors, not salesmen with a hidden agenda. We must prevent analysts from touting weak companies because they happen to be clients of their own firm for underwriting or merger advice. This is a flat-out conflict of interest, and we'll aggressively enforce new SEC rules against this practice—rules which take effect today. 36

And the stock markets should make sure that the advice analysts give, and the terms they use, have real meaning to investors. "Buy" should not be the only word in an analyst's vocabulary. And they should never say "hold" when they really mean "sell." 37

Small investors should also not have to have the deck stacked against them when it comes to managing their own retirement funds. My pension reform proposal would treat corporate executives the same as workers during so-called "blackout periods," when employees are prohibited from trading in their accounts. What's fair for the workers is fair for the bosses. (Applause.) 38

My reform proposal gives workers quarterly information about their investments. It expands workers' access to sound investment advice, and allows them to diversify 39 out of company stock. The House has passed these measures; I urge the Senate to do the same.

Tougher laws and stricter requirements will help—it will help. Yet, ultimately, the ethics of American business depend on the conscience of America's business leaders. We need men and women of character, who know the difference between ambition and destructive greed, between justified risk and irresponsibility, between enterprise and fraud.

40

Our schools of business must be principled teachers of right and wrong, and not surrender to moral confusion and relativism. Our leaders of business must set high and clear expectations of conduct, demonstrated by their own conduct. Responsible business leaders do not jump ship during hard times. Responsible leaders do not collect huge bonus packages when the value of their company dramatically declines. Responsible leaders do not take home tens of millions of dollars in compensation as their companies prepare to file for bankruptcy, devastating the holdings of their investors.

41

Everyone in a company should live up to high standards. But the burden of leadership rightly belongs to the chief executive officer. CEOs set the ethical direction for their companies. They set a moral tone by the decisions they make, the respect they show their employees, and their willingness to be held accountable for their actions. They set a moral tone by showing their disapproval of other executives who bring discredit to the business world.

42

And one of the principal ways that CEOs set an ethical tone is through their compensation. The pay package sends a clear signal whether a business leader is committed to teamwork or personal enrichment. It tells you whether his principal goal is the creation of wealth for shareholders, or the accumulation of wealth for himself.

43

The SEC currently requires the annual disclosure of a CEO's compensation. But that information is often buried in long proxy statement—proxy statements, and seldom seen—seldom seen—by shareholders. I challenge every CEO in America to describe in the company's annual report—prominently, and in plain English—details of his or her compensation package, including salary and bonus and benefits. And the CEO, in that report, should also explain why his or her compensation package is in the best interest of the company he serves.

44

Those who sit on corporate boards have responsibilities. I urge board members to check the quality of their company's financial statements; to ask tough questions about accounting methods; to demand that audit firms are not beholden to the CEO; and to make sure the compensation for senior executives squares with reality and common sense. And I challenge compensation committees to put an end to all company loans to corporate officers.

45

Shareholders also need to make their voices heard. They should demand an attentive and active board of directors. They should demand truly independent directors. They should demand that compensation committees reward long-term success, not failure. Shareholders should demand accountability not just in bad

46

times, but especially in boom times, when accountability frequently breaks down. Shareholders are a company's most important constituency, and they should act like it.

The 1990s was a decade of tremendous economic growth. As we're now learning, it was also a decade when the promise of rapid profits allowed the seeds of scandal to spring up. A lot of money was made, but too often standards were tossed aside. Yet the American system of enterprise has not failed us. Some dishonest individuals have failed our system. Now comes the urgent work of enforcement and reform, driven by a new ethic of responsibility. 47

We will show that markets can be both dynamic and honest, that lasting wealth and prosperity are built on a foundation of integrity. By reasserting the best values of our country, we will reclaim the promise of our economy. 48

Leaders in this room help give the free enterprise system an ethical compass, and the nation respects you for that. We need that influence now more than ever. I want to thank you for helping to restore the people's trust in American business. I want to thank you for your love of the country. And I want to thank you for giving me the chance to come and address you today. May God bless you all. (Applause.) 49

SAMPLE INFORMED CITIZEN ANALYSES

The following two sample Informed Citizen essays illustrate how the system can be applied in a critical essay. In these essays, I do not go through each research stage of the system, but instead report the conclusions that came from the application of those stages. The first sample is a complete example of an Informed Citizen analysis. In the consideration of one of President George W. Bush's speeches on Social Security, a number of problems in the argument developed by President Bush are identified. On the other hand, in relation to stage four of the Informed Citizen, there are no significant ethical problems with the speech.

The second example of an Informed Citizen analysis consists only of a sample application of stage four of the system to a satirical anti-Bush Internet picture portraying the 2004 election results as a battle between extremist Christians and moderate and sensible citizens supporting Democrats. I only apply stage four because the primary problem with this rhetoric is the violation of standards of ethics. The rhetoric hardly makes an argument at all. These two samples not only illustrate the application of the system, but also once again demonstrate that it is equally applicable to liberal and conservative perspectives.

PRESIDENT GEORGE W. BUSH ON SOCIAL SECURITY REFORM

On February 12, 2005, President George W. Bush presented a radio address in which he argued that there were severe problems in the present Social Security system that required major changes in the system, including the creation of private accounts for workers under the age of 50.

President Discusses Social Security in Radio Address

THE PRESIDENT: Good morning. In my State of the Union address, I discussed the need to act to strengthen and save Social Security. Since then, I have traveled to eight states and spoken with tens of thousands of you about my ideas. I have reminded you that Social Security was one of the great moral successes of the 20th century. And for those born before 1950, I have assured you that the Social Security system will not change in any way, and you will receive your checks. 1

I've also warned our younger workers that the government has made promises it cannot pay for with the current pay-as-you-go system. Social Security was created decades ago for a very different era. In 1950, about 16 workers paid into the system for every one person drawing benefits. Today, we have only about three workers for each beneficiary, and over the next few decades, baby boomers like me will retire, people will be living longer and benefits are scheduled to increase dramatically. Eventually, there will be just two workers per beneficiary. With every passing year, fewer workers will be paying ever-higher benefits to ever-larger numbers of retirees. 2

So here is the result: 13 years from now, in 2018, Social Security will be paying out more than it collects in payroll taxes; and every year afterward will bring a new and larger shortfall. For example, in the year 2027, the government will somehow have to come up with an extra $200 billion a year to keep the system afloat. By the year 2033, the annual shortfall would be more than $300 billion a year. And by the year 2042, the entire system would be bankrupt. If we do not act now to avert that outcome, the only solutions would be dramatically higher taxes, massive new borrowing or sudden and severe cuts in Social Security benefits or other government programs. 3

To keep the promise of Social Security alive for our children and grandchildren, we need to fix the system once and for all. Fixing Social Security permanently will require a candid review of the options. In recent years, many people have offered suggestions, such as limiting benefits for wealthy retirees; indexing benefits to prices, instead of wages; increasing the retirement age; or changing the benefit formulas and creating disincentives for early collection of Social Security benefits. All these ideas are on the table. 4

I will work with members of Congress and listen to any good idea that does not include raising payroll taxes. But we cannot pretend that the problem does not exist. Social Security will go broke when some of our younger workers get ready to retire, and that is a fact. And if you're a younger person, you ought to be asking your elected officials, what are you going to do about it—because every year we wait, the problem becomes worse for our children. 5

And as we fix Social Security permanently, we must make it a better deal for younger workers by allowing them to set aside part of their payroll taxes in personal retirement accounts. The accounts would be voluntary. The money would go into a conservative 6

President George W. Bush, Radio Address on Social Security Reform, February 12, 2005 mix of bond and stock funds that would have the opportunity to earn a higher rate of return than anything the current system could provide. A young person who earns an average of $35,000 a year over his or her career would have nearly a quarter million dollars saved in his or her own retirement account. And that money would provide a nest egg to supplement that worker's traditional Social Security check, or to pass on to his or her children. Best of all, it would replace the empty promises of the current system with real assets of ownership.

Reforming Social Security will not be easy, but if we approach this debate with courage and honesty, I am confident we will succeed, because our children's retirement security is more important than partisan politics.

7

In the address, Bush made two primary arguments. He initially argued that the present system cannot be maintained without either major benefit cuts or tax increases. He explained that by 2018 "Social Security will be paying out more than it collects in payroll taxes" (paragraph 2) and added that "by the year 2042, the entire system would be bankrupt" (paragraph 3). In this situation, immediate action is needed since "If we do not act now to avert that outcome, the only solutions would be dramatically higher taxes, massive new borrowing, or sudden and severe cuts in Social Security benefits or other government programs" (paragraph 3).

While Bush says that all possible solutions, except increasing payroll taxes, should be "on the table" (paragraph 4), he advocates a system in which workers under 50 would be able to "set aside part of their payroll taxes in personal retirement accounts" (paragraph 5) which would be invested in a "conservative mix of bond and stock funds" (paragraph 5) and earn a higher rate of return than under the current system. He claims that "A young person who earns an average of $35,000 a year over his or her career would have nearly a quarter million dollars saved in his or her own retirement account" (paragraph 5). The clear implication is that workers would be much better off under Bush's proposal than under the present system.

There is no question that Social Security reform is an important issue facing the country. Social Security has been among the most popular and important government programs since its creation in the 1930s. President Bush is clearly calling on the public to support major changes in that program and he does so by using strategies to suggest that his reform package could both solve the problem and produce greater returns without any additional costs. It clearly is important to test whether he makes a strong case for his position.

Testing the Quality of Bush's Argument

The most obvious strength in Bush's address is his clear explanation of the shortfall facing Social Security in the future. Bush notes that in the decade of the 1950s, there were 16 workers paying into Social Security for every person earning benefits, while in 2005 there were only three and that figure will decline in the future (paragraph 2). Here, Bush clearly lays out the reason behind future shortfalls in the trust fund of Social Security.

In other ways, however, Bush's argument is not as strong. First, it is important to recognize that it is by no means certain that the shortfall identified by the president will occur. David

Francis noted in the *Christian Science Monitor* that a decade ago, the trustees of the system thought that the trust fund would only allow for full benefits to be paid until 2030. Now, they estimate that full benefits can be paid until 2042 (Francis, 2005). The point is that better economic conditions could eliminate or at least minimize the problems cited by President Bush. In addition, a relatively painless way of solving a large part of the funding shortfall would be to eliminate the cap on wages taxed under Social Security. At the time Bush spoke, only the first roughly $90,000 (now approximately $128,600) of income was subject to Social Security taxes. If that limit were removed, the result would be to produce more revenue for the system from a group of people who could afford to pay more (Francis, 2005; Smith, 2005). It is also important to recognize that even after 2042, when the president says the system would be bankrupt, Social Security would be able to pay between 70 and 80 percent, depending upon the study, of current benefits out of taxes paid into the system each year (Furman, 2004, 2).

There are also a number of problems with the investment accounts in Bush's plan. One difficulty with the plan is that there would be transition costs in setting up the private accounts that would require an enormous increase in deficit spending. The problem is, as Hal R. Varian, a Professor at the University of California, Berkeley, has noted, that "Social Security is structured as a 'pay as you go' plan" (2005, C2). This means that benefits are paid for with the contributions of current workers. However, if those workers put money in investment accounts, the funds would not be available to pay for benefits that have been promised to people already retired forcing "huge borrowing by the federal government" (Varian, 2005, C2). This borrowing could be quite dangerous given the already enormous federal budget deficit.

One very important problem with the argument developed by the president is that he does not mention that the private accounts would be paid for by cuts in benefits. Thus, workers who invested in private accounts would have to earn a high enough rate of return in the stock market to offset the cut in benefits (Weisman, 2005, A13). There is strong data indicating that many Americans would end up being worse off. *New York Times* columnist and economics professor Paul Krugman cites research by the Center on Budget and Policy Priorities indicating that a worker earning an average income would face a roughly 10 percent cut in 2075 (Krugman, 2005, A25).

There is also a problem with the proposal that relates to the timing of retirement. If one retired at the end of a stock market boom, the worker might be in very good shape. On the other hand, if a worker had the bad luck to retire at a point such as the 2000–2001 or 2008–2009 period, when the market was down substantially, the results would be to produce "a meltdown in the value of the basic income support for retirees" (Aaron, 2005).

An additional problem relates to the assumptions of Bush's plan that he did not flesh out in the radio address. These assumptions are clearly inconsistent. Economists who have looked at the details of Bush's plan note that the estimates of a shortfall in Social Security are based on the assumption that the economy grows only at "1.9 percent as baby boomers reach retirement" (Andrews, 2005, A23). At the same time, the plan assumes that returns on the stock market will average "6.5 percent a year after inflation" (Andrews, 2005, A23). The problem is that if economic growth is only 1.9 percent a year, the stock market is unlikely to produce the high profits that Bush assumes. In fact a study by economists at the Brookings Institution projects profits of only 4.5 percent, resulting in as much as a 70 percent decrease in earnings in private accounts (Andrews, 2005, A23).

There is also a problem with Bush's claim that the funds in an individual's account could be passed "on to his or her children" (paragraph 5). What the president did not mention was that his plan would require people with accounts to buy an annuity when they entered retirement that would pay out a guaranteed amount for the rest of their life. They only could pass on any funds that were left after the purchase of the annuity ("Some inheritance," 2005, A30).

While Bush cites some strong data on problems facing Social Security, he fails to explain in detail how his proposal for investment accounts would work. Nor does he explain the basis for his claim that a worker could end up with $250,000 in his/her account or indicate that this would be sufficient to support retirement. Research indicates that there are a number of other significant problems with Bush's proposal and that he also exaggerated the degree to which the current system is threatened. Overall, he does not make a strong case for his proposed Social Security program in the speech.

Testing the Ethics of Bush's Argument

It is not enough, however, to test the quality of the case (the claims in the rhetoric). It is also important to consider whether that case is ethical. In this instance, President Bush uses rational argument in combination with value-laden appeals to build a case that the present system is fatally flawed and to suggest that some form of privatization could solve the problem easily. While there are major problems with the argument, he does not violate standards of ethics and deceive his audience. First, Bush in no way attempts to silence the other side in the debate on Social Security. It is true that he rules out future tax increases, but in making this statement he is simply supporting his conservative agenda. In no way does he label the other side in such a way as to deny them access to the public sphere. Nor does President Bush attempt to overwhelm the reason of the audience with overly emotional rhetoric or some other device. While I have noted the flaws in his argument, he does not use any device to prevent the audience from thinking through the issue. Rather, he simply makes a case for the conservative view of Social Security reform. Finally, Bush does not attack groups or individuals opposing his views. One easily can imagine a politician demonizing those opposed to Social Security reform as supporting a system that will leave seniors destitute. Bush does not take that tack, but simply argues for his view. There is nothing deceptive in the radio address, only a misguided argument, as noted above.

CONCLUSION

In his February 12, 2005 radio address, President Bush argues for reform of Social Security and diverting a portion of current revenues into private accounts. While Bush's conservative argument is not deceptive, it is not strongly grounded in solid evidence and reasoning. A review of background data on Social Security indicates that the problems facing the system are not nearly as serious as President Bush indicates and that there are severe risks associated with the system that he proposed.

WORKS CITED

Aaron, H.J. (2005, February 18). Privatize Social Security? No. Brookings Institution on-line, originally published in *New York Daily News*, 1 November 2004.

Andrews, E L. (2005, March 31). Social Security, growth and stock returns. *New York Times*, A23.

Bush, G.W. (2005, February 12). President discusses Social Security in radio address. Whitehouse.gov.

Francis, D.R. (2005, February 14). Social Security cure: procrastination. *Christian Science Monitor* on-line.

Furman, J. (2004, January 11). Does Social Security face a crisis in 2018? Center on Budget and Policy Priorities, p. 2.

Krugman, P. (2005, May 2). A gut punch to the middle. *New York Times*, A25

Smith, D. (2005, February 15). 240 million risky pieces. TomPaine.com.

Some inheritance. (2005, February 23). *New York Times*, A30.

Varian, H.R. (2005, February 10). Two issues face Social Security, and applying one answer to both is risky. *New York Times*, C2.

Weisman, J. (2005, February 3). Participants would forfeit part of accounts' profits, *Washington Post*, A13.

AN ANALYSIS OF *JESUSLAND*

APPLICATION OF STAGE FOUR OF THE INFORMED CITIZEN TO *JESUSLAND*

Jesusland visually depicts the 2004 election results and the United States as divided between fundamentalist extremists who supported President George W. Bush and sensible people who supported Senator John Kerry. These sensible people are visually labeled as part of the United States of Canada. The map draws on the fact that all of the states that supported Kerry were found on the East or West Coast of the United States or among northern states that are close to Canada. In contrast, the states that supported Bush include all of the southern United States that often has been called the "bible belt." In this rhetoric, these states are labeled "Jesusland."

Jesusland is a satirical map that uses visual symbols to draw on the audience's enthymematic knowledge of the geography of the 2004 election results. The map clearly cannot work as a rhetorical device if the audience does not share values and beliefs labeling fundamentalist Christianity as reactionary or even primitive. Absent that value judgment, the audience would be likely to reject the rhetoric out of hand. For example, some fundamentalist Christians might see the map as anything but an indictment of the nation. Instead, they might see it as an aspirational document in the sense that they would like to recreate the United States as a strongly Christian nation. Given the facts that the rhetoric seems to be aimed at only a small subset of the American people and that it strongly attacks groups within American society, it is appropriate to test whether the rhetoric meets standards of ethics. Clearly, it does not.

Jesusland implies that people who embrace political views tied to the ideas of Christ are out of the mainstream. The implication seems to be that they are extremists of some unstated type. Obviously, no data is cited to support that judgment. Rather than a developed argument, the strategy seems to be to label Bush supporters as extremists as a way of silencing them in the public sphere. Clearly, there is no justification for such rhetoric, since it denies Christians a voice without citing any data to support the charge of extremism.

It also seems clear that one goal of the rhetoric is to stop the audience of liberals and other Democrats from thinking about the real meaning of the 2004 election results. It may be comfortable for liberals to blame the election outcome on extremists, but that approach has the unfortunate effect of preventing a rational debate about why so many Americans found Bush to be an appealing candidate and also why so many did not find Kerry to be a strong candidate. In reducing this debate to a question of religious extremism, the creators of *Jesusland* wildly oversimplify the real issue and thus make it less likely that Democrats will understand the causes of the election outcome.

Finally, the rhetoric is clearly unacceptable because it labels all Bush supporters as religious extremists. Of course, some Bush supporters did come from the extreme right wing of the fundamentalist movement, but many others were supporters of traditional values, a forceful foreign

Adaptation of image originally created by G. Webb.

policy or of smaller government. Labeling all of these groups as fitting within a *"Jesusland"* ruled by Christian extremists is a profoundly unfair personal and group attack. It also is important to recognize that even the accurate labeling of someone as an "extreme" Christian is itself unethical. One of the glories of a democratic society is that there is room for many different views. Labeling a fundamentalist Christian as an extremist is unethical, just as it would be unethical to attack someone as an extremist environmentalist.

Many liberals and other Democrats undoubtedly found *Jesusland* to be an amusing work of rhetoric. But the strategies used in the rhetoric are clearly unethical. The rhetoric is aimed at silencing a group of citizens. It uses humor to prevent reflection on the election returns and it attacks a group of citizens, not for their ideas, but because of their group identity.

1   A press release from the New Democrat Coalition, a group of moderate Democrats in Congress made this point clear. They cite Congressional Budget Office numbers indicating that in 1998 the United States had a $29 billion deficit, when Social Security surpluses were excluded from the budget calculation. See New Democrat Coalition, "Fiscal Discipline and Debt Reduction Must be Top Priority," 1999, p. 1.

2   See James Bennet, "Candidate's Speech is Called Code to Controversy," *The New York Times* 25 February 1996: A22.

3   Christoph Ingraham, "Two charts demolish the notion that immigrants here illegally commit more crime," *Washington Post*, June 19, 2018, https://www.washingtonpost.com/news/wonk/wp/2018/06/19/two-charts-demolish-the-notion-that-immigrants-here-illegally-commit-more-crime/?utm_term=.c7712bb71ad0.

4   Phillip Bump, "The administration is using heavily inflated numbers to argue for a border wall," *Washington Post*, January 4, 2019, https://www.washingtonpost.com/politics/2019/01/04/administration-is-using-heavily-inflated-numbers-argue-border-wall/?utm_term=.071e17ef0514.

5   Michael T. Light, "Does Undocumented Immigration Increase Drug and Alcohol Problems?," *Public Health Post*, November 9, 2017, https://www.publichealthpost.org/research/undocumented-immigration-increase-drug-alcohol-problems/.

6   Even many conservatives agree on this point. Writing for the Cato Institute, a libertarian think-tank, David Bier systematically explained why a wall would not work to block undocumented immigration. David Bier, "Why the Wall Won't Work," *Cato Institute*, reprint of *Reason*, May 2017, https://www.cato.org/publications/commentary/why-wall-wont-work. Nor would a wall work to decrease drug shipments. See Eugene Kiely, "Will Trump's Wall Stop Drug Smuggling?," *FactCheck.org*, August 30, 2017, https://www.factcheck.org/2017/08/will-trumps-wall-stop-drug-smuggling/.

7   Manuela Tobias, "Has there been a 1,700 percent increase in asylum claims over the last 10 years?" *POLITIFACT*, June 21, 2018, https://www.politifact.com/truth-o-meter/statements/2018/jun/21/donald-trump/1700-percent-increase-asylum-claims/.

8   The poem is by Emma Lazarus. See National Park Service, "The New Colossus," n.d., https://www.nps.gov/stli/learn/historyculture/colossus.htm.

9   Elliot Spagat, "Asylum seekers find it's catch and can't release fast enough," *AP*, January 8, 2019, https://www.apnews.com/07b2dbeac9c84b089aef48525c12c3ee.

10   John Kruzel, "Majority of undocumented immigrants show up for court, data shows," *Punditfact*, June 26, 2018, https://www.politifact.com/punditfact/statements/2018/jun/26/wolf-blitzer/majority-undocumented-immigrants-show-court-data-s/.

11   Weiyi Cai and Simone Landon, "Attacks by White Extremists Are Growing. So Are Their Connections," *New York Times*, April 3, 2019, https://www.nytimes.com/interactive/2019/04/03/world/white-extremist-terrorism-christchurch.html.

12   This view is widely held. See for example Dean Obeidallah, "Trump Still Won't Name 'White Supremacist Terrorism' and His Base Loves It," *Daily Beast*, March 16, 2019, https://www.thedailybeast.com/trump-still-wont-name-white-supremacist-terrorism-and-his-base-loves-it.

13   Bryan Craig, "Reagan vs. Air Traffic Controllers," *UVA—Miller Center*, n.d., https://millercenter.org/reagan-vs-air-traffic-controllers; Richard Reeves, *President Reagan: The Triumph of Imagination* (New York: Simon & Schuster, 2005), 91.

14   See the *Oxford Dictionary of Quotations* (New York: Oxford University Press, 1979), p. 314

INDEX

speech, 56–57, 61

Atomic bomb fallout testimony (Anjain), 119–126

Attitude, defined, 49

Attractiveness, 135–136

Audacity of Hope, The (Obama), 111, 129

Audience, 6–9

    actual audience, 44–47

    external, 232–237

    implied audience, 26–28, 44

    internal, 232–233, 235, 237–238

    rhetorical advantages and barriers, 49–54

Audience-centered approach, 5–6

Audience-related barriers/ advantages, 49–51

Authenticity, 148

Authoritative evidence, 82, 293–294

B

Bambi, 118

Barriers, rhetorical

    vs. advantages, 8

    defined, 8, 49

    definition of, 49

    PBS acronym, 56, 61

    types, 49–54

    typology of, 54

Basic needs, appeal to, 194–195, 216

Basic values, appeal to, 195–196, 216–217

Baskerville, Barnet, 3

Beethoven, 161

Belief, defined, 49–51

bin Laden, Osama, 234, 237, 261, 300

Black History, 234

Black is Beautiful, 234

Black Power, 234

Blow, Charles M., 93

Brown, Dan, 6

Buchanan, Pat, 196, 300

Bundy, McGeorge, 147

Bunk detector, 312

Burford, Anne Gorsuch, 174, 178, 182, 183

Burke, Kenneth, 116, 135

Bush, George H. W., 2, 5, 196–197

Bush, George W., 13, 45, 319, 324

    corporate responsibility speech, 313

    embryonic stem cell research, 38–41

    inaugural address, 275–283

    Iraq, 2

    Jesusland application, 324–326

    social security reform address, 319–323

    testing the ethics of argument, 323

    testing the quality of argument, 321–323

C

Capitol, 234

Carter, Jimmy, 7, 202, 276

Carter-Reagan debate, 7

Challenger eulogy (Reagan), 262

Challenger speech (Reagan), 268–269

Character, credibility, 133

Characters, 114

    narrative forms of rhetoric, 124

Charisma, 136

Charleston, 49

China Syndrome, The (film), 117

Choice, rhetorical analysis, 2–4

Churchill, Winston, 167

Civil disobedience, 30, 31, 227, 230, 235, 236, 245

Civil War, 51, 62

Claims

    identification, 290

    rational argument, 78

    testing, 290–298

Cleveland, Grover, 56

Clinton, Bill, 23

Clinton, Hillary, 5, 80

Cochran, Johnny, 166

"Common Ground" address (Jackson), 201–220

    analysis of, 212–213

    strategies, 213–220

Comparisons, 83–85, 164, 293

Completeness, 5–6

Generic analysis, 253–287
case study, 259–262
Challenger address and analysis (Reagan), 262–264
Challenger eulogy and analysis (Reagan), 259–262
defined, 253
eulogy characteristics, 254
functions, 254–255
inaugural address and analysis (Bush), 269–275
model, 255–258
outline, 283
overview, 253–254
problems associated with, 254–255
process of, 258
recurrent problem, 257
useful and useless, 255
Genre, defined, 253. *See also* Generic analysis
Gingrich, Newt, 77, 101
Giuliani, Rudy, 46
Global warming, 101, 294
Gore, Al, 47
pro-environment speaker, 48
Goals analysis, 17–20, 36
"Atlanta Exposition Address" (Washington), 61–62
contextual research, 46
rhetor, 44–46
Goldwater, Barry, 177
Good character, 131, 134–135
Good will, 135

Gore, Al, 14, 47, 136
Graphic aesthetics, 160
Graphic description, 193
Great Depression, 13
Griffin, Leland, 231
Guernica (Picasso), 159
Guilt
appeal to, 197, 217, 235, 236
emotion producing strategies in Jackson's address, 217
Gulag prison system, 230
Gulf Oil disaster, 49
Gulf War, 53
Gun control, topic of advertisement, 48
audience-related barriers/advantages, 49–51
informed citizens, 312
research, 48

H

Hanks, Tom, 117
Harlan, Louis, 66
Harris, Thomas, 56
Harry Potter, 118
Health care, rational argument, 92–100
Health insurance, 94
Health Insurance Exchange, 95
Heath, Robert L., 56, 57
Heine, Dwight, 122
Heinlein, Robert A., 113
Henry, David, 177

Hiroshima, op-ed (Palchikoff), 248–249
History, appeal to, 197–198, 218
History, emotion producing strategies in Jackson's address, 218
Holocaust, emotions and, 192
Honeymoon period, 270
Huckleberry Finn (Twain), 115
Hussein, Saddam, 261

I

I Am Woman (song), 238
"I CARE" system, 1, 10, 13. *See also* Informed Citizen system; Research
analysis, 4–6, 13–14 (*See also* Analysis)
choice, 2–4
explanation and evaluation, 10
research, 7
"I Have a Dream Speech" (King), 28, 198
Immediacy, principle of, 2
Implied audience, 26–28, 37
Implied relationship, 24–25, 36
Inaugural address, 269–275
stages in evaluating, 275
Informed Citizen system, 289–324
application, 301–302, 306–310
claim
consistency, 295

identification, 290
testing, 290–298
corporate responsibility
speech (Bush), 313
importance, 301–302, 312
Jesusland application,
324–326
manipulation, 298–300
Reagan, Ronald, 311–312
reasons for, 295–296
self-protection, 289–290
social security reform address
(Bush), 319–323
stages, summary of, 301
Infrastructure, 106–107
Intermountain Health in
Salt Lake City, 95
Internal audience
confrontative rhetoric,
233, 235
confrontative strategies,
237–238
Internal (intrinsic) credibility,
133, 144–145
Irish Republican Army
(IRA), 234
Irony, 168, 183

J

Jackson, Jesse, 232
background and context,
202, 212–220
"Common Ground" address,
201–212
analysis, 212–213, 220

speech, 202–212
strategies, 213–220
confrontative rhetoric, 232
emotion-creating
strategies, 220
Japan, nuclear disaster, 51
Jarvis, Gregory, 263, 266
Jefferson, Thomas, 151, 164,
199, 221, 278, 280
Jennings, Peter, 152
Jesusland, application of stage,
324–326
Jeter, Derek, 78
Job: A Comedy of Justice
(Heinlein), 113
Job creation and unemployment,
103–108
Johnson, Lyndon, 133, 147,
167, 204
Jones, Joe, 79
Jordan, Barbara, 132, 148, 153
Jordan, Michael, 132
Jungle, The (novel), 115

K

Kabua, Ahata, 121
Kelly, Sam, 79
Kennedy, John F., 29, 167
Kennicott, Patrick, 56
Kerry, John
evaluation of testimony, 148
internal credibility, 144–145
Jesusland application,
324–326

redefinition, 146–147,
166–167
rhetoric and, 5, 8
Vietnam War, 15, 78, 137,
143, 144, 146, 204, 210
Keynesian Alchemy, 106
Keynote address (Cuomo),
169–176. *See also*
Cuomo, Mario
King, Martin Luther Jr.
audience, 232
civil disobedience, 230
confrontative rhetoric,
231, 235
history, appeal to, 197
metaphor, 163–164
as mythic figure, 219
unification, 300
Kirk, James T., 118
Krugman, Paul, 322

L

Labeling, 168, 182
Language
abstract, 193
aesthetics, 29, 159–160
"Common Ground" address
(Jackson), 215–216
Language strategies
in Cuomo's address,
179–183
alliteration, 182
allusion, 182
antithesis, 180
assonance, 182

credibility, 135–136

distinctiveness, 3

inaugural address, 271, 281, 283

informed citizen, application of, 311–312

myth, appeal to, 198–200

narrative strategy, 112, 116

objectivity, 5

research, 7

"Star Wars" address, 45

unification and, 283

Reasoning

presence of, 291

in rational argument, 77, 79, 291

Recipe, 254

Reddy, Helen, 238

Redefinition, 144, 146–148, 166–167, 182, 183, 233, 237–238, 246–247

Refutation example, 80, 96–99

as persuasive strategy, 98

use of, 98

Relevance, principle of, 3–4

Religion

appeal to, 198

emotion producing strategies in Jackson's address, 218–219

Reluctant testimony, 96, 145

Repatriation tax holiday, 107–108

Repetition, 165, 181

Representativeness, principle of, 2–3

Republicans, 32

Reputation, of rhetor, 53

Requested actions, 20, 36

Research, rhetorical

understanding context and judging effectiveness, 43–71. *See also* "Atlanta Exposition Address" (Washington)

barriers and advantages, 49–54

as critique stage, 7–10

evaluation, 54–56

goals, 44–46

in "I CARE" system, 7–10

stages, 46–48

Resnik, Judith, 263, 266

Rhetor goals, 44–46

purpose, 256–257

reputation, 53

role of, in analysis, 24–25, 33, 36–37

Rhetorical advantage

vs. barrier, 8

defined, 8, 49

types, 49–54

Rhetorical analysis categories, 36–37

Rhetorical barrier

vs. advantage, 8

defined, 8, 49

types, 49–54

Rhetorical criticism analysis, 4–6

choice, 2–4

evaluation of, 10

research, 7–10

Rhetorical question, 22, 32, 76, 165, 181, 183, 244, 247

Rhetorical self-protection, 289

Rhetoric, The (Aristotle), 191

Rhetoric categorizing. *See also* Generic analysis

purpose of, 55–56

self-protection (*See* Informed Citizen system)

tools for analysis of, 13–41

Rhythm and rhyme, 166, 182

Rongelap Island. *See* Anjain, John

Roosevelt, Franklin

aesthetics, 159

charisma, 136

death, 259

distinctiveness, 3

emotional response, 193

inaugural address, 269, 281

narrative rhetoric, 170

unification, 300

Roosevelt, Teddy, 92

Rostow, Walt, 142, 147

Rowling, J.K., 118

S